A Reflection of Reality

文学中的现实

当代中国短篇小说选读

Selected Readings in
Contemporary Chinese Short Stories

Princeton Language Program: Modern Chinese

Princeton University Press is proud to publish the Princeton Language Program in Modern Chinese. Based on courses taught through Princeton University Department of East Asian Studies and the Princeton in Beijing Program, this comprehensive series is designed for university students who wish to learn or improve upon their knowledge of Mandarin Chinese.

Students begin with *First Step*, *Chinese Primer*, or *Oh, China!* depending on their previous exposure to the language. After the first year, any combination of texts at a given level can be used. While all of the intermediate and advanced texts focus on modern life in China, and especially on the media, texts marked with an asterisk (*) in the chart below compare China to the United States and are particularly appropriate for American students.

PROGRAM OVERVIEW			
FIRST YEAR	SECOND YEAR	THIRD YEAR	ADVANCED
First Step (For beginners with no previous knowledge of Chinese)	*A New China*	*A Kaleidoscope of China*	*Anything Goes*
Chinese Primer (For beginners with no previous knowledge of Chinese)	*A Trip to China*	*All Things Considered*	*China's Own Critics*
Oh, China! (For students who speak and understand some Chinese, especially "heritage" students who speak the language at home.)	*An Intermediate Reader of Modern Chinese**	*Newspaper Readings**	*China's Peril and Promise*
			Literature and Society
			Readings in Contemporary Chinese Cinema
			A Reflection of Reality

A Reflection of Reality

文学中的现实

当代中国短篇小说选读

Selected Readings in Contemporary Chinese Short Stories

Selected and Edited by

周质平 Chih-p'ing Chou
于丽萍 Liping Yu
杨玖 Joanne Chiang

Princeton University Press
Princeton and Oxford

ISBN 978-0-691-16293-5

Library of Congress Control Number: 2014937130

British Library Cataloging-in-Publication Data is available

The publisher would like to acknowledge the authors of this volume for providing the
camera-ready copy from which this book was printed.

This book has been composed in STKaiti and Times New Roman

Printed on acid-free paper ∞

Printed in the United States of America

1 3 5 7 9 10 8 6 4 2

文学中的现实
A Reflection of Reality

目　录
Table of Contents

序

《文学中的现实》是普林斯顿大学对外汉语教研室的老师们第一次以文学作品结集作为高年级的教材。

最近十年来，由于中国经济快速的发展，许多美国学生都有去中国经商或工作的打算。对外汉语教学为了顺应这个潮流，许多学校开设了"商用中文"(Business Chinese) 课程，也出版了许多相应的课本。这一发展，就一定程度而言，体现了晚近美国高年级对外汉语教学有走"单一功能"的趋向。所谓"单一功能"，即强调语言课在词汇和语法结构的介绍上，为了达到某一特定的目标，走"特殊"(specific) 而非"一般"的方向。

我们对高年级课程的编定则采取"一般"而非"特殊"的原则。我们相信高年级课本的内容宜宽而不宜窄。一个受过完整而且良好汉语训练的学生，他的中文不仅可以"商用"，也可以"法用"、"工用"、"农用"、"艺用"……。当然，更重要的是"日用"。我们认为只有"中文商用"，而没有"商用中文"。初看这一提法，或许以为这是在玩文字游戏，殊不知这是高年级对外汉语教学不同理念之所在。

过分强调语言的功能，不免使语言课走上枯燥和单调的方向。有些人或许以为"单一功能"是条学好汉语的捷径，但日常生活包罗万象，即使是商业谈判，也是千变万化。在语言教材上，强调单一功能的结果是企图以"有限"来应付"无穷"。

普大过去所出一系列的高年级对外汉语教科书，所遵循的是"内容"取向，而非"功能"取向。我们透过所选的教材，向学生介绍近现代中国文学历史和社会的知识，使学生在学过这些课本之后，不但能习得语言的结构和使用，也能有系统地了解近现代中国文史的相关知识和社会结构的变迁。换句话说，普大的中文语言教育是"通才"式的，而不是"专业"或"职业"式的。

本书的出版是过去几年来我们课余整理积累所得。在不同时期、不同学校都使用过，师生反应都很热烈。这次集印成书又作了比较细致的修订。为便于教学，少数篇章略有删减。

本书一仍普大中文教科书惯例，简化字课文与生词同页互见，大大增进了学习的便利。

周质平
于丽萍
杨　玖
2014 年 5 月 1 日

Preface

A Reflection of Reality is the first anthology of modern Chinese short stories that the Chinese Language Program at Princeton University has developed over the past 25 years. This textbook is designed for those who have completed three years of college Chinese. Princeton University Press has published several titles for the advanced level students, such as *All Things Considered, A Kaleidoscope of China, Anything Goes, China's Own Critics, Literature and Society,* and *China's Peril and Promise.* None of these books were devoted to contemporary Chinese short stories. We have been working on this anthology for the past ten years and Chinese Linguistics Project has been distributing this textbook for adoption in the classroom by several universities.

Many advanced Chinese language textbooks have been taking a very practical approach, such as branching into Business Chinese. We believe that in order to improve students' Chinese proficiency, especially at the advanced level, a more general, non-specific, content base is necessary. *A Reflection of Reality* takes a different direction in its pedagogical approach by presenting a selection of twelve short-stories written by contemporary authors. These stories appeared in various newspapers and magazines published in China and reflect contemporary Chinese society from various perspectives in the hopes of covering all walks of life. We believe this textbook will not only improve students' language proficiency, but enhance their understanding of contemporary China. Hence, this textbook can be adopted for language as well as contemporary Chinese literature courses.

Chih-p'ing Chou
Liping Yu
Joanne Chiang

May 1, 2014

List of Abbreviations

adj. = adjective

adv. = adverb

aux. = auxiliary

AN. = Measure Word

conj. = conjunction

idm. = idiom

intj. = interjection

n. = noun

num. = number

o. = object

onom. = onomatopoeia

part. = particle

phr. = phrase

prefix = prefix

prep. = preposition

pron. = pronoun

s. = subject

suffix = suffix

v. = verb

v.- c.= verb-complement

v.- o. = verb-object

* 轻声字注音不标调号，但在注音前加一个圆点，如"桌子"：zhuō.zi。一般轻读，有时重读的字，在注音上标调号，注音前再加一个圆点。如"因为"：yīn.wèi。两字之间可插入其他成分时，加 //，如："理发"：lǐ//fà。各词条的注音都依据商务印书馆出版的《现代汉语词典》。

Characters pronounced with a neutral tone are transcribed not with a tone marker on top of the main vowel, as ordinary characters are, but with a dot before the initial consonant, such as "桌子"：zhuō.zi. Characters usually pronounced with a neutral tone but occasionally with a stress are transcribed with both a tone marker and a dot before the initial consonant, such as "因为"：yīn.wèi, where 为 is usually pronounced with a neutral tone but sometimes with a falling tone (the fourth tone). When there can be an insertion between two characters, a // is added, such as "理发"：lǐ//fà. The phonetic notation for all entries is based on *Xiandai Hanyu Cidian* published by The Commercial Press.

A Reflection of Reality

文学中的现实

当代中国短篇小说选读

Selected Readings in
Contemporary Chinese Short Stories

"人 证"

郁青

在火车上,一个很漂亮的女列车员盯着一个民工模样⑴的中年人,大声说:"查票!"

中年人浑身上下⑵一阵翻找,终于找到了,却捏在手里不想交出去。

列车员朝他手上看了一眼,怪怪地笑了笑,说:"这是儿童票。"

中年人涨红了脸,小声地说:"儿童票不是跟残疾人票价格一样吗?"

儿童票和残疾人票的价格都是全票的一半,列车员当然知道。她打量了中年人一番,问道:"你是残疾人?"

"我是残疾人。"

"那你把残疾证给我看看。"

中年人紧张起来,说:"我……没有残疾证。买票的时候,售票员就向我要残疾证,我没办法才买的儿童票。"

列车员冷笑一下:"没有残疾证,怎么能证明你是残疾人啊?"

中年人没有做声,只是轻轻把鞋子脱下,又将裤腿拉了起来——他只有半个脚掌。

Selected & edited by Chih-p'ing Chou
Prepared by Joanne Chiang

人证	rénzhèng	*n.*	testimony of a witness; (here) "certificate of human-ness"
列车员	lièchēyuán	*n.*	attendant (on a train)
盯着	dīng.zhe	*v.*	fix one's eyes on; stare at 别盯着人看，那很不礼貌。
民工	míngōng	*n.*	poor laborers who come from the countryside to work in the city
模样	múyàng	*n.*	appearance; look 儿子的模样很像父亲。
查票	chápiào	*v.-o.*	examine ticket; check ticket
浑身上下	húnshēn shàngxià	*n.*	from head to toe; all over 他被汽车撞了，浑身上下都是血。
阵	zhèn	*AN.*	a burst; a peal; a fit 一阵大风/一阵咳嗽/一阵雨/一阵掌声
翻找	fānzhǎo	*v.*	rummage all over
捏	niē	*v.*	hold between fingers, pinch
朝	cháo	*prep.*	to; towards 朝南走/朝他看了一眼
涨红脸	zhànghóng liǎn	*v.-o.*	face flushed scarlet 听了我的话，他的脸立刻涨红了。
残疾人	cánjírén	*n.*	disabled people; the physically handicapped
打量	dǎ.liang	*v.*	measure with the eyes; look somebody up and down 把他上下打量了一番
番	fān	*AN.*	measure word for actions, deeds, etc. 经过一番讨论，终于做出了决定。
残疾证	cánjízhèng	*n.*	certificate of disability
售票员	shòupiàoyuán	*n.*	booking-office clerk; ticket seller
冷笑	lěngxiào	*v.*	sneer; laugh scornfully
没做声	méi zuòshēng	*v.*	did not say a word; kept silent
脱下	tuōxià	*v.*	take off (clothes, shoes, etc.)
裤腿	kùtuǐ	*n.*	trouser legs
拉	lā	*v.*	pull
脚掌	jiǎozhǎng	*n.*	sole (of the foot)

列车员斜眼看了看，说："我要看的是证件！是上面印着'残疾证'的三个字的本本！是残联盖的钢印！"

中年人一副(3)苦瓜脸，解释说："我没有当地户口，人家不给办理残疾证。而且，我是在私人工地干活，出了事之后老板就跑了，我也没钱到医院做评定……"

列车长闻讯而来，询问情况。

中年人再一次向列车长说明，自己是一个残疾人，买了一张和残疾人票一样价格的票……

列车长也问："你的残疾证呢？"

中年人说他没有残疾证，接着就让列车长看他的半个脚掌。

列车长连看都没看(4)，便不耐烦地说："我们只认证不认人！有残疾证就是残疾人，有残疾证才能享受残疾人买票的待遇。你赶快补票吧！"

中年人一下子(5)说不出话来。

他翻遍了全身的口袋和行李，只有几块钱，根本不够补票的。他带着哭腔对列车长说："我的脚掌被机器轧掉一半之后，就再也(6)打不了工了。没有钱，连老家也回不去了。这张半价票

斜眼看	xiéyǎn kàn	v.	look at someone sideways
证件	zhèngjiàn	n.	certificate; papers; credentials
印	yìn	v.	print
本本	běn.ben	n.	booklet; brochure
残联	CánLián	n.	short for 中国残疾人联合会；China Disabled Persons' Federation

盖	gài	v.	affix (a seal), stamp a seal
钢印	gāngyìn	n.	embossed stamp
副	fù	AN.	measure word for facial expression 露出一副不高兴的样子
苦瓜脸	kǔguāliǎn	n.	facial expression of bitterness 苦瓜：bitter gourd
当地	dāngdì	adj.	local 当地时间/当地人
户口	hùkǒu	n.	permanent residency, resident permit
人家	rénjiā	pron.	they; he; she 这是他的信，你把它给人家送去吧！
办理	bànlǐ	v.	handle 办理这些事情/办理手续
工地	gōngdì	n.	construction site
干活	gànhuó	v.-o.	work; work on a job
出事	chūshì	v.-o.	meet with a mishap; have an accident 出了什么事？/他开车出了事。
评定	píngdìng	v./n.	evaluate; evaluation
列车长	lièchēzhǎng	n.	head of a train crew; conductor
闻讯而来	wénxùn érlái	phr.	hear the news and come
询问	xúnwèn	v.	ask about; inquire
不耐烦	bú nàifán	adj.	impatient
认证不认人	rènzhèng bú rènrén	phr.	only recognize/accept identification, and not the person himself/herself
赶快	gǎnkuài	adv.	quickly; at once
补票	bǔpiào	v.-o.	buy one's ticket after the normal time
翻遍	fānbiàn	v.-c.	rummage all over 我翻遍了房间，还是没找着。
口袋	kǒudài	n.	pocket
行李	xíng.li	n.	luggage; baggage
哭腔	kūqiāng	n.	tearful tone
机器	jīqì	n.	machine
轧	yà	v.	run over (by a car, train, etc.)
老家	lǎojiā	n.	native place; old home

还⑺是老乡们凑钱给我买的呢。求您高抬贵手，放过我吧！"

列车长坚决地说："那不行。"

那个女列车员趁机对列车长说："让他去车头铲煤吧！算做义务劳动。"

列车长想了想，说："好。"

中年人对面的一个老同志看不惯⑻了。他站起来，盯着列车长的眼睛，说："你是不是男人？"

列车长不解地说："这跟我是不是男人有什么关系啊？"

"你就告诉我，你是不是男人？"

"我当然是男人！"

"你用什么证明你是男人呢？把你的男人证拿出来给大家看看！"

周围的人一下都笑起来。

列车长愣了愣，说："我一个大男人在这儿站着，难道还有假不成⑼？"

老同志摇了摇头，说："我和你们一样，只认证不认人。有男人证就是男人，没男人证就不是男人。"

列车长呆住了，一时⑽想不出什么话来应对。

那个女列车员站出来替列车长解围，她对老同志说："我不是男人，你有什么话跟我说好了！"

老同志指着她的鼻子，说："你根本就不是人！"

老乡	lǎoxiāng	*n.*	fellow-townsman; fellow-villager
凑钱	còuqián	*v.-o.*	pool money; raise a fund 他想凑一笔钱在北京买一幢房子。
求	qiú	*v.*	ask; beg; request 求我帮他的忙/求你一件事
高抬贵手	gāotái guìshǒu	*idm.*	Raise your hand high in mercy! Please don't be too hard on me this time!
放过	fàng.guo	*v.*	let off; let slip 我们决不放过一个坏人。
坚决地	jiānjué.de	*adv.*	resolutely; firmly
趁机	chènjī	*adv.*	take advantage of the occasion; seize the chance 今天下午我没有课，所以，我就趁机去超市买东西。
车头	chētóu	*n.*	the front of the train; the engine
铲煤	chǎnméi	*v.-o.*	shovel coal
义务劳动	yìwù láodòng	*n.*	voluntary labor
老同志	lǎo tóngzhì	*n.*	old comrade
看不惯	kàn.buguàn	*v.-c.*	cannot bear the sight of; detest; hate to see 我看不惯这些落伍的做法。
不解	bùjiě	*v.*	not understand; puzzled
周围	zhōuwéi	*adj./n.*	surrounding 周围的人/周围的环境/周围的情况
愣	lèng	*v.*	dull; stupefied; blank
有假	yǒujiǎ	*v.*	there is falsification
摇头	yáotóu	*v.-o.*	shake one's head
呆住	dāi.zhu	*v.-c.*	be stupefied; be dumbstruck
一时	yìshí	*adv.*	for a short while; for the moment 一时想不起来/一时不知道该说什么
应对	yìngduì	*v.*	reply; answer
站出来	zhàn.chu.lai	*v.-c.*	stand out boldly
替…解围	tì…jiěwéi	*v.*	help somebody out of a predicament; save somebody from embarrassment 谢谢你替我解围。

列车员一下暴跳如雷，尖声叫道："你嘴巴干净点儿！你说，我不是人是什么？"

老同志一脸平静，狡黠地笑了笑，说："你是人？那好，把你的"人证"拿出来看看……"

四周的人再一次哄笑起来。

只有一个人没笑，就是那个只有半个脚掌的中年人。他定定地望着眼前的一切，不知何时，眼里蓄满了泪水，不知道是委屈，感激，还是仇恨。

选自《小小说月刊》2005 年第 5 期

暴跳如雷	bàotiàorúléi	*idm.*	stamp with rage; be in a frenzy of rage
尖声	jiānshēng	*n.*	shrill voice
嘴巴干净点儿	zuǐba gān.jing diǎnr	*phr.*	Watch your mouth!
平静	píngjìng	*adj.*	calm
狡黠地	jiǎoxiá.de	*adv.*	slyly; craftily; cunningly
哄笑	hōngxiào	*v.*	burst into uproarious laughter
定定地望着	dìngdìng.de wàng.zhe	*phr.*	stare with a dull look in one's eyes; stare fixedly
蓄	xù	*v.*	harbor; retain; full of
泪水	lèishuǐ	*n.*	tears
委屈	wěiqū	*n.*	the feeling of being wronged
感激	gǎnjī	*n.*	grateful feeling
仇恨	chóuhèn	*n.*	hatred; hostility

词语例句

1. ......模样：with the appearance of
   ❖ 一个很漂亮的女列车员盯着一个民工模样的中年人，大声说："查票！"
   1) 一个学生模样的人从教室里走了出来。
   2) 这孩子的模样很像他妈妈。

2. 浑身上下：from head to toe; all over
   ❖ 中年人浑身上下一阵翻找，终于找到了。
   1) 他在雨里跑了一个钟头，浑身上下都湿透了。
   2) 他浑身上下没有一个地方是干净的。

3. 一副......：(used for facial expression)
   ❖ 中年人一副苦瓜脸，解释说："我没有当地户口，人家不给办理残疾证。
   1) 他说："我用不着你帮忙！"脸上一副看不起人的样子。
   2) 一谈到他的婚姻，他就露出一副幸福得不得了的表情。

4. 连 v. 都没 v. ：do not even v.
   ❖ 连看都没看，便不耐烦地说："我们只认证不认人！"
   1) 我说完以后，他连想都没想，立刻就拒绝了我的要求。
   2) 我发现，给他做的饭菜，他连动都没动，都还在桌子上。

5. 一下子 v.：for the moment; momentarily,   all of a sudden?
   ❖ 中年人一下子说不出话来。
   1) 我一下子呆住了，不知道怎么回答。
   2) 他气得涨红了脸，一下子站起来，冲出了教室。

6. 再也不 v.了：will never v. again
   ❖ 我的脚掌被机器轧掉一半之后，就再也打不了工了。
   1) 我两年前见过他一次，以后就再也没看见过他。
   2) 我再也不敢这么做了。这一次请您高抬贵手，原谅我吧！

7. 还：even
   ❖ 这张半价票还是老乡们凑钱给我买的呢！
   1) 他是个穷光蛋，吃饭的钱还是朋友们给的呢，哪儿有钱买酒喝！
   2) 他才学了两个月，简单的句子还说不好呢，怎么能作演讲！

8. 看不惯：cannot bear the sight of; detest; hate to see

❖ 中年人对面的一个老同志看不惯了。

1) 你看他那副骄傲的样子，真让人看不惯。

2) 他看不惯那些唯利是图的人，从来不跟他们来往。

9. 难道……不成？：How could there be…?

❖ 我一个大男人在这儿站着，难道还有假不成？

1) 他是个百万富翁，难道还得跟你借钱不成？

2) 不是男人就是女人，难道还有第三种人不成？

10. 一时：for the moment

❖ 列车长呆住了，一时想不出什么话来应对。

1) 他大吃一惊，一时不知道该怎么办。

2) 我一时想不起来，明天再告诉你吧！

练习

I. 按照故事的内容，排出正确的次序：

A: （　） 出事之后，他没钱去医院做残疾评定，也回不了老家。

（　） 他是一个从乡下来的民工，出了事，老板就跑了。

（　） 可是他们凑的钱只够买一张半价票。

（　） 幸亏几个老乡同情他，凑了钱帮他买票回老家。

B: （　） 因为没有残疾证，他只好买了一张跟残疾票价格一样的儿童票。

（　） 他把被轧掉一半的脚掌给列车员看，她却说"认证不认人"。

（　） 列车员查票时，因为他没有残疾证，非要他补票不可。

（　） 后来列车长来了，但他也持同样的态度，坚持要他补票。

C: （　） 这位老同志其实是趁机把列车长和列车员狠狠地骂了一顿。

（　） 他解围的办法很巧妙，他要列车长拿出"男人证"来证明自己是个男人。

（　） 他又让女列车员拿出"人证"来证明自己是个人。

（　） 车上一位老同志看不惯列车长的态度，就站出来替这个民工解围。

II. 把正确的词语填进去：

| 朝，指着他的鼻子，浑身上下，不成，一番 |

1. 雨很大，他又没有伞，＿＿＿＿ 都湿透了。
2. 售票员不耐烦地 ＿＿＿＿ 他看了一眼，就大声地说："没钱，你买什么票！"
3. 他打量了这个陌生人 ＿＿＿＿ ，然后很不客气地问道："从哪儿来的？"
4. 我 ＿＿＿＿ ，大声地骂："你简直不是人！"
5. 我是你的老师，难道还会骗你 ＿＿＿＿ ？

| 一下子，连想都没想，盯着，一副，还 |

6. 他 ＿＿＿＿ ，马上说出了答案。
7. 我自行车 ＿＿＿＿ 买不起呢，哪儿能买汽车！
8. 他 ＿＿＿＿ 我看了半天，才想起来我是谁。
9. 我仔细向他说明学校的规定，他听了以后，脸上 ＿＿＿＿ 不高兴的样子。

10. 他 _____ 暴跳如雷，尖声叫道："你嘴巴干净点儿！"

III. 选最合适的词填进去：

1. 拿，捏
   a. 他进来的时候，手里 _____ 着一本很大的字典。
   b. 我仔细一看，发现他手里 _____ 着一张破破烂烂(tattered)的钞票(bill)。

2. 看，打量
   a. 你病得挺严重，最好去 _____ 医生，自己买药吃是不行的。
   b. 他们回头 _____ 着这个陌生人，目光里充满了怀疑。

3. 一番，一次
   a. 我只看过 _____，哪里能记得那么清楚呢！
   b. 他们热烈地讨论了 _____ ，最后决定改变原来的计划。

4. 一副，一张
   a. _____ 车票花不了多少钱，我替他买吧！
   b. 看到他那 _____ 痛苦的表情，我真有点儿不忍心。

5. 跑了，走了
   a. 撞他的人撞了他就 _____ ，因此他没得到赔偿。
   b. 你找张老师？张老师 3 点钟下课以后立刻就 _____ 。

6. 看不惯，住不惯
   a. 在这儿住了半年了，我还是 _____ 。
   b. 他那个看不起人的态度，我真 _____ 。

IV. 讨论问题：

1. 你认为这篇小说的作者对这个火车上发生的事件持什么样的态度？请你举例说明。
2. 请你根据这篇小说从以下两方面来谈谈中国的状况：
   1) 流动人口（民工）的困境，2) 残疾人受到的待遇。
3. 列车员和列车长都错了吗？
4. 请你从女列车员的角度，改写这个故事。
5. 故事的最后一部分，那个民工眼里蓄满了泪水，你认为是因为委屈，感激，还是仇恨？
6. 这是不是一篇好的短篇小说？为什么？
7. 这个故事并没说出结局。你认为结局是怎么样的？

一生的痛悔

蓝风

　　那一年我从省邮电学校毕业，被分配在大别山区一个偏远的小镇上当邮差，女朋友也随之⑴与我分手。我的心情简直糟透了，成⑵天琢磨着怎样离开这个山区，根本无心⑶工作。

　　我所负责的一条线更是名副其实的穷乡僻壤，邮件少得可怜⑷，这倒好，我总是等信件积累得差不多才劳驾⑸自己跑一趟，大概平均半个月一次吧。好在下面管理松散，没有人过问，说白了，其实根本没有人注意到一个山村小邮差的存在，但有一位老人除外。

　　这位老人住在深山里的一个村庄里，已年过花甲。每逢我送信到他们村，总⑹看见她老远就站在村口。我还没下车，她就迎了上来，小声问：“有我儿子的信吗？”

一生	yìshēng	*n.*	lifetime
痛悔	tònghuǐ	*n.*	deep regret
邮电学校	yóudiàn xuéxiào	*n.*	school of post and telecommunications
分配	fēnpèi	*v.*	assign (a job)
大别山区	Dàbiéshānqū	*n.*	Dabie Mountain, a mountainous area in Anhui Province
偏远	piānyuǎn	*adj.*	remote; faraway
小镇	xiǎozhèn	*n.*	small town
当	dāng	*v.*	work as; serve as
邮差	yóuchāi	*n.*	mailman

Selected & prepared by: Liping Yu
Edited by: Chih-p'ing Chou

随之	suízhī	adv.	following this
分手	fēnshǒu	v.-o.	break up
心情	xīnqíng	n.	mood
糟透了	zāotòu.le	v.-c.	extremely bad
成天	chéngtiān	n.	all day long
琢磨	zuó.mo	v.	turn sth. over in one's mind; ponder
无心	wúxīn	v.	not in the mood for
负责	fùzé	v.	be responsible for; be in charge of
线	xiàn	n.	line; route
名副其实	míngfùqíshí	idm.	be worthy of the name; the name matches the reality
穷乡僻壤	qióngxiāng pìrǎng	idm.	remote, backward place
邮件	yóujiàn	n.	mail
可怜	kělián	adj.	miserably; pitifully
积累	jīlěi	v.	accumulate
劳驾	láojià	v.	excuse me; May I trouble you?
下面	xiàmiàn	n.	lower level; subordinate
管理	guǎnlǐ	v.	manage; administer
松散	sōngsǎn	adj.	loose; lax
过问	guòwèn	v.	inquire about; take an interest in 不该过问他的私事
说白了	shuōbáile	phr.	frankly speaking; in short
除外	chúwài	v.	be an exception; apart from
深山	shēnshān	n.	remote mountains; deep in the mountains
村庄	cūnzhuāng	n.	village
花甲	huājiǎ	n.	sixty years of age
每逢	měiféng	v.	every encounter; every occasion
老	lǎo	adv.	very 老远/老高/老大
村口	cūnkǒu	n.	the entrance to a village
迎上来	yíng.shang.lai	v.-c.	go to meet

渐渐地我就知道了这位老人的一些事：早年丧夫，唯一的儿子在深圳打工。开始我还在包里翻找一遍，问多了我就有些不耐烦地说："没没没！" 车停都不停(7)，直奔村长家。

但老人还是不厌其烦地嘱咐我："娃子，有我儿子的信麻烦(8)你给捎来，啊？"

我送信是没有规律的，或十天或半月的，但每次总是老远地被老太太迎接着。我不知道这位老人是不是每天都这么等着，那时我根本无心琢磨这些。

在我的记忆里，还真给老人送过一回信，深圳来的。 老人拿着信小心翼翼地求我读给她听。也许是老人的神情让我良心发现，我破例耐心地给她念了，还把要紧的解释给她听："您的儿子春节忙，不回家过年。"

老人的眼里顿时(9)涌出了混浊的泪。那会儿我动了恻隐之心(10)，忙安慰她："但您的儿子很有孝心，马上要给您寄钱和年货回来。"老人顿时含着泪连连(11)点头，忙不迭地说："啊唉！啊唉！多谢娃子，多谢娃子！"

渐渐	jiànjiàn	adv.	gradually; increasingly; step by step
丧夫	sàngfū	v.-o.	lose a husband; be widowed
唯一	wéiyī	adj.	single; only; sole
翻找	fānzhǎo	v.	rummage; search
不耐烦	bú nàifán	adj.	impatient
直奔	zhíbèn	v.	head directly for
村长	cūnzhǎng	n.	village head

不厌其烦	búyànqífán	*idm.*	do not mind to take the trouble to do something.; be extremely patient 老师不厌其烦地给孩子们讲要注意安全。
嘱咐	zhǔ.fu	*v.*	urge; exhort; tell 妈妈嘱咐孩子下学以后早点回家。
娃子	wá.zi	*n.*	baby; child (a diminutive)
麻烦	má.fan	*v./adj.*	trouble somebody; bother sb. to do sth.
捎	shāo	*v.*	bring to sb.
规律	guīlǜ	*n.*	regulation; regular pattern
迎接	yíngjiē	*v.*	meet, greet
记忆	jìyì	*n.*	memory
小心翼翼	xiǎoxīnyìyì	*idm.*	cautiously; with great care
神情	shénqíng	*n.*	expression
良心发现	liángxīnfāxiàn	*idm.*	be stung by conscience
破例	pòlì	*v.*	break a rule; make an exception
耐心	nàixīn	*adv.*	patiently
解释	jiěshì	*v.*	explain
春节	Chūnjié	*n.*	Spring Festival; Chinese New Year
顿时	dùnshí	*adv.*	immediately; at once (used for past events)
涌出	yǒngchū	*v.*	well up
混浊	húnzhuó	*adj.*	muddy; turbid
动心	dòngxīn	*v.-o.*	one's emotions are stirred; one's interest is aroused
恻隐之心	cèyǐnzhīxīn	*n.*	compassion; pity
安慰	ānwèi	*v.*	comfort; console; soothe
孝心	xiàoxīn	*n.*	filial piety
年货	niánhuò	*n.*	special purchases for the Spring Festival
含着	hán.zhe	*v.*	have/fill with (tears in the eyes)
连连	liánlián	*adv.*	repeatedly; again and again
忙不迭	mángbùdié	*adv.*	hasten to do sth.看见老师来了，他忙不迭地请老师进来坐下。

　　等我将信件送到村长家时，惊奇地看到老人竟然⑫比我们先到了村长家，但不是找我，只见她高扬着信，中气十足地说：“我儿子来信了，要寄钱回来，还寄年货，大城市的年货呢，赶明儿过去尝尝鲜吧！”

　　村长笑眯眯地说：“好啊！赶明儿率领全村的男女老少都到你家去尝鲜吧！”

　　“好啊，好啊，我还得在村里再买些腊鱼腊肉，备足些才好啊。我儿子的钱快到了，快到了！”老人因激动而满脸通红。

　　这一年的冬天似乎特别的寒冷，一场又一场纷飞的大雪将大山、小村和我的心严严实实地覆盖着。我送信的次数越来越少。腊月初八这天，我在旧历年里最后一次来到老人的村庄。老人上前一把拉住我，急切地问：“有我儿子的汇款单吗？”

　　“没有。”我几乎忘了她的儿子曾给她写过那封信。也许是天气的原因，我的回答恢复到以前冷冰冰的状态，根本没有在意一位老人此时的焦虑与不安。

　　一个星期后，我将一些零散的邮件锁进抽屉，提前⑬回家过年了。

惊奇	jīngqí	*adv.*	surprised; amazed
竟然	jìngrán	*adv.*	surprisingly
高扬	gāoyáng	*v.*	raise sth. high
中气十足	zhōngqì shízú	*adj.*	full of vigor; full of spirit
赶	gǎn	*v.*	wait till a time in the future 赶明儿我们再去一次。

尝尝	cháng.chang	v.	taste
鲜	xiān	n.	delicious food
笑眯眯地	xiàomīmī.de	adv.	with a smile on one's face; smilingly
率领	shuàilǐng	v.	lead; head
腊肉	làròu	n.	bacon; cured meat
备	bèi	v.	prepare; get ready
足	zú	adj.	sufficient; ample
激动	jīdòng	v./adj.	agitate; stir; excite
满脸	mǎnliǎn	n.	entire face; whole face
通红	tōnghóng	adj.	very red
冬天	dōngtiān	n.	winter
寒冷	hánlěng	adj.	cold
大雪纷飞	dàxuěfēnfēi	phr.	the snow flakes were falling thick and fast
严严实实	yányán shíshí	adv.	tightly, closely
覆盖	fùgài	v.	cover, blanketed
腊月	làyuè	n.	the 12th lunar month
急切	jíqiè	adv./ adj.	anxiously/anxious
汇款单	huìkuǎn dān	n.	money order
恢复	huīfù	v.	resume
冷冰冰	lěngbīngbīng	adj.	ice cold; icy; frosty
状态	zhuàngtài	n.	state; condition
在意	zàiyì	v.	take notice of; pay attention to 他的话只是开玩笑，你别在意。
焦虑	jiāolǜ	adj./n.	worry; anxiety
不安	bù'ān	adj./n.	uneasy
零散	língsǎn	adj.	scattered
锁	suǒ	v.	lock
抽屉	chōu.ti	n.	drawer
提前	tíqián	v.	in advance; ahead of time

　　家的温馨暂时融化了我心头的冰山。我将那个恼人的穷山沟抛到了九霄云外，痛痛快快地过了一个喜气洋洋的春节。但好景不长，半月过后，我极不情愿地回到了大别山区，回到了那个让我沮丧的工作岗位。

　　我将年前没有送出的邮件整理了一下，准备送出去。这时，我突然发现了那位老人的儿子从深圳寄来的汇款单和包裹单，不禁⑭一愣，一种不祥的预兆袭上心头。我马不停蹄地向老人的村庄赶去。可我已经去得太晚太晚！意料之中的事情发生了，老人已经长眠于村口的坟山上了。

　　据说，老人在年前每天都在村口翘首企盼，任谁都⑮劝不走。她说"我儿子说到了就会做到，除非……除非他出什么事啦？" 说到这里，老人总是连扇自己几耳光，然后自我安慰道："不会的不会的，瞧我这乌鸦嘴。我儿子没事的，他会寄来的，我再等等，再等等！" 就这样，直到大年三十新年的爆竹响起的时候，村长再一次去劝老人时，发现老人已被雪覆盖，成了一

温馨	wēnxīn	*adj./n.*	warmth, coziness
融化	rónghuà	*v.*	thaw
冰山	bīngshān	*n.*	iceberg
恼人	nǎorén	*adj.*	annoying; irritating
山沟	shāngōu	*n.*	remote mountain valley
抛到九霄云外	pāodào jiǔxiāo yúnwài	*phr.*	recede from one's mind far into the ninth celestial sphere; vanish into the ninth region of heaven 抛：throw; toss; fling

痛痛快快	tòngtòng kuāikuāi	*adv.*	happily; delightedly
喜气洋洋	xǐqìyángyáng	*idm.*	full of joy
好景不长	hǎojǐng bùcháng	*idm.*	Good times don't last long.
情愿	qíngyuàn	*v.*	be willing to 她一点都不情愿辞职在家看孩子。
沮丧	jǔsàng	*adj.*	deject; depress
岗位	gǎngwèi	*n.*	station; post
包裹	bāoguǒ	*n.*	package; parcel
不禁	bùjīn	*adv.*	can't help (doing sth.); can't refrain from 他听到这些话，不禁笑起来。
愣	lèng	*v.*	blank; stupefied 愣了半天/愣住了
不祥	bùxiáng	*adj.*	ominous; inauspicious
预兆	yùzhào	*n.*	presage; omen
袭	xí	*v.*	raid; make a surprise attack on
马不停蹄	mǎbùtíngtí	*idm.*	make a hurried journey without stop; without a single halt 接到妈妈病重的电话，他马不停蹄地赶回家。
赶去	gǎnqù	*v.*	hurry; rush
长眠	chángmián	*v.*	sleep eternally; die
坟山	fénshān	*n.*	cemetery hill
翘首企盼	qiáoshǒu qǐpàn	*phr.*	raise one's head and stand on tiptoe – eagerly looking forward to/awaiting
任…都…	rèn…dōu…	*conj.*	no matter (how/what/ etc.)
扇	shān	*v.*	slap
耳光	ěrguāng	*n.*	a slap on the face
自我	zìwǒ	*n.*	self; oneself
道	dào	*v.*	speak, say
瞧	qiáo	*v.*	look
乌鸦嘴	wūyā zuǐ	*n.*	a person who always says something inauspicious
爆竹	bàozhú	*n.*	firecracker

尊永远的雕塑。

老人的遭遇让我麻木的心灵受到了强烈的震撼。我手捧汇款单和包裹单跪在老人的坟前痛彻心扉，号啕大哭。那是一个因生活的不遂意而变得玩世不恭的青年从骨子里流出的忏悔的泪。

选自《做人与处世》 2001 年第 3 期

尊	zūn	AN.	measure word used for statue
			一尊佛像
永远	yǒngyuǎn	adj.	forever; ever; for good
雕塑	diāosù	n.	statue; carved figure
遭遇	zāoyù	n.	(bitter) experience; (hapless) fate
麻木	mámù	adj.	numb; be dead to all feeling
心灵	xīnlíng	n.	thoughts and feelings
强烈	qiángliè	adj.	strong; intense; violent
震撼	zhènhàn	n.	shock
捧	pěng	v.	hold in both hands
跪	guì	v.	kneel
痛彻心扉	tòngchèxīnfēi	idm.	pain shoots through one's heart – a deep grief
号啕大哭	háotáo dàkū	idm.	cry loudly; cry one's eyes out
遂意	suìyì	adj.	to one's liking; fulfill one's desire
玩世不恭	wánshì bùgōng	idm.	be cynical; take a cynical attitude towards life
骨子里	gǔ.zilǐ	n.	innermost being
忏悔	chànhuǐ	v.	confess; repent; be penitent

词语例句

1. 随之：following this
   - ❖ 那一年我从省邮电学校毕业, 被分配在大别山区一个偏远的小镇上当邮差, 女朋友也随之与我分手。
   1) 由于管理松散，工作效率随之下降。
   2) 大学毕业后，许多老同学随之分散各地，难得见面。

2. 成 + Time word：whole + time word
   成天/成日/成月/成年
   - ❖ 我成天琢磨着怎么离开这个山区。
   1) 市中心成天都有很多买东西的人。
   2) 他成年在外工作，很少在家住。

3. 无心 + V：not in the mood to v.
   - ❖ 我根本无心工作。
   1) 跟女朋友分手以后，他根本无心做任何事情。
   2) 毕业以后我一直在找工作，无心做别的事情。

4. adj. 得可怜：miserably/pitifully adj.
   - ❖ 邮件少得可怜。
   1) 这个地区的老百姓穷得可怜。
   2) 整个工程的进度慢得可怜。

5. 劳驾：May I trouble you…?
   - ❖ 我总是等信件积累得差不多才劳驾自己跑一趟。
   1) 劳驾，请您帮我把信寄出去。
   2) 劳您驾，让我过去。

6. 每逢……总/都……：on every occasion; when
   - ❖ 每逢我送信到他们村，总看见她老远就站在村口。
   1) 每逢过年过节，他都给孩子买些礼物。
   2) 每逢假期，他总是回去看看父母。

7. （连）v. 都不 v.：don't even bother to v.
   - ❖ 我的车停都不停，直奔村长家。

1) 老师给他打电话，他（连）接都不接。

2) 妈妈出事了，可是他（连）问都 不问。

8. 麻烦：bother sb. to do sth.

❖ 有我儿子的信麻烦你给捎来。

1) 我最不喜欢麻烦别人。

2) 这么一点小事你就不要去麻烦老板了。

9. 顿时：at once, but only used for past events

❖ 老人的眼里顿时涌出混浊的泪。

1) 听到这个坏消息，他顿时大哭起来。

2) 老板一发脾气，他顿时不敢开玩笑了。

10. 动心：one's mind is perturbed; one's interest is aroused

❖ 那会儿，我动了恻隐之心。

1) 看见别人买跑车，我也动心了。

2) 别人都去北京了，我也动了去北京的心。

11. 连连 + v.: v. repeatedly, v. again and again

❖ 老人顿时含着泪连连点头。

1) 吃了真正的中国饭以后，他连连说："真好吃，真好吃。"

2) 他在单位里连连出事，终于被开除了。

12. 竟然：surprisingly

❖ 老人竟然比我先到村长家。

1) 这么好的电影竟然没有人看。

2) 那么冷的天气，他竟然没穿大衣。

13. 提前 + v.: v. in advance; v. ahead of time

❖ 一个星期以后，我提前回家过年了。

1) 明天的事情比较多，请你提前 来上班。

2) 由于使用了计算机，他们提前完成了任务。

14. 不禁 + v.: can't help (doing sth.); can't refrain from

❖ 这时, 我突然发现了那位老人的儿子从深圳寄来的汇款单和包裹单，不禁一愣。

1) 他完全没想到父亲会在此时出现，不禁大吃一惊。

2) 他听说了这个消息，不禁兴奋得跳了起来。

15. 任… （question word）都…： no matter (how, what, etc.)
   ❖ 老人每天都到村口去，任谁都劝不走。
   1) 任你怎么解释，这件事都是不可原谅的。
   2) 这是一件珍贵的礼物，任你花多少钱我都不卖。

练习

I. 读下面的句子，然后用划线的词语造句：

1. 我的心情简直糟透了，<u>成天琢磨着</u>怎样离开这个山区，<u>根本无心</u>工作。
2. <u>每逢</u>我送信到他们村，<u>总</u>看见她老远就站在村口。
3. 有我儿子的信<u>麻烦</u>你给我捎来。
4. 老人的神情让我良心发现，我<u>破例</u>耐心地给她念了。
5. 我<u>惊奇</u>地看到老人<u>竟然</u>比我们先到了村长家。
6. 老人的脸<u>因</u>激动<u>而</u>满脸通红。
7. 一场又一场纷飞的大雪<u>将</u>大山、小村和我的心覆盖着。
8. 我的回答<u>恢复到</u>以前冷冰冰的<u>状态</u>，<u>根本没有</u>注意到她的焦虑和不安。

II. 把划线部分改用一个四字成语：

> 名副其实，不厌其烦，小心翼翼，玩世不恭，
> 喜气洋洋，马不停蹄，翘首企盼

1. 她是一个<u>做什么事都不认真，什么事情都不在乎</u>的人。
2. 这个服务员<u>一点都不嫌麻烦</u>地帮顾客选衣服。
3. 我的老板非常厉害，所以我们总是<u>十分小心</u>地工作。
4. 我在中国只住了两个星期，可是我<u>一刻不停</u>地参观了 10 个城市。
5. 快过节了，孩子们都<u>盼望</u>着得到很多礼物。

III. 用所给的词完成句子：

1. 公司的经理辞职了以后，＿＿＿＿＿＿＿＿＿＿＿＿＿＿＿＿（随之）
2. 这个公司的管理松散，＿＿＿＿＿＿＿＿＿＿＿＿。（好在）
3. 这些腊肉坏了，＿＿＿＿＿＿＿＿＿＿＿＿＿。（劳驾）
4. 学生们还是没有听懂，所以＿＿＿＿＿＿＿＿＿＿。（不厌其烦）
5. 她很少在公共场合讲话，＿＿＿＿＿＿＿＿＿＿＿。（破例）
6. 她的好朋友们买股票赚了很多钱，所以，＿＿＿＿＿＿。（动…的心）
7. 连连工作了几天以后，她累得不得了，＿＿＿＿。（恢复到…的状态）
8. 她无论如何也不想再上学了，＿＿＿＿＿＿＿＿＿。（任…都）

IV. 用所给词语回答问题：

1. 老人是怎样盼着儿子的来信的？
   （一把拉住，不厌其烦，嘱咐，急切，不安，任……都）

2. 这个邮差是一个什么样的人？他是怎样工作的？
   （分配，偏远，根本无心，积累，不耐烦，极不情愿）

3. 老人急切的心情跟邮差懒散的工作形成了强烈的对比，你觉得老人的死对邮差会有什么影响？
   （受到……震撼，忏悔，玩世不恭）

V. 讨论问题：

1. 你怎样看中国大学生的分配制度？
2. 一个不喜欢自己的工作的人有没有权利不好好地做自己的工作？
3. 中国的老人有哪些特点？他们跟孩子的关系是怎样的？你怎么看这种关系？

遗 嘱

付爱毛

老金55岁了。

55岁的老金经营着一个巨大的建材企业，他手头儿究竟⑴有多少资产，谁也说不清。只晓得，他向慈善机构捐款，一出手就是十万二十几万的。

老金有两个儿子一个女儿，老伴儿在几年前就去世了。

老伴儿去世后，有一打儿的女人挖空心思想嫁给老金，老金一概回绝了：自己已老朽得如同一把枯柴，且患有心脏病，他清楚那些女人想要的是什么。

老金对狗十分宠爱。几十年的商人生活使他明白了一个道理：狗有时比人更值得信赖。

不过，狗与人相比总是短命的，这让老金深感遗憾。在死掉了几条狗之后，老金发誓再也不养狗了⑵。

遗嘱	yízhǔ	n.	last words; will
经营	jīngyíng	v.	operate; run a business
巨大	jùdà	adj.	huge
建材	jiàncái	n.	building materials
企业	qǐyè	n.	enterprise
手头儿	shǒutóur	n.	one's financial condition at the moment

Selected & prepared by: Liping Yu
Edited by: Chih-p'ing Chou

究竟	jiūjìng	*adv.*	exactly; after all
资产	zīchǎn	*n.*	property
晓得	xiǎo.de	*v.*	know
向	xiàng	*prep.*	to
慈善	císhàn	*adj.*	charitable; philanthropic; benevolent
机构	jīgòu	*n.*	organization; institution
捐款	juānkuǎn	*v.-o.*	donate
出手	chūshǒu	*v.*	take out (money; property; etc.)
老伴儿	lǎobànr	*n.*	one's dear old companion – one's spouse in old age
去世	qùshì	*v.*	pass away
打儿	dár	*AN.*	a dozen
挖空心思	wākōngxīn.si	*idm.*	rack one's brains
嫁给	jiàgěi	*v.*	(of a woman) marry
一概	yígài	*adv.*	without exception 所有的要求，一概不准。
回绝	huíjué	*v.*	refuse; decline
老朽	lǎoxiǔ	*adj./n.*	decrepitude, old and useless
如同	rútóng	*v.*	like; 像
枯柴	kūchái	*n.*	dry wood; dry branch
患	huàn	*v.*	suffer from (an illness)
心脏病	xīnzàngbìng	*n.*	heart disease
宠爱	chǒng'ài	*v.*	fond of (pets, children; implies the object of affection is of lower status than the one giving affection)
商人	shāngrén	*n.*	businessman
道理	dàolǐ	*n.*	principle; truth
信赖	xìnlài	*v.*	trust
短命	duǎnmìng	*adj.*	be short-lived
遗憾	yíhàn	*n./adj.*	regret; sorrow
发誓	fāshì	*v.*	swear

没有狗相伴的日子，老金显得形单影只，女儿看了心疼，便在他 63 岁生日的时候，又送了他一条狗。这条狗虽然不是什么名贵狗，但乖巧、温顺，好像天生与老金有缘⑶，一见到它，老金就很喜爱。他给小狗取名"闹闹"，每天无论多忙，他都亲自替闹闹洗澡；闹闹生病了，他又亲自带它去宠物医院看医生。

就是在那家宠物医院里，老金认识了阿方。阿方是宠物医院的护士。每次老金带闹闹去看病时，阿方姑娘都亲切地把闹闹抱进怀里，又是逗着玩儿又是抚爱的，就像一个年轻的妈妈爱抚自己的孩子那样。老金看在眼里，喜在心上。后来，老金就把阿方姑娘聘请到家里专门照顾闹闹。再后来，阿方就成了老金的妻子。结婚的这一年，老金 63 岁，阿方 23 岁。

大家都认为年轻貌美的阿方是"因狗得福"的，她嫁给老金一定另有图谋。而阿方表现出的却是另一种姿态。她在老金面前从来没有提及"钱"这个话题，也从来不肯接受老金送她的任何贵重礼物。她对老金说："这世界上只有两样是她的最爱，一是老金这个人，二是老金养的这条狗。她要用自己的行动向人们证明⑷：在这个物欲横流的社会，还存在着⑸一种纯粹的东西，那就是没有任何功利的爱。

| 相伴 | xiāngbàn | v. | follow; accompany |
| 形单影只 | xíngdān yǐngzhī | idm. | a solitary form, a single shadow -- extremely lonely |

心疼	xīnténg	*adj.*	feel sorry; be distressed
名贵	míngguì	*adj.*	precious; expensive
乖巧	guāiqiǎo	*adj.*	cute; lovely
温顺	wēnshùn	*adj.*	docile; tame
与…有缘	yǔ….yǒuyuán	*v.*	be brought together by fortune/fate 我跟他很有缘，一见面就成了好朋友。
给…取名	gěi…qǔmíng	*v.*	name someone
宠物	chǒngwù	*n.*	pet
护士	hù.shi	*n.*	nurse
姑娘	gū.niang	*n.*	girl; miss
亲切	qīnqiè	*adv.*	tender; kind
抱	bào	*v.*	hold or carry in arms
怀	huái	*n.*	bosom
逗	dòu	*v.*	play with; tease
抚爱	fǔ'ài	*v.*	caress; fondle
爱抚	àifǔ	*v.*	caress; show tender care for
聘请	pìnqǐng	*v.*	invite; hire
专门	zhuānmén	*adv.*	specially
年轻貌美	niánqīng màoměi	*idm.*	young and pretty
图谋	túmóu	*n.*	conspiracy; plot; scheme
姿态	zītài	*n.*	appearance; attitude
提及	tíjí	*v.*	mention; speak of
话题	huàtí	*n.*	topic
贵重	guìzhòng	*adj.*	valuable; precious
最爱	zuì'ài	*n.*	favorite
行动	xíngdòng	*n.*	action; operation
证明	zhèngmíng	*v.*	prove; demonstrate
物欲横流	wùyùhéngliú	*idm.*	material desires overflow
存在	cúnzài	*v.*	exist
纯粹	chúncuì	*adj.*	pure
功利	gōnglì	*n.*	material gain

（三）遗嘱

既有女人又有狗的日子，老金感到心满意足。然而，夕阳无限好，只是近黄昏。和阿方姑娘结婚还不到一年的时间，老金就心脏病突发去世了。不过，他的猝死并没有引出什么乱子来。毕竟(6)是在商场上混(7)了半辈子的人，老金自有他的精明之处。在跟阿方姑娘结婚前一个月，他就悄悄立下了遗嘱。

在老金的后事处理完后，律师和公证人就宣布了遗嘱：老金的全部不动产归(8)两个儿子所有，全部动产平均分成三份，分别归两个儿子和一个女儿所有。具体细则有遗嘱附本详细说明。

当然，作为(9)他的合法妻子，他不可能不(10)提到阿方。他在遗嘱中特别说明：他很爱他的狗。他认为在他所有的财产中，最贵重的就是那条名叫"闹闹"的狗。因为它代表着"爱"、"忠诚"以及"信任"这些最美好的东西，是多少金钱都无法替代的。

心满意足	xīnmǎnyìzú	idm.	be perfectly satisfied
夕阳无限好 只是近黄昏	xīyáng wúxiàn hǎo; zhǐshì jìn huánghūn		A sunset may be infinitely brilliant, nonetheless night follows its heels
突发	tūfā	v.	burst out or occur suddenly
猝死	cùsǐ	n.	sudden death
引出	yǐnchū	v.	give rise to; draw forth; lead to
乱子	luàn.zi	n.	disturbance; trouble
毕竟	bìjìng	adv.	after all
混	hùn	v.	drift along; muddle along

他在大学里混了四年，居然也毕业了。

半辈子	bànbèi.zi	n.	half a lifetime
精明	jīngmíng	adj.	shrewd
悄悄	qiāoqiāo	adv.	quietly
			他悄悄地走进教室，坐在后面。
立	lì	v.	make/set up (a will)
后事	hòushì	n.	funeral affairs
处理	chǔlǐ	v.	handle; deal with
公证人	gōngzhèng rén	n.	notary public
宣布	xuānbù	v.	declare; announce
全部	quánbù	adj.	entire; full
归…所有	guī…suǒyǒu	v.	be turned over to sb. to verb
			这些土地将来会归国家所有。
动产	dòngchǎn	n.	movable goods; transferable assets (as opposed to fixed assets)
平均	píngjūn	adj./v.	equally; share and share alike
分成	fēnchéng	v.	divide into
份	fènr	AN.	share
分别	fēnbié	adv.	respectively
具体	jùtǐ	adj.	concrete; specific
细则	xìzé	n.	detailed rules and regulations
附本	fùběn	n.	supplementary articles
详细	xiángxì	adj.	in detail
说明	shuōmíng	v/n.	explain; illustrate
作为	zuòwéi	v.	as; being
合法	héfǎ	adj.	legal; lawful; legitimate
财产	cáichǎn	n.	properties
代表	dàibiǎo	v./n.	represent, representative
忠诚	zhōngchéng	adj./n.	loyal; faithful, faithfulness; loyalty
信任	xìnrèn	v./n.	trust
替代	tìdài	v.	substitute for; replace

如果他突然去世的话，他要把闹闹作为一份最珍贵的遗产，留给⑾他的妻子阿方，希望阿方像他在世时那样，悉心照料它。如果阿方不同意收养它，则征询家里其它人的意见，谁愿意就把狗托付给谁⑿。实在没有人收养，就把狗送到福利院，总之不能让它流落街头。

遗嘱刚刚宣读完毕⒀，阿方就歇斯底里大叫起来，一边叫一边骂老金没有良心。说他把所有的财产都给了自己的儿子和女儿，却给自己一条该死的哈巴狗。自己付出⒁青春和美貌，耐着性子⒂陪个"老不死的"，并不是无偿的。看着这个以"贤淑"和"爱心"著称⒃的女人一瞬间变成这副嘴脸，大家深感惊诧。

等她骂够了，律师再一次郑重征询她的意见，问她愿意不愿意收养闹闹。她咬牙切齿地骂道："收养它个大头鬼⒄啦！我生平最恨的就是狗！让它去死吧！"见她坚决拒绝，律师便遵照遗嘱，当场⒅征询家里其他人的意见。老金的三个儿女由于财产的分配不是很合意，都默不作声。

珍贵	zhēnguì	*adj.*	valuable; precious
遗产	yíchǎn	*n.*	legacy; inherited goods
留	liú	*v.*	leave behind
在世	zàishì	*v.*	be living
悉心	xīxīn	*v.*	with the entire mind
照料	zhàoliào	*v.*	take care of
收养	shōuyǎng	*v.*	adopt

34

则	zé	*conj.*	then
征询	zhēngxún	*v.*	query; consult
其他	qítā	*adj.*	other
托付	tuō.fu	*v.*	entrust; commit sth. to sb.'s care
福利院	fúlìyuàn	*n.*	nursery home; (here): animal shelter
总之	zǒngzhī	*conj.*	in a word, in short; in brief
流落	liúluò	*v.*	drift about; wander about
街头	jiētóu	*n.*	street
完毕	wánbì	*v.*	finish; complete
歇斯底里	xiēsīdǐlǐ	*adj./n.*	hysterical, hysteria
骂	mà	*v.*	curse
良心	liángxīn	*n.*	conscience
该死	gāisǐ	*adj.*	goddamned
哈巴狗	hā.bagǒu	*n.*	Pekingese
耐着性子	nài.zhe xìng.zi	*adv.*	restrain oneself; patiently do sth.
无偿的	wúcháng.de	*adj.*	gratuitous; done without compensation
以…著称	yǐ...zhùchēng	*v.*	be celebrated for; be famous for 这所学校以管理严格著称。
贤淑	xiánshū	*adj.*	(of a woman) virtuous
一瞬间	yíshùnjiān	*n.*	in the twinkling of an eye
嘴脸	zuǐliǎn	*n.*	look; countenance
惊诧	jīngchà	*adj.*	amazed; surprised
郑重	zhèngzhòng	*adj.*	serious; solemn
意见	yìjiàn	*n.*	idea; opinion
咬牙切齿	yǎoyáqièchǐ	*idm.*	grit one's teeth
生平	shēngpíng	*n.*	all one's life
遵照	zūnzhào	*v.*	comply with; act in accordance to
当场	dāngchǎng	*adv.*	on the spot
分配	fēnpèi	*v.*	distribute
合意	héyì	*adj.*	agreeable; to one's liking
默不作声	mòbú zuòshēng	*idm.*	hold one's tongue; keep silence

老金家的保姆，一个伺候了老金多年的乡下阿嫂秋桂最后说："既然大家都不想养这条狗，我就带回乡下去养好了。"老金生前一直对她不薄，如今老金去了，她收养他的狗，也算为他尽一点心意。既然秋桂阿嫂愿意收养闹闹，律师就让秋桂在一份文件上签⑲了字。

秋桂签完了字，律师和公证人当场拿出另一份遗嘱附本宣布道：愿意收养闹闹者，奖励人民币五百万。

阿方听到这里，当场昏厥了过去。老金的三个儿女也都傻了似的呆住了。

选自《爱情、婚姻、家庭》2000年第10期

保姆	bǎomǔ	n.	maid; housekeeper
伺候	cì.hou	v.	serve; wait on
乡下	xiāng.xia	n.	countryside
阿嫂	āsǎo	n.	an informal way to address a middle-aged woman
薄	báo	adj.	lacking in warmth (usually used in the negative form) 待她不薄 treat her quite well
如今	rújīn	n.	nowadays; now
尽	jìn	v.	exert one's utmost effort 尽最大的努力/尽责任
心意	xīnyì	n.	kindly feelings; regard
文件	wénjiàn	n.	file; record
签	qiān	v.	sign
奖励	jiǎnglì	v.	reward
昏厥	hūnjúe	v.	faint
傻	shǎ	v.	be dumbfounded; be stunned
呆住	dāi.zhu	v.-c.	be stunned

词语例句

1. 究竟：same as 到底；exactly; after all (used in questions and statements)
    ❖ 他手头究竟有多少资产，谁也说不清。
    1) 跟你说话的那个人究竟是谁？
    2) 他虽然很能干，但究竟/毕竟/到底年纪大了，一紧张就受不了。

2. 再也不 v.了：will never do sth. again
    ❖ 在死掉了几条狗以后，他发誓以后再也不养狗了。
    1) 那个商店老骗人，我再也不去那里买东西了。
    2) 我已经等了十年了，我再也不想等了。

3. A 跟 B 有缘：A and B are brought together by fortune
    ❖ 那条狗好像天生跟老金有缘。
    1) 我跟他特别有缘，每次出门总能碰见他。
    2) 我跟他很有缘，见面不久就结婚了。

4. 向⋯证明：to prove something to somebody
    ❖ 她要向人们证明这个世界上有纯粹的爱。
    1) 她要向法官证明她没有罪。
    2) 这件事向大家证明她不是一个唯利是图的人。

5. 存在(着): exist
    ❖ 这个物欲横流的社会里还存在着没有任何功利的爱。
    1) 中国虽然发展很快，但是还存在着严重的社会问题。
    2) 他们夫妻之间存在着很深的矛盾。

6. 毕竟：after all (used in positive sentences only)
    ❖ 毕竟是在商场上混了半辈子的人，老金自有他的精明之处。
    1) 计算机毕竟是一个机器，还得有人操作。
    2) 她毕竟还是一个孩子，有很多事她根本不懂。

7. 混：drift along, muddle along
    ❖ 他毕竟是在商场上混了半辈子的人。
    1) 这个学生根本不喜欢念书，一天到晚混日子。
    2) 她没有什么学问，她的文凭是混出来的。

8．归… v.: be turned over to sb. to v.

　　归…所有/负责/管/领导

　❖ 他的全部不动产归两个儿子所有。

　1）这笔钱归学校管，不归我管。

　2）城市的环境卫生归政府负责。

9．作为… : as; being

　❖ 作为他的合法妻子，他不可能不提到阿方。

　1）作为老师，你绝对不能迟到。

　2）作为一个法官，你应该公平地对待每一个人。

10．不可能不 v.: must; be impossible not to

　❖ 他不可能不提到阿方。

　1）今天的考试很重要，他不可能不来。

　2）上大学的时候，我们是同屋，她不可能不记得我。

11．把A留给B: leave A to B

　❖ 他把那条狗留给了他的太太。

　1）我把那本书留给了我的学生。

　2）他虽然很有钱，但是他没有把钱留给孩子。

12．谁 v. ....(determinant) , 谁... : Whoever...whoever...

　❖ 谁愿意就把狗托付给谁。

　1）谁想去谁去，反正我不去。

　2）谁有钱，我就嫁给谁。

13．v. 完毕: finish v.-ing

　❖ 遗嘱刚刚宣读完毕，她就大叫起来。

　1）报告完毕，她们就讨论起来了。

　2）准备完毕，大家就出发了。

14．付出: sacrifice; give (of oneself)

　　付出（青春/美貌/代价/劳动/心血/时间）

　❖ 她付出青春美貌，并不是无偿的。

　1）为了她的孩子，她付出了大量的时间。

　2）为了能到美国来，他们付出了很高的代价。

15. 耐着性子 v.：restrain oneself and v.; patiently v.
   ❖ 这个年轻的女人耐着性子陪着那个老头。
   1）这本书很没有意思，我耐着性子终于看完了。
   2）老板讲话很没意思，但是大家也得耐着性子听。

16. 以…著称：be famous for
   ❖ 这个以"贤淑"和"爱心"著称的女人一瞬间变成了这副嘴脸。
   1）中国以自行车王国著称。
   2）日本的汽车以质量好著称于世。

17. v. 个大头鬼！：v., no way; not a chance!
   ❖ 收养它个大头鬼啦!
   1）帮个大头鬼！我恨死他了，绝对不帮他的忙！
   2）吃个大头鬼！我都快让你气死了，还吃什么饭！

18. 当场 v.：v. on the spot
   ❖ 律师便遵照遗嘱，当场征询家里其他人的意见。
   1）警察当场抓住了那个小偷。
   2）车祸很严重，她当场就被撞死了。

19. 签：sign　　签(字/名/合同/约)
   ❖ 律师请她在一份文件上签了字。
   1）她的新书刚刚出版的时候，很多人排队请她签字。
   2）签约以后，双方必须按约办事。

练习

I. 选出正确的词填空：

捐款，显得，发誓，聘请，姿态，心满意足，替代，意见，良心，乱子

1. 你穿黑衣服的时候，常常_____很瘦。
2. 有一个好工作，又有一个好太太，他感到_____.
3. 虽然他很有钱，但是他从来不为穷人_____.
4. 他虽然有一个大学毕业证，但是却没有人愿意_____他工作。
5. 这件礼物对我来说非常珍贵，任何东西都是无法_____的。
6. 他想怎么做就怎么做，从来不征求别人的_____.
7. 父母悉心地照料他，他却骂父母，他真没有_____.
8. 得了癌症以后，他_____以后再也不抽烟了。
9. 他明明很不喜欢狗，却做出很喜欢狗的_____.
10. 幸亏警察及时赶到，否则一定会出_____.

II. 用所给词语回答问题：

1. A: 你觉得阿方应该不应该得到一些遗产？(作为)

   B: _____.

2. A: 阿方跟老金生活得快乐不快乐？（耐着性子＋v.）

   B: _____.

3. A: 那个有钱人常常捐款帮助穷人吗？(当场＋v.)

   B: _____.

4. A: 事情结束后，阿方会怎么想？(如果……的话)

   B: _____.

5. A: 在大学里，所有的学生都努力学习吗？（混）

   B: _____.

6. A: 一个城市的交通问题应该由谁来负责? (归)

    B: _____.

7. A: 你会跟一个什么样的人结婚? (跟…有缘)

    B: _____.

8. A: 中国现在有什么问题? (存在着)

    B: _____.

III. 用所给的词回答问题:

1. 老金的老伴去世后，老金为什么回绝了那些追求他的女人?
(清楚，挖空心思，嫁给，老朽，患，值得，信赖，一概)

2. 阿方企图用什么样的方法来取得老金的信任?
(逗狗玩，提及，接受，贵重礼物，向…证明，物欲横流，
存在着，纯粹，功利)

3. 老金是一个什么样的人? 他所爱的人是什么样的?
(老朽，患，商场上，混，精明，有爱心，忠诚，值得信赖)

4. 老金为什么不直接把钱给阿方?
(证明，信任，爱心)

IV. 讨论问题:

1. 你觉得阿方是一个什么样的人?

2. 阿方到底是"因狗得福"还是"因狗得祸"? 这个变化是谁造成的?

3. 在这个世界上有没有没有任何功利的爱? 爱情的实质是什么?

4. 你觉得老金相信不相信阿方? 要是你是老金，你会怎么做? 为什么?

5. 有没有比法律、金钱、美貌更牢固的东西能把夫妻结合在一起? 如果

有的话，那应该是什么? 老金要证明和奖励的又是什么?

偷 父

刘心武

（一）

那晚我到家已临近午夜，进门后按亮厅里的灯，立刻感觉到不对劲儿(1)，难道……？我快步走到各处，一一按亮灯盏，各屋的窗户都好好地关闭着啊，再回过头去观察大门，没有问题呀！但是，当我到卫生间再仔细检查时，一仰头，心就猛地往下一沉(2)——浴盆上面那扇透气窗被撬开了！再一低头，浴盆里有明显的鞋印，呀！我忙从衣兜掏出手机，准备拨110报警，这时又忽然听见窸窸窣窣的声响，循声过去，便发现卧室床下有异动，我把手机倒换到左手，右手操起窗帘叉子，朝床下喊："出来！放下手里东西，只要你不伤人，出来咱们好商量(3)！"

一个人从床底下爬出来了。那是一个瘦小的少年，剃着光头，身上穿一件黑底子的圆领T恤。我看他手里空着，就允许他站立起来，用那窗帘叉指向他，作为防备，问他："你偷了些什么？把藏在身上的掏出来！"

午夜	wǔyè	*n.*	midnight
不对劲儿	bú duìjìnr	*adj.*	there is something wrong 我一看他的表情，就知道有点儿不对劲儿。

Selected by：Chih-p'ing Chou
Edited & prepared by: Joanne Chiang

灯盏	dēngzhǎn	*n.*	lamp
卫生间	wèishēngjiān	*n.*	bathroom
仔细	zǐxì	*adv.*	carefully; attentively
仰头	yǎngtóu	*v.-o.*	raise one's head
猛地	měng.de	*adv.*	suddenly; abruptly
心往下一沉	xīn wǎng xià yìchén	*phr.*	worried; one's heart sinks 他听说公司把他解雇了，心不禁往下一沉。
浴盆	yùpén	*n.*	bathtub
扇	shàn	*AN.*	measure word for door, window, etc.
透气窗	tòuqìchuāng	*n.*	vent
撬开	qiàokāi	*v.-c.*	pry open
鞋印	xiéyìn	*n.*	footprint
衣兜	yīdōu	*n.*	pocket
掏	tāo	*v.*	draw out
拨	bō	*v.*	dial (a telephone number)
报警	bàojǐng	*v.-o.*	report (an incident) to the police
窸窸窣窣	xīxīsūsū	*onom.*	a succession of slight, soft sounds, as of leaves, silks, papers, etc.
循声	xúnshēng	*adv.*	follow the sound
异动	yìdòng	*n.*	unusual movement
倒换	dǎohuàn	*v.*	switch to
操	cāo	*v.*	hold; grasp
窗帘叉子	chuānglián chā.zi	*v.*	curtain pole (for opening curtains)
朝	cháo	*prep.*	to; towards 朝他大声喊/朝外走/朝东去
好商量	hǎo shāng.liang	*adj.*	can be settled through discussion 别生气，坐下来谈，什么事都好商量。
剃着光头	tì.zhe guāngtóu	*v.-o.*	with shaved head
黑底子	hēidǐ.zi	*n.*	black background 黑底白花/蓝底红花
圆领 T 恤	yuánlǐng T xù	*n.*	round collared T-shirt
防备	fángbèi	*n.*	precautions
藏	cáng	*v.*	store; lay by 藏在口袋里/藏在身后

43

他把两手伸进裤兜，麻利地将兜袋翻掏出来，又把双手摊开，回答说："啥也没拿啊！"我又问他："你们一伙儿子吧？他们呢？"他说："傻胖钻不进来，钳子能钻懒得⑷钻，我一听钥匙响就往外钻。他们见我没逃成，准定扔下我跑远了，算⑸我倒霉！"看他一副"久经沙场"、处变不惊的模样，倒弄得⑹我哭笑不得。

我用眼角余光检查了一下我放置钱财的地方，似乎还没有受到侵犯。我保持伸出窗帘叉的姿势，倒退着，命令他跟着我的指挥来到门厅里，我让他站在长餐桌短头靠里一侧，自己站在靠外一侧，把窗帘叉收到自己这边，开始讯问。

他倒是有问必答。告诉我他们一伙儿，分工侦察。本来他到我家窗外侦察后，他们一伙得出的结论是"骨头棒子硌牙"，意思就是油水不大还难到手。确实也是，我的新式防盗门

裤兜	kùdōu	*n.*	trouser pocket
麻利	málì	*adj.*	quick and neat; dexterous
翻掏	fāntāo	*v.*	turn inside out
摊开	tānkāi	*v.-c.*	spread out
啥	shá	*n.*	what; 什么
一伙儿子	yì huǒr.zi	*n.*	partners; group
傻胖	Shǎpàng	*n.*	nickname of one of the thieves 傻：stupid 胖：fat; stout
钻	zuān	*v.*	go through; penetrate; pierce; get into
钳子	qián.zi	*n.*	tongs; pincers (here): nickname of one of the thieves
懒得	lǎn.de	*adv.*	not feel like; not be in the mood to 懒得站

起来/懒得动/懒得上街

钥匙	yào.shi	*v.*	key
逃	táo	*v.*	run away; flee
准定	zhǔndìng	*adv.*	definitely; certainly; surely
倒霉	dǎoméi	*v.*	have bad luck; be out of luck
久经沙场	jiǔjīng shāchǎng	*idm.*	have fought many battles; be a veteran of many wars　沙场：battlefield
处变不惊	chǔbiàn bùjīng	*idm.*	with presence of mind in the face of disasters
模样	múyàng	*n.*	appearance; look
哭笑不得	kūxiàobùdé	*idm.*	be able neither to cry nor to laugh; be at a loss whether to cry or to laugh
眼角	yǎnjiǎo	*n.*	the corner of the eye
余光	yúguāng	*n.*	peripheral vision
放置	fàngzhì	*v.*	lay aside; place
侵犯	qīnfàn	*v.*	disturb; encroach on
姿势	zīshì	*n.*	posture; gesture
倒退	dàotuì	*v.*	go backwards; fall back
命令	mìnglìng	*v./n.*	order; command
指挥	zhǐhuī	*n./v.*	command; direct
门厅	méntīng	*n.*	hallway; foyer
短头	duǎntóu	*n.*	the short side
靠里一侧	kàolǐyícè	*n.*	the side away from the door
讯问	xùnwèn	*v.*	interrogate; question
分工	fēngōng	*v.*	divide work
侦察	zhēnchá	*v.*	scout
结论	jiélùn	*n.*	conclusion
骨头棒子硌牙	gú.tou bàng.zi gè yá	*phr.*	(robber's idiom) refers to a place which is well guarded and difficult to steal from 骨头棒子：bone stick 硌牙：made teeth ache
油水	yóu.shui	*n.*	profit; (improper) fringe benefit
防盗门	fángdàomén	*n.*	burglar-proof door

极难撬开，各处窗户外都有铁栅，唯独(7)大意的地方就是卫生间浴盆上面的那扇透气窗。那窗是窄长的，长度大约六十厘米，宽度大约只有三十厘米，按说(8)钻进一只猫可能，钻进一个人是不可能的，没想到站在我对面的这位"瘦干狼"，他自己后来又告诉我，在游乡的马戏班子里被训练过柔术的，竟能钻进来！

"您为什么还不报警？"他问我。他能说"您"，这让我心里舒服。我把手指挪到手机按键上，问他："你想过，警察来了，你会是怎么个处境吗？"他叹口气，说出的话让我大吃一惊："嗨，惯了，训一顿，管吃管住。完了，把我遣返回老家，再到那破土屋子里熬一阵呗。"他那满无所谓，甚至还带些演完戏卸完妆可以大松一口气的表情，令我惊奇。

（二）

我就让他坐到椅子上，我坐在另一头，把窗帘叉子靠在桌子边，跟他继续交谈。他今年 14 岁。家乡在离我们这个城市很远的地方。他小学上到三年级就辍学了。 一年前开始了

铁栅	tiězhà	*n.*	iron bars
唯独	wéidú	*adv.*	only 总是为朋友们想，唯独不为自己。
大意	dàyì	*v.*	careless; negligent; inattentive 开车时千万不可大意。
窄长	zhǎicháng	*adj.*	narrow and long
长度	chángdù	*n.*	length
厘米	límǐ	*n.*	cm. (centimeter)

宽度	kuāndù	*n.*	width; breadth
按说	ànshuō	*adv.*	in the ordinary course of events; normally 按说，一个人生活花不了多少钱。
瘦干狼	Shòugānláng	*n.*	nickname of the thief 瘦干：thin; emaciated 狼：wolf
游乡马戏 班子	yóuxiāng mǎxì bān.zi	*n.*	traveling circus 马戏班子：circus
柔术	róushù	*n.*	contortionism
挪	nuó	*v.*	move; shift
按键	ànjiàn	*n.*	key; button
处境	chǔjìng	*n.*	unfavorable situation; plight
叹口气	tàn kǒu qì	*v.-o.*	sigh; heave a sigh
大吃一惊	dà chī yì jīng	*v.-o.*	be startled; be astounded
惯了	guàn.le	*v.*	used to it
训	xùn	*v.*	lecture; teach; train
管吃管住	guǎnchī guǎn zhù	*v.*	provide food and accommodation
遣返	qiǎnfǎn	*v.*	repatriate
熬	áo	*v.*	endure; go through (difficult times) 他一 连熬了好几个晚上，终于把文章写出来 了。
一阵	yízhèn	*n.*	a period of time
呗	bei	*part.*	final particle, indicating that the fact is obvious
演戏	yǎnxì	*v.-o.*	act in a play; play act; pretend
卸妆	xièzhuāng	*v.-o.*	take off a costume; remove makeup
松一口气	sōng yìkǒu qì	*v.-o.*	let out a breath; sigh (of relief) 找到工作 以后，他们可以松一口气了。
惊奇	jīngqí	*adj.*	be surprised; be amazed
家乡	jiāxiāng	*n.*	hometown
辍学	chuòxué	*v.-o.*	drop out of school 为了帮助父母维持生 活，很多农村的孩子不得不辍学。

流浪生活。现在就靠结伙偷窃为生。有几个问题他拒绝回答，那就是：他父母为什么不管他？他们一伙儿住在什么地方？他钻进我的私宅究竟想偷窃什么？如果我还不回来，他打算怎么下手？面临这些追问，他就垂下眼睑，抿紧嘴唇。

我望着被灯光照得瘦骨嶙峋、满脸灰汗的少年，问他："渴吗？"他点头，我站起来。他知道是想给他去倒水，就主动说："我不动。"我去给他取来一瓶冰可乐，又递给他一只纸杯，他不用纸杯，拧开可乐瓶盖，仰头咕嘟咕嘟喝，他喝完，我就又问他："饿吧？"他摆正身子，眯眼看我，仿佛我是个怪物。我也不等他回答，就去为他泡了一碗方便面，端到他面前。

他呼噜呼噜将那方便面一扫而光。我有点好奇地问："你们不是每天都有收获吗？难道还吃不饱？"他告诉我："有时候野马哥带我们吃馆子，吃完撑得在地上打滚儿…这几

流浪	liúlàng	v.	roam about; lead a vagrant life
靠…为生	kào…wéi shēng	v.	make a living by… 他失业以后就靠打零工为生。
结伙偷窃	jiéhuǒ tōuqiè	v.	gang up to rob
拒绝	jùjué	v.	refuse; reject
私宅	sīzhái	n.	private house
下手	xiàshǒu	v.	put one's hand to; start; set about 不知从何下手
面临	miànlín	v.	be faced with; be confronted with 面临困难/面临两种选择

追问	zhuīwèn	v.	question closely
垂	chuí	v.	hang down; droop; let fall
眼睑	yǎnjiǎn	n.	eyelid
抿紧	mǐnjǐn	v.-c.	close lightly; pucker
嘴唇	zuǐchún	n.	lips
瘦骨嶙峋	shòugǔ línxún	idm.	thin and bony; skin and bones
灰汗	huī hàn	n.	dust and sweat
渴	kě	adj.	thirsty
主动	zhǔdòng	adv.	proactive; take initiative 主动作好事/主动帮忙
冰可乐	bīng kělè	n.	iced coke
递	dì	v.	hand over; pass
拧开	nǐngkāi	v.-c.	twist open; screw open
瓶盖	pínggài	n.	bottle cap
咕嘟咕嘟	gūdūgūdū	onom.	sound of water bubbling or a person gurgling
摆正	bǎizhèng	v.-c.	settle; arrange; set in order
眯眼	mīyǎn	v.-o.	squint at
仿佛	fǎngfú	adv.	seem; as if
怪物	guàiwù	n.	monster, a freak
泡	pào	v.	pour boiling water on
方便面	fāngbiànmiàn	n.	instant noodles
端	duān	v.	hold sth. level with both hands; carry
呼噜呼噜	hū.luhū.lu	onom.	sound of slurping or wheezing
一扫而光	yì sǎo ér guāng	idm.	wipe out completely, make a clean sweep of; (here): finish off all the food
好奇	hàoqí	adj.	curious
收获	shōuhuò	n.	results; gains; (here) loot
野马哥	Yěmǎ gē	n.	nickname of one of the thieves. 野马: wild horse
撑	chēng	adj.	full to the point of bursting 我吃得撑死了，得出去走走。
打滚儿	dǎgǔnr	v.-o.	roll about; roll on the ground

天野马哥净⑼打人，一分钱也不让我们留下……"我就懂得，我，还有我的邻居们，甚至这附近整个地区，所受到的是一种有组织有控制的偷盗团伙威胁，他一定从我的眼神里看出了什么，吃完面，抹抹嘴说："您放心，有我，他们谁也不会惹您来了。"我又一次哭笑不得。

我想了想，决心放他出去。我对他说："我知道，我的话你未必⑽肯听，但是我还要跟你说，不要再跟着野马哥他们干这种违法的事了。你应该走正路。"他点头。但是我要去给他开门时，他居然说："我还不想走。"我大吃一惊，问他："为什么？"他回答的声音很小，我听来却像一声惊雷："我爸在床底下呢……"

天哪！原来⑾还有个大人在卧房床底下！我慌忙将窗帘又抢到手里，又拨110。谁知⑿这时候手机居然没信号了，怎么偏⒀在这骨节眼儿上断电！我就往座机那边移动。这工夫里，那少年却已经转身进了卧室，而且麻利地爬进了床底下。我惊魂未定，他却又从床底下爬了出来，并且回到了门厅。我这才看清，他手里捧着一幅油画，那不是我原来挂在卧室墙上的吗？他究竟是怎么一回事？我正想嚷，他对我说："我要，我要我爸，求您了！"

几分钟以后，我们又都坐在了餐桌两头，而那幅画框已经被磕坏的油画，则竖立在我们都能看清的餐具柜边。 我们

净	jìng	*adv.*	only; merely; nothing but 你不能净赚不花，买几件衣服也是应该的。
邻居	lín.ju	*n.*	neighbor
控制	kòngzhì	*v.*	control
团伙	tuánhuǒ	*n.*	gang
威胁	wēixié	*n./v.*	threaten; menace
眼神	yǎnshén	*n.*	expression in one's eyes
抹	mǒ	*v.*	wipe　他把脸上的汗水抹去。
惹	rě	*v.*	offend; provoke 惹人生气/惹他不高兴
违法	wéifǎ	*adj.*	illegal
走正路	zǒu zhènglù	*v.-o.*	follow the correct path
惊雷	jīngléi	*n.*	a sudden clap of thunder
天哪	tiān.na	*intj.*	Good Heavens!
慌忙	huāngmáng	*adv.*	in a great rush; in a flurry
信号	xìnhào	*n.*	signal
偏	piān	*adv.*	deliberately; contrary to what is expected
节骨眼儿	jié.guyǎnr	*n.*	critical juncture 事情已到了节骨眼上。/ 在这节骨眼上，他倒非常镇静。
断电	duàndiàn	*v.-o.*	interruption of power; outage
座机	zuòjī	*n.*	fixed phone
移动	yídòng	*v.*	move
惊魂未定	jīnghún wèidìng	*v.*	be still suffering from the shock
捧	pěng	*v.*	hold or carry in both hands
油画	yóuhuà	*n.*	oil painting
嚷	rǎng	*v.*	shout; yell
求	qíu	*v.*	ask; beg; request; entreat
画框	huàkuāng	*n.*	frame
磕坏	kēhuài	*v.-c.*	knocked (against sth. hard) and broken 磕掉/磕破/磕坏
竖立	shùlì	*v.*	set upright; stand
餐具柜	cānjù guì	*n..*	sideboard; buffet table

开头儿的问答是混乱的，然而逐渐意识都清明起来。

那幅油画，是我前几年临摹的荷兰画圣凡高的自画像。这幅自画像是他没自残耳朵前画的，显得特别憔悴，眼神饱含忧郁，胡子拉碴，看去不像个西方人倒像个东方农民。出于某种非常私密的原因⑭，我近来把这幅自以为临摹得最传神的油画悬挂在卧室里。少年窃贼告诉我，他负责踩点的时候，从我那卧室窗外隔着铁栅看见了这幅画，一看就觉得是他爸，就总想给偷走。这天他好不容易⑮钻了进来，取下了这幅画，偏巧⑯我回来了，他听见钥匙响就往外逃。他人好钻，画却难以一下子随人运出去，急切里，他就又抱着画钻到卧室床底下去了……

我就细问他，他爸，那真的爸，现在在哪儿呢？他妈妈呢？他不可能只有爸爸没有妈妈啊！可是他执拗地告诉我，他就是没有妈。后来我听懂了，他妈在他还不记事儿的时候，就嫌他爸穷，跟别的男人跑了。他爸把他拉扯大。他记得他爸，记得一切，记得那扎人的胡子茬，记得那熏鼻子的汗味加烟味

开头儿	kāitóur	v.-o.	begin; start; at the beginning of 凡事开头时就应该想到它的后果。
混乱	hùnluàn	adj.	confusion; disorder; havoc
意识	yì.shi	n.	sense; consciousness
清明	qīngmíng	adj.	clear and bright
临摹	línmó	v.	copy (a picture)
荷兰	Hélán	n.	the Netherlands; Holland

52

画圣	huàshèng	*n.*	sage of painting; master painter
凡高	Fán gāo	*n.*	Vincent Van Gogh
自画像	zìhuàxiàng	*n.*	self-portrayal; self-portrait
自残	zìcán	*v.*	self-mutilate
憔悴	qiáocuì	*adj.*	haggard; thin and pallid
饱含	bǎohán	*v.*	be filled with (certain emotion, feelings, etc.)　她的脸上饱含愤怒。
忧郁	yōuyù	*adj.*	melancholy
胡子拉碴	hú.zi lāchā	*adj.*	stubbly and untrimmed (beard); bristly unshaven (chin)
私密	sīmì	*adj.*	personal; private; not to be divulged
传神	chuánshén	*adj.*	vivid; lifelike; expressive
悬挂	xuánguà	*v.*	hang
窃贼	qièzéi	*n.*	thief; burglar
踩点儿	cǎidiǎnr	*v.-o.*	(robber's idiom) case the site; scope out
好不容易	hǎo bù róngyì	*adv.*	with great difficulty; have a hard time (doing sth.)
偏巧	piānqiǎo	*adv.*	it so happened that; as luck would have it 我到的时候，偏巧他不在。
急切里	jíqiè.li	*adv.*	in a moment of desperation 急切里他说出了不该说的秘密。
执拗	zhíniù	*adj.*	stubborn; pigheaded; willful
不记事儿	bú jìshìr	*adj.*	(of a child) too little to remember anything 那时我才两岁，还不记事儿。
嫌	xián	*v.*	dislike; complain of　嫌菜不好吃
跑了	pǎo.le	*v.*	run away; elope
拉扯	lā.che	*v.*	take great pains to bring up (a child) 她自己把孩子拉扯大，非常辛苦。
扎人	zhārén	*adj.*	prickly
胡子茬	hú.zichár	*n.*	a stubbly beard
熏鼻子	xūn bí.zi	*adj.*	stinking; foul-smelling 熏: be suffocated by a bad smell
汗味	hànwèir	*n.*	stink with perspiration

加酒味……。爸爸换过很多种挣钱的活路，他记得爸爸说过这样的话："不怕活路累活路苦，就怕干完了拿不到钱。"他很小就自己离开家去闯荡过。有回他正跟着⑰马戏班子在集上表演柔术，忽然他爸冲进圈子，抱起他就走。班主追上去，骂他爸："自己养不起，怪得谁？"他爸大喘气，把他扛回了家，吼他，不许他再逃跑，那一天晚上，爸爸给他买来一包吃的，是用黄颜色的薄纸包的，纸上浸出油印子。打开那纸，有好多块金黄色的糕饼，他记住了那东西的名字，爸爸郑重地告诉他的———桃酥！讲到这个细节，少年耸起眉毛问我："您吃过桃酥吗？"我真想跟他撒谎，说从来没有吃过……

（三）

他们那个村子，不记得在哪一天，忽然说村外地底下有黑金子，大家就挖了起来。他爸爸也去挖，是给老板挖，于是他讲到了去年那一天，半夜里村子忽然闹嚷起来，跟着有呜哇呜哇的汽车警笛声，他揉着眼睛出了屋……。简单地说，村外的小煤窑出事故了，他爸，还有别的许多孩子的爸，给埋在井底下了…。他们为什么没有得到补偿？矿主早跑了不见影儿，人家说他们那个小煤窑根本是非法的，不罚款已经是开恩了，还补偿⑱？

| 活路 | huólù | n. | job; work; method of survival |
| 闯荡 | chuǎngdàng | v. | make a living wandering from place to place |

集	jí	n.	country fair; market
表演	biǎoyǎn	v.	perform; act; play
冲	chōng	v.	charge; rush; dash
圈子	quān.zi	n.	circle
抱	bào	v.	cradle; hold with both arms; embrace
班主	bānzhǔ	n.	owner of the circus
喘气	chuǎnqì	v.-o.	pant; gasp
扛	káng	v.	carry on the shoulder
吼	hǒu	v.	roar; howl
浸	jìn	v.	soak; saturate
油印子	yóuyìn.zi	n.	oil stains, marks made by oil
糕饼	gāobǐng	n.	cake; pastry
郑重	zhèngzhòng	adj.	serious; solemn; earnest
桃酥	táosū	n.	a kind of shortbread
细节	xìjié	n.	details; particulars
耸	sǒng	v.	rise straight up
眉毛	méi.mao	n.	eyebrows
撒谎	sāhuǎng	v.-o.	tell a lie; lie
挖	wā	v.	dig; excavate
闹嚷	nàorǎng	v.	raise clamor; din
呜哇呜哇	wūwā wūwā	onom.	sound of siren
警笛	jǐngdí	n.	siren
揉	róu	v.	rub
煤窑	méiyáo	n.	coal pit
事故	shì.gu	n.	accident; mishap
埋	mái	v.	bury
井	jǐng	n.	pit; mine
补偿	bǔcháng	n./v.	compensation; compensate
矿主	kuàngzhǔ	n.	owner of the mine
罚款	fákuǎn	v.-o.	impose a fine 违反规定的人会被罚款
开恩	kāiēn	v.-o.	grant leniency; have mercy

少年说，他从我那卧室窗外，望见了这幅画，没想，就先叫了声"爸"。他奇怪他爸的像怎么挂在我屋里？他说他爸坐在床上，想心事的时候，就那么个模样。

少年说这些事情的时候，眼里没有一点泪光。我听这孩子讲他爸的遇难，也就是鼻子酸了酸。但是，当我听清这孩子这天钻进我的屋子，为的只是偷这幅他自以为是他父亲画像的油画，我的眼泪忍不住就溢出了眼角。

少年惊诧地望着我。我理解了他，他能理解我吗？我感到自己是那么软弱无力，我除了把这幅画送给他，还能为他，为他父亲那样的还活着的人们，为那些人们的孩子们，做些什么？

"您放我走吧，还有我爸。"少年望望窗外，请求说。

（四）

我把画送给了他。他不懂得道谢，我把门打开，他闪了出去。

关上门以后，我竟若有所失。不到半分钟，我冲了出去，撞上门，捏紧钥匙，希望能从楼梯天井望到他的身影。没有，我就一溜烟儿⑲跑下楼梯，那速度绝对是与我这把年纪不相宜的。我气喘吁吁地踏出楼门，朝前方和左右望，那少年竟已经从人间蒸发，只有树影在月光下朦胧地闪动。

我让自己平静下来。当一派寂静笼罩着我时，我问自己："你追出去，是想跟他说什么？"

心事	xīn.shi	*n.*	sth. weighing on one's mind; a load on one's mind
泪光	lèiguāng	*n.*	the shine of tears in someone's eyes
遇难	yùnàn	*v.-o.*	die in an accident; meet with misfortune 飞机出了事故，飞机上的所有的人全部遇难。
鼻子酸	bí.zi suān	*phr.*	nose irritated (as if about to cry); feel sad; sick at heart
溢	yì	*v.*	overflow; spill
惊诧	jīngchà	*adj.*	surprised; amazed; astonished
软弱无力	ruǎnruò wúlì	*adj.*	weak and feeble
请求	qǐngqiú	*v.*	ask; request; beg
道谢	dàoxiè	*v.-o.*	express one's thanks; say thank you
闪	shǎn	*v.*	flash past
若有所失	ruòyǒu suǒshī	*idm.*	feel as if sth. were missing
撞上门	zhuàng .shang mén	*v-o.*	slam the door shut
捏	niē	*v.*	hold between the fingers; pinch
楼梯	lóutī	*n.*	stairs; staircase; stairway
天井	tiānjǐng	*n.*	(here)：天窗；skylight
一溜烟儿	yíliùyānr	*adv.*	(run away) swiftly
相宜	xiāngyí	*adj.*	suitable; fitting; appropriate
气喘吁吁	qìchuǎnxūxū	*adv.*	pant for breath; be short of breath
从人间蒸发	cóng rénjiān zhēngfā	*phr.*	evaporate from the world -- vanish without a trace
朦胧	ménglóng	*adj.*	dim; hazy
派	pài	*AN.*	measure word used with scenery, sight, sound, etc. 一派繁荣的景象/一派胡言
寂静	jìjìng	*n./adj.*	quiet; still; silent
笼罩	lǒngzhào	*v.*	envelop; shroud
追	zhuī	*v.*	chase after; run after

是的，我冲出来，是想追上他补充一句叮嘱："孩子，你以后可以来按我的门铃，从正门进来！"

夜风拂到我的脸上，我痴痴地站在那里。

一句更该说的话浮上我的心头："孩子，如果我要找你，该到哪里去？"

选自《读者》2005 年第 24 期

补充	bǔchōng	v.	supplement; make-up; complement; add
叮嘱	dīngzhǔ	n./v.	exhortation; advice
门铃	ménlíng	n.	door bell
正门	zhèngmén	n.	front door
拂	fú	v.	stroke; touch lightly
痴痴地	chīchī.de	adv.	stupidly; senselessly
浮上心头	fú shàng xīntóu	phr.	come to mind. 浮：float 心头：mind; heart

词语例句

1. 不对劲儿：there is something wrong
   ❖ 那晚我到家已临近午夜，进门后按亮厅里的灯，立刻感觉到不对劲儿。
   1) 我觉得有点不对劲儿，我们得想个别的办法。
   2) 他们两人的关系很不对劲儿，恐怕不久会分手。

2. 心往下一沉：feeling disturbed; worried; one's heart sinks
   ❖ 一仰头，心就猛地往下一沉，浴盆上面那扇透气窗被撬开了！
   1) 我一看见他的脸色，心就往下一沉，我看出他又失败了。
   2) 听说他没考上大学，我的心不禁往下一沉。

3. 好商量：can be settled through discussion
   ❖ 只要你不伤人，出来咱们好商量！
   1) 什么事只要你说出来，都好商量。何必生这么大的气呢！
   2) 别哭别哭！这些事都好商量！我肯定帮你的忙！

4. 懒得：not feel like; not be in the mood to
   ❖ 钳子能钻懒得钻。
   1) 我不是不能管，是懒得管。
   2) 天气太热了，我懒得出去。

5. 算：consider; regard as; count as
   ❖ 他们见我没逃成，准定扔下我跑远了，算我倒霉！
   1) 这次算你说对了！他果然选了那个比较有名的大学。
   2) 纽约可以算是最多元化的城市。
   3) 我算运气好，赶上了最后一班车。

6. 弄得（人）adj.：made (a person react a certain way)
   ❖ 看他一副"久经沙场"、处变不惊的模样，倒弄得我哭笑不得。
   1) 他突然生起气来，弄得我不知道怎么办。
   2) 他说出这样的话，弄得人人都很紧张。

7. 唯独：only　（points out and explains how a particular person or thing is different from the general class）

　❖　我的新式防盗门极难撬开，唯独大意的地方就是浴盆上面的那扇透气窗。

　1)　他又聪明又能干，唯独脾气不好。

　2)　这个工作，环境、工资都不错，唯独离家远了一点儿。

8. 按说：in the ordinary course of events; normally

　❖　按说钻进一只猫可能，钻进一个人是不可能的。

　1)　按说我该陪你去，可是我实在没有时间。

　2)　按说一个大学毕业生应该很容易找到工作，没想到今年的情况不同。

9. 净：only; merely; nothing but

　❖　这几天野马哥净打人，一分钱也不让我们留下。

　1)　周末他净玩，什么也不干。

　2)　他的屋子里净是书。

10. 未必：maybe not; not necessarily

　❖　我知道，我的话你未必肯听，但是我还要跟你说。

　1)　父母的看法未必完全对，你得自己想想。

　2)　大城市未必是居住最理想的地方，交通堵塞、空气污染都是问题。

11. 原来：as it turns out to be

　❖　天哪！原来还有个大人在卧房床底下！

　1)　原来他的车被偷了，难怪他这几天坐公车上下班。

　2)　教室里气氛特别紧张，原来老师突然宣布要考试。

12. 谁知：who knew ...

　❖　我慌忙将窗帘又抢到手里，又拨110。谁知这时候手机没信号了。

　1)　我立刻给他打电话，谁知他不在家。

　2)　我准时到机场接他，谁知飞机晚点，我等了足足三个小时。

13. 偏：deliberately; showing the reality is contrary to one's expectation

　❖　怎么偏在这节骨眼儿上断电！

　1)　不让他那样做，他偏要那样做。

2) 你怎么偏问他？为什么不问我？

14. 出于…原因/目的/同情/好奇/关怀…： out of; arising from; due to…
   ❖ 出于某种非常私密的原因，我近来把这幅油画悬挂在卧室里。
   1) 出于好奇，我问他到底他口袋里装着什么。
   2) 出于不可告人的目的，她嫁给了那个比自己大二十几岁的老头。

15. 好不容易： with great difficulty; have a hard time (doing sth.)
    (always used to modify something in the past)
   ❖ 这天他好不容易钻了进来，取下了这幅画，偏巧我回来了。
   1) 我好不容易找到那本书，给了他，他却连看也不看。
   2) 你好不容易找到这份工作，可得好好做。

16. 偏巧： it so happened that; as luck would have it
   ❖ 这天他好不容易钻了进来，取下了这幅画，偏巧我回来了。
   1) 他需要200块钱，偏巧我就有200块钱。
   2) 他不喜欢大家庭，偏巧他的女朋友的家庭有十几口人。

17. 跟着： at once; right after
   ❖ 半夜里村子忽然闹嚷起来，跟着有呜哇呜哇的汽车警笛声。
   1) 刮了一阵风，跟着就下起了大雨。
   2) 他说完，跟着就拿出一大笔钱来。

18. 不……(就)……，还……? (rhetorical question)
   ❖ 他们那个小煤窑根本是非法的，不罚款已经是开恩了，还补偿？
   1) 你犯了这么大的错，不罚你就很幸运了，你还要人夸奖你？
   2) 你撞了人，人家没报警就算你运气好了，你还希望人家赔偿？

19. 一溜烟： (run away) swiftly
   ❖ 我一溜烟跑下楼梯。
   1) 他一看见老师来了，就一溜烟跑了。
   2) 他一溜烟跑到楼下，可还是没追上那个人。

（四）偷父

练习

I. 选择合适的词填进去：

> 挪，撬，按，走，钻，隔，拨，掏，嚷，端，抿，拂，捧，递

1. _____ 电话报警
2. 窗户被 _____ 开了
3. 从衣兜 _____ 出了一点儿钱
4. 从床底下 _____ 出来
5. 把餐桌 _____ 到靠里一侧
6. _____ 紧嘴唇
7. _____ 给他一支笔
8. 从厨房 _____ 出了一碗面
9. _____ 正路
10. 她手里 _____ 着一幅画
11. 别大声 _____
12. 两个人 _____ 着铁栅说话
13. _____ 门铃
14. 春风轻 _____ 在我的脸上

II. 选择合适的词填进去：

> 偏，原来，算，还，净

1. _____ 你聪明，居然知道怎么回答这样的问题！
2. _____ 临摹是不够的，一个真正的画家必须有自己的创作。
3. 这家饭馆什么菜都好，唯独鱼不行，可他 _____ 要吃鱼！
4. 他不是辍学了吗？难道 _____ 天天到学校去？
5. _____ 这些小窃贼都是有团伙的，太可怕了！

III. 选择合适的词语填进去：

> 瘦骨嶙峋，若有所失，窸窸簌簌，一扫而光，有问必答，处变不惊

1. 我听到床底下有 _____ 的声响。
2. 面对危机，必须能 _____ 。
3. 他很诚实，对警察的问题是 _____ 。
4. 他病了好几年，现在真是 _____ 。
5. 桌上的菜被这一群饿极了的孩子 _____ 。
6. 我多年的老朋友搬到国外去了。他走了以后我确实感到 _____ 。

IV. 完成下面的句子：

1. 他懒得_____ ，所以_____ 。
2. 他喝完冰可乐，跟着_____ 。
3. 他自以为 _____ ，其实 _____ 。

62

4. 本来的计划是 _____ ，谁知 _____ 。

5. 出于贫穷，_____ 。

6. 看他 _____ 的模样，弄得我 _____ 。

7. 按说 _____ ，可是 _____ 。

8. _____ ，让我大吃一惊。

9. 做学生的不怕 _____ ，就怕 _____ 。

10. 你的表现这么差，老板不 _____ 就 _____ 了，还 _____ 啊？

V. 用提供的词语回答问题：

1. 他为什么到医院去了？（不对劲儿）

2. 你不是要买新窗帘吗？怎么没买呢？（偏巧）

3. 你这两天怎么老看这本书呢？（好不容易）

4. 他又抽烟又喝酒，肯定是个坏人。（未必）

5. 警察抓到那个窃贼了没有？（一溜烟）

VI. 用提供的词语回答问题：

1. 作者是怎么发现有窃贼的？

     (午夜，不对劲儿，检查，鞋印，声响，爬)

2. 作者从跟窃贼的谈话中，了解到哪些事情？

     (无所谓，钱财，报警，流浪，有组织，威胁)

3. 这个小窃贼为什么想偷那幅凡高的自画像呢？

     (憔悴，挖，埋，补偿，心事，模样)

4. 作者为什么把那个小窃贼放走了？

     （理解，控制，叮嘱，违法，走正路)

VII. 讨论问题：

1. 你同情不同情这个小窃贼？为什么？

2. 作者在故事最后写了"更该说的一句话"：如果我要找你，该到哪里去？为什么这是一句"更该说的话"？

3. 家里有了窃贼，你认为应该怎么应付？作者应付的态度你认为如何？

4. 作者要用这篇小说说明什么？

5. 这个小窃贼平常之所以偷窃，显然是因为贫穷。贫穷是不是所有的窃贼偷窃的原因？

6. 窃贼横行，是法律问题还是经济问题？

两个人的历史

余 华

（一）

一九三〇年八月，一个名叫谭博的男孩和一个名叫兰花的女孩，共同坐在阳光照不到的台阶上。他们的身后是一扇朱红的大门。作为(1)少爷的谭博和作为女佣女儿的兰花，时常这样坐在一起。他们的身后总是飘扬着太太的嘟哝声，女佣在这重复的声响里来回走动。

两个孩子坐在一起悄悄(2)谈论着他们的梦。

谭博时常在梦中为尿所折磨(3)。他在梦里四处寻找便桶，在自己的房间里焦急不安。现实里放在床前的便桶，在梦里不翼而飞。不停的寻找使梦中的谭博痛苦不堪(4)。然后他来到了大街上，在人力车来回跑动的大街上，乞丐们在他身旁走过。终于无法忍受的谭博，将尿撒向了大街。

此后的情景是梦的消失。即将(5)进入黎明的天空在窗户上一片灰暗。梦中的大街事实上是他的床。谭博醒来时感觉到身下

谭博	Tánbó	*n.*	personal name
兰花	Lánhuā	*n.*	orchid; (here): personal name
阳光	yángguāng	*n.*	sunlight; sunshine

Selected & edited by: Joanne Chiang
Prepared by: Joanne Chiang

照	zhào	*v.*	shine; illuminate
台阶	táijiē	*n.*	flight of steps
扇	shàn	*AN.*	measure word for doors, windows, etc.
朱红	zhūhóng	*n.*	vermilion; bright red
少爷	shào.ye	*n.*	young master of the house
女佣	nǚyōng	*n.*	woman servant; maid
飘扬	piāoyáng	*v.*	fly; wave; flutter
嘟哝	dū.nong	*v.*	mumble to oneself
声响	shēngxiǎng	*n.*	sound; noise
悄悄	qiāoqiāo	*adv.*	quietly; stealthily
尿	niào	*n./v.*	urine, urinate
折磨	zhémó	*v.*	torment; be suffered 女朋友喜欢折磨我。
四处	sìchù	*adv.*	all around; everywhere 四处流浪/假证件四处泛滥
寻找	xúnzhǎo	*v.*	seek; look for
便桶	biàntǒng	*n.*	chamber pot
焦急	jiāojí	*adj.*	anxious; worried
现实	xiànshí	*n.*	reality; actuality
不翼而飞	búyìérfēi	*idm.*	(of an object) disappear without trace; vanish into thin air
adj.不堪	bùkān	*phr.*	extremely adj. 破旧不堪/混乱不堪
人力车	rénlìchē	*n.*	rickshaw
乞丐	qǐgài	*n.*	beggar
忍受	rěnshòu	*v.*	endure; to bear
将	jiāng	*prep.*	(literary) 把 (used to introduce the object before the verb)
撒尿	sā niào	*v.-o.*	urinate; pee
情景	qíngjǐng	*n.*	scene; sight; circumstances
消失	xiāoshī	*v.*	disappear; vanish; dissolve
即将	jíjiāng	*adv.*	(literary) about to; on the point of; soon
黎明	límíng	*n.*	dawn; daybreak
天空	tiānkōng	*n.*	sky
灰暗	huī'àn	*adj.*	murky gray; gloomy

的被褥有一片散发着热气的潮湿。于是尿床的事实使他羞愧不已。(6)

"你呢？"

男孩的询问充满热情，显然他希望女孩也有同样的梦中经历。然而女孩面对这样的询问却表现了极大的害臊，用双手捂住眼睛。

"你是不是也这样？"

男孩继续问。

他们的眼前是一条幽深的胡同，两旁的高墙由青砖砌成。并不久远的岁月已使砖缝里生长出青草。

"你说。"

男孩开始咄咄逼人。

女孩满脸羞红，她垂头叙述了与他近似的梦中情景。她在梦中同样为尿所折磨，同样四处寻找便桶。

"你也把尿撒在街上？"

男孩十分兴奋。

然而女孩摇摇头，她告诉他她最后总会找到便桶。

这个不同之处使男孩羞愧不已。他抬起头望着高墙上的天空，他看到了漂浮的云彩，阳光在墙的上头显得一片灿烂。

他想：她为什么总能找到便桶，而他却永远也无法找到？这个想法使他内心燃起了嫉妒之火。后来他又问：

"醒来时是不是被褥湿了？"

被褥	bèirù	*n.*	bedding; bedclothes
散发	sànfā	*v.*	send forth; diffuse; emit
潮湿	cháoshī	*adj.*	moist; damp
羞愧	xiūkuì	*adj.*	ashamed; abashed 羞愧不已/非常羞愧
v.不已	bùyǐ	*phr.*	endlessly v.; incessantly v.
询问	xúnwèn	*v.*	ask about; inquire
热情	rèqíng	*n.*	enthusiasm; zeal
经历	jīnglì	*n.*	experience
害臊	hàisào	*v.-o.*	feel ashamed; be bashful
捂住	wǔzhù	*v.-c.*	cover or seal with one's hand
幽深	yōushēn	*adj.*	remote and quiet 幽：dim; dark　深：deep
青砖	qīngzhuān	*n.*	black brick
砌	qì	*v.*	build by laying bricks or stones
岁月	suìyuè	*n.*	years; time
缝	fèng	*n.*	crack; crevice; fissure　地缝/砖缝
咄咄逼人	duōduō bīrén	*idm.*	overbearing; aggressive 咄咄：tut! tut! 逼：force; compel
羞红	xiūhóng	*v.*	blush from shyness
垂头	chuítóu	*v.-o.*	lower one's head
叙述	xùshù	*v.*	narrate; recount; relate
近似	jìnsì	*adj.*	similar 这幅画跟那幅有些近似 / 采取了近 似的做法
抬头	táitóu	*v.-o.*	raise one's head
望	wàng	*v.*	gaze into distance
漂浮	piāofú	*v.*	float
云彩	yún.cai	*n.*	clouds
灿烂	cànlàn	*adj.*	magnificent; splendid; resplendent 阳光灿烂 / 笑得很灿烂
燃起	ránqǐ	*v.-c.*	burn; ignite
嫉妒	jídù	*v.*	be jealous of; envy

女孩点点头。

结局还是一样。

<h2 style="text-align:center">（二）</h2>

一九三九年十一月，十七岁的谭博已经不再和十六岁的兰花坐在门前的台阶上。那时候谭博穿着黑色的学生装，手里拿着鲁迅的小说和胡适的诗。他在院里进出时，总是精神抖擞。而兰花则继承了母业，穿着碎花褂子在太太的唠叨声里来回走动。

偶尔的交谈还是有的。

谭博十七岁的身躯里青春激荡，他有时会突然拦住兰花，眉飞色舞地向她讲一些进步的道理。那时候兰花总是低头不语，毕竟⑺已不是两小无猜的时候，或者兰花开始重视起谭博的少爷地位。然而沉浸在平等互爱精神里的谭博，很难意识到⑻这种距离正在悄悄成立。

在这年十一月的最后一天里，兰花与往常一样用抹布擦洗着那些朱红色的家具，谭博坐在窗前阅读泰戈尔有关飞鸟的诗句。兰花擦着家具时尽力不发出声响，她偶尔向谭博望去的眼神有些抖动。她希望现存的宁静不会遭受破坏。然而阅读总会带来疲倦。当谭博合上书，他必然要说话了。

| 结局 | jiéjú | n. | final result; outcome; ending |
| 鲁迅 | Lǔ Xùn | n. | Lu Xun, 1881-1936, 著名作家、评论家 |

胡适	Hú Shì	*n.*	Hu Shih, 1891-1962，著名学者、思想家
诗	shī	*n.*	poem; poetry
抖擞	dǒusǒu	*v.*	enliven; rouse 精神抖擞：full of energy
继承	jìchéng	*v.*	inherit; carry on
母业	mǔyè	*n.*	mother's job
碎花褂子	suìhuā guà.zi	*n.*	short gown made of printed calico
唠叨	láo.dao	*v.*	chatter; be garrulous
身躯	shēnqū	*n.*	body; stature
青春	qīngchūn	*n.*	youthfulness
激荡	jīdàng	*v.*	agitate; surge; rage
拦住	lánzhù	*v.-c.*	block; stop somebody (from doing something) 这条河拦住了我们的去路。/ 他刚要说，我把他拦住了。
眉飞色舞	méifēi sèwǔ	*idm.*	with dancing eyebrows and radiant face – enraptured; exultant 当问起他是怎么赚到这么多钱时，他总是眉飞色舞地跟大家讲他如何赚钱的故事。
毕竟	bìjìng	*adv.*	after all
两小无猜	liǎngxiǎo wúcāi	*idm.*	(of a little boy and a little girl) be innocent playmates
沉浸	chénjìn	*v.*	immerse; steep
意识到	yìshí dào	*v.-c.*	realize; be conscious of; be aware of
成立	chénglì	*v.*	establish
抹布	mābù	*n.*	rag for wiping
阅读	yuèdú	*v.*	read
泰戈尔	Tàigē'ěr	*n.*	Rabindranath Tagore, 1861-1941. 印度有名的作家、诗人、社会活动家
眼神	yǎnshén	*n.*	expression in one's eyes
抖动	dǒudòng	*v.*	shake; tremble; vibrate
宁静	níngjìng	*n./adj.*	tranquility; peace, tranquil; peaceful
疲倦	píjuàn	*n./adj.*	tired; weary
合上	hé.shang	*v.-c.*	close; shut 合上眼睛/把书合上

在他十七岁的日子里，他常常梦见自己坐上了一艘轮船，在浪涛里颠簸不止。一种渴望出门的欲望在他清醒的时候也异常强烈。

现在他开始向她叙述自己近来时常在梦中出现的躁动不安。

"我想去延安。"他告诉她。

她迷茫地望着他。显而易见，延安二字带给她的只是一片空白。

他并不打算让她更多地明白一些什么，他现在需要知道的是她近来梦中的情景。这个习惯是从一九三〇年八月延伸过来的。

她重现了一九三〇年的害臊，然后告诉他近来她也有类似的梦。不同的是她没有置身海轮中，而是坐在由四人抬起的轿子里，她脚上穿着颜色漂亮的布鞋。轿子在城内各条街道上走过。

他听完微微一笑，说：

"你的梦和我的梦不一样。"

他继续说：

"你是想着要出嫁。"

那时候日本人已经占领了他们居住的城市。

（三）

一九五〇年四月，作为解放军某文工团团长的谭博，腰间系着皮带，腿上打着绑腿，回到了他的一别就是⑼十年的家中。

此刻全国已经解放，谭博在转业之前回家探视。

艘	sōu	AN.	measure word for boats or ships
轮船	lúnchuán	n.	steamer; steamship
浪涛	làngtāo	n.	wave
颠簸	diānbǒ	v.	bump; toss; jolt 路很糟糕，车颠簸得厉害。/风更大了，船颠簸起来。
渴望	kěwàng	v.	thirst for; long for
欲望	yùwàng	n.	desire; passion
清醒	qīngxǐng	v.	be wide-awake
异常	yìcháng	adv.	extremely; exceedingly
强烈	qiángliè	adj.	strong
躁动不安	zàodòng bù'ān	v.	move restlessly
延安	Yán'ān	n.	Yan'an, the base of Communist Party in 1937-1947
迷茫	mímáng	adj.	perplexed; dazed
显而易见	xiǎn'éryìjiàn	adv.	obviously; evidently; clearly
空白	kòngbái	n.	blank space
延伸	yánshēn	v.	extend; stretch
置身	zhìshēn	v.	place oneself; stay (at a certain place or situation) 置身于群众之中/置身事外
抬	tái	v.	(of two or three persons) carry, lift; raise
轿子	jiào.zi	n.	sedan chair
占领	zhànlǐng	v.	occupy; capture
解放军	Jiěfàngjūn	n.	the Chinese People's Liberation Army
文工团	wéngōngtuán	n.	song and dance ensemble; art troupe; cultrual troupe
系	jì	v.	fasten; tie 系鞋带/系扣子/系好安全带
打	dǎ	v.	tie up 打绑腿/打行李
绑腿	bǎngtuǐ	n.	leg wrappings; puttee
转业	zhuǎnyè	v.-o.	transfer to civilian work
探视	tànshì	v.	visit

那时候兰花依然居住在他的家中，只是不再是他母亲的女佣，而是开始独立地享受起自己的生活。谭博家中的两间房屋已划给兰花居住。

谭博英姿焕发走入家中的情景，给兰花留下了深刻的印象。此时兰花已经儿女成群，她已经丧失了昔日的苗条，粗壮的腰扭动时抹杀了她曾经有过的美丽。

在此之前，兰花曾梦见谭博回家的情景，居然和现实中的谭博回来时一模一样。因此在某一日中午，当兰花的丈夫出门之后，兰花告诉了谭博她梦中的情景。

"你就是这样回来的。"兰花说。

兰花不再如过去那样羞答答。她在叙述梦中的情景时，丝毫⑩没有含情脉脉的意思，好像在叙说一只碗放在厨房的地上，语气十分平常。

谭博听后也回想起他在回家路上的某个梦。梦中有兰花出现，但兰花依然是少女时期的形象。

"我也梦见过你。"谭博说。

他看到变得十分粗壮的兰花，不愿多费唇舌去叙说她从前的美丽。有关兰花的梦，在谭博那里将永远地消失。

（四）

一九七二年十二月，垂头丧气的谭博以反革命分子的身份⑪回到家中。母亲已经去世，他是来料理后事的。此刻兰花的儿女

72

已长大成人。兰花依然如过去那样没有职业。当谭博走入家中

时，兰花正在洗塑料布，以此挣钱糊口。

划	huà	v.	assign; allocate
英姿焕发	yīngzī huànfā	idm.	dashing and spirited
丧失	sàngshī	v.	lose; forfeit　丧失了信心/丧失了资格
苗条	miáotiáo	adj.	(of a woman) slender; slim
粗壮	cūzhuàng	adj.	sturdy; thickset; brawny
扭动	niǔdòng	v.	sway; writhe
抹杀	mǒshā	v.	obliterate
一模一样	yìmúyíyàng	idm.	exactly alike 他们两个人的衣服一模一样。
羞答答	xiūdādā	adj.	coy; shy; bashful
丝毫	sīháo	adv.	（usually used in the negative）in the slightest degree 丝毫不感兴趣/丝毫没有惭愧的意思
含情脉脉	hánqíng mòmò	idm.	(soft eyes) exuding tenderness and love
语气	yǔqì	n.	tone; manner of speaking
回想	huíxiǎng	v.	recollect
形象	xíngxiàng	n.	image; form; figure
多费唇舌	duōfèi chúnshé	v.	take a lot of talking or explaining
垂头丧气	chuítóu sàngqì	idm.	be crestfallen; be dejected　没有通过考试，她一天到晚垂头丧气的。
反革命分子	fǎn gémìng fènzǐ	n.	a counterrevolutionary
身份	shēnfèn	n.	identity; status; capacity
去世	qùshì	v.	die; pass away
料理	liàolǐ	v.	arrange; manage; take care of
后事	hòushì	n.	funeral affairs　料理后事: make arrangements for a funeral
塑料布	sùliàobù	n.	plastic cloth
糊口	húkǒu	v.	make a living

谭博身穿破烂的黑棉袄在兰花身旁经过时，略略⑫站住了一会儿，向兰花胆战心惊地笑了笑。

兰花看到他后轻轻"哦"了一声。

于是他才放心地向自己屋内走去。过了一会儿，兰花敲响了他的屋门，然后问他：

"有什么事需要我？"

谭博看着屋内还算整齐的摆设，不知该说些什么。

母亲去世的消息是兰花设法通知他的。

这一次，两人无梦可谈。

（五）

一九八五年十月。已经离休回家的谭博，整天坐在院子里晒太阳。还是秋天的时候，他就怕冷了。

兰花已是白发苍苍的老人了，可她依然十分健壮。现在是一堆孙儿孙女围绕她了。她在他们之间长久周旋，丝毫不觉疲倦；同时在屋里进进出出，干着家务活。

后来她将一盆衣服搬出来，开始洗衣服。

谭博眯着眼睛，看着她的手臂有力地摆动。在一片"唰唰"声里，他忧心忡忡地告诉兰花，他近来时常梦见自己走在桥上时，桥突然塌了。走在房屋旁时，上面的瓦片向他脑袋飞来。兰花听了没有说什么，依然洗着衣服。

谭博问：

74

"你有这样的梦吗？"

"我没有。" 兰花摇摇头。

选自《余华作品集》，北京：中国社会科学出版社，1994.12

破烂	pòlàn	*adj.*	tattered; ragged; worn-out
棉袄	mián'ǎo	*n.*	cotton-padded jacket
略略	lüèlüè	*adv.*	slightly; briefly
胆战心惊	dǎnzhàn xīnjīng	*idm..*	be terror-stricken; tremble with fear
哦	o	*intj.*	Oh!; Hi!
敲	qiāo	*v.*	knock
摆设	bǎi.she	*n.*	decorations; furnishings
设法	shèfǎ	*v.*	try; think up a method
通知	tōngzhī	*v.*	notify; inform
离休	líxiū	*v.*	retire
晒太阳	shài tài.yang	*v.-o.*	sun-bathe
白发苍苍	báifà cāngcāng	*idm.*	white-haired
堆	duī	*AN.*	a heap of; a pile of
围绕	wéirào	*v.*	encircle; go round
周旋	zhōuxuán	*v.*	socialize; deal with
家务活	jiāwù huó	*n.*	housework
盆	pén	*n.*	basin; tub
眯	mī	*v.*	squint
手臂	shǒubì	*n.*	arm
摆动	bǎidòng	*v.*	swing; sway
唰唰	shuāshuā	*onom.*	sound of swishing
忧心忡忡	yōuxīn chōngchōng	*idm.*	care-laden; heavyhearted
塌	tā	*v.*	collapse
瓦片	wǎpiàn	*n.*	pieces of tile
脑袋	nǎo.dai	*n.*	head

《两个人的历史》中所提到的几个年代：

1930　北伐战争（Northern Expedition, 1926-1927）刚结束，中国南北统
　　　一。

1939　日军已经占领了北京。抗日战争（Anti-Japanese War, 1937-1945）
　　　正在进行。

1950　1949 年，共产党打败了国民党的军队，"解放战争"得到胜利，
　　　建立了中华人民共和国。

1972　文化大革命（The Great Cultural Revolution, 1966-1976）正在进
　　　行。打倒反革命分子，打倒封建主义，破四旧（破除旧思想、旧
　　　文化、旧风俗、旧习惯）。

词语例句：

1. 作为...: as
   ❖ 作为少爷的谭博和作为女佣女儿的兰花，时常这样坐在一起。
   1) 作为一个大学生，对社会有一定的责任。
   2) 作为一个现代人，对国际问题应该有一定的认识。

2. 悄悄（地): quietly
   ❖ 两个孩子坐在一起悄悄谈论着他们的梦。
   1) 她悄悄地离开了会场，几乎没有人注意到。
   2) 她悄悄地把全部的经过都跟我说了。

3. 为...所 v. : be v.-ed by
   ❖ 她在梦中同样为尿所折磨。
   1) 这个国家的资源都为政府所控制。
   2) 他的看法奇特，不为人们所理解。

4. adj. 不堪: extremely adj.
   ❖ 不停的寻找使梦中的谭博痛苦不堪。
   1) 连续工作了十几个钟头以后，她疲倦不堪，一上床就睡着了。
   2) 那几个乞丐穿得破烂不堪，非常可怜。

5. 即将：be about to; be on the point of
   ❖ 即将进入黎明的天空在窗户上一片灰暗。
   1) 学期即将结束，学生们都在准备回家。
   2) 你即将毕业，对毕业后的生活，有什么计划？

6. v.不已: v. endlessly; v. incessantly
   ❖ 尿床的事实使他羞愧不已。
   1) 她为自己无意中伤害了好友而后悔不已。
   2) 大家看了这幅精美的画，都赞叹不已。

7. 毕竟: after all; all in all; in the final analysis
   ❖ 那时候兰花总是低头不语，毕竟已不是两小无猜的时候。
   1) 他毕竟是一个十七岁的男孩，总是精神抖擞。
   2) 她毕竟在北京住过二十几年，对北京的名胜古迹知道得很详细。

8．意识到: be conscious of; realize

❖ 然而沉浸在平等互爱精神里的谭博，很难意识到这种距离正在悄悄成立。

1）我一看到他的脸色，就意识到他对这件事是有意见的。

2）她刚来，还没意识到办公室里大家的关系并不和谐。

9．一 v. 就是…. : once (an action) takes place, it easily reaches (a certain extent)

❖ 谭博腰间系着皮带，腿上打着绑腿，回到了他的一别就是十年的家中。

1）他一离开就是十年，如今回来，头发都白了。

2）她疲倦不堪，一睡就睡了十二个钟头。

10．丝毫: (usually used in the negative) in the slightest degree, a bit

❖ 她在叙述梦中的情景时，丝毫没有含情脉脉的意思。

1）他谈到过去的错误，却丝毫没有后悔的意思。

2）你们没有丝毫的证据，怎么能说他犯了罪?

11．以…的身份: in (a certain) capacity

❖ 一九七二年十二月，垂头丧气的谭博以反革命分子的身份回到家中。

1）他以学生代表的身份参加了教师大会。

2）她以官方代表的身份在会议上发表谈话。

12．略略: slightly; briefly

❖ 谭博从兰花身旁经过时，略略站住了一会儿。

1）他说到失败的原因时，略略犹豫了一下。

2）他对大家略略点了点头，就开始说话。

练习：

I. 用下面的词语来描述一个情况：

1. 焦急不安　　　　2. 不翼而飞　　　　3. 眉飞色舞
4. 一模一样　　　　5. 垂头丧气　　　　6. 胆战心惊
7. 显而易见　　　　8. 忧心忡忡

II. 用下面的副词 (adverb) 造句：

1. 悄悄地　　　　　2. 不停地　　　　　3. 热情地
4. 永远　　　　　　5. 尽力　　　　　　6. 略略

III.　用下面的动词 (verb) 造句：

1.为...所折磨　　　2. 消失　　　　　　3. 羞愧　　　　　　4. 叙述
5. 意识到　　　　　6. 渴望　　　　　　7. 丧失

IV. 读下面的句子，然后用划线的词语造句：

1. 作为少爷的谭博和作为女佣的兰花，时常这样坐在一起。
2. 那时兰花总是低头不语，毕竟已不是两小无猜的时候。
3. 谭博回到了他的一别就是十年的家中。
4. 她在叙述梦中的情景时，丝毫没有含情脉脉的意思。
5. 谭博从兰花身旁经过时，略略站住了一会儿。

V. 回答问题：
1. 1939、1950、1972 年时，谭博和兰花的关系与 1930 年时的关系有什么不同？在你看来，造成不同的原因是什么？
2. 这个小说中的"梦"有什么作用？你认为作者想用男孩和女孩的梦的不同来说明什么？
3. 这两个人哪一个是主角？哪一个人的生活比较幸福？
4. 你愿意采取哪一个人的生活态度？为什么？
5. 作者用这篇小说到底要表现什么？这是不是一篇好小说？为什么？

伤　痕

卢新华

（一）妈妈是叛徒

除夕的夜里，车窗外什么也看不见，只有远的近的，红的白的，五彩缤纷的灯火在窗外时隐时现(1)。这已经是一九七八年的春天了。

她有些倦意了，但仍旧睡不着。在她的对面，坐着一对回沪探亲的青年男女，他们疲倦地互相依靠着睡了。车厢的另一侧，一个三十多岁的妇女正在打着盹儿，在她的身旁睡着一个四五岁的小女孩儿。忽然，小女孩儿伸了一下腿，在梦中喊着："妈妈！"她的妈妈一下惊醒过来，低下头来亲着小女孩儿的脸问："宝宝，怎么了？"小女孩儿没吱声儿，舞了舞小手，又睡了。

她依旧没有睡意，看着身旁的那对青年，瞧着对面那个小女孩儿和她的妈妈，一股孤独、凄凉的感觉向她压迫过来。特别是小女孩梦中"妈妈"的叫声，仿佛是一把尖利的小刀，又刺痛了她的心。"妈妈"这两个字，对于她已是何等(2)的陌生；而"妈妈"这两个字，却又唤起她对生活多么热切的期望。她想像着妈妈已经花白的头发和满是皱纹的脸，她多么想

伤痕	shānghén	*n.*	scar
叛徒	pàntú	*n.*	traitor
五彩缤纷	wǔcǎi bīnfēn	*idm.*	be blazing with color; colorful
时隐时现	shíyǐn shíxiàn	*phr.*	appear at times, disappear at times
倦意	juànyì	*n.*	feeling of exhaustion
仍旧	réngjiù	*adv.*	still; yet; as before
沪	Hù	*n.*	Shanghai
探亲	tànqīn	*v.-o.*	go home to visit one's family or go to visit one's relatives
疲倦	píjuàn	*adj.*	exhausted
车厢	chēxiāng	*n.*	carriage
一侧	yícè	*n.*	one side
打盹儿	dǎdǔnr	*v.-o.*	nod off
惊醒	jīngxǐng	*v.*	startle awake
亲	qīn	*v.*	kiss
吱声儿	zhīshēngr	*v.-o.*	utter sth.; make a sound
舞	wǔ	*v.*	move; wave (hand)
睡意	shuìyì	*n.*	sleepiness
瞧	qiáo	*v.*	look
股	gǔ	*AN.*	a whiff of; a burst of 一股怒气/一股香味
孤独	gūdú	*adj.*	lonely
凄凉	qīliáng	*adj.*	lonely and desolate
压迫	yāpò	*v.*	oppress; press down upon
仿佛	fǎngfú	*adv.*	as if 仿佛睡着了
尖利	jiānlì	*adj.*	sharp
刺	cì	*v.*	stab
何等	héděng	*adv.*	how, what 何等有利/何等快乐
陌生	mòshēng	*adj.*	unfamiliar; strange
唤起	huànqǐ	*v.*	evoke 唤起大家的注意/唤起国民奋斗的精神
热切	rèqiè	*adj.*	fervent; earnest
皱纹	zhòuwén	*n.*	wrinkles

扑进她的怀里，请求她的宽恕。可是，……她痛苦地摇摇头，又重新将视线移向窗外。

九年了。……她痛苦地回忆着。

那时，她是强忍着对自己"叛徒妈妈"的愤恨，怀着极度矛盾的心情(3)，没有毕业就报名上山下乡了。她怎么也想像不到(4)革命多年的妈妈，竟会是这样的人。

她希望这也许是假的。听爸爸生前说，妈妈曾经在战场上冒着生命危险(5)在炮火下抢救过伤员，怎么可能在敌人的监狱里叛变自首呢？

自从妈妈定为叛徒以后，她开始失去了最好的同学和朋友；家也搬进一间黑暗的小屋，同时，因为妈妈，她的红卫兵也被撤了，而且受到从未有过的歧视和冷遇。所以，她心里更恨她，恨她历史上的软弱和可耻。虽然，她也想到妈妈和爸爸对她这个独生女的深情。可是现在，妈妈使她蒙受了莫大的

扑进…的怀里	pū jìn...de huáilǐ	v.	throw oneself into someone else's arms
宽恕	kuānshù	n./v.	pardon; forgive; excuse
重新	chóngxīn	adv.	again　重新考虑/重新组织
视线	shìxiàn	n.	line of sight
移向	yíxiàng	v.	shift to
回忆	huíyì	v./n.	recall the past; memory
强	qiǎng	adv.	make an effort; by force 强作镇静/强笑

忍	rěn	v.	bear; put up with
愤恨	fènhèn	n.	indignant resentment; enmity
怀着…的心情	huái.zhe...de xīnqíng	v.-o.	with the feeling of 怀着极度悲伤的心情
极度	jídù	adv.	extreme　极度怀疑/极度紧张
上山下乡	shàngshān xiàxiāng	idm.	(of educated urban youth) go and work in the countryside and mountain areas
生前	shēngqián	n.	during one's lifetime; before one's death
战场	zhànchǎng	n.	battle field
冒着…的危险	mào.zhe...de wēixiǎn	v.-o.	risk the danger of 冒着被发现的危险/冒着生命的危险
炮火	pàohuǒ	n.	artillery fire; gunfire
抢救	qiǎngjiù	v.	rescue; save
伤员	shāngyuán	n.	the wounded
监狱	jiānyù	n.	prison
叛变	pànbiàn	v.	turn traitor
自首	zìshǒu	v.	surrender; give oneself up to the enemy
定为	dìngwéi	v.	decide, fix; (here) convicted
搬	bān	v.	move
黑暗	hēi'àn	adj.	dark
红卫兵	hóngwèibīng	n.	the Red Guard
撤	chè	v.	dismiss sb. from a post 由于他贪污，他被撤职了。
从未	cóngwèi	adv.	never;　从来没有 从未失败过/从未怀疑过
歧视	qíshì	n./v.	discrimination; discriminate
冷遇	lěngyù	n.	cold shoulder; cold reception
软弱	ruǎnruò	adj.	weak; feeble
可耻	kěchǐ	adj.	shameful; disgraceful
深情	shēnqíng	n.	deep affection
蒙受	méngshòu	v.	suffer; sustain
莫大	mòdà	adj.	greatest

耻辱。她必须按照心内心外的声音，批判自己小资产阶级的思想感情，彻底(6)和她划清界限。她需要立即离开她，越远越快越好。

离开上海时，她只是一个十六岁的小姑娘，瓜子型的脸，扎着两根短短的小辫，在所有上山下乡的同学中，她显得格外地年幼和脆弱。她望了一下行李架上自己的两件行李。她想像着，妈妈现在大概已经回到了家里，也一定发现了那留在桌上的纸条：

我和你，也和这个家彻底(6)决裂了，你不用再找我。

晓华

一九六九年六月六日

她想像着，妈妈也许会哭，或许很伤心。她不由(7)又想起了从小妈妈对自己的爱抚。可是，谁叫她当叛徒的(8)！她忽然又感到，不应该可怜她，即使是自己的母亲。这时她才注意到周围的同学：有的睡了，有的在看书。她对面的座位上，一个年龄和她相仿的男同学，正愣愣地望着她。她有些羞涩地低下头。然而，那男同学却热情地问她："你是哪一届的？""六九届。"她抬起头。"六九届？"那男同学显然觉得有些奇怪："那……你？"

"我提前⑼毕业了。"她勇敢地审视了一下这个男同学的容貌：中等的个儿，天真活泼的眼睛。她问他："你叫什么？"

耻辱	chǐrǔ	*n.*	shame; disgrace; humiliation
批判	pīpàn	*v.*	criticize
资产阶级	zīchǎn jiējí	*n.*	bourgeoisie; the capitalist class
划清界限	huàqīngjièxiàn	*phr.*	make a clear distinction; draw a clear line of demarcation
瓜子脸	guāzǐliǎn	*n.*	oval face; pretty face with an oval shape
扎小辫	zhā xiǎobiàn	*v.-o.*	tie up one's pigtails
格外	géwài	*adv.*	especially 格外有趣/格外高兴/格外认真
脆弱	cuìruò	*adj.*	fragile; delicate
行李架	xínglǐjià	*n.*	luggage rack
决裂	juéliè	*v.*	break with
伤心	shāngxīn	*adj.*	grieved, hurt
不由	bùyóu	*adv.*	can't help but 不由流下眼泪/不由笑了起来
爱抚	àifǔ	*n./v..*	caress; show tender care for
可怜	kělián	*v.*	pity; have pity on
周围	zhōuwéi	*adj./n.*	surrounding
相仿	xiāngfǎng	*adj.*	similar
愣愣地	lènglèng.de	*adv.*	blankly
羞涩	xiūsè	*adj.*	shy
热情	rèqíng	*adv.*	warmly
届	jiè	*n.*	class year, graduating class
审视	shěnshì	*v.*	look at carefully; examine; gaze at
容貌	róngmào	*n.*	appearance; looks
中等个儿	zhōngděnggèr	*n.*	medium height
天真	tiānzhēn	*adj.*	innocent; naive
活泼	huópō	*adj.*	lively; active; full of life

"苏小林。你呢？""王晓华。"她回答了他的反问，脸上不由又掠过一股羞涩的红晕。听了他们的谈话，一个看书的同学便也插进来问，"王晓华，你怎么提前毕业了？"她愣了片刻，止不住⑩红着脸将实情告诉了他们。她说完，低下头，一种将遭冷遇的预感便涌上心来。然而，同学们却热情地安慰了她。苏小林更激动地说："王晓华，你做得对。不要紧，到了农村，我们大家都会帮助你的。"她感激地朝他们点点头。

（二） 在农村插队

于是，在温暖的集体生活的怀抱里，她渐渐忘记了使她厌恶的家庭，和一起来的上海同学们在辽宁省的一个农村里扎下了根。

她进步很快，第二年就填写了入团志愿书。可万万⑾没想到，因为妈妈的叛徒问题，公社团委没有批。她了解到这点后，含着泪水找到团支部书记说："我没有妈妈，我已和我的家庭断绝了一切关系，这是你知道的……"苏小林和其他几个同学也在一旁证实道："去年，她妈妈知道她到这儿来后，

苏小林	Sū Xiǎolín	n.	person's name
王晓华	Wáng Xiǎohuá	n.	person's name
反问	fǎnwèn	v./n.	ask in reply; counter with a question
掠过	lüèguò	v.	skim over; sweep across
红晕	hóngyùn	n.	flush, blush

插（话）	chā (huà)	v.	interpose
片刻	piànkè	n.	a short while; an instant; a moment 等了片刻/讨论了片刻
止不住	zhǐbúzhù	v.-c.	can't stop from; can't keep from 止不住哭了起来/止不住破口大骂
遭	zāo	v.	suffer
预感	yùgǎn	n.	premonition; presentiment
涌	yǒng	v.	well up; surge
安慰	ānwèi	v./n.	comfort; console
激动	jīdòng	adj.	excited
感激	gǎnjī	v.	feel grateful; be thankful
插队	chāduì	v.-o.	go to live and work in a production team
温暖	wēnnuǎn	adj.	warm
集体	jítǐ	adj.	collective 集体生活/集体活动
怀抱	huáibào	n.	embrace
厌恶	yànwù	v.	detest
辽宁	Liáoníng	n.	Liaoning Province
扎根	zhāgēn	v.	take root
填写	tiánxiě	v.	fill in (a form)
入团	rùtuán	v.-o.	join the Chinese Communist Youth League
志愿书	zhìyuànshū	n.	application form
万万	wànwàn	adv.	absolutely 万万不能忘记/万万不可以
公社	gōngshè	n.	commune
团委	tuánwěi	n.	Communist Youth League Committee
批	pī	v.	ratify; approve
含着泪水	hán.zhe lèishuǐ	v.-o.	with tears in the eyes
团支部	tuán zhībù	n.	branch of Youth League
书记	shūjì	n.	party secretary
断绝	duànjué	v.	break off; sever
证实	zhèngshí	v.	confirm; verify

吃的、穿的寄了一大包，可她还是原封不动地给退了回去。而且，她妈妈哪一次来信她连看都不看⑫，都是随时收到随时打回的。""但是，"团支部书记显出为难的样子说："公社团委接到了上海的信，而且，省里一直强调……"他脸上现出一副苦笑。

她茫然了。

到了第四年的春天，她才勉强⑬地入了团。但她的一颗火热的心至此已经有些灰冷了。

春节又到了。这是她最痛苦的日子。一起的青年都回家探亲了，宿舍里只剩下她孤独的一个人。　她能获得一点安慰的是，这里的贫下中农是那样真诚地关心她，爱护她，鼓励她，而且，还有小苏经常来看她。他们在几年的生活和劳动中，建立了越来越深厚的情谊。她也把他看作自己最可以信赖的亲人，常常向他倾吐一些内心的苦闷。特别是中秋那天晚上，她和小苏从海边散步回来以后，更这样想了。

他们沿着⑭海边走了很久，然后并排在沙滩上坐了下来。小苏突然问："晓华，你想不想家？"她愣了一下，抬起头："不……你怎么问起这个？"小苏低了头，缓缓地说："晓

| 原封不动 | yuánfēng búdòng | *idm.* | be left intact; untouched; with the original seal still unbroken |

退	tuì	*v.*	return 把信退回去
随时	suíshí	*adv.*	at all times; any time
打回	dǎhuí	*v.*	send back
为难	wéinán	*adj.*	feel awkward; feel embarrassed
强调	qiángdiào	*v.*	emphasize; stress
苦笑	kǔxiào	*v.*	forced smile
茫然	mángrán	*adj.*	at a loss 感到很茫然，不知道该怎么办
勉强	miǎnqiǎng	*adv.*	with difficulty 勉强说了几句话
火热	huǒrè	*adj.*	burning hot; fervent
至此	zhìcǐ	*adv.*	to this extent; at this point
灰冷	huīlěng	*adj.*	downhearted; dispirited
痛苦	tòngkǔ	*adj.*	agony; pain; suffering
获得	huòdé	*v.*	gain
贫下中农	pínxiàzhōngnóng	*n.*	贫农：lower class peasants 下中农： lower-middle class peasants
真诚	zhēnchéng	*adj.*	true; genuine; sincere
爱护	àihù	*v.*	cherish; treasure; take good care of
鼓励	gǔlì	*v.*	encourage
建立	jiànlì	*v.*	build; establish; set up
深厚	shēnhòu	*adj.*	deep; profound
情谊	qíng.yi	*n.*	friendly feelings; affection
信赖	xìnlài	*v.*	trust; have faith in
亲人	qīnrén	*n.*	one's family member
倾吐	qīngtǔ	*v.*	pour; exchange ideas without reservation
苦闷	kǔmèn	*adj./n.*	depressed; downhearted; depression; downheartedness
沿着	yán.zhe	*prep.*	along
并排	bìngpái	*adv.*	side by side
沙滩	shātān	*n.*	beach
想家	xiǎngjiā	*v.-o.*	homesick; to miss home
缓缓地	huǎnhuǎn.de	*adv.*	slowly

华，我看你还是写封信回去问问，林彪迫害了许多老干部，说不定你妈妈也在其中呢。"她没有回答他的话，想起自己的一切，止不住又是一阵⑮伤痛。小苏扭过头，看到泪珠又涌在她的眼里，便安慰她说："晓华，不要难过。"可是，他自己忍不住也擦了擦眼角的泪珠。终于，他把自己内心积压很久的话儿说了出来："晓华，你也没有亲人，如果你相信我的话，就，就让咱们作朋友吧……""真的？你不……？"她吃惊地瞪大了含着喜悦的双眼怀疑地问。"真的。"小苏肯定地点点头说，"晓华，相信我吧！"她激动地望着他，不由地扑到他的怀里……

她的脸上重新有了笑容，宿舍里，田间又有了她的歌声，而且面庞上也有了红润，显出青春的俏丽。

第二年秋天，因为身体不好和工作的需要，她调到了村里的小学任教。一个下午，她在公社参加教育工作会议后，来到小苏的宿舍。门半开着，屋里却空无一人。她收起他换下的衣服，准备给他洗一洗，扭头却看到床头柜上的日记本。她随手拿过来翻着，却看到昨天的日记上这样写道："…今天，我感到很头疼。上午，李书记对我说，县委准备调我到宣传部去工作，正在搞我的政审。他说，我跟晓华的关系，县委强调了，说这是世界观的问题，也是个阶级路线问题，要是还要继续下去的话，调宣传部的事还要再考虑考虑。我真不明白."

林彪	Lín Biāo	*n.*	Lin Biao, 1907-1971, named as Mao's successor in 1966
迫害	pòhài	*v.*	persecute
老干部	lǎo gànbù	*n.*	old cadre
阵	zhèn	*AN.*	a moment of
伤痛	shāngtòng	*n.*	pain, sadness
扭过头	niǔ .guo tóu	*v.*	turn one's head
泪珠	lèizhū	*n.*	teardrops
内心	nèixīn	*n.*	heart
积压	jīyā	*v.*	store up; (here) repress (e.g. emotions)
瞪大双眼	dèngdà shuāngyǎn	*v.-o.*	open one's eyes wide
喜悦	xǐyuè	*n.*	happiness, joy
笑容	xiàoróng	*n.*	smile
田间	tiánjiān	*n.*	field; farm
面庞	miànpáng	*n.*	face
红润	hóngrùn	*adj.*	flush; tender and rosy (skin, cheeks, etc)
青春	qīngchūn	*n.*	youth
俏丽	qiàolì	*n.*	(of a young woman) handsome; pretty
调	diào	*v.*	shift; transfer 被调到别的单位
任教	rènjiào	*v.*	teach
空无一人	kōngwúyìrén	*phr.*	empty; nobody there
床头柜	chuángtóuguì	*n.*	nightstand
随手	suíshǒu	*adv.*	conveniently; without extra trouble 随手关灯/随手把衣服放在床上
翻着	fān.zhe	*v.*	browse; look over
县委	xiànwěi	*n.*	County Party Committee
宣传部	xuānchuán bù	*n.*	publicity department
搞	gǎo	*v.*	make; do 搞学习/搞生产
政审	zhèngshěn	*n.*	political examination; background check
世界观	shìjiè guān	*n.*	worldview
路线	lùxiàn	*n.*	route

看到这里，她像木头一样地呆住了。

她猛然合上本子，立即离开了那间屋子，昏昏沉沉地回到了学校。

当她躺到自己宿舍的铺上时，她再也止不住伤心地哭了。

第二天，吃过早饭，她请了假，到公社找到公社书记，平静地对他说："李书记，我和小苏的关系从今往后完全断了，请不要因为我影响了小苏的前途。"

这以后，她几乎完全变了一个人，比先前更沉默寡言了。表情也近乎麻木起来。虽然，小苏为了她而没有同意调到县里去工作，仍旧那样真情地爱着她，但她对他却有意⑯避而不见了。

她现在才真正理解了她所处的地位和她的身份。虽然她和家庭断绝了关系，但她是始终无法挣脱那个"叛徒妈妈"的家庭给她套上的绳索的。而且，她也清楚了，如果她爱上了一个人，那么那根绳索也会带给那个人的。为了这点，她觉得自己不应该连累他。她已经决定：要永远关上自己爱情的心窗，不再对任何人打开。

又是两年过去了，粉碎"四人帮"以后，她感到自己精神上逐渐轻松了些，嘴角也有了笑纹。然而，当她陷入沉思的时候，脸上仍然挂着一股难言的忧郁。

呆住	dāizhù	*v.-c.*	be in a daze; be stunned
猛然	měngrán	*adv.*	abruptly; suddenly
合上	héshàng	*v.-c.*	close (a book)
昏昏沉沉	hūnhūn chénchén	*adv.*	feel in a daze
铺	pù	*n.*	plank bed
请假	qǐngjià	*v.-o.*	ask for leave
前途	qiántú	*n.*	future; prospects
沉默寡言	chénmò guǎyán	*idm.*	of few words; reticent; reserved
表情	biǎoqíng	*n.*	expression
近乎	jìnhū	*v.*	approach; be close to
麻木	mámù	*adj.*	apathetic; be dead to all feeling
有意	yǒuyì	*adv.*	purposely; deliberately
避而不见	bìérbújiàn	*v.*	avoid seeing someone
身份	shēnfèn	*n.*	status
始终	shǐzhōng	*adv.*	from beginning to end 我始终不了解他.
挣脱	zhēngtuō	*v.*	break loose
套上	tàoshàng	*v.*	harness; (metaphor): impose a burden
绳索	shéngsuǒ	*n.*	rope
连累	liánlèi	*v.*	implicate; get sb. into trouble
粉碎	fěnsuì	*v.*	crush; smash
四人帮	Sìrénbāng	*n.*	the Gang of Four
逐渐	zhújiàn	*adv.*	gradually
轻松	qīngsōng	*adj.*	light; relaxed
嘴角	zuǐjiǎo	*n.*	corner of one's mouth
笑纹	xiàowén	*n.*	laugh line
陷入	xiànrù	*v.*	sink into; land oneself in
沉思	chénsī	*n.*	meditation; contemplation
挂着	guà.zhe	*v.*	hang; put up; (here): wear certain expression on one's face 脸上挂着笑容
难言	nányán	*adj.*	difficult to describe, indescribable
忧郁	yōuyù	*n.*	heavyheartedness; dejection

一天，她正在批改作业本，忽然一个教师递给她一封从江苏寄来的信。谁写的？她怀疑地拆开一看，竟是妈妈写的。她的地址变了。要是以前，她也许会一下把信撕掉，但现在她却止不住读了下去……

晓华儿：

你和妈妈已经断绝关系八年了，妈妈不怪你。在这封信中，妈妈只想告诉你，在党中央的英明领导下，我的冤案已经昭雪了。我的"叛徒"的罪名是"四人帮"为了达到他们篡权的目的强加给我的，现在已经真相大白了。

孩子，我们已经八年多没见面了，我很想去看看你，但我的身体已经不允许了，因此，我盼望你能回来一趟，让我看你一眼。孩子，早日回来吧。祝你近好。

妈妈

一九七七年十二月二十日

她读着手中的信，不由呆了。"这是真的？真的吗？"她的心一下子⑴激烈地颤动起来。"回不回去呢？"她有些犹豫不决了。

直到除夕前两天，她又收到妈妈单位的一封公函，她才匆忙收拾了一下儿，买了当天的车票，离开了学校。

现在，她坐在这趟开往上海的列车上，心情又怎能平静呢？

她激动，她喜悦，但她也痛苦和难过……

批改	pīgǎi	*v.*	correct (students' homework)
递	dì	*v.*	hand over
江苏	Jiāngsū	*n.*	Jiangsu Province
拆开	chāikāi	*v.-c.*	tear open (a letter)
地址	dìzhǐ	*n.*	address
撕掉	sīdiào	*v.-c.*	tear up
党中央	dǎng zhōngyāng	*n.*	central authorities of the Communist Party
英明	yīngmíng	*adj.*	wise; brilliant
领导	lǐngdǎo	*v./n.*	lead; exercise leadership
冤案	yuān'àn	*n.*	unjust case; injustices
昭雪	zhāoxuě	*v.*	rehabilitate; redress a wrong or an injustice
罪名	zuìmíng	*n.*	crime; accusation; charge
篡权	cuànquán	*v.*	usurp the power
达到…的目的	dádào...de mùdì	*v.-o.*	achieve or attain the goal of…
强加	qiángjiā	*v.*	impose
真相大白	zhēnxiàngdàbái	*idm.*	the whole truth has come out
允许	yǔnxǔ	*v.*	allow
盼望	pànwàng	*v.*	look forward to; long for
激烈	jīliè	*adv.*	intense; fierce; violent
颤动	chàndòng	*v.*	tremble; shake
犹豫不决	yóuyùbùjué	*idm.*	hesitate; dubious; remain undecided
单位	dānwèi	*n.*	work unit
公函	gōnghán	*n.*	official letter
匆忙	cōngmáng	*adv.*	hastily; in a hurry
收拾	shōu.shi	*v.*	pack

（三）回家

清晨六点多钟，列车昂然驶进了上海站。

今天是春节，妈妈在家里干什么呢？妈妈是不爱睡懒觉的，她一定已经起了床。当她突然地出现在门口时，也许妈妈正在吃早饭呢。于是，她便轻轻地喊一声："妈！"妈妈一定会吃惊地转过头来，"呀！晓华！"而惊喜的眼泪一定涌在妈妈脸上。

她这样兴奋地想着。

她找到了816弄1号，走近屋门去叩门。屋里没有人，邻居告诉她说："新搬来的王校长昨天发病住到医院去了。"她吃了一惊，忙问："什么科？什么房间？""内科二号。"她便急火火地往医院赶去。

因为是春节，医院走廊里空荡荡的。她跑向前面走来的几个穿白衣服的医生问："医生，王校长在哪个病房？"一个戴眼镜瘦瘦的医生盯着她看了一下，像想起什么似的，忽然拿起手中的纸条说："喔，正好，你是从王校长学校来的，是吧？那好，麻烦你拍个电报告诉王校长的女儿，这是地址，告诉她，她的母亲今天早上已经去世了，让她……"

"什么？什么？"晓华脱口惊叫一声，瞪直了眼睛，发疯似地奔到2号房间，砰地一下推开门。一屋的人都猛然回过头来。她也不管这些是什么人，挤到病床前，抖着双手揭起了盖在妈妈头上的白布。

…… 啊！ 这就是妈妈 …… 已经分别了九年的妈妈！

…… 啊！ 这就是妈妈 …… 现在永远分别了的妈妈！

"妈妈！妈妈！妈妈……"她呼唤着："妈妈！你看看吧，看看吧，我回来了…… 妈妈……"她猛烈地摇撼着妈妈的臂膀。

可是，再也没有任何回答。

昂然	ángrán	*adv.*	upright and unafraid
驶	shǐ	*v.*	drive
弄	nòng	*n.*	alley
叩门	kòumén	*v.-o.*	knock at the door
内科	nèikē	*n.*	internal medicine
急火火	jíhuǒhuǒ	*adv.*	hurriedly
空荡荡	kōngdàngdàng	*adj.*	spacious and deserted
拍电报	pāi diànbào	*v.-o.*	send a telegram
脱口	tuōkǒu	*adv.*	blurt out; say without thinking
发疯似地	fāfēngshì.de	*adv.*	as if going crazy
奔	bēn	*v.*	rush; run
砰地一下	pēng.deyíxià	*phr.*	with a big bang
抖着	dǒu.zhe	*v.*	trembling; shivering
揭	jiē	*v.*	uncover
盖	gài	*v.*	cover
分别	fēnbié	*v.*	leave each other
呼唤	hūhuàn	*v.*	call
猛烈地	měngliè.de	*adv.*	fiercely
摇撼	yáohàn	*v.*	shake something violently

词语例句

1. 时 (而) v./adj. 时(而) v/adj : at times……; at times……..

    时好时坏， 时冷时热， 时快时慢，时高时低， 时松时紧，
    时而有趣， 时而乏味； 时而火热， 时而冰冷；
    - ❖ 五彩缤纷的灯火在窗外时隐时现。
    1) 最近的天气时冷时热，很多小孩子都生病了。
    2) 她对男朋友的态度很奇怪，时而火热，时而冰冷。

2. 何等(的) +adj.：how adj. (questions word used as intensifier)
    - ❖ "妈妈"这两个字，对于她已是何等的陌生。
    1) 再也见不到妈妈的孩子是何等的可怜。
    2) 提前三年就毕业的孩子是何等的聪明。

3. 怀着……的心情：with feelings of (excitement/pain…) （兴奋、激动、喜悦、痛苦）
    - ❖ 她怀着极度矛盾的心情报名上山下乡了。
    1) 开学的第一天，学生们都怀着兴奋的心情来到了学校。
    2) 父亲怀着痛苦的心情告诉孩子们母亲去世的消息。

4. 怎么也不 v.：impossible in any case; there is no way (used in a negative sentence)
    - ❖ 她怎么也想象不到，革命多年的妈妈，竟会是这样的人。
    1) 我怎么也不明白，他居然会打自己的母亲。
    2) 他怎么也不会欺骗你的。你放心吧!

5. 冒着……的危险：risk the danger of…..
    - ❖ 妈妈曾经在战场上冒着生命危险在炮火下抢救过伤员。
    1) 这个记者冒着被开除的危险，揭露了政府贪污腐化的现象。
    2) 她冒着被淹死的危险，跳到河里把那个孩子救了出来。

6. 彻底：thoroughly
    - ❖ 她必须彻底跟母亲划清界限。
    1) 考完试以后，学生们可以彻底放松一下儿。
    2) 妻子对有婚外恋情的丈夫彻底失去了信任。

7. 不由+v.：can't help but; cannot but

❖　她不由又想起了从小妈妈对自己的爱抚。

1) 他看过这篇文章以后，不由想起自己的遭遇。

2) 孩子要走了，妈妈不由哭了起来。

8.　谁叫＋ sb. ＋ v.！ : Who asked you to?! No one asked you to! (question word used as intensifier)

❖　可是，谁叫她当叛徒的！

1) 你现在后悔了。谁叫你当时不听老师的话的！

2) 警察罚你是应该的。谁叫你乱停车的！

9.　提前＋ (time word) ＋ v.: v. ahead of time, beforehand

❖　我提前毕业了。

1) 要是你搬家了，请你提前告诉我你的地址。

2) 那个聪明的学生提前一个小时就交考试卷子了。

10.　止不住＋ v. : can't stop from; can't keep from

❖　她愣了片刻，止不住红着脸将实情告诉了他们。

1) 她看到了那个孩子的母亲，就止不住回想起自己的母亲。

2) 他止不住立刻把好消息告诉了大家。

11.　万万： (usually in negative) absolutely

❖　可万万没想到，因为妈妈的叛徒问题，公社团委没批。

1) 她万万没有想到自己的好朋友居然骗了自己。

2) 你万万不可把这件事告诉她。

12.　连 v. 都不 v. : don't even bother to v.

❖　妈妈的来信她连看都不看，都是随时收到随时打回的。

1) 她处处受到别人的冷遇，她跟别人说话的时候，别人连理都不理她。

2) 那个男人送给她的礼物，她连拆都不拆就扔了。

13.　勉强： barely enough

❖　到了第四年的春天，她才勉强地入了团。

1) 她的成绩很差，只能勉强上一个一般的大学。

2) 她的工资只能勉强维持生活。

14.　沿着＋ place word ＋ v.: v. along a place

❖　他们沿着海边走了很久，然后在沙滩上并排坐了下来。

1）你一直沿着这条路开，开半个小时就到了。

2）学生们很喜欢沿着河边的那条小路跑步。

15. 一阵 +（凄凉、激动、伤心、喜悦、难过）: a moment of ...

   ❖ 想起自己的一切，止不住又是一阵伤痛。

   1）看着母亲满是皱纹的脸，她的心里一阵难过。

   2）想到马上要看到心上人，她的心里一阵激动。

16. 有意：intentionally, deliberately

   ❖ 虽然他仍旧那样真情地爱着她，但她对他却有意避而远之。

   1）她有意低下头，假装没看见他。

   2）在那个晚会上，她有意打扮得很漂亮。

17. 一下子：all of a sudden

   ❖ 她的心一下子激烈地颤动起来。

   1）他把吃下去的东西又一下子都吐出来了。

   2）她看见他脸上的表情，一下子明白了他真正的目的。

练习

I. 选出合适的词语填空：

沉默寡言	脆弱	厌恶	安慰	身份
彻底	预感	激动	激烈	仿佛

1. 为了能多赚一点钱，他每天都不得不拼命地工作，他真_____这样的生活。
2. 在美国，上一个大学并不难，但是上名牌大学的竞争却是非常_____的。
3. 虽然好朋友们都来_____她，但是她的心里仍旧很难过。
4. 她一向_____，很少跟别人说话。
5. 她非常_____，她常常会因为一点小小的事情就哭个不停。
6. 今天她接到了很多奇怪的电话，她有一种不好的_____.
7. 要_____解决交通堵塞的问题，最好的办法是发展公共交通。
8. 大街上到处都是五彩缤纷的灯火，夜晚看起来_____跟白天一样。

II. 把正确的词圈出来：

1. 听到孩子们唱的歌，使我（回忆，回忆起）我自己的童年。
2. （即使，既然）是老师，他们的水平也不一定都比学生高。
3. 开学的第一天，很多学生的脸上都（怀着，挂着）兴奋的神情。
4. 因为她是一个外国人，所以学校没有（批，批改）她的申请。
5. 这个学生手里拿着一张地图，她（显得，显然）是一个新生。
6. 我是 80 （届，年级）的毕业生。
7. 女儿很久没回家了，母亲每天都（盼望，希望）着女儿早点回家。
8. 因为她说话有口音，所以常常（获得，遭到）很多人的歧视。
9. 听了老师的解释以后，我（始终，终于）明白了这句话的意思。
10. 如果你有问题，你可以（随手，随时）给我打电话。
11. 他（万万，千万）也没有想到，自己的好朋友居然背叛了自己。
12. 这个淘气的孩子（逐渐，缓缓）地懂事了。

III. 用所提供的词语回答问题：

1. 这篇小说的题目是"伤痕"，对王晓华来说，文革给她留下了怎样的伤痕？
   （自从…以后；失去；受到…冷遇；蒙受…耻辱；彻底；划清界限；断绝；连累；影响…前途）
2. 晓华虽然受到了很多的歧视跟冷遇，小苏一直真情地爱着她。写一写他们之间的关系。
   （建立…情谊；把…看作…；信赖；影响…前途；断绝；调到；仍旧）
3. 晓华是怎样跟妈妈划清界限的？妈妈又是怎样对她的？
   （决裂；寄；v都不v.；随时；原封不动；退回；不怪她；盼望）
4. 晓华的妈妈是一个怎样的人？文革中她为什么受到了迫害？
   （冒着…危险，抢救；篡权；迫害；强加；罪名；冤案，昭雪）

IV. 讨论问题：

1. 文革中，晓华因为妈妈的"问题"吃了很多苦，你怎样看这种因为父母的问题而连累孩子的社会现象？
2. 文革结束以后，晓华发现自己失去了妈妈，你觉得她会不会也失去小苏？为什么？
3. 文革给中国人民带来了难以想像的灾难，你觉得中国应该不应建一个文革博物馆？为什么？

二十五年后

高行健

　　他绝没有想到，这样快，就结束了，前后不过十来分钟光景，不，也就整整十分钟。他在传达室填写了会客单，神经质地看了下表，十点零七分。他按照传达室老头的指点，从走廊进去，左手对面第三个门，这样明确，不难找到。办公室的房门敞开。这正是做工间操的时间，满院子里⑴的人在做第四套，不，第五套广播体操。而他认识她的时候，才在推广第一套广播体操，他刚进大学。离他们分别的那年，1957 年，也已经整整 25 年了，四分之一个世纪。这就是人生。是的，是的，谁能想到还能见面？可 25 年来，他就一直期待这次会见。

　　办公室房门敞开，人都到院子里去做操了，只有一位剪短发的中年妇女背对着房门，坐在临窗的一张办公桌前。他战兢兢问道："请问，冯亦萍同志在吗？"

　　这女人转身，用诧异的目光，是的，是的，用诧异的目光打量着他："你找她有什么事？"

　　她就是冯亦萍，哪怕⑵再过 25 年，他也还能认出她那双眼睛，那双使他不敢正视的眼睛。当然，也还有她那轮廓分明

十来分钟	shíláifēnzhōng	*n.*	十几分钟；a couple of minutes; 10 to 20 minutes
光景	guāngjǐng	*n.*	(used after time and numerical expressions) about; around 离这儿有十里光景
传达室	chuándáshì	*n.*	reception office
填写	tiánxiě	*v.*	fill in; write
会客单	huìkè dān	*v.*	guest register 会客：receive guests
神经质地	shénjīngzhì.de	*adv.*	nervously
老头	lǎotóu	*n.*	old man
指点	zhǐdiǎn	*n.*	directions
走廊	zǒuláng	*n.*	hallway; corridor
明确	míngquè	*adj.*	clear and definite; explicit 明确的说明
敞开	chǎngkāi	*v.-c.*	open wide
工间操	gōngjiāncāo	*n.*	work-break exercises
体操	tǐcāo	*n.*	gymnastics, setting-up exercises to radio music
推广	tuīguǎng	*v.*	popularize; spread
期待	qīdài	*v.*	expect
会见	huìjiàn	*n.*	meeting; get-together
剪	jiǎn	*v.*	cut (with scissors)
背对着	bèiduì.zhe	*adv.*	with the back towards 背对着窗户坐着
临窗	línchuāng	*adj.*	by the window
战兢兢	zhànjīngjīng	*adv.*	trembling with fear
冯亦萍	Féng Yìpíng	*n.*	personal name
转身	zhuǎnshēn	*v.-o.*	(of a person) turn around
诧异	chàyì	*adj.*	be surprised; be astonished 感到十分诧异
目光	mùguāng	*n.*	gaze; look
打量	dǎ.liang	*v.*	measure with the eye; look somebody up and down
哪怕	nǎpà	*conj.*	even; even if; even though
正视	zhèngshì	*v.*	look squarely at
轮廓	lúnkuò	*n.*	outline; contour
分明	fēnmíng	*adj.*	be clear; be distinct; be unmistakable

的嘴角，如今已松弛了，可毕竟(3)还是分明的，尤其是那时候，当她出声傻笑的时候，那是非常鲜明的。

他还是鼓足了勇气说："不认识我了？我是你大学时代的老同学啊！"

她噢了一声，回忆起来了。尽管也老了，讲话还是那么快，声音还是那么明亮。她连忙给他拉椅子。

"我以为再也见不到你了。"他松了口气，说着便坐下。他不能这样站着，得坐下，从头说起。

他来得正好，他是选好了这工间操时间到的。他在街上已经转了十多分钟，就为的等这工间操时间到。这时候大家都休息，办公室里也好(4)谈话呀。或者，她万一(5)出来到街上买菜，他知道城里上班的人都好利用这时间买菜什么的。他在大门口外转了几分钟，没见到她出来，十点零五分，他便向传达室走去。

"噢，你现在在哪儿啊？"她问。

可他怎么说起呢？他说他"改正"了。

"噢，总算。"她说。

"是的，总算(6)改正了。"他笑道："25 年了。"

"啊，可不，57、67、77……可不，25 年啦！"

"要不是(7)这样，我也不会来看你的。"他说。

"过去的就让它过去吧。"她叹息道。

"那当然，不这样，有什么法子呢？总算过去了，也连累了你。"他必须首先表达这番歉意。

"噢，我没事。"她立即说。

"不，我很对不起你，这些年来，我一直……"他打断她的话。

嘴角	zuǐjiǎo	*n.*	corners of the mouth
松弛	sōngchí	*adj.*	limp; flabby; slack
毕竟	bìjìng	*adv.*	after all; all in all
傻笑	shǎxiào	*v.*	laugh foolishly; to giggle; to smirk
鲜明	xiānmíng	*adj.*	clear-cut; distinct; distinctive
鼓足勇气	gǔ zú yǒngqì	*phr.*	muster up the courage
噢	o	*intj.*	Oh
回忆	huíyì	*v.*	look back upon; recollect
松口气	sōng kǒuqì	*v.*	let out one's breath; relax
从头说起	cóngtóu shuōqǐ	*v.*	relate (the story) from the very beginning
好	hǎo	*adj.*	be easy (to do); be convenient: 书放在这儿好拿。/ 这个问题好回答。
转	zhuàn	*v.*	stroll; take a short walk
改正	gǎizhèng	*v.*	rehabilitate (here): refers to rehabilitation of those branded Rightists in the 1957 Anti-Rightist Campaign
总算	zǒngsuàn	*adv.*	at last; finally
叹息	tànxī	*v.*	sigh
道	dào	*v.*	say (书面语, usually used for the dialogue in a novel)
连累	lián.lei	*v.*	implicate; involve; get somebody into trouble　怕连累别人/被连累
番	fān	*AN.*	measure word for actions, deeds, etc. 下了一番工夫
歉意	qiànyì	*n.*	regret; apology
打断	dǎduàn	*v.*	interrupt; cut short

"对我没多大影响，不就是划了个中右吗？这后来我才知道的，在我的档案里，划了个中右。"

"当时你可为我讲了话。"他坚持道。他必须把这份歉意表达到。

"那时候，大家都还是孩子，懂什么呀!"她说。

"可我总记得当时班里对我的批判会上你说的那几句话。"

"说什么了？我都不记得了。"她笑道，甩了一下头发。她年轻的时候，在班里当众讲话时总是这样。

"你是我们的好班长，我们老同学见到，都这么谈起你。"他说。

"是吗？"她很高兴。

"是的，"他说："唉，25 年啦……"他不应该叹息，可这成了习惯，成了毛病。他立刻收敛，他得高兴才对。25 年来，他不就盼这个时刻吗？谈谈"反右斗争"之前，谈谈那些年大学生活中美好的回忆。啊，那时候女同学们都穿布拉吉，男女同学们在宿舍里经常一块儿唱〈山楂树〉，还有〈小路〉，啊，还有每星期六的舞会，张灯结彩的，哪像现在跳舞还好像是不怎么正经似的。那时候都是由青年团、学生会出面组织，堂而皇之，在大礼堂里，挂着彩带，像过节似的。

"你还带我跳过舞呢!"他说。

106

划	huà	v.	be branded as; determine (class status)
中右	zhōngyòu	n.	middle-of-the-road but slightly to the right (here): the most harmless type of Rightist
档案	dàng'àn	n.	file; record
讲话	jiǎnghuà	v.-o.	speak in defense of 为朋友讲话/为右派讲话
坚持	jiānchí	v.	persist in; persevere in; insist on
批判会	pīpànhuì	n.	criticism meeting
甩	shuǎi	v.	swing
当众	dāngzhòng	adv.	in the presence of all; in public
班长	bānzhǎng	n.	class monitor
毛病	máobìng	n.	bad habit; shortcoming
收敛	shōuliǎn	v.	restrain oneself
盼	pàn	v.	hope for; long for
时刻	shíkè	n.	a point of time; hour; moment
反右斗争	fǎnyòu dòuzhēng	n.	the Anti-Rightist Campaign (1957)
布拉吉	bùlājí	n.	another name for 连衣裙 (a transliteration of Russian *platye*); women's dress
山楂树	shānzhāshù	n.	hawthorn tree; (here): name of a song
舞会	wǔhuì	n.	dance; ball
张灯结彩	zhāngdēng jiécǎi	idm.	be decorated with lanterns and colored streamers
正经	zhèng.jing	adj.	decent; respectable
青年团	qīngniántuán	n.	the Communist Youth League
学生会	xuéshēnghuì	n.	student union; student association
出面	chūmiàn	v.-o.	act in one's own capacity or on behalf of somebody 他出面组织了一个学生会。/ 双方由民间团体出面，对贸易问题进行讨论。
堂而皇之	táng'ér huángzhī	idm.	openly and legally
大礼堂	dàlǐtáng	n.	auditorium
彩带	cǎidài	n.	colored ribbon; streamer
过节	guòjié	v.-o.	celebrate a festival

"这会儿都成老太婆了。"她笑了。

那眼神神采焕发，她依然是她，尽管鬓角也有了银丝。可他知道他自己的头发早都花白了。

"你毕业后分到哪里去了？"她问。

"我没毕业。"他说。

"噢，我知道。我是说你后来分到哪儿了？"她连忙解释道。

"在一个农场劳动了两年，后来就在附近的一个农村中学教书。"

"以后呢？"

"以后一直在农村。"

她也叹了一口气，便不再问了。

不，他要把这一切都告诉她！这些年来他之所以能支撑下来，全是因为她。他至今还保留当时写给她又没有勇气交给她的那封信。而他这次来看她并没有别的意思，他早已在农村结婚了，也早有了孩子。他还要说，他的妻子是个善良的农村妇女，他要说她当时不顾⑧他戴着右派份子的帽子，肯同他结婚，也是他这些年来极大的安慰。他妻子是个善良而通达的女人，他保留的那封信，他妻子也知道。他还珍藏她那几张照片，不，应该说是同学们大家郊游时拍的有她在一起的照片。他指给他妻子看过，他妻子也知道他怀念她，不，别打断，让他说下去，他要说，他妻子也还知道她在批判会上为他辩解

108

过，因此受到了连累，也倒了霉。他当然知道她已经结婚了，她不能不结婚，她应该结婚，应该找个她理想的人。他希望她幸福，他绝不会来打扰她的家庭的幸福。再说这怎么可能呢？

这会儿	zhèihuǐr	*n.*	(informal) now; at the moment 你从前同意，怎么这会儿又反对了呢？
老太婆	lǎotàipó	*n.*	(informal) old woman
眼神	yǎnshén	*n.*	expression in one's eye 从他的眼神可以看出他很高兴。
神采焕发	shéncǎi huànfā	*idm.*	glowing with health and radiating vigor
依然	yīrán	*adv.*	still; as before
鬓角	bìnjiǎo	*n.*	hair on the temples
银丝	yínsī	*n.*	(here) grey hair
花白	huābái	*adj.*	(of hair or beard) grey
支撑	zhīchēng	*v.*	support; prop up 全家的生活全靠他一人支撑。
勇气	yǒngqì	*n.*	courage; nerve
善良	shànliáng	*adj.*	kind-hearted; good and honest
戴帽子	dài mào.zi	*v.-o.*	bear the label of; be branded as; be labeled 戴上反革命的帽子
右派份子	yòupài fēnzǐ	*n.*	Rightists
安慰	ānwèi	*n./v.*	consolation; comfort
通达	tōngdá	*adj.*	be reasonable; be sensible 他是一个通达的人，一点儿也不保守。
珍藏	zhēncáng	*v.*	consider valuable and collect appropriately
郊游	jiāoyóu	*v./n.*	go on an excursion
拍	pāi	*v.*	take (a picture)
怀念	huáiniàn	*v.*	cherish the memory of; think of
辩解	biànjiě	*v.*	try to defend; provide an explanation
倒霉	dǎoméi	*v.-o.*	fall on evil days; fall on hard times
打扰	dǎrǎo	*v.*	disturb

他已经深深扎根农村了。

他是个农民。不过，他要说他如今没有政治包袱了，他也并不指望再回来过城里人的生活。他们家有自己的菜园子，吃的都是新鲜菜，不像城市里蔬菜这么贵。他有两个孩子，负担够重的了，像城里人那样生活他负担不起。不过，去年他调了一级，是在承认他大学毕业的资格的基础上再调了一级。他现在可以说一身轻快，他只希望大儿子能考上大学，女儿能念完中学，将来找到个工作，他就心满意足了。生活就是生活，你没法抱怨。各人有各人自己的命运，他不是个不安分守己的人。如今，夜里要是听不见他家后门池塘里青蛙的叫声，他还睡不着觉呢。他这次出来是参加省里的中学教材会议的。去年，他从小胖子那里打听到她的下落。

"胖子你还记得吗？"他问。

"小胖子啊，他在班上最调皮了。"她回答道。"刚粉碎四人帮的那年，他来过，为他自己的事平反奔波。"

"他的问题现在解决了吗？"他问。

"早解决了，当上研究室的副主任啦！他吃亏就在于⑼不接受57年的教训。"她说。

"这些年，你还好吗？"他又问。

"总算平平安安的。"

"这就好。"他说。

扎根	zhāgēn	*v.-o.*	take root
如今	rújīn	*n.*	now; nowadays
包袱	bāo.fu	*n.*	millstone round one's neck; burden; weight 思想包袱/ 不要把成绩当包袱
指望	zhǐ.wang	*v.*	look to; count on
蔬菜	shūcài	*n.*	vegetable
调级	tiáojí	*v.-o.*	adjust a wage scale (usually upwards); promote
承认	chéngrèn	*v.*	acknowledge; recognize
基础	jīchǔ	*n.*	basis; foundation
一身	yìshēn	*adv.*	the whole body
轻快	qīngkuài	*adj.*	relaxed
心满意足	xīnmǎn yìzú	*idm.*	be fully satisfied and content
抱怨	bàoyuàn	*v.*	complain
命运	mìngyùn	*n.*	fate; destiny
安分守己	ānfèn shǒujǐ	*idm.*	abide by the law and behave oneself; accept one's position in life
池塘	chítáng	*n.*	pond; pool
青蛙	qīngwā	*n.*	frog
叫声	jiàoshēng	*n.*	call; cry; shout
小胖子	xiǎo pàng.zi	*n.*	fatty; (here): a nickname
打听	dǎ.ting	*v.*	ask about; inquire about
下落	xià.luo	*n.*	whereabouts
调皮	tiáopí	*adj.*	naughty; mischievous
粉碎	fěnsuì	*v.*	smash; crush
四人帮	Sìrénbāng	*n.*	the Gang of Four
平反	píngfǎn	*v.*	redress (a mishandled case)
奔波	bēnbō	*v.*	rush about; be busy running about
副主任	fù zhǔrèn	*n.*	deputy director
吃亏	chīkuī	*v.-o.*	at a disadvantage; in an unfavorable situation
教训	jiàoxùn	*n.*	lesson; moral
平平安安	píngpíng'ān'ān	*adj.*	safe and sound; without mishap

　　她淡淡地笑了。这倒使他不知所措。他怎么说呢？这些年来他不就期待这样的笑容吗？就期待能见她一面！25 年来，她带着她的笑容就一直生活在他心里。他拎着铺盖卷儿离开学校的时候，都没告诉她一声，他不会给她留下地址的，因为他自己都不知道要到什么地方去，也就根本没那种非分的妄想。可当时却没敢去看她一眼。 他这些年来对她的思念， 她当然无从⑩知道。她也不知道他曾经偷偷爱她，而他未敢递出的那封信因为漏雨，因为潮湿发霉，也早已变得黄迹斑斑。但这毕竟是他一生中最美好的回忆。

　　他从家动身的前一天晚上，鼓足勇气对他妻子说，他想就便弯道去看一看她，这事他不能瞒着同他共过患难的妻子。妻子却不假思索，说："也该去看看人家，你现在不是没事了吗？"他本想带点乡里的土产，他们那里的红枣是出名的甜。再就是香油，听说城市里的人过春节的时候才配给二两，香油对城里人是珍贵的。他到县里去托人办事的时候，总带上斤把自家种的芝麻磨的香油。但是，临出门，他突然觉得拎着这些

淡淡地	dàndàn.de	adv.	indifferently; cool
不知所措	bùzhīsuǒcuò	idm.	be at wits' end; be at a loss what to do
笑容	xiàoróng	n.	smile; smiling expression
拎	līn	v.	(dialect) carry; lift 拎着一个书包
铺盖卷儿	pū.gaijuǎnr	n.	bedding roll; bedroll; luggage roll
地址	dìzhǐ	n.	address

非分	fēifèn	adj.	presumptuous; overstepping one's bounds
妄想	wàngxiǎng	n.	vain hope; wishful thinking
思念	sīniàn	v.	think of; long for; miss
无从	wúcóng	adv.	have no way (of doing something) 我们不了解情况，无从回答有关的问题。/这件事太复杂，一时无从说起。
递出	dìchū	v.-c.	send out; give
漏雨	lòuyǔ	v.-o.	(of a house) rain leaking in
潮湿	cháoshī	adj.	moist; damp; humid
发霉	fāméi	v.-o.	go moldy; become mildewed
黄迹斑斑	huángjìbānbān	adj.	stained with yellow spots
动身	dòngshēn	v.-o.	go on a journey
就便	jiùbiàn	adv.	at somebody's convenience; while you're at it 你去买书的时候，请就便替我也买一本。
弯道	wāndào	v.	detour
瞒	mán	v.	hide the truth from
患难	huànnàn	n.	trials and tribulations; adversity; hardship
不假思索	bùjiǎsīsuǒ	idm.	without thinking; without hesitation; readily
土产	tǔchǎn	n.	local product
红枣	hóngzǎo	n.	red date
香油	xiāngyóu	n.	sesame oil
春节	Chūnjié	n.	Chinese New Year
配给	pèijǐ	v.	ration
两	liǎng	AN.	a traditional unit of weight
珍贵	zhēnguì	adj.	precious
托	tuō	v.	ask; entrust 托人买书/托人照顾孩子
斤把	jīnbǎ	n.	about one jin, a jin or so 斤：jin, a traditional unit of weight, equivalent to 1.102 pounds.
芝麻	zhī.ma	n.	sesame
磨	mó	v.	grind

东西去看她，土气，会被人觉得寒酸。他不能以这种面目出现在她面前，便把妻子准备好的红枣和香油都留在桌上了。

他应该问她丈夫的情况，这是礼节。再有，要问问她的孩子，她应该有孩子了。也许都已经上了大学，城市里的孩子受教育的条件比乡里好得多。她不会不抓紧自己孩子的教育。但是他都没有问。他不知道为什么没有问。他不知道该问些什么，他甚至不知道此刻谈什么才好。他不知道为什么来看她，他不清楚。可这之前，在她那淡淡的一笑之前，这一切都是清清楚楚的，深思熟虑过的。此刻，他却不知所措了。他只好一笑，后来他说，那是一种苦笑，因为他的眼角、额头到脸上都布满了皱纹，他知道他不笑的时候倒更好看一些。

走廊里熙熙攘攘，做工间操的人都回到办公室里来了。第四套还是第五套广播体操？又何必⑾去管它是第几套呢？总之，生活又回到了它的轨道上来了。啊，生活！

"25年了。"他呐呐道。

"可不，25年啦！"她回答着。

人们都回到自己的办公桌前坐下。他立即站起来让座，因为他坐了别人的座。这人向他摆摆手，说："你坐，你坐。"

"不，我没事，我该走了。"他对她说。

"你是出差来的？"她问。

"顺便⑿来看看。"

"你再坐一会儿。"可她也起身了。

"你们都忙啊，我走了！"他说，口气肯定。

土气	tǔqì	*adj.*	rustic; uncouth; countrified
寒酸	hánsuān	*adj.*	(of a poor scholar) shabby and miserable
面目	miànmù	*n.*	appearance; look; aspect
礼节	lǐjié	*n.*	courtesy; etiquette
抓紧	zhuājǐn	*v.-c.*	firmly grasp; pay close attention to 抓紧学习/抓紧时间
深思熟虑	shēnsīshúlǜ	*idm.*	consider carefully 经过深思熟虑的思考以后，他决定先工作，然后再上大学。
苦笑	kǔxiào	*n.*	a wry smile
额头	étóu	*n.*	forehead
布满	bùmǎn	*v.-c.*	be covered all over with; spread all over 桌子上布满尘埃。
皱纹	zhòuwén	*n.*	wrinkle
熙熙攘攘	xīxīrǎngrǎng	*adj.*	bustling with activity; with people bustling about 马路上熙熙攘攘，热闹极了。
何必	hébì	*adv.*	why must
轨道	guǐdào	*n.*	track
呐呐	nènè	*v.*	murmur
让座	ràngzuò	*v.-o.*	offer one's seat to somebody 他给一位抱孩子的妇女让了座。
摆手	bǎishǒu	*v.-o.*	shake one's hand in admonition or disapproval 他向我摆手，叫我不要说话。
出差	chūchāi	*v.-o.*	go on a business trip
顺便	shùnbiàn	*adv.*	do something in addition to what one is already doing without much extra effort 你去图书馆的时候，顺便把这本书还了。
起身	qǐshēn	*v.-o.*	stand up
口气	kǒuqì	*n.*	tone; manner of speaking
肯定	kěndìng	*adj.*	positive; affirmative

"你在这里还要待几天吧？"她问。

"不，明天就走，学校里还有事。"他补充道。"你留步吧！见了你就很高兴。"他又说。

"你难得⑬来呀，送送你。"她坚持道。

他默默走着。她默默送他。

到了机关大门口，她大声说："怎么走得这样急？老李，下回再来，可得到我们家去做客呀！"

他说他也许听错了，不，他又说这两个字他不会听错的，因为他并不姓李，他姓张。同学们当中，25年前，大家都叫他张圈。大家都爱起绰号，而他的姓名张志远一念快了，就成了张圈，他说他们这位班长发号施令的时候就喊他"圈儿"，她是非常喜欢恶作剧的，那当然是25年以前，如今连他的姓名都忘了。可这能怪人家吗？你难道记得你25年前同班同学每一个人的姓名吗？

他谢过了她，又说了一些告别的话。她也对他说下次再来一定要到她家去吃饭，今天实在来不及⑭了，下次一定得来，一起好好叙叙旧。他一再⑮向她挥手告别，大声请她回去。她始终⑯含笑站在台阶上，目送他。

后来，电车就来了。是那种两节头的很长很长的电车。当电车驶过大门口的时候，他就再也没有回头。他说他好像记得看了下表，是无意识的，大概是十点十七分，因为他印象中，

总共就待了十分钟。就这样同二十五年前告别了，同二十五年

补充	bǔchōng	v.	supplement
留步	liúbù	v.-o.	(said by a departing guest to host) don't bother to see me out; don't bother to come any further
难得	nándé	adv.	seldom; rarely
送	sòng	v.	see somebody off or out 送他回家/ 把客人送到门口
默默	mòmò	adv.	silently
机关	jīguān	n.	office; organization
做客	zuòkè	v.-o.	be a guest (usually used to invite somebody) 你下次来，一定得到我家来作客。
圈	quān	n.	circle; ring; (here): personal name
起绰号	qǐ chuòhào	v.-o.	give somebody a nickname
发号施令	fāhàoshīlìng	idm.	issue orders; order people about
喊	hǎn	v.	call (a person); yell
恶作剧	èzuòjù	v.	play practical jokes, prank
告别	gàobié	v.	bid farewell to; say good-bye 到了八点，我们就向主人告别回家。
来不及	lái.bují	v.-c.	there is not enough time (to do something); too late (to do something)
叙旧	xùjiù	v.-o.	talk about the old days
一再	yízài	adv.	repeatedly; again and again
挥手	huīshǒu	v.-o.	wave
始终	shǐzhōng	adv.	from beginning to end; all along 我始终不明白他的意思。
含笑	hánxiào	v.-o.	have a smile on one's face
台阶	táijiē	n.	a flight of steps
目送	mùsòng	v.	follow somebody with one's eyes
电车	diànchē	n.	tramcar; streetcar
两节头	liǎngjiétóu	n.	with two cars
驶	shǐ	v.	(of a vehicle, etc.) speed by
无意识	wúyì.shi	adv.	unconsciously

来一直萦绕在他心头的梦告别了。这是荒谬的,又是真实的。他觉得空虚了,又觉得轻快了。

他停在一家百货商店门前,他说,那大玻璃橱窗里陈列着衬出女人的身腰的各种时装。他要买点什么。他突然觉得应该给他妻子买件这样的新衣服。自从他们结婚后,他就没有给妻子买过一件礼物。每月那点工资都如数交给了妻子。一家大小的衣服也都由她来做。他们曾经狠存了一阵子钱,为了买一台缝纫机。他决定要给妻子买一件做好了的成衣,一件像橱窗里陈列的漂亮的女式服装。他身上带着出差费,还有他妻子交给他路上花的五十块钱。要给小女儿买一双高筒的雨鞋,再买一床染得像人造毛样的棉毯。家里那床旧的,大儿子带走了,他在县中寄宿读书,而县城里卖的那种棉毯一洗就掉颜色。还要买两盒点心送给县教育局的王局长。这次出席省里的中学教材会议,人家够器重他的了。这都是妻子的嘱托。但是他还是决定先要给妻子买一件新衣服,一件领子上扎了花边的新衣服。

1982 年 6 月 25 日于北京

选自《高行健短篇小说集》2001 年 8 月

萦绕	yíngrào	*v.*	hover; linger
荒谬	huāngmiù	*adj.*	absurd
空虚	kōngxū	*adj.*	hollow; void
橱窗	chúchuāng	*n.*	display window; shop window
陈列	chénliè	*v.*	display; exhibit
衬出	chènchū	*v.-c.*	set off by contrast; serve as a foil to
身腰	shēnyāo	*n.*	waistline; waist
时装	shízhuāng	*n.*	fashionable dress
如数	rúshù	*adv.*	exactly the number or amount
狠	hěn	*adv.*	resolutely; firmly; severely
一阵子	yízhèn.zi	*n.*	a period of time; a spell
缝纫机	féngrènjī	*n.*	sewing machine
成衣	chéngyī	*n.*	ready-to-wear
出差费	chūchāifèi	*n.*	allowances for a business trip
高筒雨鞋	gāotǒng yǔxié	*n.*	rain boots
床	chuáng	*AN.*	measure word for bedding
染	rǎn	*v.*	dye
人造毛	rénzàomáo	*n.*	artificial wool
棉毯	miántǎn	*n.*	cotton blanket
寄宿	jìsù	*v.*	board/stay (for students); 寄宿学校＝boarding school
掉颜色	diào yánsè	*v.-o.*	lose color; fade
盒	hé	*AN.*	a box of
点心	diǎnxīn	*n.*	pastry; light refreshments
教育局	jiàoyùjú	*n.*	Education bureau
出席	chūxí	*v.*	attend; be present (at a meeting, social gathering, etc.)
器重	qìzhòng	*v.*	think highly of (one's juniors or subordinates)
嘱托	zhǔtuō	*v.*	exhortation
领子	lǐng.zi	*n.*	collar
扎	zhā	*v.*	suture; sew up
花边	huābiān	*n.*	lace

词语例句

1. 满 + place word：entire (place) filled with / full of…
   ❖ 满院子里的人在做第四套广播体操。
   1) 满屋子里的人都朝她望过去。
   2) 满电影院里的人都大声笑起来。
   3) 他跌倒在地上，满手都是泥。

2. 哪怕: even; even if; even though; no matter how
   ❖ 哪怕再过 25 年，他也还能认出她那双眼睛。
   1) 哪怕你不承认，我也知道这件事是你做的。
   2) 哪怕是再大的困难，我们也能克服。

3. 毕竟: after all; all in all
   ❖ 她那轮廓分明的嘴角，如今已松弛了，可毕竟还是分明的。
   1) 他虽然出国三十年了，但思考方式还是中国的，毕竟是个中国人。
   2) 毕竟是个诗人，他对各种事物的观点跟别人就是不一样。

4. 好：be easy (to do); be convenient
   ❖ 这时候大家都休息，办公室里也好谈话呀！
   1) 这本书很不好买。
   2) 这个问题好回答。
   3) 把书都放在书架子上才好找。

5. 万一：just in case; if by any chance
   ❖ 或者，她万一出来到街上买菜。
   1) 这件事万一让他知道了，那就糟糕了。
   2) 万一他不认识你了，那可怎么办呢?

6. 总算: at long last; finally
   ❖ "是的，是的，总算改正了。"他笑道："25 年了。"
   1) 奋斗了 10 年，他总算有了一些成就。
   2) 过了 25 年，我总算又见到了过去的老朋友了。

7. 要不是: if it were not for; but for
   ❖ "要不是这样，我也不会来看你的。"他说。
   1) 要不是他的指示这么明确，我也不可能这么快就找到了。

2) 要不是领导帮忙，他怎么可能得到那套两居室的房子！

8. 不顾: disregard; ignore; in defiance of; in spite of
   ❖ 他要说她当时不顾他戴着右派份子的帽子，肯同他结婚，也是他这些年来极大的安慰。
   1) 她不顾父母的反对，坚持跟男朋友同居。
   2) 政府不顾国际社会的批评，坚决执行计划生育的政策。

9. 在于: lie in; rest with
   ❖ 他吃亏就在于不接受 57 年的教训。
   1) 他成功的根本原因就在于他事前做了充分的准备。
   2) 社会的进步在于人们对现实的不满。

10. 无从: have no way (of doing sth.); not be in a position (to do sth.)
    ❖ 他这些年来对她的思念，她当然无从知道。
    1) 没有法律的依据，这件事我们无从处理。
    2) 这个问题的背景极为复杂，我一时无从说起。

11. 何必: there is no need; why
    ❖ 又何必去管它是第几套呢？总之，生活又回到了它的轨道上来了。
    1) 你拒绝他的要求就是了，何必生气呢！
    2) 你何必用这么多时间打扫房间？为什么不花点钱请人替你做？

12. 顺便: conveniently; while you are at it; without extra effort
    ❖ 我顺便来看看你。
    1) 你去图书馆的时候，请顺便替我把这本书还了。
    2) 我可以顺便给你买一点菜，并不麻烦。

13. 难得: seldom; rarely
    ❖ 你难得来呀，（我）送送你。
    1) 虽然我住得离纽约很近，但是难得到纽约去一趟。
    2) 我们难得有时间出去看电影。

14. 来不及: there's not enough time (to do sth.); it's too late
    ❖ 她也对他说下次再来一定要到她家去吃饭，今天实在来不及了。
    1) 昨天早上我起晚了，来不及吃早饭就上班去了。
    2) 你明天要考试，今天晚上才预备怎么来得及呢？

15．一再：again and again; repeatedly
   ❖ 他一再向她挥手告别，大声请她回去。
   1) 她父亲一再提醒她，千万别忘了打电话。
   2) 美国政府一再指责中国忽视人权状况。

16．始终：from beginning to end; from start to finish; all along
   ❖ 她始终含笑站在台阶上。
   1) 在中国工作期间，他始终没有离开过北京。
   2) 手术过程中病人始终是清醒的。

(七) 二十五年后

练习

I. 选合适的词语填进去：

> 连累，妄想，下落，填写，敞开，表达
> 打断，抓紧，布满，花白，萦绕，松

1. 才 40 岁，他的头发却已经 _____ 了。

2. 他不过是个乡下人，你劝劝他，千万不要有非分的 _____ 。

3. 战争结束了，他到处打听家人的 _____ 。

4. 真对不起，我不该 _____ 你。 让你受 那么多苦。

5. 尽管事情过去20年了，这份感情一直 _____ 在他心头。

6. 别 _____ 他的话，让他说下去。

7. 你得先 _____ 存款单，然后到窗口去存钱。

8. 天气很热，又没有电，所以，家家户户的房门都是 _____ 的。

9. 我之所以写这封信给你，是要向你 _____ 歉意。

10. 你得 _____ 时间复习功课， 否则你就考不上好大学。

11. 他脸上 _____ 了皱纹，完全是一个乡下的老农民。

12. 我看见孩子高高兴兴地回来了，这才 _____ 了一口气。

II. 选择合适的四字词填进去：

> 不敢正视，鼓足勇气，神采焕发，心满意足，安分守己
> 不知所措，发号施令，不假思索，深思熟虑，熙熙攘攘

1. 他偷偷地爱了她十年了，今年终于 _____ 向她求婚了。

2. 我现在没什么要求，只要孩子们考上大学，毕业后找到好工作，

   我就 _____ 了。

3. 孩子做错了事情，回到家里 _____ 父母。

4. 这一切都是经过 _____ 才决定的，并不是随便产生的想法。

123

5. 我只想嫁给一个 _____ 的人，过一个平平安安的生活。

6. 街上 _____ ，简直像过年一样热闹。

7. 你只不过是一个小小的班长，凭什么对我们 _____ ？

8. 我问他什么时候动手，他 _____ 地说："明天！"

9. 她突然大声哭起来，使他 _____ 。

10. 赢了比赛以后，球员们个个 _____ ，开了一个热热闹闹的记者会。

III. 用所提供的词语回答问题:

1. 你跟他十年没见面了，你还记得他的样子吗？ （哪怕）

2. 你改行经商，怕不怕失败呢？ （万一）

3. 你的研究报告到底做完了没有？ （总算）

4. 你得到这么好的工作机会，跟你父母有关系吗？ （要不是）

5. 为什么你不在报告中讨论中国古代社会？ （无从）

6. 我为了练习演讲比赛，昨天花了 10 个小时的时间。 （何必）

7. 你上了大学以后，经常出国吗？为什么？ （难得）

8. 这么重要的场合，你怎么穿得这么随便？你该换一件衣服。 （来不及）

9. 你为什么那么感激他？ （不顾）

10. 他们从前不是老朋友吗？怎么连姓名都忘了？ （毕竟）

IV. 用所提供的词语回答问题:

1. "他"的这二十五年是怎么过的？
   （戴着...的帽子，农村，珍藏，怀念，结婚，负担，心满意足，抱怨）

2. "他"为什么要去看"她"？
   （批判，辩解，倒霉，歉意，保留，勇气，期待，美好的回忆）

3. "他"想带什么礼物给"她"？为什么没带？
   （土产，珍贵，临出门，土气，寒酸）

4. "他"和"她"当年的大学生活是怎么样的？
   （宿舍，舞会，张灯结彩，郊游，反右斗争，毕业，安分守己）

5. 他们两个人在分别 25 年后，互相想念的感情一样不一样？
   （盼望，认出，诧异，思念，告别，姓名，荒谬，真实）

V. 讨论问题：

1. 在你看来，他跟她（冯亦萍）之间的爱情算不算是真正的爱情？这种跟他与妻子之间的感情有什么不同？

2. 小说中的男主角在什么时候感情起了很大的变化？是什么样的变化？你对这个变化有什么看法？

3. 从这篇小说里，你看到农村和城市有什么不同？

4. 你认为作者要表达的是什么？

讹诈

梁晓声

老会计半年后退休。

他供职的公司，是一家国有的药品公司，正紧锣密鼓筹备"上市"。"上市"前体制进行⑴转变，将以股份公司的性质重新挂牌。几天来公司经理忙碌又兴奋，一会儿召集某部门开会，一会儿找某几个人谈话。一种莫测高深的气氛笼罩在公司上下，有人喜欢有人忧。然而老会计却觉得自己似乎是局外人。体制转变和"上市"，并不能带给他值得激动不已的利益。他在公司是那种有他不多没他不少的角色。像他这样一些员工，顺水搭船，获得微不足道的股份罢了。他也不担心失去什么。

半年后就退休了嘛。

但他确实期待着经理找他，对他做一番当面的指示。因为公司有一笔"小金库"资金，东挪西攒的，近百万。此事

讹诈	ézhà	v.	blackmail; extort
会计	kuài.ji	n.	accountant
供职	gòngzhí	v.	serve; work at

Selected & prepared by: Liping Yu
Edited by: Chih-p'ing Chou

紧锣密鼓	jǐnluómìgǔ	*idm.*	wildly beating gongs and drums; intense publicity campaign
筹备	chóubèi	*v.*	arrange, prepare
上市	shàngshì	*v.-o.*	go on the market
体制	tǐzhì	*n.*	system of organization, system
转变	zhuǎnbiàn	*v.*	change; transition
股份公司	gǔfèn gōngsī	*n.*	publicly-traded company
挂牌	guàpái	*v.-o.*	listed (on the market)
经理	jīnglǐ	*n.*	manager
忙碌	mánglù	*adj.*	busy
召集	zhàojí	*v.*	call together
莫测高深	mòcè gāoshēn	*idm.*	too profound to be understood; too high and deep to be measured; unfathomable
气氛	qì.fen	*n.*	atmosphere; mood
笼罩	lǒngzhào	*v.*	envelop; shroud; hover over
局外人	júwàirén	*n.*	stranger, outsider
激动	jīdòng	*v.*	excite; stir; agitate
v.不已	bùyǐ	*suffix*	endlessly; ceaselessly 激动不已/痛哭不已/赞叹不已
利益	lì.yi	*n.*	advantage; interest; profit
顺水搭船	shùnshuǐ dāchuán	*idm.*	sail with the wind; go with the flow
微不足道	wēibùzúdào	*idm.*	unworthy; insignificant; negligible
番	fān	*AN.*	a course; a turn 这是他的一番好意，你就接受了吧！
当面	dāngmiàn	*adv.*	face to face, in one's presence 当面说清楚/当面交给他
指示	zhǐshì	*n.*	instructions
金库	jīnkù	*n.*	coffers; chest; vault (小金库: petty cash account)
东…西…	dōng... xī...	*v.*	...here ...there 东奔西跑/东一个西一个
挪	nuó	*v.*	move
攒	zǎn	*v.*	accumulate; save
东挪西攒	dōngnuó xīzǎn	*v.*	accumulate money from here and there

除了经理和老会计心中有数，再无第三者知道。近百万中包括不少关系单位奉送给公司的回扣。经理常对他说："这种钱我是不会占为己有的。别人更无权支配。等积累多了，全公司来一次公平分配，每个员工都有份儿！"

经理的话常使老会计感动。

多好的头儿啊。

如今这么廉洁的头儿可不多了。

所以，经理让他报销什么花费时，他从无耽延，一向当即照办。再好的头儿，也(2)难免(3)要进行"特殊消费"啊。如今的"公关"方式讲究这个呀。不是谁洁身自好不洁身自好的问题啊。何况(4)，支出在"小金库"的账上......

由于只有自己一人掌管着"小金库"，老会计常觉得自己是经理的心腹。起码是心腹之一。经理陪客，都带上他。他其实厌酒，也不善言谈，不能替经理推杯换盏，也不能活跃席间气氛。他便想，经理竟还带上他，那么纯粹是抬举他了。这么一想，心里很满足。尤其是，当经理默默无言地，将一只手

心中有数	xīnzhōng yǒushù	idm.	know what's what; have a clear idea about sth.
奉送	fèngsòng	v.	offer as a gift
回扣	huíkòu	n.	sales commission; kickback
占为己有	zhànwéi jǐyǒu	phr.	take as one's own
无权	wúquán	adv.	have no right
支配	zhīpèi	v.	arrange; allocate; budget

积累	jīlěi	*v.*	accumulate
分配	fēnpèi	*n.*	distribution; allocation; assignment
员工	yuángōng	*n.*	staff; personnel
有份儿	yǒufènr	*v.-o.*	have one's share in 这些钱是大家一起赚的，当然人人有份儿。
感动	gǎndòng	*v.*	be moved; be touched
头儿	tóur	*n.*	head; chief
廉洁	liánjié	*adj.*	honest; integrity; purity
报销	bàoxiāo	*v.*	write off expenses, apply for reimbursement
花费	huāfèi	*n.*	money spent; expenditures
耽延	dānyán	*v./n.*	delay
当即	dāngjí	*adv.*	immediately
公关	gōngguān	*n.*	public relations 公共关系
讲究	jiǎng.jiu	*v.*	pay special attention to; be particular about
洁身自好	jiéshēn zìhào	*idm.*	lead an honest and clean life; keep oneself pure from vice
何况	hékuàng	*conj.*	what is more
支出	zhīchū	*n./v.*	expenses; outflow
账	zhàng	*n.*	account book
掌管	zhǎngguǎn	*v.*	be in charge of
心腹	xīnfù	*n.*	trusted subordinate; trusted aide
起码	qǐmǎ	*adv.*	at least 起码需要2000元/起码得花10天的时间
不善言谈	bùshàn yántán	*idm.*	not good at talking
推杯换盏	tuībēi huànzhǎn	*idm.*	participate in celebratory drinking (at parties or official functions)
活跃	huóyuè	*v.*	enliven; invigorate
席间	xíjiān	*n.*	during the meal
便	biàn	*adv.*	then; in that case; 就
纯粹	chúncuì	*adv.*	purely
抬举	tái.ju	*v.*	praise or promote sb. to show favor; favor sb.
默默无言	mòmòwúyán	*idm.*	keep silent; without saying a word

亲昵地拍在他肩上时，他简直就有点儿觉着得宠了……

经理终于找他了。

经理是在电梯口碰见他的。

他说："经理，这几天忙苦了吧？"

经理说："是啊是啊，晕头转向。"

只他和经理两人乘电梯。进入电梯，他想请经理对"小金库"做出指示，只见经理一副费心劳神的样子，不便开口。

经理却主动说："咱俩还有点事儿谈呢。今晚到我家谈吧。别忘了带账本。"

经理的一只手一如既往地在他肩上拍了拍。

于是老会计的心里又感到极大满足。

经理最烦别人到他家里去谈工作，这是公司上下都明白的。

例外的对待使老会计有点受宠若惊。

晚上。在经理家，经理开了一瓶高级的法国葡萄酒，与老会计隔桌相对而坐。边喝边谈。 尽量⑸挑感情色彩浓的话说。经理的夫人和孩子不在家，经理说他们看文艺演出去了……

聊着聊着，自然就切入了正题。

经理将预先备好的两万元钱取来，放在老会计面前，让老会计收好再谈。

老会计以为又是该入"小金库"的钱，没想便放入了手提包里。

经理重新坐在他对面时说："给你的钱。你个人的钱。"

老会计一愣。

"半年后你就退休了，没功劳还有苦劳。所以那是你分内

亲昵地	qīnnì.de	*adv.*	intimately
肩	jiān	*n.*	shoulder
得宠	déchǒng	*v.*	be in sb.'s good grace
晕头转向	yūntóu zhuànxiàng	*idm.*	be confused and disoriented
乘电梯	chéng diàntī	*v.-o.*	take the elevator
费心劳神	fèixīn láoshén	*idm.*	take a lot of care; take a lot of trouble
主动	zhǔdòng	*adv.*	(do sth.) on one's own initiative; (do sth.) of one's own accord
账本	zhàngběn	*n.*	account book
一如既往	yìrújìwǎng	*idm.*	just as in the past
受宠若惊	shòuchǒng ruòjīng	*idm.*	feel extremely flattered; be surprised at the unexpected honor
葡萄酒	pútáo jiǔ	*n.*	wine
浓	nóng	*adj.*	great; strong 香味很浓/兴趣很浓
文艺演出	wényì yǎnchū	*n.*	entertainment performance
切入	qiērù	*v.*	cut to; cut through to
正题	zhèngtí	*n.*	subject of a talk
手提包	shǒutíbāo	*n.*	handbag
愣	lèng	*v.*	stupefied
功劳	gōngláo	*n.*	merits and contribution
苦劳	kǔláo	*n.*	toil
分内	fènnèi	*adj.*	one's duty, one's own share 关心学生是老师分内的事。

的钱。你心安理得地接受就是了。”

“由我给你⑹，你怕什么呢？我又不是在向你行贿？”

“……”

“别多虑。是从‘小金库’里出的钱……”

想起经理曾说过“每个员工都该有份儿”，老会计不再狐疑。他确乎心安理得起来。他笑了。

接下来的事便顺理成章了——按照经理的指示，他一笔一笔地将“小金库”的钱从账上高明地转移了。他曾被抽借到别的单位协助纪检部门查账，颇精通将假账做得看去仿佛很清楚很规范似的……

他因为有些醉了，也因为心安理得地接受了两万元而高兴，一觉酣睡至天明。

醒来，目光落在被两万元撑鼓的手提包上，回忆昨晚迈入经理家和迈出经理家的全过程，渐渐地不那么心安理得了……

他明白------只有他和经理两个人知道的“小金库”的钱，已从账目上流失了。所剩不过是零头，好象原先就只有那么点儿钱。

他明白------ 经理是企图趁机⑺转移而且独占。

他明白------ 他实际上参与了经济犯罪。

他明白------ 如果他不接受那两万元钱，有朝一日他还可以在法律面前替自己辩护。但他已经将两万元钱带回自己家了啊!

心安理得	xīn'ānlǐdé	idm.	feel at ease and justified
行贿	xínghuì	v.	bribe
份儿	fènr	n.	share
狐疑	húyí	v.	doubt; be suspicious
确乎	quèhū	adv.	really; indeed
顺理成章	shùnlǐ chéngzhāng	idm.	follow as a matter of course; in a clear and ordered pattern
按照	ànzhào	prep.	according to 按照公司的规定，只有星期五才可以穿牛仔裤上班。
高明	gāomíng	adj./adv.	brilliant; bright; wise
转移	zhuǎnyí	v.	transfer
抽	chōu	v.	take out, select
协助	xiézhù	v.	help; assist
纪检	jìjiǎn	n.	disciplinary inspection
部门	bùmén	n.	department; branch
颇	pō	adv.	pretty, quite, rather
精通	jīngtōng	adj.	good at
仿佛	fǎngfú	adv.	as if; seem 仿佛睡着了
规范	guīfàn	adj.	orthodox; conforming with the norm
酣睡	hānshuì	v.	sleep soundly
撑鼓	chēnggǔ	v.-c.	fill to the point of bursting
回忆	huíyì	v.	call to mind; recollect
迈入	màirù	v.-c.	step into
账目	zhàngmù	n.	items of an account
流失	liúshī	v.	drained away; depleted
零头	líng.tou	n.	fractional amount
企图	qǐtú	v.	attempt; seek; try
趁机	chènjī	adv.	take the opportunity to; seize the chance to
独占	dúzhàn	v.	take as one's own
有朝一日	yǒuzhāoyírì	idm.	one day; some time in the future 有朝一日，我也会有我自己的公司。
辩护	biànhù	v.	speak in defense of; defend; justify

那么他不是已经没有了替自已辩护的资格了吗？

他明白------做得再高明的假账，只要认真仔细地查，最终总是会被查账人发现破绽的。正所谓"狐狸再狡猾也斗不过好猎手"。他曾做过几次"猎手"，而现在是"狐狸"了。

他想到了儿子。儿子争气，在重点大学读硕士研究生，是优秀学生会干部，将被公费送出国攻博......

他想到了女儿。女儿已经大学毕业，是一所重点中学的英语教师。而女婿是该中学最年轻的副校长。互敬互爱的，一对感情和美的小夫妻......

他想到了自己。当了一辈子会计，和钱打了一辈子交道，却从未在钱字上动过歪念。过去的年代，多次获得"模范"。

......他想到了他老伴儿。老伴儿死于癌症，死前对他说："我最不放心的是你的身体；最放心的是你会领着儿女们走正道......"

他想到了在大学里读硕士的儿子需要钱......

他想到了即将分娩的女儿需要钱......

两万元------ 多乎哉？不多也！

对于有些人，两万元是区区之数。

对于儿子和女儿，如果他忽然说给他们每人一万元钱------他想像得出，儿子和女儿将多么的被他这位父亲所感动......

但，要是代价是......

（八）讹诈

老会计不敢想下去了......

都道是"常在河边站，哪能不湿鞋"------ 可他在钱这条

往往诱人自溺的"大河"边站了一辈子，又何曾湿过鞋底儿？

资格	zīgé	*n.*	qualification
破绽	pò.zhan	*n.*	burst seam; flaw
狐狸	hú.li	*n.*	fox
狡猾	jiǎohuá	*adj.*	sly; cunning
斗不过	dòu bú guò	*v.-c*	can not beat
猎手	lièshǒu	*n.*	hunter
争气	zhēngqì	*v.*	not to let someone down; strive to excel　供你上学不容易，你得争气，得个好成绩。
重点大学	zhòngdiǎn dàxué	*n.*	key university
硕士	shuòshì	*n.*	Master's degree
优秀	yōuxiù	*adj.*	outstanding; excellent
公费	gōngfèi	*adv.*	at public expense; at state expense
攻博	gōng bó	*v.-o.*	study for a Ph.D
女婿	nǚ.xu	*n.*	son-in-law
从未	cóngwèi	*adv.*	have never
动	dòng	*v.*	move, stir
歪念	wāiniàn	*n.*	wicked idea; evil thought
模范	mófàn	*n.*	an exemplary person or thing; model
老伴儿	lǎobànr	*n.*	one's dear old companion – one's spouse in old age
即将	jíjiāng	*adv.*	be about to
分娩	fēnmiǎn	*v.*	deliver; give birth
区区之数	qūqūzhīshù	*n.*	a small amount; a pittance
代价	dàijià	*n.*	price; cost
诱	yòu	*v.*	seduce, lure
溺	nì	*v.*	drown
何曾	hécéng	*adv.*	when (used in rhetorical question to indicate negation) 我何曾说过这么不合理的话！

135

他越不敢往下想越不能不往下想，而越往下想则越害怕……

他害怕得都没有打开手提包看一看那两万元钱。

第二天，在预先探知经理办公室没别人的时间里，他拎着手提包去见经理。

实际上我们讲述的这一件事，至此已接近尾声了。

然而却也刚刚开始。

是的，刚刚开始，因为导致老会计死于杀手刀下的真正原因------那一种"黑色"的，越希望被正确理解便越被严重误解和曲解的夺命情节，才刚刚介入这一件事。

老会计径直走到经理那张宽大的办公桌前，从手提包内取出两万元钱，轻轻放在桌上，以极低极低的声音说："经理，我觉得我不能接受这两万元钱……"经理的第一个反应是霍地从老板椅上弹跳而起，神色慌张地去插上办公室的门。

经理走回到老会计身旁，斜眼瞧瞧桌上那两万元钱，随即瞪着老会计，以更低的声音说："嫌少是不是？"从经理那方面，只有得出以上结论才符合他的经验向他揭示的某种逻辑。"经理，我……我不是…我真的不是…我只不过…"

老会计口拙舌笨起来，他一时⑻不知该如何正确地表达自己的意思了。

"你，你嫌少你也不应该这样啊！"

"经理，我发誓我不是嫌少……"

老会计不但口拙舌笨，而且面红耳赤了。他越是极力想

探知	tànzhī	v.	find out by inquiry
拎	līn	v.	carry
尾声	wěishēng	n.	the end
导致	dǎozhì	v.	lead to
杀手	shāshǒu	n.	killer
误解	wùjiě	v.	misunderstand
曲解	qūjiě	v.	misunderstand
夺命	duómìng	v.	take someone's life
情节	qíngjié	n.	circumstances; plot
介入	jièrù	v.	intervene; get involved
径直	jìngzhí	adv.	directly; straight
霍地	huò.de	adv.	quickly, suddenly
弹跳而起	tántiàoérqǐ	v.	spring up
神色	shénsè	n.	facial expression
慌张	huāngzhāng	adj.	flurried; flustered
插上	chāshàng	v.	lock (the door)
斜眼瞧	xiéyǎn qiáo	v.	look sideways at sb.
瞪	dèng	v.	stare at
嫌	xián	v.	dislike, mind
结论	jiélùn	n.	conclusion
符合	fúhé	v.	conform to; fit; suit
揭示	jiēshì	v.	unveil
逻辑	luó.ji	n.	logic
口拙舌笨	kǒuzhuó shébèn	idm.	be awkward in speech; inarticulate
一时	yìshí	adv.	for the time being, for a while
发誓	fāshì	v.-o.	swear
面红耳赤	miànhóng ěrchì	idm.	flushed (often with embarressment or anger)

137

表白自己来到经理办公室不是嫌两万元钱太少，却越是给经理一种他嫌钱少的印象……

经理从腰间摘下一串钥匙，扭开一个抽屉的暗锁，从中取出了一捆钱，连同老会计放在桌上的两万元，一齐替老会计收进了手提包。

经理的嘴附在老会计耳上悄语："一会儿几位部门领导都要到我这里来开会，有什么想法儿你晚上到我家去谈好吗？你我之间，难道还不可以开诚布公吗⑼？"

经理不容⑽老会计再说什么，左手从背后按在老会计左肩上，右手从背后按在老会计右肩上，将老会计亲亲密密地"送"出了办公室……

当夜，老会计失眠了。他将手提包放在床头柜上，歪头瞧着它发呆。它因为多装了一万元而显得更鼓了。老会计也更加不安了，更加不敢拉开它的拉链了。

"苍天在上，我不是嫌少……"

他不由得自言自语地说了一句……

几天后的中午，老会计离开公司，在马路旁的公用电话亭往经理办公室拨了一次电话。电话线很照顾他，一拨就通。

"经理吗？您现在说话方便吗？"

经理正独自在办公室午休。他立刻听出了老会计的声音。尽管⑾只一个人在办公室里，他还是心虚地用另一只手捂上了话筒。

"方便，可你在哪儿给我打电话？！"

"在外边。在马路旁的公用电话亭……经理，您误解我了，

我不是嫌少，无功受禄，我怎么会嫌少呢？请您耐心听我解

表白	biǎobái	v.	justify oneself; vindicate
摘	zhāi	v.	remove
钥匙	yào.shi	n.	key
扭开	niǔkāi	v.-c.	wrench the door open
暗锁	ànsuǒ	n.	built-in lock
捆	kǔn	AN.	bundle; bunch
悄语	qiāoyǔ	v.	speak in a low voice
开诚布公	kāichéng bùgōng	idm.	speak frankly and sincerely
不容	bùróng	v.	not allow; not tolerate 不容怀疑/不容干涉
亲亲密密	qīnqīnmìmì	adv.	intimately
失眠	shīmián	v./n	insomnia; inability to sleep
发呆	fādāi	v.	stare blankly
拉链	lāliàn	n.	zipper
苍天在上	cāngtiān zàishàng	n.	only heaven knows
不由得	bùyóu.de	adv.	can't help; cannot but 他说得那么可怜，我不由得掉下了眼泪。
自言自语	zìyánzìyǔ	v.	talk to oneself; think out loud
独自	dúzì	v./n	alone, by oneself
午休	wǔxiū	v.	noon break, midday rest
心虚	xīnxū	adj.	with a guilty conscience
捂	wǔ	v.	cover (with hand)
话筒	huàtǒng	n.	mouthpiece; microphone
无功受禄	wúgōng shòulù	idm.	get a reward without deserving it
耐心	nàixīn	adj.	patient

释，我……我……"

"得啦得啦，别解释了！下班以后，我在办公室等你。有话当面说！"

经理那头啪地搁了电话。

老会计在马路旁的电话亭前手握着话筒发愣。

还跑到马路上去在公用电话亭给我打起电话来了！

经理绕着办公桌走了一圈，又走了一圈，内心里忽然间产生一种类似被讹诈的感觉……

当公司租用的那一层写字楼彻底安静下来以后，老会计幽灵似的出现了……

经理显出一副恭候良久的样子⑫。

经理客气地说："坐吧。现在只有你我二人，你究竟想要多少才满足，开门见山吧！"

那一种客气的态度，使老会计顿时⑬感到，他已不再是心腹了。他们以前的亲密关系已改变了。

老会计不禁⑭心生出大的无奈、沮丧和悲哀。

老会计以一种近乎冤屈的语调说："经理，我怎么才能向您解释清楚呢？"

经理慢条斯理地说："既然连自己都觉得解释不清楚，那就别解释了。现实中有些事本来就是完全不需要解释的。你不解释，我还清楚；你一解释，我倒糊涂了……"

经理说着，探手于西服内兜，二指夹出一个存折，伸在老会计眼前晃了几晃……

得啦	dé.la	v.	All right! That's enough.
搁	gē	v.	put; (here): hang up
发愣	fālèng	v.-c.	stupefied
圈	quān	n.	circle; ring
类似	lèisì	adj.	similar
幽灵	yōulíng	n.	ghost; spirit
显出	xiǎnchū	v.	display, show 显出很高兴的样子/显出很生气的样子
恭候良久	gōnghòu liángjiǔ	idm.	wait respectfully for a long time
开门见山	kāimén jiànshān	idm.	The door opens on a view of mountains - go straight to the point 我不喜欢绕来绕去，有话请你开门见山地说。
顿时	dùnshí	adv.	immediately; suddenly 老师严肃地走进了教室，教室里顿时安静了下来。
不禁	bùjīn	adv.	can't help doing sth. 不禁一笑/不禁大吃一惊
无奈	wúnài	n./adj.	feeling of helplessness; have no choice; helpless
沮丧	jǔsàng	n./adj.	depression; dejection; depressed; dejected
悲哀	bēi'āi	n./adj.	grief; sadness; sorrowful
冤屈	yuānqū	n.	wrongful treatment; injustice
语调	yǔdiào	n.	intonation; tone
慢条斯理	màntiáosīlǐ	adv.	slowly and methodically
探手	tànshǒu	v.	reach into
西服	xīfú	n.	(western-style) suit
内兜	nèidōu	n.	inside pocket
存折	cúnzhé	n.	bankbook
晃	huàng	v.	shake

经理又说："中午接到你从外边打来的电话，知道我下午办的第一件事是什么吗？我亲自去到银行里，将我家的一个存折，改成了你的名字。我一时也搞不到许多现金，只能以这种方式满足你了。如果你真的不嫌少，那你就收下。如果你收下了，那你就别再来向我解释。就算我求你，啊？"

经理说罢，将存折放在了桌角。

老会计的目光，从经理脸上，转移向了存折，却没伸手去碰它。

"满足不满足，你总得拿起来看看啊！"

经理的态度客气而又彬彬有礼，客气得老会计周身发寒。

老会计太为难了。

如果他照直说自己怕受牵连，那么也就等于是在当着经理的面，说经理指示他做的那件事是犯罪。

但是，若经理反问："你凭⑮什么认为我企图将那笔钱占为己有？"

他将被问得张口结舌，无言以答。

如果经理没有那一种企图，又为什么对他如此慷慨？

"我再说一遍，请拿起来看一看。如果你真的不嫌少了，那你就收下。"

老会计拿起存折，翻开看了一眼，存着一万元。

这时电话响了……

经理接电话时，老会计收起存折走了。

他已两次想亲自退回经理最初给他的两万元，结果却使两万变成了四万元。如果他当时不离开，经理将认为他还不满足。如果他继续解释，情形一定很僵，他不愿将两人之间的关系搞得太僵。他只不过希望在被充分理解的前提之下⑯，得以从一件使自己不安的事中摆脱。于是当时悄然离开成了一种明智，一种权宜之举……

求	qiú	*v.*	beg
彬彬有礼	bīnbīnyǒulǐ	*idm.*	refined and courteous; behaving in a refined and civil manner
周身发寒	zhōushēn fāhán	*idm.*	entire body wracked with shivers
为难	wéinán	*adj.*	feel awkward; be in a quandary
照直	zhàozhí	*adv.*	straightforward
牵连	qiānlián	*v.*	involve (in trouble); implicate (in a crime)
反问	fǎnwèn	*v.*	ask (a question) in reply
凭	píng	*prep.*	according to, on the basis of
张口结舌	zhāngkǒu jiéshé	*idm.*	be agape and tongue-tied; be at a loss for words
无言以答	wúyányǐdá	*v.*	unable to answer
慷慨	kāngkǎi	*adj.*	generous
僵	jiāng	*adv.*	have reached a stalemate; deadlocked
前提	qiántí	*n.*	premise
得以	déyǐ	*aux.*	so that ... can ...; so that ... may ...他和他的恋人在分别25年以后，终于得以相见。
摆脱	bǎituō	*v.*	break away from, shake off
权宜之举	quányízhījǔ	*n.*	expedient act 租车只是一个权宜之举，你最终还是得有一辆自己的车。

回到家里，他戴上花镜再看那存折，却原来不是存着一万，而是存着十万！

他当即往经理办公室拨电话，经理已不在；往经理家中拨电话，经理还没回家......

第二天老会计没上班。

第二天经理又接到了老会计一次电话。老会计在电话里又作解释，他说天地良心，已经有十三万元属于他了，他怎么还会嫌少呢？女儿女婿至今住在一间老平房里，十三万元快够他们买套两居室的商品房了呀！但事情不是钱不钱的问题啊！

老会计越急切地想解释清楚，却越加地语无伦次。

经理打断了他的话。

经理以冷冰冰的语调说："你终于变得坦率了，这挺好。我十分感谢你照直谈到了你女儿女婿的房子问题。我向你保证，房子他们会有的！"

经理一说完就摔下了电话，同时恨恨地骂了一句："老流氓！"此时的经理，不是似乎感到，而是确信自己被诓诈了。

他恼怒地扯断了电话线......

三天后老会计收到了一份专递信件，里边只有一把缠着纸条的钥匙。纸条上，电脑打印着一处地址。

老会计按照纸条去看了那套房子。很宽敞的一套两居室楼房。如果对女儿和女婿说是他们的了，小两口一定会喜出望外的。他曾听人议论公司为经理多买了一套房子，想必这一套便是了……

又过了几天，全公司热热闹闹地召开庆贺体制转变成功的大会。在会上经理被宣布为新成立的股份公司的总裁。

当人们纷纷围向经理碰杯祝酒时，秘书将经理请到一旁，低声说办公室里有电话在等他接。

"你不会说我不在吗？"

经理生气了。

花镜	huājìng	*n.*	reading glasses
天地良心	tiāndìliángxīn	*idm.*	speak the truth; from the bottom of one's heart
语无伦次	yǔwúlúncì	*idm.*	speak incoherently; babble like an idiot 他喝多了，说起话来语无伦次。
坦率	tǎnshuài	*adj.*	candid; straightforward
老流氓	lǎoliúmáng	*n.*	old hooligan
恼怒	nǎonù	*v./adv.*	angry; indignant
扯断	chěduàn	*v.-c.*	rip out; disconnect
专递信件	zhuāndì xìnjiàn	*n.*	express mail
缠	chán	*v.*	wrap; bind
宽敞	kuānchǎng	*adj.*	spacious; roomy
喜出望外	xǐchū wàngwài	*idm.*	be overjoyed; happy beyond expectations
议论	yìlùn	*v.*	talk; discuss
召开	zhàokāi	*v.*	call a meeting
庆贺	qìnghè	*v.*	celebrate
宣布	xuānbù	*v.*	declare, announce
总裁	zǒngcái	*n.*	director general
碰杯祝酒	pèngbēi zhùjiǔ	*v.*	clink glasses and drink a toast

"对方说有很重要的事与您谈。"

那个"对方"非是别人，正是老会计。

"经理，您也会收到一份专递信件。里边有属于你的房子的钥匙，还有那存折。您前两次给我的三万元钱，我存入存折了。容我最后一次解释，我并不嫌少。"

"喂，喂！"

轮到老会计将电话挂断了。

经理口中咬牙切齿挤出两个字是------"妈的！"

经理颓然坐在他的老板椅上，想到了"人心不足蛇吞象"那一句成语，内心里感到一种将被牢牢地粘住并被步步紧逼地讹诈着的恐惧......

他全身不由得抖了一下......

老会计遇害不久，经理被推上了被告席。

罪名是"雇佣谋杀"。

在事实面前，他供认不讳。

他的律师替他请求减刑。理由是------他杀人的动机，毕竟也是由于受到了一次接一次的讹诈。

于是律师娓娓讲述讹诈过程，强调被一次接一次地讹诈时，内心生出的恐惧会对人造成多么巨大的心理压力......

站在被告席上的男人双手捂脸哭了。

他原本的企图是------将那笔只有他和老会计知道的"小

金库"的钱占为己有，再以个人的名义买入公司的股份。也许，这种做法，十年后会使他成为千万富翁......却怎么也没想到⒄自己会被一个自己一向认为言听计从的人所讹诈。

对方	duìfāng	*n.*	the other side; the other party
轮	lún	*v.*	take turns (here): this time it was the accountant's turn to hang up the phone
挂断	guàduàn	*v.-c.*	hang up the phone
咬牙切齿	yǎoyáqièchǐ	*idm.*	gnash the teeth in anger
妈的	mā.de	*intj.*	damn!
颓然	tuírán	*adv.*	dejectedly; disappointedly
牢牢	láoláo	*adv.*	firmly
粘	zhān	*v.*	glue; stick; paste
步步紧逼	bùbùjǐnbī	*v.*	press on at every stage
恐惧	kǒngjù	*n.*	fear; dread
抖	dǒu	*v.*	shiver
遇害	yùhài	*v.*	be murdered
被告席	bèigàoxí	*n.*	defendant's seat
罪名	zuìmíng	*n.*	charge, accusation
雇佣谋杀	gùyōng móushā	*n.*	orchestrated murder; hiring someone to kill someone else
供认不讳	gòngrèn búhuì	*idm.*	confess everything; candidly confess
减刑	jiǎnxíng	*v.*	reduce a penalty
动机	dòngjī	*n.*	motivation; cause
娓娓	wěiwěi	*adv.*	tirelessly
讲述	jiǎngshù	*v.*	relate
以⋯名义	yǐ...míngyì	*n.*	in the name of
千万富翁	qiānwàn fùwēng	*n.*	billionaire
言听计从	yántīng jìcóng	*idm.*	always follow sb.'s advice; act upon whatever sb. says

是的，站在被告席上的男人，更加感到自己是被一次次讹诈过的了。

十三万元加上一套商品房，在他还没成为千万富翁之前，他给予讹诈者的确乎不能算少了！

听众席上也有人在哭。

是老会计的儿子、女儿和女婿……

他们想不通他们的父亲何以⑱会变得那么贪，何以一次次地不能满足一次次地讹诈他人？

那一时刻法庭极静。

分明许多旁听者都对谋杀案主犯或多或少⑲地有些同情了。

分明那一时刻，似乎也是对另一个人的讹诈提出的指控了！

一个一次次退钱的人，其实并不是因为别人给他的钱数少，而是一心要与非法所得划清界限------今天谁还相信这样的事？要证明这样的事是一个事实，比要辩护一名罪犯无罪困难十倍。

法庭没有减刑。

但不少旁听者离开法庭时相互说："那老家伙也死的活该！"

人们的话象涂了毒的刀一样深深刺入老会计的儿子、女儿和女婿的心里。

他们是那么地觉得羞耻。

于是，连他们的内心里，也有些鄙视并恨老会计了……

选自《人民文学》2000年第11期

何以	héyǐ	*pron.*	why
贪	tān	*adj.*	greedy; avaricious
分明	fēnmíng	*adv.*	clearly
或多或少	huòduō huòshǎo	*adv.*	more or less
指控	zhǐkòng	*v.*	charge, accuse
一心	yìxīn	*adv.*	whole heartedly　他一心要学音乐。
划清界限	huàqīng jièxiàn	*phr.*	make a clear distinction; draw a clear line of demarcation
活该	huógāi	*v.*	serve sb. right
涂	tú	*v.*	spread on; smear
刺入	cìrù	*v.*	stab
羞耻	xiūchǐ	*adj.*	shame
鄙视	bǐshì	*v.*	despise; disdain

词语例句

1. 进行： carry on, conduct 进行＋（讨论、教育、研究、访问、调查）
   ❖ 上市前体制进行转变。
   1) 美国总统对中国进行了五天的访问。
   2) 中学生吸毒的情况很严重，学校应该对这个情况进行调查。

2. 再……也……： at any rate; no matter how adj., still …
   ❖ 再好的头儿，也难免要进行特殊消费啊。
   ❖ 做得再高明的假账，只要认真仔细地查，最终总是会被查账人发现破绽的。
   ❖ 狐狸再狡猾也斗不过好猎手。
   1) 他父母认为生活再困难也要供孩子上大学。
   2) 时间再晚，今天也得把这些事情做完。

3. 难免： hard to avoid
   ❖ 再好的头儿，也难免要进行特殊消费啊。
   1) 他这么不小心，难免失败。
   2) 犯错误是难免的。

4. 何况： what is more
   ❖ 这不是洁身自好不洁身自好的问题啊。何况，支出在"小金库"的账上。
   1) 你今天就住在这儿吧。这儿有地方住，何况你明天又不上班。
   2) 你应该去接她。这儿这么难找，何况她从来没有来过。

5. 尽量： as far as possible; try one's best to
   ❖ 他们边喝边谈，尽量挑感情色彩浓的话说。
   1) 请大家尽量发表意见。
   2) 所有的问题，我们一定尽量解决。

6. 由＋ sb. ＋ v.： v. by someone
   ❖ 由我给你，你怕什么呢？
   1) 李老师生病了，所以今天的中文课由王老师上。
   2) 单位里的钱是由老会计掌管。

7. 趁机: take advantage of the opportunity to; seize the chance to
❖ 经理是企图趁机转移而且独占。
1) 警察上厕所的时候，小偷趁机跑了。
2) 放假的时候，很多人都出去玩了。所以，小偷会趁机到家里偷东西。

8. 一时: for the time being, a short time
❖ 他一时不知该如何正确地表达自己的意思了。
1) 我肯定有他的电话，可是一时找不到。
2) 我一时想不起他的名字了。

9. 难道……吗？: Could it be said that ...? (rhetorical question)
❖ 你我之间，难道还不可以开诚布公吗？
1) 我昨天刚刚告诉你的事，难道你今天就忘记了吗？
2) 你总是不去上课，难道你就不怕老师生气吗？

10. 不容 + v: do not allow; do not permit
❖ 经理不容老会计再说什么。
1) 这个作业明天一定得交，不容拖延。
2) 他很不礼貌，不容我把话说完就把电话挂了。

11. 尽管: though; even though; in spite of
❖ 尽管只一个人在办公室里，他还是心虚地用另一只手捂上了话筒。
1) 他们两个人尽管经常吵架，但是却没有离婚。
2) 尽管外边很冷，但是屋里却很暖和。

12. 显出……的样子: show, display a certain appearance
❖ 经理显出一副恭候良久的样子。
1) 他显出一副不在乎的样子，其实，他心里很生气。
2) 在女人面前，他常常显出一副很有礼貌的样子。

13. 顿时: immediately; suddenly; at once
❖ 那一种客气的态度，使老会计顿时感到，他已不再是心腹了，他们从前的亲密关系已改变了。
1) 老师一来那些淘气的孩子们顿时不说话了。

2）接到女朋友的电话，他的心情顿时好了起来。

14. 不禁：can't help doing
   ❖ 老会计不禁心生出大的无奈、沮丧和悲哀。
   1）老师说的话太有意思了，学生们不禁大声笑了起来。
   2）一阵冷风刮来，我不禁打了一个冷颤。

15. 凭：rely on; depend on; base on
   ❖ 你凭什么认为我企图将那笔钱占为己有？
   1）这家饭馆凭它的有利位置赚了很多钱。
   2）所有的人都得凭票上飞机。
   3）他从来不上课，他凭什么得A？

16. 在……的前提下：on the premise of
   ❖ 他只不过希望在被理解的前提之下，得以从一件使自己不安的事中摆脱。
   1）在互相尊重的前提下，我们进行学术交流。
   2）在合法的前提下，我愿意帮你做一切事情。

17. 怎么也不/没……：no matter how; in no way
   ❖ 他怎么也没想到自己会被一个自己一向认为言听计从的人所讹诈。
   1）钢琴太难了，我怎么也学不会。
   2）这个东西，我怎么也想不出来它为什么这么贵。

18. 何以：why; how
   ❖ 他们想不通他们的父亲何以会变得那么贪，何以一次次地不能满足，一次次地讹诈他人？
   1）她总说要去中国，何以至今还没有去？
   2）何以见得他考不上大学？

19. 或多或少：more or less; to a greater or lesser extent

   ❖ 许多旁听者都对谋杀案主犯或多或少地有些同情了。
   1）他的失败，跟得不到家庭的支持或多或少有点关系。
   2）你或多或少得花一点钱，才能办好这件事。

练习

I. 填进正确的字：

1. 微不___道　　　2.一如既_____　　　3.受___若惊　　　4. 顺___成章

5. ___红耳赤　　　6. ___门见山　　　7.彬彬有___

II. 选词填空：

1. 得了第一名，她的心情很_____(激动，感动).

2. 大家都被他舍己救人的故事____了。(激动，感动)

3. 体制转变和上市并不能带给他值得 ____不已的利益。(激动，感动)

4. 她被妈妈的爱心_____得哭了。(激动，感动)

5. 你_____要多少钱才满足啊？(究竟，毕竟)

6. 今天晚上的比赛_____谁赢谁输还很难说。(究竟，毕竟)

7. _____屋里只有他一个人，他还是心虚地捂上了话筒。(尽管，不管)

8. _____别人去不去上课我都去上课。(尽管，不管)

9. _____单位离家很远，他总是骑车上班。(尽管，不管)

10. _____单位离家多远，他都骑车上班。(尽管，不管)

11. 我有钱是有钱，但是我___拿不出那么多现金。(一时，顿时)

12 接到父亲病逝的电话，母亲_____昏了过去。(一时,顿时)

13. 学中文不能只凭___的兴趣，得坚持下去才行。(一时,顿时)

14. 听老师一讲，大家_____明白了。(一时，顿时)

III. 读下面的句子，然后用划线的部分造句：

1. 尽管屋里只有他一个人，他还是心虚地捂上了话筒。

2. 你不解释，我还清楚；你一解释，我倒糊涂了。

153

3. 你凭什么认为我企图将那笔钱占为己有？

4. 这不是洁身自好不洁身自好的问题啊。何况，支出在"小金库"的账上。

5. 常在河边走，哪有不湿鞋的？

6. 狐狸再狡猾也斗不过好猎手。

IV. 选择合适的成语取代划线的部分，保持原意不变：

心安理得	慢条斯理	晕头转向	微不足道
开诚布公	心中有数	语无伦次	一如既往

1. 我个人所能做的事确实是很少很少的，这次成功都是靠大家。

2. 我知道该怎么办，你不必担心。

3. 我一天到晚事情多得不得了，忙得不知道该做什么，不该做什么。

4. 改革开放虽然出现了很多问题，但是中国还会像以前一样坚持改革开放。

5. 这个小贩虽然常常骗客人，但是他却觉得这样做事合情合理，心里没有不舒服的感觉。

6. 要是你对我有意见，你应该诚恳地告诉我，不应该在背后说我的坏话。

7. 他无论做什么事都是慢慢的，好像从来不着急似的。

8. 在很多人面前说话，他很紧张。说着说着就说乱了，一会儿说这个，一会儿说那个。

V. 用提供的词语回答问题：

1. 经理为什么要给老会计两万块钱？
   （向……行贿，做假账，趁机，转移，独占）

2. 老会计为什么不愿意接受这笔钱？
   （参与，犯罪，受牵连，和钱打交道，未动过歪念，划清界限）

3. 老会计退钱的时候，遇到了什么麻烦？
   （一心，划清界限，摆脱，越……越，误解，讹诈）

VI. 讨论问题：

1. 在法庭上，旁听者是同情杀人犯还是同情老会计？为什么？

2. 在这个黑白颠倒的社会里，允许不允许真、善、美的存在？还有没有一个值得信任的东西？

3. 这篇小说反映了现代中国社会的什么问题？

风雪茫茫

牛正寰

（一）

金牛媳妇坐在炕上给丈夫补鞋的时候，对丈夫提出，想乘⑴农闲回趟娘家，春节前回来过年。起初，金牛不同意，说农活儿没什么可做的，可家里的事儿还多着呢！得把麦子磨了，得收拾冬菜⋯媳妇听了这话，就道：

"磨麦，我不在你一个人还磨不了啊⑵？冬菜我早就收拾好了。辣椒、芹菜，还有几十棵白菜，够你们吃一冬了。"

"你不吃了？"

"我？不是说过要回娘家去吗？"

"那，你就不回来了？"

她的心猛然跳了一下，忙说：

"谁说我不回来？我回来就过年，三几天过去，就又该有新菜了。"

"那 ⋯⋯" 金牛还想找点儿理由，又说：

"过年娃们都有新衣服穿。你不在，咱们根柱就得穿旧的。"

媳妇打开了柜子，取出一个包袱，一边儿拿出衣帽鞋袜，一边儿说：

"我都给他做好了。这是棉袄棉裤，这是新鞋。帽子是你上次到镇上买的。"金牛一时找不出什么话来，只好说：

"那，那你就去吧！什么时候走？"

"明天吧！"

茫茫	mángmáng	*adj.*	boundless and indistinct 茫茫的黑夜/前途茫茫
炕	kàng	*n.*	kang - a heatable brick bed
补	bǔ	*v.*	mend or repair 补衣服/把破了的地方补好
乘	chéng	*v.*	take advantage of 乘机会学一点儿经验
农闲	nóngxián	*n.*	slack season (in farming)
娘家	niáng.jia	*n.*	a married woman's parents' home
春节	Chūnjié	*n.*	the Spring Festival; Chinese Lunar New Year
活儿	huór	*n.*	work; job 在田里干活儿
麦子	mài.zi	*n.*	wheat
磨	mó	*v.*	grind
冬菜	dōngcài	*n.*	preserved, dried cabbage or mustard greens
道	dào	*v.*	say (the words quoted); 说
辣椒	làjiāo	*n.*	hot pepper
芹菜	qíncài	*n.*	celery
白菜	báicài	*n.*	Chinese cabbage
猛然	měngrán	*adv.*	suddenly; abruptly 猛然发现
娃	wá	*n.*	(dialect) child; baby
根柱	Gēnzhù	*n.*	personal name
柜子	guì.zi	*n.*	cupboard; cabinet
包袱	bāo.fu	*n.*	cloth-wrapper, a bundle wrapped in cloth
棉袄	mián'ǎo	*n.*	cotton-padded jacket

丈夫同意了，金牛媳妇收拾这收拾那(3)，整整忙了一天。她把屋里屋外收拾好，又到隔壁二妈家去了一趟，告诉二妈，自己要回娘家去了，让她帮着照顾一下根柱爷儿仨的生活。回来才做晚饭。吃饭时，公公已从金牛嘴里知道她要回娘家去，拿出一捆自家种的烟叶，说：

"把这带给没见过面的亲家尝尝。告诉他们，情况好了就到咱们家来玩儿。"

根柱听说妈要回娘家，吵着要跟了去。金牛见根柱吵闹，抱起他说：

"乖，等你大了，咱们三人一起到舅舅家去。"后来又答应明天带他去看火车，这才算哄住了。

金牛不愿让女人回娘家，是真不愿离开她。这也难怪。自从媳妇从外乡到他家四年多来，家里的一切事都不用他操心。早晨出工，一碗热汤两个馒头早就摆在桌子上。下工回来，媳妇把又白又细的面条盛在大碗里放在他面前。媳妇对公公很孝敬。老人牙不好，她烙饼特地烙几个又薄又软的。对从小失去亲娘，三十岁上才娶老婆的金牛来说，她太重要了。

媳妇娘家在渭河上游地方，和这儿邻省。六〇年春来到这儿。 那天， 金牛下工回来，村头大柳树下围了好多人，树下的石头上坐着一个年约二十二三的女子。两条小辫，蓝底白花的夹袄，黑布裤子，虽说上下都打了补丁，却也很合身。

爷儿仨	yérsā	n.	(informal) three men of two or more generations
公公	gōng.gong	n.	husband's father
捆	kǔn	AN.	a bundle of
烟叶	yānyè	n.	tobacco leaf
亲家	qìng.jia	n.	parents of one's daughter-in-law or son-in-law
乖	guāi	adj.	well-behaved (child)
舅舅	jiù.jiu	n.	mother's brother
哄	hǒng	v.	coax; humor; soothe
操心	caōxīn	v.	worry about 让父母操心/为他操心
出工	chūgōng	v.-o.	go to work
馒头	mán.tou	n.	steamed bun
面条	miàntiáo	n.	noodle
盛	chéng	v.	fill; ladle 盛在碗里/把面条盛出来
烙	lào	v.	bake in a pan
饼	bǐng	n.	round flat bread
特地	tèdì	adv.	specially 特地给她打了一个电话/特地来看你
薄	báo	adj.	thin; flimsy
亲娘	qīnniáng	n.	mother
渭河	Wèihé	n.	Weihe River
上游	shàngyóu	n.	upper reaches (of a river)
邻省	línshěng	n.	neighboring province
村头	cūntóu	n.	the entrance of the village
柳树	liǔshù	n.	willow
围	wéi	v.	enclose; surround; encircle
石头	shí.tou	n.	stone; rock
辫子	biàn.zi	n.	plait; braid
蓝底白花	lándǐ báihuā	n.	white flower on a blue background
夹袄	jiā'ǎo	n.	lined jacket
补丁	bǔdīng	n.	patch
合身	héshēn	adj.	fit

159

她细而长的眼睛由于饥饿失去了本来的光彩。她的脚前是一个小包袱，从里边露出破旧的衣服。她的身后，一个二十七八的男人靠在树上。

"我们是从渭河上边过来的。"男的说："挨饿挨了一年多了。挖野菜，野菜光了，剥树皮，树皮也光了。没办法，能跑出来的就跑出来了。这是我妹子，她走不动了。哪位好心人收留她，也算做了好事。"两滴眼泪从女的眼里落到脚上。

隔壁二妈在人群里看见金牛，附在他耳朵上说："你把她留下。模样儿好，又是外乡来的，花不了多少钱。"金牛脸上一红，摆手说："人家是有困难，咱们不能占这个便宜。"说着要走。二妈急忙拦住他说："看你，都三十了，还说这样的话！你没听见她哥说是做好事吗？"那男的声音又断续传了过来："回去……饿死……收留她让她活命，她什么都会干……"金牛想了想，说："那好，二妈，你去说说。"

金牛收留了这个姑娘。从那天起，那兄妹俩就住在金牛家。这地方风俗，娶媳妇一定得给聘礼。这姑娘虽是逃荒来的，金牛爹还是从箱子底摸出二百元钱，要二妈交给姑娘的哥哥，并且要请大家喝喜酒。那男的却无论如何也⑷不要这钱。说他们是逃荒来的，妹子能找个忠厚人家安身，他就放心了。如果一定要给聘礼，那就给他一斗麦。钱拿回去没用，粮还能救家里人。金牛父子只好给了他一百五十斤麦。金牛要他吃完

喜酒再走，他硬是⑸不肯，只说救人要紧，以后他还会来。金
牛爹让金牛和那妹子送她哥哥，走到村口柳树下，那女的哭得
泪人似的。那男的饿得很虚弱，背着麦子抬不起头来，劝他妹
子道："你留在这儿，过不久我再来。他这人老实。" 他用手

细	xì	*adj.*	thin; slender
饥饿	jī'è	*n.*	hunger; starvation
光彩	guāngcǎi	*n.*	luster; splendor; brilliance
露出	lòuchū	*v.*	show; reveal 露出紧张的样子
挨饿	ái'è	*v.-o.*	suffer from hunger
挖	wā	*v.*	dig 挖出来/挖得很深
野菜	yěcài	*n.*	edible wild herbs
剥	bō	*v.*	skin; shell; peel 剥皮/把皮剥干净
收留	shōuliú	*v.*	take somebody in; have somebody in one's care
滴	dī	*AN.*	a drop of
附	fù	*v.*	get close to; be near
模样	múyàng	*n.*	look; appearance
摆手	bǎishǒu	*v.-o.*	wave 他摆手叫我走开。
占便宜	zhàn pián.yi	*v.-o.*	gain extra advantage by unfair means
拦住	lánzhù	*v.-c.*	bar; block
断续	duànxù	*adv.*	off and on; intermittently
风俗	fēngsú	*n.*	custom
聘礼	pìnlǐ	*n.*	betrothal gifts (from the bridegroom's to the bride's family)
逃荒	táohuāng	*v.-o.*	flee from famine
忠厚	zhōnghòu	*adj.*	honest and tolerant; sincere and kindly
安身	ānshēn	*v.-o.*	make one's home; take shelter
斗	dǒu	*AN.*	a unit of dry measure for grain
粮	liáng	*n.*	grain; food
虚弱	xūruò	*adj.*	weak; debilitated

抹一抹脸，不知是抹汗还是抹眼泪。哥哥走了，妹子还倚着柳树哭。金牛拿她没办法。劝她吧，不知该说什么；拉她回去吧⑹，又觉得不合适。看她样子实在伤心，便说："那你也跟他一块儿走吧！"听了这话，她依旧站在那儿不动，只是哭。金牛左右为难。二妈连说带劝⑺，连拉带扯，把她带回了金牛家。

一年以后，金牛添了个胖儿子，起名叫根柱。根柱三岁了，金牛媳妇没回过一次娘家。根柱他舅（就是那个男的）倒是来过四五次。每次金牛都给他四五十元，再让他背百十斤麦回去。根柱他舅走，金牛媳妇总恋恋不舍。根柱他舅总劝她好好跟金牛过，过一两年等情况好了再回去看看。家里人都好，要她安心。金牛是个忠厚善良的人，照理说应该主动陪她回娘家。可是娶媳妇、生孩子，再加上根柱舅一年来两趟，花了不少钱；两个人的车票四五十元，不能空手到岳家去，买这买那，又是一笔开销。哪里去弄这笔钱呢？

金牛躺在炕上，怎么也睡不着，叫了声："孩子他妈"

"嗯，你睡吧！我想把这两双鞋做好。"

"你真的明天走？"

"嗯。"

"别去了。明年麦子收了，咱们带着根柱一起去。"

媳妇停了手里的活，说："你白天不是同意了吗？"

"哎……"金牛又不会说了。停了一会儿，他坐起来穿上衣服。她问："你要干嘛？"

"你要回就回吧！我找二妈借点钱你拿着。"

她不让他去借钱。说这些年金牛给她家的不少了，这次她能回去看看就好。金牛又问："鸡蛋呢？""就在那儿。"她指了指墙脚，问："你饿了？我给你做两个荷包蛋。""不用了。你忙你的(8)，反正(9)我也没事。"

金牛取了鸡蛋，就去煮蛋。她忙着做活，也就不管了。金牛一会儿看看锅里煮的鸡蛋，一会儿看看媳妇。她做好一只鞋，把睡熟的根柱的脚拉过来比了比，不知怎的，眼圈一红，连忙用手擦了擦眼睛。

抹	mǒ	v.	wipe
汗	hàn	n.	sweat
倚	yǐ	v.	lean on or against
左右为难	zuǒyòuwéinán	idm.	in a dilemma; in an awkward predicament
连说带劝	liánshuōdàiquàn	v.	talking and urging
连拉带扯	liánlādàichě	v.	dragging and pulling
恋恋不舍	liànliànbùshě	idm.	be reluctant to part with
照理说	zhàolǐshuō	adv.	as it should be 照理说，我不该问你。
空手	kōngshǒu	adv.	empty-handed
岳家	yuèjiā	n.	family of one's wife's parents
开销	kāixiāo	n.	expense
墙脚	qiángjiǎo	n.	the foot of a wall
荷包蛋	hébāo dàn	n.	poached egg
煮	zhǔ	v.	boil
睡熟	shuìshú	v.-c..	in deep sleep
眼圈	yǎnquān	n.	rim of the eye

金牛和她向来话少，今天就算说话最多了。锅里煮的鸡蛋，并不是自己想吃，而是要给她带在路上吃。自她到金牛家后，他实在挑不出她的毛病，只是她话少，笑得更少。金牛起先以为她不习惯，后来日子长了，觉得这是跟他一样的脾气，也就不在意了。现在看她难过，便笨拙地劝道：

"别做了。没做完，回来再做。明天一早就要上路呢！"

她叹了口气，说：

"我走了，你可要把孩子照顾好。不要让别的孩子欺负他。"

金牛说："嗯。"

"孩子小，犯了错，你不要打他。"

"看你说到哪儿去了⑩？我怎么舍得？"

屋里又是一阵沉默。金牛煮好了鸡蛋，看她还在灯下做活，便拿走了她手中的鞋，说："睡吧！看把你累坏了。"说完，熄了灯，把她拉在自己身旁睡下。

第二天清早，金牛背着根柱去送行。媳妇只带着她来时带来的包袱，装着几件旧衣服和公公送的烟叶，肩上挂着一个袋子，装着金牛昨晚煮的鸡蛋和几块饼。　一路上根柱一会儿爬到爸爸背上，一会儿偎在妈妈怀里，这呀那呀问个不停，金牛媳妇细心地一样一样讲给他听。村子离车站十多里，他们走了快三个小时。到了车站，金牛去买票。

　　"呜…呜…"一声长鸣，客车进站了。根柱连忙把头埋进妈妈怀里。她搂着他往后退了两步。根柱说："妈，你快上，车要开了。"金牛气喘吁吁地跑过来，把票往她手里一塞，接着就把她推到车上。车已经开了，她大声说："根柱，你要听爸爸的话！"站在站台上的金牛忙对孩子说："快说，让妈早点回来！"车速加快了，根柱稚气的声音在喊："妈！早点回来！"她的眼眶涌出了泪水。

挑毛病	tiāo máobìng	v.-o.	find fault; pick at　挑别人的毛病
脾气	pí.qi	n.	temperament; disposition
不在意	bú zàiyì	v.	not to take notice of ; not to take to heart
笨拙	bènzhuó	adj.	clumsy; stupid
欺负	qī.fu	v.	bully with
犯错	fàncuò	v.-o.	make a mistake
偎	wēi	v.	snuggle up to
耐心	nàixīn	adv.	patiently
呜	wū	onom.	toot; hoot; zoom
长鸣	chángmíng	n.	a booming sound
怀	huái	n.	bosom
搂	lǒu	v.	hug; cuddle; embrace
气喘吁吁	qìchuǎn xūxū	adv.	pant; puff hard
稚气	zhìqì	adj.	childish
眼眶	yǎnkuàng	n.	eye socket
涌	yǒng	v.	gush; well; pour　涌出了眼泪

（二）

金牛媳妇找了一个靠窗的位子坐下。车走了几站，便到了西安。上来的人把座位都坐满了。她把脸贴着玻璃窗，怕遇见认得她的人。路两旁的树落尽了叶子，干枯的树身一棵棵落在车后。车行太快了，她的目光不能在哪棵树上停下来。有一个问题就像眼前的树一样，一次又一次地反复出现："我走了，对得起他吗？"答案显然找不出来，她只好把目光从树身上移开，去看那一望无际的麦田。秋天种下的麦子，已经长成了三寸长的绿苗，看着这快过冬的青苗，她一下就想到了根柱："唉！我真造孽！根柱也是根嫩苗啊！没有了妈，怎么过得下去？"她仿佛已听到根柱哭着找妈的声音："妈呀……妈呀……"不对，这不是根柱的声音，这是另一个跟根柱一样大的孩子的哭声："妈呀……妈呀……这分明是四年前的锁娃呀！黑瘦的手在脸上抹着眼泪，她抱着他，在春日的阳光下晒着，一丝气力也没有。"妈呀……妈呀……"孩子的哭声让她心痛。她能给他吃什么呢？什么也没有。他哭着哭着⑾，睡着了。丈夫回来了，看着睡着的锁娃问："吃了？""没有。"她用微弱得连自己都听不清楚的声音答道。听到她的回答，他走进屋子拿了个大碗出来说："我去看看，今天给不给汤。"

"别去了。几十天不见粮食。除了队长、炊事员，谁能喝到一口汤？"

自从大炼钢铁以来，私人家里的锅都砸光了，全村几百口人都在食堂里吃饭。去年冬天以来，只有清汤喝。近来，连清汤都没有了。

"那怎么办？就有一点儿树皮，孩子吃什么？"阳光

干枯	gānkū	adj.	dried-up; withered
反复	fǎnfù	adv.	repeatedly; again and again
一望无际	yíwàng wújì	idm.	stretch as far as the eye can see 一望无际的大草原
苗	miáo	n.	seedling
造孽	zàoniè	v.-o.	do evil; commit a sin
嫩苗	nènmiáo	n.	tender seedling
分明	fēnmíng	adv.	clearly; evidently 这分明是我的东西，怎么在你这儿？
锁娃	Suǒwá	n.	personal name
晒	shài	v.	(of the sun) shine upon 在外头晒太阳 / 他晒黑了。
丝	sī	AN.	a thread of
微弱	wēiruò	adj.	faint; feeble; weak
队长	duìzhǎng	n.	team leader
炊事员	chuīshì yuán	n.	a cook or a kitchen staff
大炼钢铁	Dàliàn gāngtiě	n.	steelmaking. In 1958, Mao Zedong initiated the Big Leap Forward campaign and proclaimed that China could overtake and surpass Britain in the output of steel and other major industrial products in 15 years. Local government leaders ordered people to sacrifice their iron cooking utensils and farming equipment to make iron and steel.
砸	zá	v.	smash
清汤	qīngtāng	n.	clear soup

下，他们呆看着自己的影子。过了半天，她费了很大的力气才说："我到陕西去，也许一家人能活。""什么？"他怕自己没听清，大声问。"我到陕西去。"这一次她不犹豫了，口气坚定地说。他无力地蹲了下去。她接着说："你看，去了陕西的人都有办法弄来粮食，我们总不能就这样等死。孩子才两岁…"她说不下去了。他的眼光离开了妻子，看着地面，似乎下了决心，说："去就去，我送你。"听了这话，她反而慌了："去了，得另嫁人，你…你能行？"

　　过了好一阵，她见他不出声，哽咽着说："能救活全家大小，我死了也甘心。我走了，你就当没有我，等以后日子好了，再娶一个。只要多疼疼孩子就行。"他听她说这些，并不接话，叹了口气说："说走就走⑫。留在这儿也是饿死。明天走，我送你到陕西，对外人就说我是你哥。"

　　火车进入甘肃，她看到这熟悉的土地，心里有说不出的滋味。她睡着了，一个接连一个的梦。一会儿是在渭水下游那个家，金牛在夺她手中的包袱，向她大吼："你为什么骗我？你怎么忍心扔下我们父子俩？"一会儿是在渭水上游自己以前的家，她伸手要抱锁娃，他却不让她抱，挣脱了她，恐惧地向前跑。她大声喊："锁娃！我是妈呀！"

　　她惊醒了，抬起头，向窗外一望，离开了四年多的家乡就在眼前…

（三）

过了腊月二十三，家家户户都忙着杀猪，预备年菜。金牛左等右等⑬，媳妇还是没回来，已经快两个月了。根柱吵得要命，金牛只好胡乱做了一点儿年菜。除夕那天，隔壁的二妈

陕西	Shǎnxī	n.	Shaanxi Province
犹豫	yóuyù	v.	hesitate
口气	kǒuqì	n.	tone
坚定	jiāndìng	adj.	firm; steadfast 态度坚定/语气很坚定
蹲	dūn	v.	squat on the heels　蹲在地上/蹲下去
慌	huāng	v.	be flurried; be flustered; be confused
哽咽	gěngyè	v.	choke with sobs
甘心	gānxīn	v.	be reconciled to; resign oneself to; be content with
甘肃	Gānsù	n.	Gansu Province
滋味	zīwèi	n.	taste; flavor
下游	xiàyóu	n.	lower reaches (of a river)
夺	duó	v.	take by force; wrest
吼	hǒu	v.	roar; howl
忍心	rěnxīn	v.	be hardhearted enough to　不忍心打孩子
扔下	rēngxià	v.	abandon; leave behind
挣脱	zhèngtuō	v.-o.	struggle to get free; try to throw off
恐惧	kǒngjù	adv.	be frightened
惊醒	jīngxǐng	v.	wake up with a start
腊月	làyuè	n.	the twelfth month of the lunar year
家家户户	jiājiāhùhù	n.	each and every family
胡乱	húluàn	adv.	carelessly; casually; at random 胡乱写了几个字/胡乱吃了一点东西
除夕	chúxī	n.	New Year's Eve

过来给他们包了饺子。大年初一，第一碗饺子给爹吃了，第二碗给了根柱，金牛自己却连一个也吃不下去。他想："说好了回来过年，到今天却连封信都没有，恐怕是出了什么事吧？病了？不对，病了家里会有信来。车在路上出了事？要是火车翻了车可不得了。"他给自己这个想法吓得脸色发白。他又担心："是不是遭了意外？他们那一带这两年不太平，有抢劫的。她一个女人家不常出门，是不是碰到了坏人？"想到这儿，他非常后悔没送她回去。"唉！都是为了几个钱！没有钱可以想办法，没有了人可怎么办？"越是这样想，他越是不安。到了初三，他对爹说要去接媳妇回来。爹说去看看也好，快去快回。

锁娃妈正在厨房里做吃的。亲戚朋友知道她回来了，约好了今天来喝酒庆贺庆贺。她正在切煮好的肉，丈夫进来了，在她身后低声说：

"来了！"她头也不回，说：

"来了？来了就来了。我马上就切好了，你急什么？"

丈夫又说："他来了。"

"谁？"

"他……，根柱爸。"

"啊？那，那怎么办？…你见到他了？"

"嗯，他一来就到了那屋。"他指指北屋："我对他说你忙着，我去找，就出来了。"

"咱们怎么办？"

"把他先款待着再说。"

她跟他出了厨房，进了北屋。

金牛见媳妇来了两个月，身体明显地胖了。两个月没见，她显得更年轻了。过去苍白的脸色红润起来。凸出的胸脯，被围裙勒紧的腰身，都那么有精神。只是见了他，不知怎的，脸上缺少表情。她进了屋来就没正眼看一下金牛，低着头，右手拿围裙不断擦左手的手背。

"没想到你来了……"

"等你回去过年，等不到你。怕你出了事，我就来了。"

金牛用亲热的口气说完，不住地上下打量她。她注意到

翻车	fānchē	v.-o.	(of a car) turn over
太平	tàipíng	adj.	peaceful
庆贺	qìnghè	v.	celebrate　庆贺新年/庆贺生日
款待	kuǎndài	v.	treat cordially; entertain
苍白	cāngbái	adj.	pale
红润	hóngrùn	adj.	ruddy; rosy
凸出	tūchū	adj.	raised; protruding
胸脯	xiōngpú	n.	chest; breast
围裙	wéiqún	n.	apron
勒	lēi	v.	tie or strap something tight
腰身	yāoshēn	n.	waistline; waist
亲热	qīnrè	adv.	affectionately; intimately
打量	dǎ.liang	v.	look somebody up and down

他看她，头垂得更低了：

"我，我原准备回去呢，后来又拖到了过年，想过完年再……回去。"她为了骗他而感到罪过，话说到这儿，连自己都听不清了。金牛以为她是因为没按时回去怕他责怪，连忙说：

"在哪儿过年不都一样？你好几年没回娘家，回来过年也好。只是没封信，我不放心，所以来了。"她不知说些什么好。丈夫在一旁说：

"快去烧水，让他姑父先喝茶。"锁娃妈听说，赶紧退了出去。

一会儿，亲戚们三三两两地来了。锁娃爹端菜倒酒，招呼大家吃喝。亲戚们这个一杯那个一杯地敬金牛⑭，他都一一喝了。他看到了媳妇，心里畅快，食欲很好，加上大家热情招待，他不住地吃着喝着，有七八分醉了。锁娃爹对他说：

"你昨天坐了夜车，今天又闹了一天，累了，就在这儿睡吧！"

金牛想问媳妇什么时候跟他回去，想到她肯定还在厨房里洗碗，等一会儿再问。可是一上床，眼皮再也睁不开，就打起呼噜来了。一觉醒来，觉得口渴，点上灯，找水喝，却碰掉了桌子上的一本书，书里掉出一张照片来。上边是根柱妈和他舅并排坐着，照片右上角写着"结婚纪念"四个字。

被欺骗被抛弃的怒火猛然在胸中燃烧起来。"我要问个明白！"他穿好衣服，拉开门就要往外走。一股冷风吹进来，酒完全醒了。夜，黑沉沉的，北风发出呜呜的声音，下雪了。他把门又关上，回到炕边坐下。他陷入苦涩的回忆中，一直到

垂	chuí	v.	hang down; let fall 垂下来/垂到地上
拖	tuō	v.	delay; drag on
按时	ànshí	adv.	on time; on schedule
责怪	zéguài	v.	blame
烧水	shāoshuǐ	v.-o.	heat water
姑父	gū.fu	n.	the husband of one's father's sister
退	tuì	v.	retreat; move back
端	duān	v.	hold something level with both hands
招呼	zhāo.hu	v.	take care of (the guests)
畅快	chàngkuài	adj.	free from inhibitions and happy; carefree
食欲	shíyù	n.	appetite
招待	zhāi.dai	v.	entertain (guests) 招待客人/招待朋友
眼皮	yǎnpí	n.	eyelid
打呼噜	dǎ hū.lu	v.-o.	snore
口渴	kǒukě	v.	thirsty
点灯	diǎndēng	v.-o.	light a lamp
并排	bìngpái	adv.	side by side
怒火	nùhuǒ	n.	flames of fury; fury
燃烧	ránshāo	v.	burn
股	gǔ	AN.	a gust of (wind)
陷入	xiànrù	v.	sink into; be caught in
苦涩	kǔsè	adj.	pained; agonized; anguished, bitter and astringent
回忆	huíyì	n.	recollection

外头传来一声鸡啼。他站起来，扣好衣服，来到西房门前，用力敲着门。

"谁？什么事？"屋里传来女人的声音，接着门开了。金牛推开女人，怒冲冲地站着。锁娃爹已经知道金牛是为什么来了，拉着他叫"他姑父"，金牛气愤地吼道：

"真丢人！还叫得出口！"

锁娃妈夫妇俩拉着他的胳膊，把他按到炕沿上坐下，说："你先别生气……"两个人哆哆嗦嗦站在金牛面前，却说不出话来。　丈夫究竟是男人，勉强镇定下来，改口叫了声"大哥"，说：

"大哥，那个时候一家人没法可想，为了活命，就做出了这样的事。"

他无声地哭着。锁娃妈呜呜咽咽地说：

"我该死，我死了就好了！天啊！……"

她的哭声惊醒了炕上睡的锁娃，爬起来就喊："妈呀！"也跟着爸妈哭起来。金牛忙把锁娃抱回破被里。手一摸，一片冰凉的土炕，他心软了，想了一夜的话，这时一句也说不出来，只得重重地"咳"了一声，又坐在炕沿上。丈夫见金牛这样的举动，苦苦地哀求道：

"原谅我们吧，大哥。我们不是恶人，不是诈骗犯。不为了活命，谁忍心把自己的老婆拿去换粮食啊！实在没路了呀！"

金牛没料到竟会遇到这样的人。他想用最脏的字眼骂，用拳头打，可是这一对夫妇像绵羊一样站在他的脚下，用真诚的眼泪和令人心碎的话向他求饶。 他的心里没主意了。忽然他发出令人吃惊的大笑：

"哈哈哈！我这是做什么呀！哈哈！"

鸡啼	jītí	*n.*	the crow of a cock
扣	kòu	*v.*	button up
怒冲冲	nù chōngchōng	*adv.*	furiously; in a rage
丢人	diūrén	*v.-o.*	lose face; be disgraced
胳膊	gē.bo	*n.*	arm
按	àn	*v.*	push down
炕沿	kàngyán	*n.*	the edge of a kang
哆哆嗦嗦	duō.duo suō.suo	*adv.*	tremblingly
勉强	miǎnqiǎng	*adv.*	manage with an effort 勉强笑了一下/ 勉强说出了一个理由
镇定	zhèndìng	*v.*	calm down; cool down
改口	gǎikǒu	*v.-o.*	withdraw or modify one's previous remark
呜呜咽咽	wūwūyèyè	*adv.*	sobbingly
心软	xīnruǎn	*v.*	be softhearted; be tenderhearted
举动	jǔdòng	*n.*	move; movement
苦苦地	kǔkǔ.de	*adv.*	painstakingly; piteously
哀求	āiqiú	*v.*	beseech; implore
诈骗犯	zhàpiànfàn	*n.*	swindler
字眼	zìyǎn	*n.*	wording; diction
拳头	quán.tou	*n.*	fist
绵羊	miányáng	*n.*	sheep
心碎	xīnsuì	*v.*	be broken-hearted
求饶	qiúráo	*v.-o.*	beg for mercy

两行眼泪却从他眼角流下来。夫妻俩听到这话，一起说："您原谅我们吧！您的恩德我们这辈子报答不完，让孩子再接着报答！"

金牛站起来，长叹一声，说：

"我该走了！"

"上哪儿去？"锁娃妈问。

"我还留在这干嘛？⑮回去！"金牛用出奇平静的声音说。

夫妻俩再三苦留，要他多住几天，金牛只是不听。锁娃爹只好叫妻子去拿些东西给金牛带在路上吃。自己又把棉衣脱下，要金牛穿上，金牛不肯穿。锁娃妈给金牛装了一袋馒头，金牛拿过来背在肩上，头也不回地走了。

金牛慢慢地走到车站。一路上只感到脑袋木木的，什么也不能想。车站上冷冷清清，候车室里也没有人。雪盖住了铁轨，盖住了旷野，白茫茫的世界里只有他一个冰冷冷的人。他感到了一生从没有过的冷冻。他躲进了候车室，在长椅上坐下，上牙跟下牙不停地相碰。

"有往东去的旅客吗？"票房的小窗口传来了售票员的声音。不等他站起来，木窗啪的一声又关上了。轰隆隆的车声由远而近，又由近而远...

金牛一阵冷，一阵热，一阵清醒，一阵昏迷。向东去的

火车开过来有三四趟，他都没有上去。他不想就这么回去，但
究竟要做什么，他也说不清。

　　黑夜来临了。他漫无目的地在雪地上游荡，不知怎么又
走到了锁娃家门口。他抬手想敲门，想进去跟他们把事情讲
明，他不能没有她，根柱也不能没有妈。但抬起的手并没有去
碰那木门，而是无力地垂下来。他懊丧地离开了门口。大雪不
停地下着，寒风不停地吹着，金牛拖着沉重的脚步，漫无目的
地在雪中行走......

选自《灵与肉》——当代中国大陆作家丛刊 2

眼角	yǎnjiǎo	*n.*	the corner of the eye
恩德	ēndé	*n.*	favor; kindness
出奇	chūqí	*adv.*	unusually; extraordinarily
脑袋	nǎo.dai	*n.*	(informal) head
木	mù	*adj.*	numb; wooden
冷冷清清	lěnglěng qīngqīng	*adj.*	cold and cheerless; desolate
候车室	hòuchēshì	*n.*	waiting room (in a railway or bus station)
盖	gài	*v.*	cover　把...盖上/把...盖起来
铁轨	tiěguǐ	*n.*	rail
旷野	kuàngyě	*n.*	wilderness
旅客	lǚkè	*n.*	passenger
轰隆隆	hōng lōnglōng	*onom.*	sound of rumbling or rolling
昏迷	hūnmí	*v.*	faint; be in a coma
来临	láilín	*v.*	arrive; to come
漫无目的	mànwúmùdì	*adv.*	aimlessly
游荡	yóudàng	*v.*	wander; stray
懊丧	àosàng	*adj.*	feel dejected or depressed

词语例句

1. 乘：to take advantage of; to avail oneself of
   - ❖ 金牛媳妇坐在炕上给丈夫补鞋的时候，对丈夫提出，想乘农闲回趟娘家。
   1) 今年秋天我要到中国西部去旅游，也想乘这个机会看看西部开发的情况。
   2) 他要乘放假的时间把这几本书看完。

2. 还...啊（吗）？：...still...? (rhetorical question)
   - ❖ 我不在你一个人还磨不了啊？
   1) 这么简单的事，你还不会做啊？
   2) 你是一个大人，还比不上一个小孩子啊？
   3) 我把所有的钱都给你，还不行吗？

3. v. 这 v. 那：v. this and v. that
   - ❖ 金牛媳妇收拾这收拾那，整整忙了一天。
   1) 他买这买那，一个周末花了好几百块钱。
   2) 搬了家以后，我整理这整理那，忙得不得了。

4. 无论如何也... : in any case; at any rate; whatever happens
   - ❖ 金牛爹从箱子底摸出二百元钱，要二妈交给姑娘的哥哥，那男的却无论如何也不要这钱。
   1) 我无论如何也得在四月底把论文做完，否则就毕不了业了。
   2) 他送了重礼，而她却无论如何也不肯接受。

5. 硬是 v. : just v.; simply v.
   - ❖ 金牛要他吃完喜酒再走，他硬是不肯。
   1) 医生要他多休息，可他硬是不听。
   2) 他无论如何不肯接受这笔钱，硬是把钱退了回去。

6. A 吧，...；B 吧，...: if A…; if B…(weighing the options)
   - ❖ 劝她吧，不知该说什么；拉她回去吧，又觉得不合适。
   1) 他的演讲是关于污水处理。去吧，实在没有兴趣；不去吧，又觉得对不起朋友。
   2) 那时天还没亮。起来吧，怕吵了别人；不起来吧，又实在睡不着。

7．连 v.1.带 v.2.： v.1 and v.2

　❖　二妈连说带劝，连拉带扯，把她带回了金牛家。

　　1)　他连跑带跳，到了爷爷奶奶面前。

　　2)　他连说带唱，表演得非常精彩。

8．　你 v.你的: You do your thing.

　❖　不用了。你忙你的，反正我也没事。

　　1)　你干你的吧，我会照顾这个孩子的。

　　2)　你看你的书，我走了。

9．反正： anyway; in any case;

　❖　你忙你的，（我来做吧，）反正我也没事。

　　1)　她乘农闲回了一趟娘家。反正离得近，来回很方便。

　　2)　你就在这儿多住几天吧，反正家里也没什么要紧的事。

　　3)　无论你怎么说，反正我不答应。

10．看你说到哪儿去了？： What on earth are you talking about? (rhetorical)

　❖　看你说到哪儿去了？我怎么舍得？

　　1)　看你说到哪儿去了？我怎么可能给自己找这么大的麻烦？

　　2)　看你说到哪儿去了？她怎么会连自己的孩子都不爱？

11． v.着 v.着: as one is v.-ing

　❖　他哭着哭着，睡着了。

　　1)　她说着说着，眼泪一滴一滴地流了下来。

　　2)　我们走着走着，忽然发现小张不见了。

12． 说 v.就 v.: to say v. and do it / follow through with; v. immediately

　❖　说走就走。留在这儿也是饿死。

　　1)　说干就干！你扫地，我擦桌子，怎么样？

　　2)　你别说买就买，最好多试几件。

13．左 v.右 v.: (repetition of the same action) (wait around, look around, etc.)

　❖　金牛左等右等，媳妇还是没回来。

　　1)　她左试右试，就是没有一件合适。

　　2)　我左看右看，还是看不出有什么特别的地方。

14. 这个一杯那个一杯: a (drink) here, a (drink) there

❧ 亲戚们这个一杯那个一杯地敬金牛，他都一一喝了。

1) 学生们这个问一句，那个问一句，老师都耐心地回答了。

2) 晚会上，这个唱歌，那个跳舞，人人都玩得很高兴。

15. S. 还 ... 干嘛？： why still + v.?　　　　(rhetorical question)

❧ 我还留在这儿干嘛？回去！

1) 你还站在这儿干嘛？还不快去上课？

2) 你们还坐着干嘛？快去叫出租汽车吧！

（九）风雪茫茫

练习

I. 选正确的词填进去：

A: 补，抹，剥，哄，占，端，操，挖

      1. 把脸上的汗水 ＿＿＿＿ 去   2. 在山上 ＿＿＿＿＿ 野菜

      3. 把香蕉皮 ＿＿＿＿ 掉   4. 从厨房里 ＿＿＿＿＿ 出两盘菜

      5. 衣服上 ＿＿＿＿ 了好些补丁   6. ＿＿＿＿ 小孩

      7. 不用你 ＿＿＿＿ 心   8. 不可以 ＿＿＿＿ 别人的便宜

B: 犯，搂，盛，拦，吼，晒，蹲，挑

      1. 把饭 ＿＿＿＿ 在碗里   2. 他老 ＿＿＿＿ 别人的毛病

      3. ＿＿＿ 了错，改了就好   4. 躺在草地上 ＿＿＿＿ 太阳

      5. 他对她大声 ＿＿＿＿ 着   6. 母亲把孩子 ＿＿＿＿ 在怀里

      7. ＿＿＿ 在地上   8. 警察把车 ＿＿＿＿ 住

II. 读下面的句子，然后用划线的部分造句：

1. 她的心<u>猛然</u>跳了一下，忙说："谁说我不回来？"

2. 老人牙不好，她烙饼<u>特地</u>烙几个又薄又软的。

3. 那男的声音又<u>断续</u>传了过来："回去…饿死…收留她让她活命，她什么都会干。"

4. 有一个问题就像眼前的树一样，一次又一次地<u>反复</u>出现。

5. 这<u>分明</u>是四年前的锁娃呀！黑瘦的手在脸上抹着眼泪，她抱着他，在春日的阳光下晒着。

6. 根柱吵得要命，金牛只好<u>胡乱</u>做了一点儿年菜。

7. 她进了屋来就<u>没正眼</u>看一下金牛。

8. 金牛以为她是因为没<u>按时</u>回去怕他责怪，连忙说："在哪儿过年不都一样？"

9. 丈夫究竟是男人，<u>勉强</u>镇定下来。

III. 用括号中的词语回答问题：

1. 明年夏天，除了旅游以外，你还要做什么？　（乘）

2. 这件事，你真的要通知他吗？　（无论如何也…）

3. 这件事他不同意吗？要是你多跟他谈几次呢？　（硬是）

4. 你到底接受不接受他的建议？　（A 吧，…；B 吧，…）

5. 今天是周末，别待在宿舍里，咱们去看电影！　（说 v. 就 v.，反正）

6. 你太太要回娘家，你也要一块儿去吧？　（照理说）

IV. 把正确的词语填进去：

> 气喘吁吁，左右为难，冷冷清清，恋恋不舍，一望无际

1. 太太要我这么做，父母要我那么做，我真是 _____ 。

2. 这次离开故乡，不知什么时候才能回来，因此离去时 _____ 。

3. 他 _____ 地跑进来，眼睛里露出兴奋的光彩。

4. 在船上的三个月，每天都能看见 _____ 的大海。

5. 放了暑假，平时热闹的宿舍变得 _____ 。

V. 回答问题：

1. 从故事中可以看到陕西人过春节时有哪些习俗？

2. 这个故事中，哪一个人最值得同情？为什么？

3. 金牛媳妇对金牛的感情和对原来丈夫的感情有没有什么不同？

4. 从哪些事可以看出来金牛是个忠厚善良的好人？

5. 从哪些事可以看出来金牛媳妇是个好女人？

6. 金牛媳妇在陕西四年的生活，过得快乐吗？

7. 金牛媳妇回了甘肃，就抛弃了根柱，对根柱是否太残忍了？

8．那天早上，发现了媳妇的秘密后，金牛"忽然发出令人吃惊的大笑"，然后"两行眼泪却从他眼角流下来"。他又哭又笑，是因为什么？

9．你认为金牛最后应该怎么处理这个状况？

10．这篇小说为什么用"风雪茫茫"作为题目？

11．作者的写法有什么特点？这篇小说是不是一个好的文学作品？为什么？

被爱情遗忘的角落

张 弦

主要人物

沈存妮	Shěn Cúnnī	小豹子的女朋友，沈山旺的大女儿
沈荒妹	Shěn Huāngmèi	沈山旺的二女儿
沈山旺	Shěn Shānwàng	存妮和荒妹的父亲
菱花	Línghuā	存妮和荒妹的母亲
祥二爷	Xiáng èr yé	村中的一位老人
小豹子	Xiǎo Bào.zi	存妮的朋友，家贵的儿子
家贵叔	Jiāguì shū	小豹子的父亲
家贵婶	Jiāguì shěn	小豹子的母亲
许瞎子	Xǔ xiā.zi	村中的会计
许荣树	Xǔ Róngshù	荒妹的男朋友，新来的团委书记
二舅妈	èr jiù mā	荒妹的舅妈

（一）存妮和小豹子

尽管已经跨入了二十世纪七十年代的最后一年，在天堂公社的青年们心目中 (1)，"爱情"，还是个陌生的、神秘的、羞于出口的字眼。所以，在公社礼堂召开的"反对买办婚姻"大会上，当报告人——新来的团委书记大声地说出了这个名词的时候，听众都不约而同地一愣。接着，小伙子们调皮地相互挤挤眼，呵呵呵放声大笑起来，姑娘们则急忙垂下头，绯红了脸，吃吃地笑着，并偷偷地交换个羞涩的眼光。

Selected & prepared by: Liping Yu
Edited by: Chih-p'ing Chou

遗忘	yíwàng	v.	forget
角落	jiǎoluò	n.	corner
跨入	kuàrù	v.	stride into
世纪	shìjì	n.	century
年代	niándài	n.	decade
天堂	tiāntáng	n.	heaven (here): a place name
公社	gōngshè	n.	commune
心目	xīnmù	n.	mind; mental view
陌生	mòshēng	adj.	strange; unfamiliar
神秘	shénmì	adj.	mysterious
羞于出口	xiūyú chūkǒu	v.	too shy to talk about 羞: shy; feel ashamed
字眼	zìyǎnr	n.	wording
礼堂	lǐtáng	n.	auditorium
召开	zhàokāi	v.	convene (a meeting)
买办婚姻	mǎibàn hūnyīn	n.	mercenary marriage
团委	tuánwěi	n.	Communist Youth League Committee
书记	shū.ji	n.	Secretary of the Communist Youth Committee
不约而同	bùyuē'ér tóng	idm.	take the same action or view without consulting each other first 新年的时候，他们不约而同地回到家里。
愣	lèng	v.	be struck dumb
调皮	tiáopí	adj.	naughty; mischievous
挤眼	jǐyǎnr	v.-o.	wink 他对我挤挤眼，我知道他又有意见要说了。
垂	chuí	v.	hang; lower
绯红	fēihóng	adj./v.	bright red
羞涩	xiūsè	adj.	shy; bashful

　　只有墙角靠窗坐着的长得很秀气的姑娘 —— 天堂大队九小队团小组长沈荒妹，没有笑。她面色苍白，一双忧郁的大眼睛迷惘地凝望着窗外。好像什么也没听见，一切都与她无关。但突然间，她的眼睛充满了泪水。——"爱情"这个她所不理解的词儿，此刻是如此强烈地激动着她这颗少女的心。她感到羞辱，感到哀伤，还感到一种难言的惶恐。她想起了她的姐姐，使她永远怨恨而又永远怀念的姐姐存妮。唉！如果生活里没有小豹子，没有发生那一件事，一切该多么好！姐姐一定会并排坐在她的身旁，毫无顾忌地男孩子般(2)地大笑。散会后，会用粗壮的臂膀搂着她，一块儿到供销店挑上两支橘红色的花线，回家绣枕头……

　　在五个姐妹中，存妮是最幸运的。她赶在一九五五年家乡的丰收之后来到世上。满月那天，家里不费力地办了一桌酒。年轻的父亲沈山旺抱起小花被裹着的宝贝，兴奋地说：

墙角	qiángjiǎo	*n.*	corner of the wall
秀气	xiù.qi	*adj.*	delicate; elegant
大队	dàduì	*n.*	production brigade
小队	xiǎoduì	*n.*	production team
团	tuán	*n.*	Communist Youth League
组长	zǔzhǎng	*n.*	group leader
苍白	cāngbái	*adj.*	pale
忧郁	yōuyù	*adj.*	melancholy
迷惘	míwǎng	*adj.*	be perplexed; be at a loss; befuddlement
凝望	níngwàng	*v.*	gaze

强烈	qiángliè	*adj.*	strong; intense; violent
激动	jīdòng	*v.*	stir; excite; move
羞辱	xiūrǔ	*v./n.*	put to the shame; insult
哀伤	āishāng	*v./n.*	distressed; sad; grieved
惶恐	huángkǒng	*n.*	terror; fear
怨恨	yuànhèn	*v.*	have a grudge against sb. 你没考上大学，不能怨恨别人，只能怨恨自己。
怀念	huáiniàn	*v.*	cherish the memory of; think of
并排	bìngpái	*adv.*	side by side; lie alongside 并排坐着/并排前进
顾忌	gù.ji	*n./v.*	scruple; apprehension;worry 想好了就去做，不要顾忌这个，顾忌那个的。
散会	sànhuì	*v.-o.*	meeting is adjourned; meeting ends
粗壮	cūzhuàng	*adj.*	thick and sturdy
臂膀	bìbǎng	*n.*	arm
搂	lǒu	*v.*	hug; embrace
供销店	gōngxiāodiàn	*n.*	store
桔红色	júhóngsè	*n./ adj.*	tangerine (color), reddish orange (color)
花线	huāxiàn	*n.*	colored thread
绣	xiù	*v.*	embroider
枕头	zhěn.tou	*n.*	pillow
赶	gǎn	*v.*	be in time for; run into a situation 要是赶上上下班时间，路上很堵。
丰收	fēngshōu	*n.*	bumper harvest
满月	mǎnyuè	*v.*	(of a baby) be a month old
费力	fèilì	*adj.*	need or use great effort;be strenuous 不费力：effortless 他毫不费力地就把院子收拾好了。
花被	huābèi	*n.*	colored quilt
裹	guǒ	*v.*	wrap 天很冷，她把自己紧紧裹在大衣里。
宝贝	bǎo.bei	*n.*	darling; baby

　　"……我把菱花送到接生站，抽空儿到信用社去存上了钱，再回来时，毛娃儿就落地了！头生这么快，这么顺当，谁也想不到哩！有人说起名叫个顺妮吧！我想，我们这样的穷庄稼汉，开天辟地头一遭儿进银行存钱！这时候生下了她，该叫她存妮。等她长大，日子不定 (3) 有多好呢！"

　　他发自内心的快乐，感染了每一个前来贺喜的人。当时，他是"靠山庄合作社"的副社长，乐观、能干，浑身都是天不怕地不怕的勇气和力量。山坡上那一片经他嫁接的山梨，第一次结果就是个丰收。小麦和玉米除去公粮还自给有余。二十几户人家的小村，人人都同他一样快乐，同他一样充满信心地憧憬着美好的未来。

　　等到五年以后，荒妹出世时，景况就大不相同了。"靠山庄合作社"已改成天堂公社天堂大队九小队。"天堂"这个好听的名字，是县委书记亲自起的。 取意于"共产主义是天堂，人民公社是桥梁"。那时候，包括队长沈山旺在内的所有社员，

接生站	jiēshēng zhàn	*n.*	midwife's station
抽空儿	chōukòngr	*v.-o.*	manage to find time
信用社	xìnyòngshè	*n.*	credit cooperative
落地	luòdì	*v.*	fall to the ground; be born
头生	tóushēng	*adj.*	firstborn 他是家里头生的孩子，所以，特别受到宠爱。
顺当	shùn.dang	*adj.*	smoothly; without a hitch
庄稼汉	zhuāng.jia hàn	*n.*	peasant; farmer

开天辟地	kāitiānpìdì	*idm.*	since the beginning of history
头一遭儿	tóu yìzāor	*adj.*	the first time 头一回; 头一次
内心	nèixīn	*n.*	inward; heart
感染	gǎnrǎn	*v.*	influence; infect; affect
贺喜	hèxǐ	*v.*	congratulate on a happy occasion
靠山庄	Kàoshān zhuāng	*n.*	place name
合作社	hézuòshè	*n.*	co-op; cooperative
副社长	fù shèzhǎng	*n.*	deputy chief of staff
乐观	lèguān	*adj.*	optimistic; hopeful; bright
浑身	húnshēn	*adv.*	all over; from head to foot 浑身都是汗/浑身脏得要命
勇气	yǒngqì	*n.*	courage
力量	lì.liang	*n.*	physical strength
山坡	shānpō	*n.*	hillside; mountain slope
嫁接	jiàjiē	*v.*	graft
山梨	shānlí	*n.*	mountain pear
小麦	xiǎomài	*n.*	wheat
玉米	yùmǐ	*n.*	corn
公粮	gōngliáng	*n.*	agricultural tax paid in grain
自给有余	zìjǐyǒuyú	*v.*	be self-sufficient and achieve a surplus
憧憬	chōngjǐng	*v./n.*	long for; look forward to 憧憬着幸福的明天/充满对未来的憧憬
未来	wèilái	*n.*	future
景况	jǐngkuàng	*n.*	circumstances
县委	xiànwěi	*n.*	County Party Committee
起名字	qǐ míng.zi	*v.-o.*	give a name
取意于	qǔyìyú	*v.*	derive its meaning from
共产主义	gòngchǎn zhǔyì	*n.*	Communism
人民公社	rénmín gōngshè	*n.*	People's Commune
桥梁	qiáoliáng	*n.*	bridge

都深信进"天堂"不过咫尺之遥，只需毫不痛惜地把集体的山梨树，连同每家房前屋后的白果、板栗统统锯倒，连夜送到公社兴办的炼钢厂。仿佛一旦那奇妙的，呼呼叫着的土炉子里喷出了灿烂的钢花，那么 (4)，他们就轻松地步过"桥梁"，进入共产主义了。但结果却是那堆使几万担树木成为灰烬的铁疙瘩，除了牢牢地占住家田之外，没有任何效用。而小麦、玉米又由于干旱，连种子也没有收回；锯倒梨树栽下的山芋，长得同存妮的手指头差不多粗细。菱花怀着快生的孩子从外地讨饭回来，沈山旺已经因"攻击大办钢铁"被撤了职。他望着呱呱坠地的孱弱的第二个女儿，浮肿的脸上露出了苦笑："唉，谁叫(5)她赶上 (6) 这荒年呢？真是个荒妹子呵！……"

咫尺之遥	zhǐchǐzhīyáo	idm.	very close; close at hand
痛惜	tòngxī	v.	deeply regret; deplore
集体	jítǐ	n.	collective household
连同	liántóng	conj.	together with; along with 我把借他的钱连同利息一起还给了他。
白果	báiguǒ	n.	ginkgo tree
板栗	bǎnlì	n.	Chinese chestnut
统统	tǒngtǒng	adv.	wholly; completely 统统出去/统统讲出来
锯倒	jùdǎo	v.-c.	cut down with a saw
连夜	liányè	n.	that very night; the same night 连夜赶到城里去/连夜做完
兴办	xīngbàn	v.	initiate; set up
炼钢厂	liàngāngchǎng	n.	steel plant
仿佛	fǎngfú	adv.	as if

一旦	yídàn	adv.	now that; once
			一旦被人发现就麻烦了。
奇妙	qímiào	adj.	marvelous; wonderful
土炉子	tǔ lú.zi	n.	earthen furnace; earthen stove
喷出	pēnchū	v.	spurt out
灿烂	cànlàn	adj.	glorious; resplendent; splendid; bright
担	dàn	AN.	measure word used to modify things carried on a shoulder pole
			一担水，一担米
灰烬	huījìn	n.	ash
铁疙瘩	tiěgē.da	n.	iron lump
牢牢	láoláo	adv.	firmly; safely
			你要把老师教的东西牢牢记在脑子里。
占住	zhànzhù	v.	occupy; hold
效用	xiàoyòng	n.	effectiveness; usefulness
干旱	gānhàn	n.	drought
种子	zhǒng.zi	n.	seed
栽	zāi	v.	plant 去年栽的树，今年就结了这么多苹果。
山芋	shānyù	n.	sweet potato
粗细	cūxì	n.	thickness
怀着孩子	huái.zhe hái.zi	v.-o.	be pregnant
讨饭	tǎofàn	v.-o.	beg for food
攻击	gōngjī	v.	attack
撤职	chèzhí	v.-o.	dismiss sb. from his post; remove sb. from office
呱呱坠地	guāguā zhuìdì	idm	(of a child) be born
孱弱	chánruò	adj.	delicate; weak
浮肿	fúzhǒng	v./n.	swollen; bloated
露出	lùchū	v.	reveal; show
苦笑	kǔxiào	n.	forced smile
荒年	huāngnián	n.	famine year

　　也许是得力于怀胎和哺乳时的营养吧，存妮终于泼泼辣辣
地长大了。真是吃树叶也长肉，喝凉水也长劲儿。十六岁的生日
还没过，她已经发育成个健壮、丰满的大姑娘了。一条桑木扁担，
代替了又一连生下三个妹妹的多病的妈妈，帮助父亲挑起了家
庭的重担。一年一度最苦的活——给国营林场挑松毛下山，她
的工分儿在妇女中数第三。每天天不亮下地，顶着星星回来，吞
下一钵子山芋或者玉米糊，头一挨枕边就睡着了。尽管年下分红
时，家里的超支数位总是有增无减(7)，连一分钱的现款也拿不到
手，但她总是乐呵呵地不知道什么叫愁。高兴起来，还搂着荒妹，
用丰满的胸脯紧贴着妹妹纤弱的身子，轻轻地哼一曲妈妈年轻
时代唱的山歌。

得力于	déliyú	v.	benefit from 他的成功得力于平时的勤学苦练。
怀胎	huáitāi	v.-o.	be pregnant
哺乳	bǔrǔ	v.	breast-feed
营养	yíngyǎng	n.	nutrition
泼辣	pōlà	adj.	bold and forceful
树叶	shùyè	n.	tree leaf
劲儿	jìnr	n.	physical strength
发育	fāyù	v.	develop physically (in puberty) 现在的孩子发育得很早。
健壮	jiànzhuàng	adj.	robust; healthy and strong
丰满	fēngmǎn	adj.	plump; full-grown; well-developed
桑木	sāngmù	n.	mulberry
扁担	biǎn.dan	n.	shoulder pole
代替	dàitì	v.	replace
挑起	tiāoqǐ	v.	carry on the shoulder

重担	zhòngdàn	*n.*	heavy burden; heavy responsibility
一年一度	yì nián yí dù	*adj.*	once a year; yearly 一年一度的庆祝活动/ 一年一度的节日
活儿	huór	*n.*	job; labor
国营	guóyíng	*v.*	state-operated; state-run
林场	línchǎng	*n.*	tree farm
松毛	sōngmáo	*n.*	pine needles
工分儿	gōngfēnr	*n.*	work point (given in lieu of wages as recognition of work performed)
下地	xiàdì	*v.-o.*	go to the fields
顶着星星	dǐngzhe xīng.xing	*v.-o.*	with the stars above on the sky 顶着星星回了家。
吞下	tūnxià	*v.*	swallow down
钵子	bō.zi	*n.*	big earthen bowl
挨	āi	*v.*	get close to 我家挨着一个学校，常常很吵。
年下	niánxià	*n.*	the Chinese lunar New Year holidays
分红	fēnhóng	*v.-o.*	share out profits 他们单位年终分红的时候，大家分到了很多钱。
超支	chāozhī	*v.*	live beyond one's income; overspend 上个月我们家已经超支了，这个月我们得省着一点花。
有增无减	yǒuzēng wújiǎn	*idm.*	increase steadily 老师不让学生迟到，但是迟到的学生有增无减。
现款	xiànkuǎn	*n.*	cash
乐呵呵	lèhēhē	*adj.*	buoyant; happy and gay
愁	chóu	*n.*	worry
胸脯	xiōngpú	*n.*	chest
贴	tiē	*v.*	nestle up to; snuggle up to
纤弱	xiānruò	*adj.*	slim and fragile
哼	hēng	*v.*	hum
山歌	shāngē	*n.*	folk song

生活中往往有一些蹊跷的事，十分偶然却有着明显的根源；令人惊诧又实在平淡无奇。存妮和小豹子之间发生的事，就是这样。

小豹子是村东家贵叔的独生子，名叫小宝，和存妮同年。这个体格剽悍的小伙子，干起活来有一股吓死人的拼劲。有一次挑松毛，赶上一场冬雨，家贵婶在前面滑了一跤，扁担也撅折了。小宝过来扶起母亲，把两担松毛并在一起，打了个赤膊，咬着牙，挑下了山。一过秤，三百零五斤！大家吃惊地说，小宝子真能拼，简直是头小豹子！就这样喊出了名。

七四年的初春，队上的干部清早就到公社去批孔老夫子了，青壮劳力全部上了水库工地。保管员祥二爷留下存妮帮他整理仓库。老头儿一面指点着姑娘干活，一面唠叨着：

“干部下来走一圈，手一指：‘这儿!’，这就开山劈石忙乎一年。山洪下来，冲个稀里哗啦！明年干部又来，手一指，'那儿！'…… 也不看看风水地脉!”

蹊跷	qī.qiao	*adj.*	odd; queer
偶然	ǒurán	*adj.*	accidental; by chance
根源	gēnyuán	*n.*	root; source; origin
惊诧	jīngchà	*adj.*	amazed; surprised
平淡无奇	píngdànwúqí	*idm.*	very ordinary; appear trite and insignificant 他说的话虽然平淡无奇，但是却很有道理。
同年	tóngnián	*adj.*	of the same age
体格	tǐgé	*n.*	physique; build

剽悍	piāohàn	*adj.*	agile and strong
小伙子	xiǎohuǒ.zi	*n.*	lad; young fellow
拼劲	pīn.jinr	*n.*	great zeal; hard working spirit
赶上	gǎnshàng	*v.*	run into 我们到的时候,正赶上村子里有庆祝活动。
滑跤	huájiāo	*v.-o.*	slip
撅折	juēshé	*v.-c.*	break
扶起	fúqǐ	*v.*	prop up sb.; help sb. up 护士把病人扶起来吃药。
并在一起	bìngzàiyìqǐ	*v.-c.*	combine together 因为学生人少,学校把这两个班并在一起。
打赤膊	dǎ chìbó	*v.-o.*	be stripped to the waist
过秤	guòchèng	*v.*	weigh on a scale
豹子	bào.zi	*n.*	leopard; panther
喊	hǎn	*v.*	call (a person)
干部	gàn.bu	*n.*	cadre
批	pī	*v.*	criticize; refute
孔老夫子	Kǒng lǎo fūzǐ	*n.*	(informal) Confucius
劳力	láolì	*n.*	manpower
水库	shuǐkù	*n.*	reservoir
工地	gōngdì	*n.*	work site; construction site
保管员	bǎoguǎnyuán	*n.*	storekeeper; stockman
仓库	cāngkù	*n.*	storehouse; warehouse
指点	zhǐdiǎn	*v.*	give advice (directions); show sb. how to do sth. 老师耐心地给学生指点出作业中出现的问题。
唠叨	láo.dao	*v.*	chatter; prattle; gab
山洪	shānhóng	*n.*	mountain torrents
冲	chōng	*v.*	wash away; flush
稀里哗啦	xī.li huālā	*onom.*	sound of rushing water
风水	fēngshuǐ	*n.*	feng shui; geological elements
地脉	dìmài	*n.*	geographical position

"不是说'愚公移山'吗？"存妮有口无心地答讪说。

"移山能填饱肚子那也成！……来，把这堆先过筛，慢点，别撒了！……瞧这玉米，山梨树根上长的，瘦巴巴的，谁知 (8) 出得了芽儿不？老人又抱怨起玉米种子来。

"不是说 '以粮为纲' 吗？"姑娘仍有口无心地答着。心想，跟老头儿干活，虽然轻巧，却远不如(9)在水库和年轻伙伴一起挑土来得热闹。

这时，仓库门口出现了个健壮的身影："派点活给我干吧！祥二爷。"

"小豹子！"存妮高兴地喊："你不是昨天抬石头扭了脚吗？"

祥二爷说："回家歇着吧！"

"歇着我难受。"小豹子憨厚地微笑说："只要不挑担子，干点轻活碍不着！"说着，他抄起木锨就帮存妮过筛。

祥二爷高兴地蹲在一旁抽了支烟，交待几句便走了。整理仓库、筛种子这些活儿，在两个勤快的十九岁的青年手里，真不算一回事儿(10)。不多久，种子装进了麻袋，山芋干也在场上

| 愚公移山 | yúgōng yíshān | *idm.* | the foolish old man moved the mountains – the determination to win victory and the courage to surmount every difficulty |
| 有口无心 | yǒukǒu wúxīn | *idm.* | speak good words but be unsympathetic; say what one does not mean |

答讪	dā.shan	v.	strike up a conversation with sb. 他想跟她交朋友，就过去跟她答讪。
填饱肚子	tiánbǎo dù.zi	v.-o.	fill oneself with food
成	chéng	adj.	行; all right; okay
过筛	guòshāi	v.	sift out
撒	sǎ	v.	spill; drop
瞧	qiáo	v.	look; see
出芽儿	chūyár	v.-o.	bud
抱怨	bào.yuan	v.	complain; grumble
以粮为纲	yǐliáng wéigāng	v.	take food production as the key link. 以粮为纲，全面发展 was one of China's key policy developments in the 60s.
轻巧	qīng.qiao	adj.	easy; simple
伙伴	huǒbàn	n.	partner; companion
热闹	rè.nao	adj./n.	fun; lively; bustling with activity
身影	shēnyǐng	n.	figure
派	pài	v.	assign (a duty; task) 老板派他去外地工作。
扭	niǔ	v.	sprain; twist
歇着	xiē.zhe	v.	stop (work, etc.); knock off; at roost
憨厚	hānhòu	adj.	be simple and honest
微笑	wēixiào	v./n.	smile
碍不着	àibùzháo	v.-c.	not in the way 他受了一点小伤，碍不着正常上班。
抄起	chāoqǐ	v.	take up; grab
木锨	mùxiān	n.	wooden shovel
蹲	dūn	v.	squat on the heels
交待	jiāodài	v.	tell; leave words; order
勤快	qín.kuai	adj.	diligent; hardworking
麻袋	mádài	n.	gunnysack
山芋干	shānyùgān	n.	dried sweet potato
场	cháng	n.	threshing ground; level open space

晾开。小豹子说了声："歇歇吧！"就把棉袄铺在麻袋上，躺了下来。

存妮擦擦汗，坐在对面的麻袋上。她的棉袄也早脱了，穿着件葵绿色的毛线衣。这是母亲的嫁妆。虽然已经拆洗过无数次，添织了几种不同颜色的线，并且因为太小而紧绷在身上。但在九队的青年姑娘中，还是件令人羡慕的奢侈品。

小豹子凝视着她那被阳光照耀而显得(11)格外红润的脸庞，凝视着她丰满的胸脯，心中浮起一种异样的、从未经验过的痒丝丝的感觉。使他激动，又使他害怕。于是，他没话找话地说：

"前天吴庄放电影，你没去？"

"那么老远，我才不去呢！"她似乎为了躲开他那热辣辣的目光，垂下头说，一面摘去袖口上拖下来的线头。

吴庄是邻县的一个大队，上那里要翻过两座山。像小豹子那样的年轻人也得走一个多钟头。它算不上是个富队，去年十个工分只有三角八，但这已使天堂的社员很羡慕了。青年们尤其向往的是，沿吴庄西边的公路走，不到三十里，就是个火车站。去年春节，小豹子约了几个伙伴到那里去看火车。来回跑了半天，在车站等了两钟头，终于看到了穿过小站飞驰而去的

晾开	liàngkāi	v.-c.	dry by spreading out
棉袄	mián'ǎo	n.	cotton-padded jacket
铺	pū	v.	spread

脱	tuō	v.	take off
葵绿色	kuílǜsè	n.	grass green
嫁妆	jià.zhuang	n.	dowry
拆洗	chāixǐ	v.	remove the padding/lining of a piece of clothing, wash it, and put it back together
无数	wúshù	adj.	countless; innumerable
添	tiān	v.	add
织	zhī	v.	knit
紧绷	jǐnbēng	v.	tighten
羡慕	xiànmù	v.	envy; admire 我是一个穷学生，我很羡慕有钱人的生活。
奢侈品	shēchǐpǐn	n.	luxury goods; luxuries
凝视	níngshì	v.	gaze fixedly; stare
阳光	yángguāng	n.	sunshine; sunlight
照耀	zhàoyào	v.	shine
格外	géwài	adv.	especially
红润	hóngrùn	adj.	flushed; ruddy
脸庞	liǎnpáng	n.	face
浮起	fúqǐ	v.	float, (a feeling) well up inside 孩子考上了大学，妈妈脸上浮起了笑容。
痒丝丝	yǎngsīsī	adj.	itchy
躲开	duǒkāi	v.	avoid; dodge 躲开他/躲开他的目光
热辣辣	rèlàlà	adj.	burning hot
摘去	zhāiqù	v.	pick; take off
袖口	xiùkǒu	n.	wrist; cuff of a sleeve
拖下来	tuōxiàlái	v.-c.	run loose
线头	xiàntóur	n.	the end of a thread
邻县	línxiàn	n.	neighboring county
翻过	fān.guo	v.	cross over; climb over
向往	xiàngwǎng	v.	look forward to
穿过	chuānguò	v.	pass through; go through
飞驰	fēichí	v.	speed along; dash forward

草绿色客车而感到心满意足。九队的社员们几乎都没有这种眼福。至于乘火车，那只有外号儿叫瞎子的许会计才有过这样令人羡慕的经历。

"我也不想去！《地道战》、《地雷战》、《南征北战》，看了八百次啦！每句话我都会背！……"小豹子伸了个懒腰，叹着气说，"不看，又干啥呢？扑克牌打烂了，托人上公社供销店开后门儿，到现在也没买到！"

除了看电影、打百分儿之外，这里的青年，劳动之余(12)再也没事可干了。队里订了一份本省的报纸，也只有许瞎子开会时用得着。他总是把报上的"孔子曰"读成"孔子日"，当然不会有人来纠正这位全队唯一的知识分子。过去，这里还兴唱山歌，如今早已属于"黄色"之列，不许唱了。

忽然，小豹子兴奋地坐起来："喂，听许瞎子说，他以前看过外国电影。嗨，那才叫好看哪！"他咧着嘴，又嗤的一声笑了：

"那上面，有……"

"有什么？"存妮见他那副有滋有味(13)的模样，禁不住(14)问。

"嘻嘻嘻，……我不说。"小豹子红着脸，独自笑个不停。

| 心满意足 | xīnmǎnyìzú | idm. | be perfectly content; be completely satisfied 夏天我要是能去北京旅行，我就心满意足了。 |

有眼福	yǒu yǎnfú	n.	have the good fortune of seeing sth. rare or beautiful
外号儿	wàihàor	n.	nickname
瞎子	xiā.zi	n.	a blind person
会计	kuài.ji	n.	accountant
伸懒腰	shēn lǎn.yao	v.-o.	stretch oneself
干啥	gànshá	v.-o.	what to do
打扑克牌	dǎ pūkèpái	n.	play cards
烂	làn	v.	worn out 穿烂了/洗烂了/打烂了
托人	tuōrén	v.-o.	entrust; trust 她托我寄这封信。
开后门儿	kāi hòuménr	v.-o.	buy things in short supply through improper channels
百分儿	bǎifēnr	n.	a popular card game
订	dìng	v.	subscribe 订杂志/订报纸
本省	běnshěng	n.	our province; this province
用得着	yòng.dezháo	v.-c.	find sth. useful; need
曰	yuē	v.	(classical Chinese) say
纠正	jiūzhèng	v.	correct
兴	xīng	v.	become popular 70年代男人兴穿中山装，现在不兴了。
黄色	huángsè	adj.	pornographic
属于…之列	shǔyú… zhī liè	v.	be part of; pertain to 这些行为都属于性骚扰之列。
咧着嘴	liě.zhezuǐ	v.-o.	grin
嗤	chī	onom.	sound of chuckling
有滋有味	yǒuzī yǒuwèi	idm.	with great interest; 滋味：taste; flavor 饿的时候，吃什么都有滋有味。不饿的时候，吃什么都没滋没味。
模样	múyàng	n.	appearance; look
禁不住	jīnbúzhù	v.	can't help (doing sth.) 禁不住笑了起来
嘻	xī	onom.	hehe
独自	dúzì	adv.	alone; by oneself

"有什么？说呀！"

"说了……你别骂！"

"你说呀。"

"有……"他又格格地笑，笑得弯了腰。存妮已经料想着他会说出什么坏话来，伸手抓起一把土粒儿。果然(15)，小豹子鼓足勇气喊："有男人女人抱在一起亲嘴儿！嘿嘿嘿……"

"呸！下流！"存妮顿时涨红了脸，刷地把手中的土粒撒过去。

"真的，许瞎子说的！"小豹子躲闪着。

"不害臊！"又是一把撒过来。带着玉米碎屑的土粒落在他肩膀上、颈项里。他也还了手，一把土粒准确地落在存妮解开的领口儿上。姑娘绷起了脸，骂道："该死的！你！……"

小豹子讪讪地笑着，脱了光脊梁，用衬衣揩抹着铁疙瘩似的胸肌。存妮也撅着嘴开始脱毛衣，把粘在胸上的土粒抖出来……。刹那间，小豹子像触电似地呆住了。两眼直勾勾地瞪着，呼吸突然停止，一股热血猛冲到他的头上。原来(16)姑娘脱毛衣

弯腰	wānyāo	v.-o.	stoop; bend at the waist
料想	liàoxiǎng	v.	expect; presume
土粒	tǔlì	n.	a clump of earth
果然	guǒrán	adv.	as expected; as things turn out 天气预报说今天有雨，果然下午就下起雨来了。
鼓足勇气	gǔzúyǒngqì	phr.	pluck up one's courage
亲嘴儿	qīnzuǐr	v.-o.	kiss

呸	pēi	*intj*	pah; bah (used to express disdain, annoyance or stern disapproval)
下流	xiàliú	*adj.*	dirty; off color; obscene
顿时	dùnshí	*adv.*	immediately; at once
涨红了脸	zhànghóng .le liǎn	*v.-o.*	flush
刷地	shuā.de	*adv.*	with a swish
躲闪	duǒshǎn	*v.*	dodge; evade 他没有躲闪开，被一辆车给撞了。
不害臊	bú hàisào	*v.*	You've got some nerve! 害臊：feel ashamed; be bashful
碎屑	suìxiè	*n.*	crumb
肩膀	jiānbǎng	*n.*	shoulder
颈项	jǐngxiàng	*n.*	neck
还手	huánshǒu	*v.-o.*	strike back
领口儿	lǐngkǒur	*n.*	collar band; neckband
绷起了脸	bēngqǐ.le liǎn	*v.-o.*	pull a long face
该死的	gāisǐ.de	*v.*	God damn (you)!
讪讪地	shànshàn .de	*adv.*	looking embarrassed
光	guāng	*adj.*	naked; stripped
脊梁	jǐ.liang	*n.*	back
揩抹	kāimǒ	*v.*	wipe
疙瘩	gē.da	*n.*	lump, knot
胸肌	xiōngjī	*n.*	chest muscle; pectoral
撅嘴儿	juēzuǐr	*v.*	pout one's lips
粘	zhān	*v.*	stick to
刹那	chànà	*n.*	instant; split second
触电	chùdiàn	*v.-o.*	get an electric shock
直勾勾	zhígōugōu	*adv.*	with fixed eyes 直勾勾地看着
瞪着	dèng.zhe	*v.*	goggle at
呼吸	hūxī	*v./n.*	breathe, breath; respiration
猛冲	měngchōng	*v.*	charge; dash abruptly

时掀起了衬衫，竟露出半截儿白皙的、丰美而富有弹性的乳房……。就像出涧的野豹一样，小豹子猛扑上去。他完全失去了理智，不顾一切地紧紧搂住了她。姑娘大吃一惊，举起胳膊来阻挡。可是，当那灼热的、颤抖着的嘴唇一下子贴在自己湿润的唇上时，她感到一阵神秘的眩晕，眼睛一闭，伸出的胳膊瘫软了。

一切反抗的企图都在这一瞬间烟消云散。一种原始的本能，烈火般地燃烧着这一对物质贫乏、精神荒芜，而体魄却十分强健的青年男女的血液。传统的礼教、理性的尊严、违法的危险以及少女的羞耻心，一切的一切，此刻全都烧成了灰烬。

……

掀起	xiānqǐ	v.	lift
半截儿	bànjiér	AN.	half
白皙	báixī	adj.	white-skinned; fair-complexioned
弹性	tánxìng	n.	elasticity; resilience
乳房	rǔfáng	n.	breast
涧	jiàn	n.	gully; ravine
野豹	yěbào	n.	wild leopard; wild panther
猛扑上去	měngpū shàngqù	v.	charge; pounce on 我家的大狗向小偷猛扑上去，把小偷吓跑了。
理智	lǐzhì	n.	reason; sense

不顾一切	búgùyíqiè	*idm.*	regardless of all consequences 他不顾一切地冲进房子，救出 自己的孩子。
大吃一惊	dàchīyìjīng	*v.-o.*	stun; be astonished; be taken completely by surprise
阻挡	zǔdǎng	*v.*	obstruct; stop; block
灼热	zhuórè	*adj.*	scorching hot
颤抖	chàndǒu	*v.*	shiver; tremble; shake
嘴唇	zuǐchún	*n.*	lips
湿润	shīrùn	*adj.*	moist
眩晕	xuànyūn	*n.*	dizziness
瘫软	tānruǎn	*v.*	(of arms and legs) become weak and limp 手脚瘫软
反抗	fǎnkàng	*v.*	resist
企图	qǐtú	*n.*	attempt
烟消云散	yānxiāo yúnsàn	*idm.*	disappear (vanish) like mist and smoke
原始	yuánshǐ	*adj.*	primitive
本能	běnnéng	*n.*	instinct; intuition
般	bān	*n.*	sort; kind; like
燃烧	ránshāo	*v.*	burn
物质	wù.zhì	*n.*	material
贫乏	pínfá	*adj.*	poor; short; lacking
荒芜	huāngwú	*adj.*	lie waste; go out of cultivation 荒 芜的田地
体魄	tǐpò	*n.*	physique; build
强健	qiángjiàn	*adj.*	strong and healthy
血液	xuèyè	*n.*	blood
礼教	lǐjiào	*n.*	the Confucian ethical code
尊严	zūnyán	*n.*	reverence
违法	wéifǎ	*v.*	break the law
危险	wēixiǎn	*n./adj.*	danger, dangerous
羞耻心	xiūchǐxīn	*n.*	sense of shame
此刻	cǐkè	*n.*	at the moment

（二）爱情？羞耻？与死亡？

瘦巴巴的玉米长出了稀疏的苗子。锄过头遍，十四岁的荒妹开始发现姐姐变了：她不再无忧无虑地大笑，常常一个人坐在床边发呆，同她讲话，好像一句也没听见；有时看见她脸色苍白、低头抹泪，有时却又红晕满面地在独自发笑……。最奇怪的是一天夜里，荒妹一觉醒来，发现身边姐姐的被窝儿是空的。第二天问她，她急得脸上红一阵白一阵的，还硬说⑴荒妹是做梦。这一阵，妈妈的腰子病发了。爸爸忙着去吴庄的舅舅家借钱，张罗着请医生。家里乱糟糟的，谁也顾不上注意存妮的变化。只有荒妹，在她稚嫩的心灵里，隐隐地预感到将有一种可怕的祸事要落到姐姐的头上。

祸事果然不可避免地来临了。而且，它远比荒妹所想象的要可怕得多。

那是玉米长出半人高的时节，累了一天的社员，晚饭后聚集在队部，听许瞎子凑着⑴⑻煤油灯念"孔子曰"。荒妹没等开完会，早就溜回了家，照应三个妹妹睡下，自己也去睡了。但不一会就被一阵喧嚣惊醒：吵嚷声、哄笑声、打骂声、哭喊声、

瘦巴巴	shòubābā	*adj.*	thin; emaciated
稀疏	xīshū	*adj.*	few and scattered; thin
苗子	miáo.zi	*n.*	young plant; seedling
锄	chú	*v.*	hoe

无忧无虑	wúyōu wúlǜ	*idm.*	carefree; without sorrow and anxiety
发呆	fādāi	*v.*	stare blankly 他一个人坐在家里发呆。
抹泪	mǒlèi	*v.-o.*	wipe away tears
红晕	hóngyùn	*n.*	flush
被窝儿	bèiwōr	*n.*	covers; bedclothes
硬 v.	yìng	*adv.*	v. obstinately 明明是他拿的，可是他硬 说没拿。
腰子病	yāo.zi bìng	*n.*	kidney disease
张罗	zhāng.luo	*v.*	take care of; attend to 他才 20 岁，家里 人就给他张罗结婚的事情。
乱糟糟	luànzāozāo	*adj.*	chaotic
顾不上	gù.bushàng	*v.-c.*	have no time for 父母每天忙着上班，根 本顾不上孩子的学习。
稚嫩	zhìnèn	*adj.*	childlike and tender
心灵	xīnlíng	*n.*	soul; heart
隐隐地	yǐnyǐn.de	*adv.*	faintly; vaguely
预感	yùgǎn	*v./n.*	have a hunch
祸事	huòshì	*n.*	disaster; calamity
落到	luòdào	*v.*	befall; fall upon
来临	láilín	*v.*	come; arrive; be here
聚集	jùjí	*v.*	gather; assemble; collect
队部	duìbù	*n.*	headquarters of the production team
凑着	còu.zhe	*v.*	move close to
煤油灯	méiyóudēng	*n.*	kerosene lamp
溜	liū	*v.*	sneak off 下午的课一点都没有意思， 所以，他早早地就溜回了家。
照应	zhào.ying	*v.*	see after 她又得上班，又得照应三个小 孩子，她简直忙死了。
喧嚣	xuānxiāo	*n.*	noise
吵嚷	chǎorǎng	*v.*	shout in confusion; make a rackct
哄笑	hōngxiào	*v.*	(of many people) laugh together
打骂	dǎmà	*v.*	beat and scold

诅咒声、夹杂着几乎全村的狗吠和山里传来的回声，从来也没有这样热闹过。荒妹惊慌地捻亮了灯，可怕的喧嚣越来越近，竟到了大门外面。突然，姐姐一头冲进门来，衣衫不整、披头散发，扑倒在床上嚎啕大哭。接着，光着脊梁、两手反绑着的小豹子，被民兵营长押进门来。在几道雪亮的手电筒光照射下，荒妹看到他身上有一条条被树枝抽打的血印。他直挺挺地跪下，羞愧难容，任凭(19)脸色铁青的父亲刮他的嘴巴。母亲这时已经瘫坐在凳上，捂着脸呜咽着。门外，黑压压地围满了几乎全村的大人和小孩。七嘴八舌(20)，詈骂、耻笑、奚落和感慨……。吓得发抖的荒妹终于明白了：姐姐做了一件人世间最丑最丑的丑事！她忽然痛哭起来。她感到无比地羞耻、屈辱、怨恨和愤懑。最亲爱的姐姐竟然给全家带来了灾难，也给她带来了无法摆脱的不幸。

诅咒	zǔzhòu	v.	curse; swear; wish sb. evil
夹杂	jiāzá	v.	be mixed up with; get tangled up with
狗吠	gǒufèi	n.	dog bark
回声	huíshēng	n.	echo; reverberation
捻亮	niǎnliàng	v.	turn up the wick (of a lamp)
披头散发	pītóu sànfà	idm.	disheveled hair; with hair hanging loose
扑倒	pūdǎo	v.	throw oneself on
嚎啕大哭	háotáodàkū	idm.	cry one's eyes out; wail
反绑	fǎnbǎng	v.	with one's hands tied behind one's back
民兵	mínbīng	n.	militia; people's militia
营长	yíngzhǎng	n.	battalion commander
押	yā	v.	escort 警察押着银车离开银行。

雪亮	xuěliàng	*adj.*	bright as snow
手电筒	shǒudiàntǒng	*n.*	flashlight
照射	zhàoshè	*v.*	shine
树枝	shùzhī	*n.*	branch; twig
抽打	chōudǎ	*v.*	whip; lash
血印	xuèyìn	*n.*	bloodstain
直挺挺	zhítǐngtǐng	*adv.*	stiff 直挺挺地躺在地上
跪下	guì.xia	*v.*	kneel down
羞愧难容	xiūkuì nánróng	*phr.*	extremely ashamed
任凭	rènpíng	*v.*	allow; let (sb. do as he pleases) 任凭孩子胡闹/任凭感情支配
铁青	tiěqīng	*adj.*	ashen; ghastly pale
刮嘴巴	guā zuǐ.ba	*v.-o.*	slap one's face
捂着脸	wǔ.zheliǎn	*v.-o.*	cover up one's face
呜咽	wūyè	*v.*	sob; whimper
黑压压	hēiyāyā	*adv.*	with a dense mass of people 公园里黑压压地挤满了人。
围	wéi	*v.*	surround 学生把老师围在中间。
七嘴八舌	qīzuǐbāshé	*idm.*	with seven mouths and eight tongues -- all sorts of gossip; all talking at once 大家七嘴八舌地说个不停，他简直不知道该听谁的。
詈骂	lìmà	*v.*	curse
耻笑	chǐxiào	*v.*	sneer at; ridicule
奚落	xīluò	*v.*	scoff at; taunt; jeer at
感慨	gǎnkǎi	*v.*	sigh with emotion
发抖	fādǒu	*v.*	shiver; shake; tremble
屈辱	qūrǔ	*adj.*	humiliated, humiliation
愤懑	fènmèn	*adj.*	depressed and discontented; resentful
灾难	zāinàn	*n.*	calamity; catastrophe; disaster
摆脱	bǎituō	*v.*	break away; cast off; get rid of 摆脱干扰/摆脱困境/摆脱贫困

那最初来临的女性的自尊，在她幼弱的心灵上还没有成型，因而(21)也就格外(22)地敏感，格外地容易挫伤。荒妹大声地哭着，伤心的眼泪像决堤的河流。一面用自己也听不清的含混的声音，哼着"不要脸！丢了全家的人！……不要脸，丢了全队的人！……不要脸！不要脸！！……"

事情闹腾到半夜。

后来，她昏昏地睡了。朦胧中，又听到队长驱散众人的声音、家贵叔家贵婶向父母求情道歉的声音、祥二爷劝慰和提醒的声音："千万别难为(23)孩子家，防备着她想不开！……"妈妈的责骂也渐渐变成了低声的安慰。荒妹终于贴着泪水浸湿的枕头睡去，又不断地被恶梦所惊扰。在最后的一个恶梦中，她猛然听到从远处传来两声急促的呼喊：

"救人哪！救人哪！……"

荒妹猛地跳了起来，东方已经大亮。床上不见存姐，也没有了守着她的母亲。她忽地爬起来，赤着脚就往外奔，跟着前面的人影跑到村边的三亩塘前。啊！姐姐，已经被大伙儿七手八脚捞了上来，直挺挺躺在那里。这么快，这么轻易(24)地死了！

自尊	zìzūn	*n.*	self-respect; self-esteem
成形	chéngxíng	*v.*	take shape
敏感	mǐngǎn	*adj.*	sensitive; susceptible
挫伤	cuòshāng	*v.*	be injured; be wounded 老师总批评孩子，会挫伤孩子的自尊心。

决堤	juédī	v.-o.	(of a dike) be breached; burst
含混	hánhùn	adj.	indistinct; vague
不要脸	búyàoliǎn	sl.	lose all sense of shame; You should be ashamed of yourself.
丢人	diūrén	v.	lose face
闹腾	nào.teng	v.	be rowdy; create a disturbance
朦胧	ménglóng	adj.	dim; hazy
驱散	qūsàn	v.	disperse; dispel; break up
求情	qiúqíng	v.	plead; ask for a favor
道歉	dàoqiàn	v.	apologize to
劝慰	quànwèi	v.	console; soothe
难为	nán.wei	v.	embarrass; press 他不会唱歌，就别难为他了。
防备	fángbèi	v.	guard against
想不开	xiǎng.bukāi	v.-c.	take a matter to heart; take things too hard 别为了一点小事而想不开。
责骂	zémà	v.	scold; blame
安慰	ānwèi	v./n.	comfort; console; soothe
浸湿	jìnshī	v.	soaked
惊扰	jīngrǎo	v.	disturb
猛然	měngrán	adv.	abruptly; suddenly
急促	jícù	adj.	short and quick; abrupt
呼喊	hūhǎn	n.	yell; call out; shout
救人	jiùrén	v.-o.	Help!
赤脚	chìjiǎo	v.-o.	barefoot
奔	bēn	v.	run
三亩塘	Sānmǔ táng	n.	name of the local pond
七手八脚	qīshǒu bājiǎo	idm.	seven hands and eight feet –hussle and bustle; disorderly 他们七手八脚地把箱子都搬了进来。
轻易	qīngyì	adv.	lightly; rashly; easily 我们不能轻易地否定一个学生。

母亲抱着姐姐嘶哑地哭嚎着，发疯似地喊着。多少次被乡亲们拉起来，又瘫倒在地上。父亲呆坐在塘边，失神地瞪着平静的水面，一动也不动，仿佛是一截枯干的树桩。

朝霞映在存妮的湿漉漉的脸上，使她惨白的脸色恢复了红润。她的神情非常安详，非常坦然，没有一点痛苦、抗议、抱怨和不平。她为自己盲目的冲动付出了最高昂的代价，现在她已经洗净了自己的耻辱和罪恶。固然，她的死是太没有价值了。但是(25)生活对她来说又有什么值得留恋的呢？在纵身于死亡的深渊前，她还来得及(26)想到的事，就是把身上那件葵绿色的破毛衣脱下来，挂在树上。她把这个人间赐予她的唯一的财富留给了妹妹，带着她的体温和青春的芳馨……

事情还没有完。大约过了半个月吧，家贵叔家里又传出了凄凉的哀哭，——两个公安员把小豹子带走了。全村又一次受到震动。他们从田野里奔来，站在路旁，惶恐地、默默无言地注视着小豹子手腕上那一双闪闪发光的东西。只有家贵夫妇一把眼泪一把鼻涕地跟在他们的独生子后面。

嘶哑	sīyǎ	*adj.*	hoarse
哭嚎	kūháo	*v.*	cry loudly
发疯	fāfēng	*v.*	go crazy; become insane
乡亲	xiāng.qin	*n.*	villagers; people from the same village
失神	shīshén	*v-o.*	dejected; in low spirits
枯干	kūgān	*adj.*	withered; haggard
树桩	shùzhuāng	*n.*	stump

朝霞	zhāoxiá	*n.*	rosy clouds of dawn
映	yìng	*v.*	mirror; reflect
湿漉漉	shīlūlū	*adj.*	wet
惨白	cǎnbái	*adj.*	pale
恢复	huī.fu	*v.*	resume; recover
安祥	ānxiáng	*adj.*	composed; be resolute and serene
坦然	tǎnrán	*adj.*	have no misgiving; calm
抗议	kàngyì	*v.*	protest; object
不平	bùpíng	*adj.*	resentful; discontent
盲目	mángmù	*adj.*	blind
冲动	chōngdòng	*n.*	impulse; impulsive motion
高昂	gāo'áng	*adj.*	high-priced; expensive
罪恶	zuì'è	*n.*	crime; evils; guilt
留恋	liúliàn	*v.*	be reluctant to leave (a place); can't bear to part from sb.
纵身	zòngshēn	*v.*	jump; leap
深渊	shēnyuān	*n.*	abyss; chasm
来得及	lái.dejí	*v.*	there's still time; be able to do in time 现在开始预备还来得及。
赐予	cìyǔ	*v.*	bestow; grant
体温	tǐwēn	*n.*	body temperature
青春	qīngchūn	*n.*	youth; youthfulness
芳馨	fāngxīn	*n.*	fragrance; sweet-smelling aroma
凄凉	qīliáng	*adj.*	lonely and desolate
哀哭	āikū	*n.*	wail
公安员	gōng'ānyuán	*n.*	policeman
震动	zhèndòng	*v.*	shock
默默无言	mòmò wúyán	*idm.*	silently; without saying a word
注视	zhùshì	*v.*	gaze at; look attentively at; watch with concern
手腕	shǒuwàn	*n.*	wrist
闪闪发光	shǎnshǎn fāguāng	*idm.*	sparkle; glitter

"同志，同志！" 沈山旺放下锄头追了上来。这位五十年代的队长是见过点世面的。虽然女儿的死使他突然老了十年，而且对生活更冷漠了。但此刻，他的责任感使他不能沉默。他向公安员说："同志，我们并没有告他呀！"

公安员严峻地瞪他一眼，轻蔑地说："去，去，去！什么告不告！强奸致死人命犯！什么告不告！……"

小豹子却很镇静，抬着头，两眼茫然四顾。突然，他略一停步，就猛地飞奔起来，向对面的荒坡冲去。

"站住！往哪儿跑！" 公安员喝着，连忙追了上去。

但是小豹子不顾一切地奔着，杂乱的脚步踏倒了荒草和荆丛。最后，他扑倒在存妮的那座新坟上，恸哭起来，两手乱抓，指头深深地抠进湿润的黄土里。公安员跑来喝了几声，他才止住泪。然后，直跪在坟前，恭恭敬敬地磕了三个头。

追上来	zhuīshànglái	v.	catch up
见世面	jiànshìmiàn	v.-o.	see life; see the world; be world-wise
冷漠	lěngmò	adj.	be cold and detached; unconcerned; indifferent
沉默	chénmò	v.	remain silent
告	gào	v.	accuse; bring charges
严峻	yánjùn	adj.	stern; severe; rigorous
轻蔑	qīngmiè	adj.	scornful; disdainful
强奸	qiángjiān	v./n.	rape
致死	zhìsǐ	v.	causing death
镇静	zhènjìng	adj.	composed
茫然四顾	mángrán sìgù	v.	look around blankly
略	lüè	adv.	briefly 他的事情我略知一二。
飞奔	fēibēn	v.	dash
荒坡	huāngpō	n.	barren hill
喝着	hè.zhe	v.	shout an order
杂乱	záluàn	adj.	mixed and disorderly
踏倒	tàdǎo	v.	step down
荒草	huāngcǎo	n.	weeds
荆丛	jīngcóng	n.	thistles and thorns
坟	fén	n.	grave; tomb
恸哭	tòngkū	v.	wail; cry one's heart out
抠	kōu	v.	dig with a finger
恭恭敬敬	gōnggōng jìngjìng	adv.	with the utmost respect
磕头	kētóu	v.-o.	kowtow

（三）荒妹和许荣树

散了会，荒妹怀着沉重的心情走出公社礼堂的大门。天堂公社是本县的角落，天堂九队又是角落的角落。她望了望低垂在松林里的夕阳，担心天黑以前赶不到家了，就断然放弃去供销社逛逛的计划，从后街直穿麦田，快步奔小路上山。

"沈荒妹，等等！一块儿走吧！"身后传来团支部书记许荣树的喊声。他家住八队，与九队只隔着个三亩塘。荒妹当然很希望有人与她同行这段漫长的山路，冬天的傍晚，这山坳是十分荒凉的。但她不希望同路的是个小伙子，特别不希望是许荣树。所以略微迟疑了一下，反而加快了脚步。在麦田尽头儿荣树赶上来时，她警惕地移开身去，使他俩之间保持四尺开外的距离。

存姐的死，绝不(27)仅仅给她留下蔡绿色的毛衣。在她的心灵上留下了无法摆脱的耻辱和恐惧。她过早地接过姐姐的桑木扁担，纤弱的身体不胜重负地挑起家庭的担子，稚嫩的心灵也不胜重负地承受着精神的重压。她害怕和憎恨所有青年男子，见了他们绝不交谈，远而避之。她甚至鄙视那些对小伙子并不害怕和憎恨的女伴们。她成了一个难以接近的孤僻的姑娘. 但是，青春毕竟不可抗拒地来临了。 她脸上黄巴巴的气色已经

怀着…的心情	huái.zhē…de xīnqíng	v.-o.	with a feeling of... 怀着哀伤的心情；怀着激动的心情
沉重	chénzhòng	adj.	heavy
低垂	dīchuí	v.	hang low
断然	duànrán	adv.	flatly; resolutely 断然采取了措施
放弃	fàngqì	v.	abandon; give up
逛逛	guàng.guang	v.	stroll around
麦田	màitián	n.	wheat field
隔	gé	v.	be separated by
漫长	màncháng	adj.	very long
山坳	shān'ào	n.	mountain ridge
荒凉	huāngliáng	adj.	bleak and desolate; barren
略微	lüèwēi	adv.	slightly; a little
迟疑	chíyí	v.	hesitate
尽头儿	jìntóur	n.	the end
警惕地	jǐngtì.de	adv.	vigilantly
＿＿开外	kāiwài	suffix	...and above; and beyond 他有六十开外/离城里五公里开外
耻辱	chǐrǔ	n.	shame; disgrace; humiliation
恐惧	kǒngjù	n.	fear; dread
不胜重负	búshèng zhòngfù	idm.	can't bear the heavy burden
承受	chéngshòu	v.	bear; sustain
重压	zhòngyā	n.	heavy weight; high pressure
憎恨	zēnghèn	v.	detest; hate
交谈	jiāotán	v.	talk with each other; converse 跟人交谈
远而避之	yuǎn 'ér bìzhī	v.	stay at a distance and avoid sb.
鄙视	bǐshì	v.	despise; disdain
孤僻	gūpì	adj.	unsociable and eccentric
不可抗拒	bùkě kàngjù	adv.	irresistibly

217

褪去，露出红润而透着柔和的光泽；眉毛长得浓密起来；枯涩的眼睛也变得黑白分明，水汪汪的了。她感到胸脯发胀，肩背渐渐丰满，穿着姐姐那葵绿色的毛线衣，已经有点绷得难受了。她的心底常常升起一种新鲜的隐秘的喜悦。看见花开，觉得花儿是那么美，不由地摘一朵戴在头上；听到鸟叫，也觉得鸟儿叫得那么好听，不由呆呆地听了一会儿。什么都变得美好了：树叶、庄稼、野草以及草上的露珠……，周围的一切都使她激动。她常常偷偷地在妈妈那面破镜子里打量自己，甚至在塘边挑水时，也忍不住对自己苗条的身影投以满意的微笑。她开始同女伴们说笑，过年过节也让她们挽着手一起逛一逛公社的供销店。尽管对小伙子仍保持着警惕，但也渐渐感到他们并不是那么讨厌的了。……就在这时，许荣树在她的生活中出现了。

还是她很小的时候，就认识了荣树。那是她到设在八队的小学上一年级，男孩子们欺侮了她，一个同存妮差不多年龄的高班男同学，跑来打抱不平，还用袖口擦掉了她的眼泪。这个男同学就是荣树。后来因为妈妈生下了最小的妹妹，她二年级还没上完就辍了学。当她背着小妹妹在三亩塘附近割猪草时，荣树看到了总是偷偷离开伙伴们，抢过她手上的镰刀，飞快地割上一大抱，扔在她的筐里，就急急走开。过了两年，八队传来锣鼓声，荒妹带着妹妹们去看。只见他穿着过大的新军装，戴着红花，沿着三亩塘边上的小路去当兵了。

　　直到去年的一次团支部会上，她才又一次见到荣树。他几

褪去	tuìqù	*v.*	(of color) fade
柔和	róuhé	*adj.*	soft; gentle; mild
光泽	guāngzé	*n.*	luster; gloss
眉毛	méi.mao	*n.*	eyebrow; brow
浓密	nóngmì	*adj.*	dense
枯涩	kūsè	*adj.*	be dull and heavy
水汪汪	shuǐwāng wāng	*adj.*	(of children's or young women's eyes) bright and intelligent
发胀	fāzhàng	*v.*	swell
隐秘	yǐnmì	*adj.*	secret; concealed
喜悦	xǐyuè	*n.*	happy; joyous
不由	bùyóu	*adv.*	can't help
庄稼	zhuāng.jia	*n.*	crops
露珠	lùzhū	*n.*	dewdrop
打量	dǎ.liang	*v.*	look up and down; measure with the eye
苗条	miáo.tiao	*adj.*	slender; willowy; slim
挽手	wǎnshǒu	*v.-o.*	hold hands
设	shè	*v.*	set up; establish
欺侮	qīwǔ	*v.*	bully
打抱不平	dǎ bào bùpíng	*idm.*	help victims of injustice; defend sb. against an injustice
辍学	chuòxué	*v.*	discontinue one's studies; drop out
割草	gēcǎo	*v.-o.*	cut grass
镰刀	liándāo	*n.*	sickle
筐	kuāng	*n.*	basket
锣鼓声	luógǔ shēng	*n.*	the sound of gong and drum
沿着	yán.zhe	*prep.*	(walk) along
当兵	dāngbīng	*v.-o.*	be a soldier

天前刚从部队复员。进了大队会议室的门，羞涩地向大家一瞥，就像荒妹她们那批刚入团的姑娘们一样，悄悄在屋角坐下了。这时几个同他相熟的活跃分子围过来，硬要他讲讲战斗生活。只见他窘得满脸通红，忙腼腆地推辞着说："当了几年和平兵，又没打过仗，说啥呀！……"全然没有青年人心目中那种革命军人的威武气派。但不知为什么，这却引起了荒妹的好感。　当选举团支委进行表决，念到许荣树的名字时，她勇敢地把手举得笔直，以此表达她真诚的愿望。

到下一次的团支部活动时，新上任的支部书记许荣树却提出了他与众不同的主张，并因此引起了曾当过民兵营长的党支部副书记的不满。

过去，天堂公社青年团的活动，除开会之外，只有一个内容：劳动。——事先准备了些积肥、抬石块之类的重活，先开会，再干活。这种无偿的劳动往往进行到很晚。但荣树打破了这个规矩，他说："青年人有自己的特点。我建议：今晚看电影！"大家乍一听，愣了。接着便哄笑着鼓起掌来。他想得真周到，事先已经在公社附近一家工厂订了票（他有个战友复员到这家工厂），开了个短会，就领着大家出发了。小伙子和姑娘们三五成群，欢天喜地，笑语喧哗。有人大胆地哼起了山歌，简直像过节一样。荒妹这才生平第一次坐在有靠背、有扶手的椅子上，舒舒服服地看了一场电影。而且当天夜里，也是生平第

部队	bùduì	*n.*	military unit
复员	fùyuán	*v.*	demobilize
瞥	piē	*v.*	glance at
活跃分子	huóyuèfènzǐ	*n.*	activist
战斗	zhàndòu	*n.*	battle
窘	jiǒng	*adj.*	embarrassed
满脸通红	mǎnliǎn tōnghóng	*idm.*	blush until one's entire face is red
腼腆	miǎntiǎn	*adj.*	shy; bashful
推辞	tuīcí	*v.*	decline (an invitation, appointment, etc.)
打仗	dǎzhàng	*v.-o.*	fight a war
全然	quánrán	*adv.*	completely; entirely
威武	wēiwǔ	*adj.*	mighty
气派	qìpài	*n.*	manner; style; air
表决	biǎojué	*v.*	vote
笔直	bǐzhí	*adj.*	perfectly straight
与众不同	yǔzhòng bùtóng	*idm.*	out of the ordinary; different from others
主张	zhǔzhāng	*n.*	proposal; opinion
积肥	jīféi	*v.-o.*	collect manure (to use as fertilizer)
重活儿	zhònghuór	*n.*	heavy job
无偿	wúcháng	*adj.*	gratuitous; free
规矩	guī.ju	*n.*	rule; custom; established practice
乍	zhà	*adv.*	first; for the first time 乍一看/乍建 的工厂/新来乍到
鼓掌	gǔzhǎng	*v.-o.*	clap one's hands; applaud
周到	zhōudào	*adj.*	considerate; thoughtful
战友	zhànyǒu	*n.*	comrade-in-arms
欢天喜地	huāntiānxǐdì	*idm.*	be full of joy; be elated and happy
笑语喧哗	xiàoyǔ xuānhuá	*idm.*	uproarious talk and laughter
大胆	dàdǎn	*adj.*	bold; daring; audacious
生平	shēngpíng	*n.*	all one's life; life-time

一次，一个青年男子走进了她甜蜜的梦境。他有点像电影里那个带领青年修水库的男主角，更像她的团支部书记。他憨厚地笑着，同她说了些什么，离她很近。醒来时，月光照在她的床边，温柔而明净。她的心里，生平第一次泛起了一片甜丝丝的柔情。但又立即因此而感到惶恐。"这是怎么回事？"她懊恼地想："唉，唉！幸亏只是个梦！……"

然而当她担任团小组长之后，荣树就真的常来找她了。荒妹的态度一如既往地严肃而冷淡。从不请他进屋，一个门外，一个门里，保持着四尺开外的距离。谈的不过(28)是通知开会之类的事，一问一答，公事公办。讲完，荣树走了，荒妹总要装出做事的样子，到门外偷偷目送他远去。她隐约希望他多谈一会儿，进来坐一坐，谈些别的，又害怕他这样做。随着接触的增多，这种矛盾的心情越加发展起来。有一天，她回家晚了，小妹妹对她说："荣树哥来过啦！"正好(29)母亲也刚回来，忙问："他又来干什么？"父亲说："他来找我的。问我嫁接山梨的事。几年能结梨？一亩山地能收多少钱？ 我说，那不是资本主义的路吗？他说，这不叫资本主义，报上就这么讲的！这孩子！……"

父亲似乎不以为然地摇着头，但荒妹却觉察到他对这个青年是有好感的，心中暗暗感到高兴。然而母亲的脸色却很难看，她皱着眉头说："他，可是个不大安分的人！……"

荒妹早就听说过荣树为限制社员养鸡的事同八队队长（他的叔父）吵起来，有人说他太狂，不服从领导等等，但她从没在意。今天母亲这样说，使她生起气来。想分辩几句，又看

靠背	kàobèi	n.	back of a chair
扶手	fúshǒu	n.	armrest
甜蜜	tiánmì	adj.	sweet
明净	míngjìng	adj.	clear and bright
泛	fàn	v.	float; drift
甜丝丝	tiánsīsī	adj.	pleasantly sweet
柔情	róuqíng	n.	tender feelings
懊恼	àonǎo	adj.	chagrined; annoyed
担任	dānrèn	v.	take the office of; hold the post of
一如既往	yìrújìwǎng	idm.	just as in the past; continue as always 虽然没有考上大学，但是他还一如既往地刻苦学习。
冷淡	lěngdàn	adj./n	cold; indifferent
公事公办	gōngshì gōngbàn	idm.	do business according to official principles
装出…的样子	zhuāng chū …de yàng.zi	v.-o.	pretend; make believe 他装出生气的样子，其实心里很高兴。
目送	mùsòng	v.	gaze after; watch sb. go
隐约	yǐnyuē	adv.	indistinctly; faintly
资本主义	zīběnzhǔyì	n.	capitalism
摇头	yáotóu	v.-o.	shake one's head
觉察	juéchá	v.	detect; perceive
皱眉头	zhòu méitóu	v.-o.	knit one's brow; frown
安分	ānfèn	adj.	be contented with one's lot
限制	xiànzhì	v.	restrict; limit
狂	kuáng	adj.	arrogant
在意	zàiyì	v.	mind; take to heart
分辩	fēnbiàn	v.	defend against a charge

到母亲狐疑的眼光总在盯住自己，只好闷闷地低头吃饭，装出毫不关心的样子。晚饭后，母亲在房里对父亲嘀嘀咕咕，她听到门缝里传出了这样一句："已经有闲话啦！要当心她走上存妮的路！……"

荒妹只觉得心头被扎了一刀似的，扑在床上哭了。她怨恨姐姐做了那种死了也洗刷不净的丑事；怨恨妈妈不明白女儿的心；她更怨恨自己，为什么竟然会喜欢一个小伙子？这是多么不应该、多么可耻呀！"不要脸！喜欢上了一个男人！…… 不要脸！！" 她恨恨地骂自己，把脸深深地埋在被子里，不让伤心的哭声传出来。

她下定决心，从明天起，再不理睬他！有什么事，让他找副组长去！他会觉得奇怪，觉得委屈(30)吗？ 随他去 (31) 吧！谁让他是个男人呢！……

过不了多久，她真的恨起荣树来了。那是偶尔在队部听到许瞎子说："荣树这孩子真不知天高地厚 (32)，又跟副书记吵起来了！"有人问："为了什么？" 许瞎子说："哼！他要为小豹子伸冤呢！"

"什么？！"荒妹大吃一惊，几乎喊出声来。小豹子被判刑，是自作自受，罪有应得，并不是什么冤假错案，翻不了的。这几乎是人们共同的看法，荒妹不可能有别的看法。由于姐姐的死，她只有对小豹子更多一份仇恨。可是荣树，一个共产党员，

一个她所尊敬的团支部书记，怎么会为小豹子这样的坏人讲话

呢？他同情小豹子？还是得了家贵夫妇的什么好处？……她气

得发抖，要去当面质问荣树。但当她在三亩塘边，看见荣树

狐疑	húyí	adj.	suspicious
盯	dīng	v.	gaze at; stare at
闷闷	mènmèn	adj.	in low spirits
嘀嘀咕咕	dídígūgū	v.	babble on and on
门缝	ménfèng	n.	the crack between a door and its frame
闲话	xiánhuà	n.	gossip
当心	dāngxīn	v.	beware of; be careful
扎	zhā	v.	stab
理睬	lǐcǎi	v.	pay attention to; show interest in 他很骄傲，不理睬别人。
委屈	wěi.qu	adj.	feel wronged; be misunderstood
随他去吧	suítāqùba	phr.	Do as he pleases.
天高地厚	tiāngāo dìhòu	idm.	high as heaven, deep as earth – the complexity of things 他简直不知道天高地厚，居然跟自己的老师吵起来了。
伸冤	shēnyuān	v.-o.	redress an injustice; right a wrong
判刑	pànxíng	v.-o.	sentence
自作自受	zìzuò zìshòu	idm.	suffer through one's own misdeeds
罪有应得	zuìyǒu yīngdé	idm.	culpable; deserving of one's punishment 他受到的处罚是罪有应得，没有人能救他。
冤	yuān	adj.	be treated wrongly
翻案	fān'àn	v.-o.	reverse a verdict
仇恨	chóuhèn	n.	hatred; loathing
好处	hǎochù	n.	gain; profit
质问	zhìwèn	v.	question; interrogate

憨笑着向她迎面走来时，那股勇气又突然消失了。那件事怎么说得出口？又怎么好对他说呀？于是忙转过身，装做到别的地方去，绕了个大圈子回到了家。接着(33)，她又后悔起来。

就这样，气他、恨他、不睬他、害怕他，又不由自主地想念他……交替地变化着、矛盾着。这就是十九岁的农村姑娘的心。如果把这说成是爱情，那么，对于生活在别的地方的青年男女们，也许是难以理解的。但荒妹是在天堂九队这个角落的角落里。这里的姑娘，在荒妹的这个年龄，也多半有过像荣树和荒妹那样隐秘的爱情、矛盾和痛苦。然而不久就会什么都消失了，平静了。——来了一位亲戚或者什么人，送了一件葵绿色或者玫红色的毛线衣，进行一番大体相似的讨价还价而达成协定。然后，在某一天，由这位亲戚或者什么人领来了一个小伙子，再陪同这相互不敢正视一眼的双方一起去吴庄或者什么地方，照一张合影相片。到了议定的日子，她就离开了父母，离开了这个角落。……

这是一条这里的人们习以为常并公认为正当的道路，却被今天大会的报告人说成是"买办婚姻"。他还说什么"爱情"！姐姐和小豹子，那叫"爱情"吗？不，不！那是可耻的、违法的呀！那么，难道还有什么别的路吗？……荒妹感到茫然。她不能不想到荣树。此刻，他就在她的身后，默默地陪她同行。同来开会的女伴都去供销社了。寂静的山路上，只有他们俩。她听到自己怦怦的心跳。

忽然，荣树站住了脚，放眼四顾，用浑厚的嗓音唱起来：

我爱这蓝色的海洋，祖国的海疆多么宽广！……

憨笑	hānxiào	v.	smile openly, smile artlessly
消失	xiāoshī	v.	disappear
后悔	hòuhuǐ	v.	regret
不由自主	bùyóu zìzhǔ	idm.	beyond one's control; in spite of oneself 他一看见她，就不由自主地紧张起来。
交替	jiāotì	v.	by turn; in turn
玫红色	méihóngsè	n.	rose red
相似	xiāngsì	v.	resemble; be similar
讨价还价	tǎojià huánjià	idm.	haggle over the price of sth.
达成协定	dáchéng xiédìng	v.-o.	come to an agreement; come to terms
陪同	péitóng	v.	go with; accompany
正视	zhèngshì	v.	look straight into sb.'s eye
合影	héyǐng	v./n.	take a group photo; group photo
习以为常	xíyǐwéicháng	idm.	be accustomed to; be a matter of common practice
正当	zhèngdàng	adj.	reasonable; sensible
茫然	mángrán	adj.	in the dark; at a loss
寂静	jìjìng	adj.	quiet; still; silent
怦怦	pēngpēng	onom.	(of the heart) pit-a-pat
放眼四顾	fàngyǎn sìgù	v.	look all around
浑厚	húnhòu	adj.	deep and booming
嗓音	sǎngyīn	n.	voice
海洋	hǎiyáng	n.	sea; ocean
祖国	zǔguó	n.	motherland
海疆	hǎijiāng	n.	coastal areas and territorial waters
宽广	kuānguǎng	adj.	broad; extensive; vast

荒妹吓了一跳。但听着听着(34)，热情奔放的歌声感染了她。不由自主回过头，露出赞许的微笑。

"看着山上的这片松林，我想起了大海啦！想起了在军舰上的日子！……"他自语似地微笑着说："看着海，心里就会觉得宽阔起来。要是乡亲们都能看看海，该多好呵！"

荒妹微笑地听着。她的警惕在悄悄地消失。

"荒妹，你去前街了吗？集上卖鸡蛋、卖蔬菜的，没人撵了！知道吗？农村政策要改啦！山坡地一定得退田还山，种梨树。山旺大叔这位好把式又要发挥作用啦！先在你家自留地上栽起树苗来！……"他说得很凌乱，也很兴奋："山旺婶身体不好，可以砍些荆条在家编篮子，换点零花钱。你大妹妹明年可以出工了吧！两个小妹妹可以放几只羊！我有个战友在公社当干事，他告诉我，很快就要传达中央的文件，要让农民富裕起来！……你不信？"

他两眼闪着乐观的光芒，声音像淙淙溪水，亲切感人。荒妹没有相信这些话。对于富裕起来，她从没有抱过希望，甚至根本没有想过。从她懂事以来，富裕之类的话总是同资本主义

热情	rèqíng	n.	warmth; enthusiasm
奔放	bēnfàng	adj.	bold and unrestrained
赞许	zànxǔ	v.	approve; praise
军舰	jūnjiàn	n.	warship
悄悄地	qiāoqiāo.de	adv.	without being noticed 时间悄悄地过去了。

集	jí	*n.*	fair; market; bazaar
蔬菜	shūcài	*n.*	vegetable
撵	niǎn	*v.*	drive away; oust
退田还山	tuìtián huánshān	*v.*	return land to the mountains- 由于过度开发造成生态环境的严重破坏，中国政府在 90 年代推行"退田还山""退田还湖"来阻止进一步的恶化
好把式	hǎobǎ.shi	*n.*	person skilled in a trade
发挥作用	fāhuī zuòyòng	*v.-o.*	give full scope to; play a role in 他在改善读书风气上发挥了很好的作用。
自留地	zìliúdì	*n.*	household plot; small plots of land allocated to commune members for private use
凌乱	língluàn	*adj.*	in disorder; in a mess
砍	kǎn	*v.*	chop
荆条	jīngtiáo	*n.*	twigs of the chaste tree
编篮子	biān lán.zi	*v.-o.*	weave baskets
零花钱	línghuāqián	*n.*	pocket money
出工	chūgōng	*v.-o.*	go to work 他每天一早就出工，很晚才回来。
放羊	fàngyáng	*v.-o.*	herd sheep
干事	gàn.shi	*n.*	secretary (a governmental or official post)
传达	chuándá	*v.*	pass on; relay; convey 今天学校开会传达一个新的文件。
文件	wénjiàn	*n.*	document
富裕	fù.yu	*adj.*	prosperous; well-to-do; well-off
闪	shǎn	*v.*	sparkle; shine 她的眼里闪着泪光。
光芒	guāngmáng	*n.*	brilliant rays
淙淙溪水	cóngcóng xīshuǐ	*n.*	gurgling stream
抱希望	bào xīwàng	*v.-o.*	entertain a hope 他对将来抱着很大的希望。

联在一起遭受批判的。使她激动的是荣树这样清楚地知道她的家庭，并且这样关心。他就是用这个来回答她的冷淡、戒备和怀恨的！她愧疚了，觉得脸上在发烧。……

"是啊！不富裕起来，一辈子过着穷日子，就什么也谈不上 (35) ！"他深为感慨地摇摇头："就拿小豹子来说 (36) 吧，能全怪他吗？穷、落后、没有知识、蠢！再加上老封建！老实的小伙子，下了大牢！你姐姐，就更冤啦！……"

一听他说起这个，姑娘顿时觉得受了羞辱。她愤愤地瞪他一眼，吼道："不许你说这个！不许你说我姐姐！……"

她竭力忍住快要流出来的眼泪，猛地冲上山顶，放开大步向下奔去，弄得 (37) 荣树莫名其妙。

联	lián	v.	be connected; be related 你不应该把资本主义同犯罪联在一起。
遭受	zāoshòu	v.	suffer
批判	pīpàn	n.	criticism
戒备	jièbèi	v./n.	guard; be on the alert; take precautions
怀恨	huáihèn	v./n.	nurse a hatred (for); harbor resentment 他对老板的批评始终怀恨在心。
愧疚	kuì jiù	v./adj.	have a guilty conscience
蠢	chǔn	adj.	stupid; clumsy
封建	fēngjiàn	adj./n.	feudal-minded; feudalism
老实	lǎo.shi	adj.	honest
下大牢	xià dàláo	v.-o.	be put into jail
愤愤地	fènfèn.de	adv.	resentfully; indignantly
吼	hǒu	v.	uproar; roar
竭力	jiélì	adv.	do one's best (utmost) to 竭力反对/竭力宣传
莫名其妙	mòmíng qímiào	idm.	be unable to make heads or tails of something; absurd

（四）压不住的爱情

走近家门，天已经完全黑了，她的心情也渐渐平静下来。小妹妹老远就向她扑来，紧接着母亲也迎了出来，脸上挂着喜气洋洋的笑容。这使荒妹感到奇怪。贫困、操劳和多病的母亲过早地衰老了，特别是姐姐的死，使她的脸上除了愁苦之外，只有木然的发愣的神情。发生了什么值得她这样高兴的事？

"快，快去看看你的床上！"母亲几乎笑出声来。

床上放着一件簇新的毛线衣，天蓝色的。在幽暗的煤油灯下发出诱人的光泽。荒妹抓在手里，还没有来得及感受到它那轻柔和温暖，就立即像触了电似地甩开了。她吃惊地喊："谁的？"

"你的！"母亲正从锅里盛出热气腾腾的玉米粥。神采飞扬地瞟了她一眼说："你二舅妈送来的。……"

"二舅妈？！……"荒妹打了个寒噤，两腿发软，颓然坐在床沿上，呆住了。二舅妈前不久来过，同母亲嘀咕了老半天，一面不断地上上下下打量着她。她当时就敏感到那眼光里好像有什么神秘的意味。果然，现在送了毛线衣来！

母亲挨着她坐下，用难得的柔声说："是二舅他们吴庄三队的，比你大三岁。他哥哥在北关火车站当工人，一月拿五十多块！……"

荒妹感到冰冷的汗水在脊背上缓缓地爬。她浑身颤抖，耳

边 "嗡嗡" 直响 (38)，什么也听不清了。

平静	píngjìng	*adj.*	calm; quiet
紧接着	jǐnjiē.zhe	*adv.*	right after
迎	yíng	*v.*	greet; go to meet
喜气洋洋	xǐqì yángyáng	*idm.*	full of joy
操劳	cāoláo	*v.*	overwork oneself; work oneself too much 母亲操劳过度，过早地衰老了。
衰老	shuāilǎo	*v.*	grow old
愁苦	chóukǔ	*n.*	anxiety; distress
木然	mùrán	*adj.*	stupefied
发愣	fālèng	*v.*	dazed
簇新	cùxīn	*adj.*	brand new
幽暗	yōu'àn	*adj.*	dim; gloomy
诱人	yòurén	*adj.*	attractive
甩开	shuǎikāi	*v.-c.*	throw off; shake off
盛	chéng	*v.*	fill a bowl (with rice or other food)
热气腾腾	rèqì téngténg	*idm.*	steaming hot
神采飞扬	shéncǎi fēiyáng	*idm.*	in high spirits
瞟	piǎo	*v.*	glance sideways at
寒噤	hánjìn	*n.*	shiver (with cold or fear)
颓然	tuírán	*adv.*	dejected; disappointed
老半天	lǎobàntiān	*n.*	quite a while
意味	yìwèi	*n.*	meaning; significance; implication
挨着	āi.zhe	*v.*	close to ; next to 他的家挨着公园。
冰冷	bīnglěng	*adj.*	ice-cold
汗水	hànshuǐ	*n.*	sweat; perspiration
嗡嗡	wēngwēng	*onom.*	drone; buzz; hum
响	xiǎng	*v.*	make a sound; ring

"我不要！"她挣扎地喊："不！我不要！"

她把毛线衣扔向母亲，母亲却仍然微笑着拉住她说："又(39)不是现在就要你过门儿！端午节来见见面，送衣裳来。十六套！……订了婚，再送五百块现钱！"

"不，不，不！"一种耻辱感陡然升上荒妹的心。她感到窒息的恐怖。她不知该怎么办，只有让委屈的泪水急速地流出来，只有愤愤甩开母亲抚慰的手臂，跑开去。

门口，站着心情沉重的父亲和三个睁大眼睛呆望着她的妹妹。她捂住脸，冲出了门，站在院子里，依着塌了半截的猪圈的土墙，大声地哭起来。

"怎么啦？怎么啦？"母亲急急地跟出来，拉起她的手："荒妹，你是个懂事的孩子。咱家有啥？ 妈有病，三个妹妹光知道张着嘴要吃。养猪没饲料，喂了半年多，连本儿也没捞回来！攒几个鸡蛋拎上街，挨人撵来撵去，心里慌得像做了贼。去年分红，又是超支，一分现钱也没到手。我想给你买双袜子都……"

母亲也啜泣起来，数落着："你姐姐不争气，这个家靠谁？房子明年再不翻盖实在不行了。欠着债，哪有钱？二舅妈说，五百块钱一到手，就……"

"钱，钱！"姑娘激动地喊："你把女儿当东西卖！"母亲顿时噎住了。她浑身无力，扶着半截土墙缓缓地坐倒在地

上。"把女儿当东西卖！" 这句话是那样刺伤了她的心，又是

那样地熟悉！是谁在女儿一样的年纪， 含着跟女儿一样的激

愤喊过？是谁？ —— 唉唉！不是别人，正是她自己呀！……

挣扎	zhēngzhá	v.	struggle
过门儿	guòménr	v.	move in to one's husband's household upon marriage
端午节	Duānwǔjié	n.	dragon boat festival
衣裳	yī.shang	n.	clothes
订婚	dìnghūn	v.-o.	engage
陡然	dǒurán	adv.	suddenly; abruptly
窒息	zhìxī	v.	suffocate
恐怖	kǒngbù	n.	terror; horror
急速	jísù	adv.	hurried; rapid
抚慰	fǔwèi	v.	comfort; console
塌	tā	v.	fall down; collapse
猪圈	zhūjuàn	n.	pigsty
土墙	tǔqiáng	n.	cob wall; earthen wall
饲料	sìliào	n.	fodder; food
本儿	běnr	n.	capital; principal
捞回来	lāo huílái	v.	gain back
攒	zǎn	v.	save; accumulate
挨	ái	v.	suffer; endure 挨饿/挨打/挨批评
啜泣	chuòqì	v.	sob; whimper
数落	shǔ.luo	v.	rebuke; scold sb. by enumerating his/her wrongdoings
争气	zhēngqì	v.	upright; try one's best to do right
翻盖	fān gài	v.	renovate (a house)
噎住	yēzhù	v.-c.	choked up; throat closed up
缓缓	huǎnhuǎn	adv.	slowly; gradually
刺伤	cìshāng	v.-c.	jab and hurt
激愤	jīfèn	n./adj.	wrathful; indignant

那是在土改工作队进了吴庄的那个冬天，菱花去看歌剧《白毛女》的那天晚上，认识了憨厚、英俊的青年长工沈山旺。从那一刻起，她突然明白了平时唱的山歌里"情郎"一词的含义。十九岁的菱花不仅勇敢地参加了斗地主的大会，而且勇敢地在夜晚去玉米地同她的情郎相会了。可是她原先是父母作主同北关镇杂货铺的小老板订了婚的。男方听到风声送了五十块银元来，硬要年内成亲。菱花大哭大闹，公然承认她自己看中了靠山庄的穷小子，公然宣布跟他进山里去受苦，一辈子不回"老封建"的娘家门！把父母气呆了，关起房门又骂又打。她哭着、闹着、在地下滚着，把银元抛洒一地。激愤地嚷："你们，是要把女儿当东西卖呀！"

那是反封建的烈火已经把"父母之命、媒妁之言"连同地主的地契债据一起烧毁了的年代。宣传婚姻法的挂图在乡政府门口贴着。舞台上的刘巧儿和同村的童养媳都是菱花的榜样。憨厚、英俊的沈山旺捧着美好、幸福的前途在等待着她。菱花有的是 (40) 冲破封建枷锁的勇气！

土改	tǔgǎi	n.	The land reform of the mid-1950s, which compelled individual farmers to join collectives, and was generally a failure in terms of production.
工作队	gōngzuòduì	n.	work team
歌剧	gējù	n.	opera
英俊	yīngjùn	adj.	handsome and spirited
长工	chánggōng	n.	long-term laborer; farm hand by the year

情郎	qínglǎng	*n.*	lover
含义	hányì	*n.*	meaning; connotation
斗地主	dòu dìzhǔ	*v.-o.*	settle scores with the landlords
相会	xiānghuì	*v.*	meet
作主	zuòzhǔ	*v.*	decide; take the responsibility for a decision 这事她作不了主。
杂货铺	záhuòpù	*n.*	general store
风声	fēngshēng	*n.*	rumor
银元	yínyuán	*n.*	silver dollar
成亲	chéngqīn	*v.-o.*	get married
公然	gōngrán	*adv.*	brazenly; openly
承认	chéngrèn	*v.*	admit
看中	kànzhòng	*v.*	take a fancy to; settle on
娘家	niáng.jia	*n.*	a married woman's parents' home
滚	gǔn	*v.*	roll
抛洒	pāosǎ	*v.*	throw; toss
烈火	lièhuǒ	*n.*	raging flames
父母之命 媒妁之言	fùmǔzhī mìng méi shuòzhī yán	*idm.*	parental commands and matchmaker's word - an arranged marriage
地契	dìqì	*n.*	title deed for land
债据	zhài.ju	*n.*	an IOU; promissory note
烧毁	shāohuǐ	*v.*	burn down; burn up
挂图	guàtú	*n.*	hanging banner; wall chart
舞台	wǔtái	*n.*	stage
刘巧儿	Liú Qiǎo ér	*n.*	a person's name
童养媳	tóngyǎngxí	*n.*	a girl taken into the family as a daughter-in-law to be
榜样	bǎngyàng	*n.*	example; model
捧着	pěng.zhe	*v.*	carrying in both hands
前途	qiántú	*n.*	future; prospects
冲破	chōngpò	*v.-c.*	break through
枷锁	jiāsuǒ	*n.*	yoke; shackles

"他们，要把女儿当东西卖！" 第二天，在刚刚粉刷一新的乡公所里，不需要任何别的，只凭(41)她菱花这一句话！土改工作队就含着鼓励的微笑，发给她和山旺一人一张印着毛主席像的结婚证。……

万万想不到(42)今天，时隔三十年的今天，女儿竟用这句话来骂自己了？

"这是怎么回事？日子怎么又过回头了？……"她感到震惊而惶惑，慢慢抬起了头，仰望着暮冬的夜空。几颗寒星发出凄清、黯淡的光，嘲讽似地向她眨着眼。她仿佛忽然得到什么启示似地一颤，捶胸顿足痛哭起来。一面喃喃地自语：

"报应报应！这就叫报应呀！"

她干枯的双眼里涌出了浓浊的泪。里面饱含着心灵深处的苦恨。她恨荒妹，恨存妮，恨她们的父亲。她恨自己的苦命，恨这块她带着青春和欢乐的憧憬来到的土地，这块付出了大半生辛勤劳动、除了哀愁什么也没有给她的土地！……

荒妹反而镇静起来,劝慰母亲说："妈！公社街上，卖鸡蛋、卖菜的没人撵啦！你可以砍些荆条编土筐拿去卖。妹妹可以去放羊。山田改了种果树，爹是个好把式！…… 要让我们农民富裕起来！荣树说的，中央有这个文件！……" "文件，文件！今天这，明天那！见多啦！见够啦！我们不照样(43)还是穷！荒妹，妈不愿意叫你像妈这样过一辈子呀！"母亲抽泣着，也渐

渐平静起来："孩子，你是个懂事的姑娘。妈看出来，荣树对你有心，你也看着他中意。可你想想，吃不饱饭，这些都是空

粉刷一新	fěnshuāyìxīn	*phr.*	be painted anew
乡公所	xiānggōngsuǒ	*n.*	village hall
凭	píng	*prep.*	base on
印	yìn	*v.*	print
万万	wànwàn	*adv.*	absolutely (usually followed by a negative) 万万没想到
震惊	zhènjīng	*v.*	shock; amaze; astonish
仰望	yǎngwàng	*v.*	look up at
暮冬	mùdōng	*n.*	late winter
凄清	qīqīng	*adj.*	lonely and sad
黯淡	àndàn	*adj.*	dim; faint; gloomy
嘲讽	cháofěng	*v.*	satirize; mock
眨眼	zhǎyǎn	*v.-o.*	blink
启示	qǐshì	*n.*	inspiration; enlightenment
捶胸顿足	chuíxiōng dùnzú	*idm.*	beat one's breast and stamp one's feet (in deep sorrow, etc)
喃喃自语	nánnán zìyǔ	*v.*	mutter sth. to oneself
报应	bào.ying	*n.*	retribution
涌出	yǒngchū	*v.*	gush; well up
浓浊	nóngzhuó	*adj.*	thick and turbid
饱含	bǎohán	*v.*	be filled with; contain; harbor (certain emotion, feelings, etc.)
苦命	kǔmìng	*n.*	hard lot
辛勤	xīnqín	*adj.*	hardworking; industrious
哀愁	āichóu	*n.*	sorrow; sadness
照样	zhàoyàng	*adv.*	in the same old way; all the same 他病了，但是还照样上班。
抽泣	chōuqì	*v.*	sob
有心	yǒuxīn	*v.*	have a mind to; set one's mind on
中意	zhòngyì	*v.*	be to one's liking; catch the fancy of 那几件衣服她全不中意。

的哟！你妈悔不该当初 (44)……唉！如今得了报应啦！……"

风停了。妈妈衰弱的身子依着荒妹。母女俩无声地呆坐着，各自沉浸在自己的心事之中。"妈，你回去吧！"荒妹低声说。她的眼睛向八队的那一片村舍凝视着，探寻着其中的一间房子："我还有点事！……"

然后，她倔强地向三亩塘的方向走去。刚才发生的事，使她突然聪明了，成熟了。一切成见，包括要为小豹子伸冤这样使她强烈反感的事情，现在都觉得合理了。她相信荣树是会讲出他的道理来的。他知道得很多很多，甚至连大海都知道！那么，他所深信不移的要让农民富裕起来的文件，荒妹又有什么可怀疑的呢？他一定还会出个最好的主意，告诉她该怎么办！

三亩塘的水面上，吹来一阵轻柔的暖气。这正是大地回春的第一丝信息吧！它无声地抚慰着塘边的枯草，悄悄地拭干了急急走来的姑娘的泪。它终于真的来了吗？来到这被爱情遗忘了的角落？

选自《上海文学》1980年第 1 期

悔不该当初	huǐ bù gāi dāngchū	phr.	regret having done sth.; regret a previous mistake
沉浸	chénjìn	v.	immerse; soak
心事	xīnshì	n.	sth. weighing on one's mind; cares; concerns
探寻	tànxún	v.	seek
倔强	juéjiàng	adj.	stubborn; unbending
成熟	chéngshú	adj.	ripe; mature
成见	chéngjiàn	n.	prejudice
反感	fǎn'gǎn	adj.	be averse to; be disgusted with 对这种人很反感/对他的话很反感
深信不移	shēnxìnbùyí	idm.	believe firmly
出主意	chū zhú.yi	v.-o.	offer advice; make suggestions
轻柔	qīngróu	adj.	soft; gentle
大地回春	dàdìhuíchūn	idm.	spring returns to the earth
拭干	shìgān	v.-c.	wipe dry

词语例句

（一）

1. 在……的心目中：in sb.'s mind; in sb.'s eye
   ❖ 在天堂公社的青年们心目中，"爱情"，还是个陌生的、神秘的字眼。
   1) 在我的心目中，他还是个孩子。
   2) 在老师的心目中，他始终是个好学生。

2. ……般：as if; like
   ❖ 姐姐一定会并排坐在她的身旁，毫无顾忌地男孩子般地大笑。
   1) 他说完以后，台下响起了暴风雨般的掌声。
   2) 他对朋友像春天般温暖。

3. 不定：not certain
   ❖ 等她长大了，日子不定有多好呢！
   1) 你带着点钱，到了街上你不定要买什么呢！
   2) 那本书图书馆不定有没有呢！

4. 一旦……那么/就：once, in case
   ❖ 仿佛一旦那土炉子喷出钢花，那么，他们就进入共产主义了。
   1) 买保险的好处是：一旦发生意外，也不必着急。
   2) 你一旦从医学院毕业，立刻就能找到很好的工作。

5. 谁叫（人）……：who told you to (rhetorical question)…? (Serves you right.)
   ❖ 谁叫她赶上这荒年呢？
   1) 谁叫你不相信我的话？现在我可帮不了你的忙了。
   2) 谁叫你不早点起来？你今天肯定会迟到。

6. 赶上：run into a situation (good or bad)
   ❖ 谁叫她赶上这荒年呢？
   1) 我到她家去的时候，正赶上她家在吃饭。
   2) 他们回家的路上，赶上下大雨。

7. 有 A 无 B：have A and lack B
   有增无减，有害无益，有备无患
   ❖ 一年下来，家里的债有增无减。
   1) 抽烟是一个有害无益的习惯。

2） 早点动手，有备无患。

8. 谁知：who knows; nobody knows
   ❖ 瞧这玉米，瘦巴巴的，谁知出得了芽不?
   1） 这是他提出的办法，谁知行不行?
   2） 早上天气那么好，谁知下午会下起雨来?

9. 远不如：far inferior; less adj. than...
   ❖ 跟老头干活，虽然轻巧，却远不如在水库和年轻的伙伴一起挑土来得热闹。
   1） 我现在的记性远不如二十年前了。
   2） 这里的房子远不如南方的那么便宜。

10. 不算一回事儿：a piece of cake
    ❖ 整理仓库、筛种子这些活儿，在两个勤快的十九岁的青年手里，真不算一回事儿。
    1） 这不算一回事儿，我几分钟就能做完。
    2） 写一篇500字的文章，对他来说真不算一回事儿。

11. 显得：look, seem, appear
    ❖ 小豹子凝视着她那被阳光照耀而显得格外红润的脸庞。
    1） 她的生活很艰苦，所以她显得很老。
    2） 穿上新衣服，他显得很精神。

12. v.之余：after v.
    ❖ 除了看电影、打百分之外，这里的青年，劳动之余再也没事可干了。
    1） 他工作之余还自学外语。
    2） 大家兴奋之余，在一起合影。

13. 有 A 有 B：有…有… (is used in front of two synonyms for emphasis)
    有滋有味/有名有姓/有条有理/有说有笑/有职有权
    ❖ 存妮见他那副有滋有味的模样，禁不住问。
    1） 她很有效率，什么事都安排得有条有理。
    2） 老同学们有说有笑地度过了一个愉快的夜晚。

14. 禁不住：can't help
    ❖ 存妮见他那副有滋有味的模样，禁不住问。

1) 老朋友见面，禁不住高兴得大叫起来。
2) 看见那个可怜的孩子，她禁不住哭了起来。

15. 果然：as expected
    ❖ 存妮已经料想到他会说出什么坏话来，果然，他说出了下流话。
    1) 使用了电脑以后，工作效率果然高多了。
    2) 天气不好，出来买东西的人果然少多了。

16. 原来：so; turn out to be
    1) 刹那间，小豹子像触电似地呆住了。原来姑娘脱毛衣时掀起了衬衫，竟露出半截乳房。
    2) 原来是你！真没想到。
    3) 难怪生意这么好，原来这家商店在打折。

（二）

17. 硬 v.：v. obstinately
    ❖ 第二天问她，她急得脸上红一阵白一阵的，还硬说荒妹是做梦。
    1) 不让他去，他硬要去。
    2) 他硬不承认错误。

18. 凑：move closer to
    ❖ 社员们听许瞎子凑着煤油灯念"孔子曰"。
    1) 学生们都凑在老师跟前，听老师说话。
    2) 我看女朋友的来信，他却也凑过来看。

19. 任凭：allow; let (sb. do as he pleases)
    ❖ 他直挺挺地跪在地上，任凭父亲刮他的嘴巴。
    1) 家长不能任凭孩子胡闹。
    2) 大家都应该发表意见，不能任凭他一个人胡说。

20. 七…八…：(suggest confusion/disorder, lots of activities)
    七手八脚/七嘴八舌/七上八下/七长八短/七扭八歪
    ❖ 七嘴八舌，詈骂，耻笑，奚落和感慨。
    1) 大家七手八脚一下子就把活儿干完了。
    2) 他写的字七扭八歪的，真难看。
    3) 这么晚了，孩子还没有回来，她的心里七上八下的。

21. 因而：as a result
    ❖ 她的自尊还没有成形，因而格外地敏感。
    1) 工作太忙，因而没有时间出去玩。
    2) 由于那里有很多工厂，因而河水污染得很严重。

22. 格外：especially
    ❖ 那最初来临的女性的自尊，还没有成形，因而格外地敏感，也格外地容易挫伤。
    1) 农村的孩子考上名牌大学格外地不容易。
    2) 圣诞节前，各个商店都格外地忙。

23. 难为：embarrass; give sb. hard time
    ❖ 千万别难为孩子，防备她想不开。
    1) 让一个十岁的孩子做这么多事，简直太难为孩子了。
    2) 他只学了一年外语，让他当翻译太难为他了。

24. 轻易：lightly, rashly
    ❖ 存妮这么快，这么轻易地就死了。
    1) 她很喜欢说谎，你们不要轻易相信她的话。
    2) 她向来很节俭，从不轻易地扔掉任何东西。

25. 固然……，但是……：it is true that …, however…
    ❖ 固然，她的死是太没有价值了。但是生活对她来说又有什么值得留恋的呢?
    1) 固然这个做法有些问题，但是我们没有其他的办法啊!
    2) 你说的固然没错，但是他说的更有道理。

26. 来得及/来不及：be able to do sth. in time/ too late to do sth.
    ❖ 在纵身于死亡的深渊前，她还来得及想到的事，就是把身上的毛衣留给妹妹。
    1) 八点的火车已经来不及了，但是九点的车还来得及。
    2) 昨天我实在太忙了，来不及给你打电话了。

（三）

27. 绝（不/没）：absolutely, by all means
    ❖ 存妮的死，绝不仅仅给她留下葵绿色的毛衣。
    1) 孩子逃学绝不是一个小问题。

2） 我绝没有看不起这个工作的意思。

28． 不过: merely, no more than
   ❖ 他们谈的不过是通知开会之类的事。
   1） 他不过四十岁，头发就全白了。
   2） 你别生气，他不过是随便说说。

29． 正好: happen to; chance to; as it happens
   ❖ 有一天，她回家晚了，小妹妹对她说："荣树哥来过啦！"正好母亲也刚回来。
   1） 我一觉醒来，正好是12点。
   2） 我去的时候，正好他也在那儿。

30． 委屈: 感到/觉得委屈/ 受了委屈/很委屈   feel wronged
   ❖ 他会觉得奇怪，觉得委屈吗?
   1） 他工作很努力，但是老板对他没有任何好感，他觉得很委屈。
   2） 他在单位里受了委屈，回到家里就跟太太发脾气。

31． 随（人）.v: let sb. do as he likes
   ❖ 随他去吧！谁让他是一个男人呢！
   1） 随你怎么说，反正我不去。
   2） 自助餐随你怎么吃都那么多钱。

32． 真不知天高地厚: don't know the complexity of things
   ❖ 荣树这孩子真不知天高地厚，又跟副书记吵起来了！
   1） 你呀! 真不知道天高地厚，居然想找警察的麻烦!
   2） 像他那样不知天高地厚的人，什么事情也干不成。

33． 接着: follow, carry on, next
   ❖ 接着,她又后悔起来。
   1） 快考试了，学生一个接着一个地问问题。
   2） 请你接着他的话继续讲。

34． v.着 v.着: as one is v.-ing
   ❖ 听着听着，热情奔放的歌声感染了她。
   1） 说着说着，她不禁流下眼泪来。
   2） 走着走着，他发现已经快到车站了。

35. 什么也谈不上：to be in no position to talk about anything
    ❖ 不富裕起来，一辈子过着穷日子，就什么也谈不上！
    1) 要是不上大学，那就什么也谈不上！
    2) 你连自己也养不起，那什么也谈不上！

36. 就拿……来说吧！take …for example
    ❖ 就拿小豹子来说吧，能全怪他吗？
    1) 找工作可不容易。就拿我来说吧，毕业以后，足足过了半年才找到工作。
    2) 大学学费很高。就拿普大来说吧，一年得花四万多块钱。

37. 弄得（人）……：cause (sb.) to become
    ❖ 她竭力忍住快要流出来的眼泪，猛地冲上山顶，放开大步向下奔去，弄得荣树莫名其妙。
    1) 他的话莫名其妙，弄得我糊里糊涂。
    2) 他公然地这么说，弄得我很不好意思。

（四）

38. 直 v.：v continuously
    ❖ 她浑身颤抖，耳边嗡嗡直响，什么也听不清了。
    1) 他听了那些话，气得直哭。
    2) 他兴奋极了，直说个没完。

39. 又：（used in a negative sentence to intensify the tone）
    ❖ 又不是现在就要你过门！
    1) 我又没说是你不对，你生什么气！
    2) 他又没兴趣，何必跟他谈呢！

40. 有的是：have plenty of
    ❖ 她有的是冲破封建枷锁的勇气。
    1) 她有的是钱。
    2) 三条腿的狗没有，两条腿的人有的是。

41. 凭：base on, take as the basis
    ❖ 只凭她这一句话，工作组就给他们一张印着毛主席像的结婚证。
    1) 就凭她的努力也应该考上大学。
    2) 所有的人都应该凭票上车。

42. 万万想不到：It is unthinkable/unfathomable…

    ❖ 万万想不到，时隔三十年的今天，女儿竟用这句话来骂自己了。

    1) 我万万想不到，他会欺骗父母。

    2) 万万想不到，这个月股票跌得这么厉害。

43. 照样：still, as before

    ❖ 今天这，明天那！见多了！见够了！俺们不照样还是穷！

    1) 他天天都在街上跑步，就是下雨也照样跑。

    2) 现在他虽然有工作了，但是还是照样没钱。

44. 当初：originally, at that time

    ❖ 你妈悔不该当初。

    1) 深圳当初是一个小镇，现在变成一个现代化的大城市了。

    2) 我当初要是学医就好了。

练习

I. 选择适当的成语填空：

   1. 2003 年中国人登上太空是 _____（开天辟地，习以为常，平淡无奇）的一件大事，中国人都觉得非常骄傲。

   2. 听到中国队得了冠军的好消息，大家都_____（七嘴八舌，莫名其妙，不约而同）地欢呼起来。

   3. 退休以后，她还像以前那样 _____（平淡无奇，不约而同，一如既往）地早睡早起，看书看报。

   4. 年轻人觉得是_____（习以为常，不约而同，一如既往）的事，老年人往往看不惯。

   5. 考上大学人人都很高兴，但是她却_____（莫名其妙，不约而同，神采飞扬）地哭了起来。

   6. 听到别人唱歌，这个喜欢唱歌的人也_____（不由自主，七嘴八舌，不约而同）地唱了起来。

   7. 这本来是一件_____（平淡无奇，默默无闻，莫名其妙）的事情，可是经她一说却十分有意思。

   8. 对于考上名牌大学，我从来不抱任何希望，只要能考上普通的大学我就_____(心满意足，神采飞扬，烟消云散)了。

   9. 她穿的衣服_____，（与众不同，一如既往，平淡无奇），所以，马上引起了大家的注意。

   10. 在小摊儿上买东西，你一定得_____，（讨价还价，有增无减，烟消云散）否则一定会吃亏的。

II. 选择适当的词语填空：

1. 出车祸的时候，她的脑子里一片_____（茫然，坦然，断然），根本不知道该怎么办。
2. 考上大学非常不容易，但是她却_____（断然，了然，颓然）放弃了上大学的机会，决定做别的事。
3. 听了别人对她的攻击，她的心里_____（陡然，坦然，木然）升起巨大的愤怒。
4. 警察让他停车，他却_____（公然，木然，了然）动手打警察。
5. 他_____（坦然，猛然，断然）承认了自己的错误。
6. 昨天本来天气很好，可是_____（坦然，突然，茫然）下起了大雨，很多人都被淋湿了。

III. 读下面的句子，然后用划线的部分造句：

1. 尽管已经是70年代的最后一年，在他们的心目中，爱情，还是一个陌生的，神秘的羞于出口的字眼。
2. 那时候，包括队长在内的所有的社员，都深信"天堂"不过咫尺之遥。
3. 他们只需要毫不痛惜地把集体的山梨树，连同房前屋后的白果，板栗统统锯倒，连夜送到钢厂。
4. 也许得力于怀胎和哺乳时的营养吧，存妮终于泼泼辣辣地长大了。
5. 跟老头干活，虽然轻巧，却远不如在水库和年轻伙伴一起挑土来得热闹。
6. 九队的社员们几乎都没有这种眼福，至于乘火车，那只有外号叫瞎子的许会计才有过这样令人羡慕的经历。
7. 过去，这里还兴唱山歌儿，如今早已属于"黄色"之列，不许唱了。
8. 原来姑娘脱毛衣时掀起衬衫，竟露出半截白皙的、丰美而富有弹性的乳房……
9. 千万别难为孩子家，防备着她想不开！
10. 散会后，荒妹怀着沉重的心情走出公社礼堂的大门。
11. 那是反封建的烈火已经把"父母之命，媒妁之言"连同地主的地契一起烧毁的年代。
12. 不需要任何别的，只凭她这一句话！土改工作队就发给他们一人一张印着毛主席像的结婚证。

IV. 用下列词语回答问题：

1. 存妮跟小豹子相爱以后，她有什么变化？为什么有这样的变化？
    （毫无顾忌，泼辣，无忧无虑；发呆，苍白，红晕，抹泪）

2. 小豹子和存妮干完活儿休息的时候，小豹子突然对存妮有一种什么样
    的感觉？
    （浮起，异样，从未体验过，痒丝丝，激动，害怕，热辣辣，
    直勾勾，呼吸，停止，热血，猛冲，失去理智）

3. 存妮和小豹子之间的爱情是怎样产生的？为什么全村的人都觉得
    他们之间的爱情是可耻的？
    （物质贫乏，精神荒芜，除了……以外，没有什么可v.的，
    体魄健壮，盲目冲动，原始本能，"父母之命，媒妁之言"）

4. 存妮为什么要自杀？她的死是为了解脱她自己还是为了反抗旧的封
    建传统？你怎么看她的死？
    （想不开，丢人，带来灾难；老封建，村民，吵嚷，哄笑，
    打骂，诅咒，洗净耻辱和罪恶，落后，没知识，轻易，没有价值）

5. 存妮的死对荒妹有什么影响？
    （在心灵上，留下，无法摆脱，耻辱和恐惧，承受，精神重压，憎恨，
    戒备，冷淡，鄙视，难以接近，孤僻）

6. 荒妹对荣树的感情是什么样的？
    （矛盾，甜丝丝的柔情，惶恐；隐约希望，保持距离；
    不由自主，想念，气他，恨他，不睬他；交替变化）

7. 山里人习以为常的婚姻是什么样的？你怎样看这样的婚姻？
    （买办婚姻，亲戚，送东西，讨价还价，达成协定，见面，腼腆，窘，
    满脸通红，不敢正视，合影，选日子，结婚）

8. 母亲菱花在这三十年间有什么变化？她为什么要荒妹做一件自己三
    十年前抗争过的事情？
    （有的是，冲破封建枷锁的勇气，不要……而要，嫁给憨厚，英俊的
    穷小子，贫困，吃不饱，空的，后悔,当初）

9. 荒妹跟存妮有什么不同？她的未来会是怎么样？

（默默承受重担，倔强，聪明，成熟，深信不移，追求）

10. 在这三十年里，存妮的家庭发生了一些什么变化？这种变化说明了
    什么？
    （存钱，办酒席，自给有余，浑身都是劲儿，充满信心；讨饭，
    浮肿，超支，欠款，衰老，发愣，愁苦，倔强，成熟，大地回春，
    拭干，爱情，被遗忘的角落）

V. 讨论问题：

1. 存妮、荒妹这两个名字反映了怎样的中国历史变迁？
2. 传统的礼教、理性、尊严对母亲、存妮、荒妹有哪些不同的影响？
3. 物质基础和感情基础是维持幸福婚姻的两个必要条件，你同意这个看
   法吗？母亲为什么后悔她的婚姻？传统的农村人的婚姻又有哪些不
   幸？
4. 你认为荒妹和许荣树的将来是怎么样的？他们的奋斗会成功吗？
5. 这是不是一篇好的小说？它的特点在哪里？

本次列车终点

王安忆

一

"前方到站，是本次列车终点站——上海……"

"上海到了。"打瞌睡的人睁开了眼睛。

"到终点站了。"急性子的人脱了鞋，站在椅子上取行李了。

那伙从新疆来的中年人开始制定活动方案："找到旅社，首先洗澡。打电话去重型机械厂联系。然后——吃西餐！"

"对，吃西餐！"他们全都兴奋起来。这伙人，是从全国各地大学毕业后去到新疆的，有北京人，有福州人，有江苏人。虽然说话还保持着乡音，可从外表到性格却都像新疆人了：皮肤粗糙，性格豪放。陈信随意问问他们新疆的情况，他们便兴致勃勃地大谈起来：新疆各个民族是多么风趣，那里的歌儿多么好听，舞多么好看，小姑娘多么活泼。他们谈锋很健，说得

列车	lièchē	*n.*	train
终点	zhōngdiǎn	*n.*	terminal point; destination
前方	qiánfāng	*n.*	the place ahead
终点站	zhōngdiǎn zhàn	*n.*	terminus
打瞌睡	dǎ kēshuì	*v.-o.*	doze off; nod; fall into a doze
睁开	zhēngkāi	*v.-c.*	open (eyes)

Selected & edited by Joanne Chiang
Prepared by Joanne Chiang

急性子	jíxìng.zi	*adj.*	of impatient disposition; impetuous
行李	xíng.li	*n.*	luggage; baggage
伙	huǒ	*AN.*	measure word for group; crowd; band 一伙工人/一伙中学生
新疆	Xīnjiāng	*n.*	Xinjiang Province, in the northeast part of China
制定	zhìdìng	*v.*	draw up; formulate; draft
活动	huódòng	*n.*	activity
方案	fāng'àn	*n.*	scheme; plan
旅社	lǚshè	*n.*	hotel; hostel
重型机械厂	zhòngxíng jīxièchǎng	*n.*	heavy-duty machinery factory
联系	liánxì	*v.*	contact; touch 我常用电子邮件跟父母联系。
西餐	xīcān	*n.*	Western-style food or meal
福州	Fúzhōu	*n*	Fuzhou, capital of Fujian Province
江苏	Jiāngsū	*n.*	Jiangsu Province
乡音	xiāngyīn	*n.*	accent of one's native place
外表	wàibiǎo	*n.*	outward appearance
性格	xìnggé	*n.*	nature; disposition
皮肤	pífū	*n.*	skin
粗糙	cūcāo	*adj.*	(of skin) rough
豪放	háofàng	*adj.*	bold and uninhibited
陈信	Chén Xìn	*n.*	personal name
随意	suíyì	*adv.*	casually; randomly; informally
兴致勃勃	xìngzhìbóbó	*adj.*	be in the best of spirits; be in high spirits
风趣	fēngqù	*adj.*	witty and humorous
小姑娘	xiǎo gū.niang	*n.*	young girl
活泼	huópō	*adj.*	lively; vivacious
谈锋很健	tánfēng hěn jiàn	*phr.*	in high spirits to talk

十分有趣。

"小伙子，在上海呆多少时间哪？"其中的北京人拍拍陈信的肩膀。

陈信正对着窗外出神，回过头笑了："这次来，就不回去了。"

"调回来了？"

"调回来了。"

"老婆孩子呢？"

"哪儿有啊！"陈信红红脸，"要有还⑴能回来？"

"真有决心。"他又重重地拍了拍陈信的肩，"你们上海人，离了上海就活不了。"

"上海是我们的故乡呀！"他说。

"可除了故乡外，还有个很大的世界呢！"

陈信不说话，笑笑。

"人，要善于⑵从各种各样的生活里吸取乐趣。到哈尔滨，就溜冰；到广州，就游泳；去新疆，吃抓羊肉；去上海，吃西餐……命运把你安排在哪里，你就把哪里的欢乐发掘出来，尽情享受。这就是人生的乐趣啊！"

陈信仍然是笑笑。他心不在焉的，眼睛看着窗外疾速掠过的

小伙子	xiǎohuǒ.zi	*n.*	(informal) young man; lad
呆	dāi	*v.*	same as 待，stay
拍	pāi	*v.*	clap; pat; beat
肩膀	jiānbǎng	*n.*	shoulder

出神	chūshén	v.-o.	be in a trance; be lost in thought
回头	huítóu	v.-o.	turn one's head; turn around
调回来	diào huí.lai	v.-c.	be transfered back
老婆	lǎo.po	n.	(informal) wife
红脸	hóngliǎn	v.-o.	blush
有决心	yǒu juéxīn	v.-o.	be resolute; be determined 他是个很有决心的人。
故乡	gùxiāng	n.	native place; hometown
善于	shànyú	v.	be good at; be adept in 善于分析问题/ 善于解决问题
吸取	xīqǔ	v.	absorb; draw 吸取经验/ 吸取先进技术
乐趣	lèqù	n.	delight; pleasure; joy
哈尔滨	Hā'ěrbīn	n.	Harbin, capital of Heilongjiang Province
溜冰	liūbīng	v.-o.	skate; skating
广州	Guǎngzhōu	n.	Guangzhou, capital of Guangdong Province
游泳	yóuyǒng	v.-o.	swim
抓羊肉	zhuā yángròu	n.	a famous dish made of mutton 抓：grab (with hands)
命运	mìngyùn	n.	destiny; fate
安排	ānpái	v.	arrange; plan; settle
欢乐	huānlè	n.	happy; joy
发掘	fājué	v.	scout for; excavate; unearth; explore
尽情	jìnqíng	adv.	to one's heart's content; as much as one likes 尽情发挥/ 尽情表现
人生	rénshēng	n.	life
心不在焉	xīnbúzàiyān	idm.	be absent-minded
疾速	jísù	adv.	fast; quick; with high-speed
掠过	lüèguò	v.	sweep past; fly past 飞机从上空掠过。

田野。那是被细心分割成一小块一小块，绣花似的⑶织上庄稼的田野，一片黄，一片青，一片绿。土地的利用率真高，并且划分得那么精致细巧。看惯北方一望无际辽阔的沃土的眼睛，会觉得有点狭隘和拥挤，可也不得不承认，这里的一切像是水洗过似的清新、秀丽。这就是江南，这就是上海的郊外。哦，上海！

二

火车驶过田野，驶进矮矮的围墙，进市区了。工厂、楼房、街道、公共汽车、行人……。上海，越来越近，越来越具体了。陈信的心，怦怦地跳动起来。十年前，他从这里离开，上海越来越远越来越渺茫的时候，他何曾⑷想过回来。似乎没有想，可又似乎是想的。在农村，他拉犁，收麦，挖河，……后来终于上了师范专科学校，毕业了，分到那个地方的一所中学。

田野	tiányě	*n.*	field; open country
细心	xìxīn	*adv.*	carefully; attentively
分割	fēn gē	*v.*	cut apart; break up
绣花	xiùhuā	*v.-o.*	embroider; do embroidery
n./pron./v. 似的	shì.de	*part.*	(used after a noun, pronoun, or verb to indicate similarity) similar to; like 他说话像女人似的。/他打起呼噜来像打雷似的。
织	zhī	*v.*	knit; weave
庄稼	zhuāng.jia	*n.*	crops
划分	huàfēn	*v.*	divide; partition
精致细巧	jīngzhì xìqiǎo	*adj.*	fine; exquisite; delicate

一望无际	yíwàng wújì	*idm.*	stretch as far as eye can see; a boundless stretch of 一望无际的大海/一望无际的田野
辽阔	liáokuò	*adj.*	vast; extensive
沃土	wòtǔ	*n.*	fertile soil
狭隘	xiá'ài	*adj.*	narrow
拥挤	yōngjǐ	*adj.*	crowded
承认	chéngrèn	*v.*	admit; acknowledge; recognize
清新	qīngxīn	*adj.*	pure and fresh 空气很清新。
秀丽	xiùlì	*adj.*	beautiful; handsome; pretty 风景秀丽/秀丽的山川
江南	Jiāngnán	*n.*	regions south of the Yangtze River, famous for its natural beauty
郊外	jiāowài	*n.*	the countryside around a city; outskirts; suburb
哦	o	*intj.*	oh! (expressing realization, understanding, etc.)
驶	shǐ	*v.*	(of a vehicle, etc.) speed; speed by; drive
围墙	wéiqiáng	*n.*	closure; wall; fence
市区	shìqū	*n.*	downtown area
具体	jùtǐ	*adj.*	concrete; specific
怦怦地	pēngpēng.de	*adv.*	(of the beating of the heart) thump; go pit-a-pat
渺茫	miǎománg	*adj.*	distant and indistinct; vague
何曾	hécéng	*adv.*	did ever (used in rhetorical questions)我何曾说过这样的话！／我何曾不想这么做！
拉犁	lālí	*v.-o.*	pull the plough; plough (the field)
收麦	shōumài	*v.-o.*	harvest the wheat
挖河	wāhé	*v.-o.*	excavate a river
师范专科学校	shīfàn zhuānkē xuéxiào	*n.*	teachers college; teachers training college

应该说有了自食其力的工作，有了归宿，努力可以告终，可以建立新的生活。然而，他却没有找到归宿的安定感，他似乎觉得目的地还没到达。他还在盼望着什么，等待着什么。当"四人帮"打倒后，大批知青回上海的时候，他才意识到自己在等什么，目的地究竟是什么。

十年中，他回过上海，探亲，休假，出差。可每次来上海，却只感到同上海的疏远。他是个外地人，陌生人。上海人多么瞧不起外地人。他受不了上海人那种占绝对优势的神气，受不了那种傲视。而在熟人朋友面前，他也同样地受不了那种怜悯和惋惜。因为在怜悯和惋惜后面，仍然是傲视。他又不得不折服，上海是好，是先进，是优越。百货公司里有最充裕、最丰富的商品；人们穿的是最时髦、最摩登的服饰；饭店的饮食是

自食其力	zìshíqílì	*idm.*	support oneself; earn one's own living
归宿	guīsù	*n.*	destination of one's life voyage
告终	gàozhōng	*v.*	come to an end 这些试验以失败而告终。
安定感	āndìnggǎn	*n.*	sense of stability
目的地	mùdìdì	*n.*	destination
到达	dàodá	*v.*	arrive; get to; reach
盼望	pànwàng	*v.*	hope for; long for
等待	děngdài	*v.*	wait; await
四人帮	Sìrénbāng	*n.*	Gang of Four, the chief culprit of the Great Cultural Revolution
打倒	dǎdǎo	*v.*	overthrow

知青	zhīqīng	*n.*	short for 知识青年，educated youth; school graduates
意识到	yì.shidào	*v.-c.*	be conscious (or aware) of; awake to; realize 事情失败了，他才意识到自己的基本观念都错了。
探亲	tànqīn	*v.-o.*	go home to visit one's family or go to visit one's relatives
休假	xiūjià	*v.-o.*	have a holiday; take a vacation 休了一个星期的假
出差	chūchāi	*v.-o.*	be on a business trip 他出差到北京去了。/出了四天差
同	tóng	*prep.*	with 同他谈谈
疏远	shūyuǎn	*adj.*	drift apart; become estranged
陌生人	mòshēngrén	*n.*	stranger
瞧不起	qiáo.buqǐ	*v.-c.*	same as 看不起；look down upon
占绝对优势	zhàn juéduì yōushì	*phr.*	have an absolute advantage in sth.
神气	shén.qi	*n.*	expression; air; manner
傲视	àoshì	*v.*	turn up one's nose at; show disdain for
熟人	shúrén	*n.*	a familiar face; friend
怜悯	liánmǐn	*v.*	take pity on; have compassion for
惋惜	wǎnxī	*adj.*	feel sorry for sb. or about sth.; have pity for
折服	zhéfú	*v.*	be convinced; be filled with admiration
先进	xiānjìn	*adj.*	advanced
优越	yōuyuè	*adj.*	superior; advantageous 条件很优越/ 处于优越的地位
充裕	chōngyù	*adj.*	abundant; ample
时髦	shímáo	*adj.*	fashionable; stylish
摩登	módēng	*adj.*	modern; fashionable
服饰	fúshì	*n.*	dress and personal adornment

最清洁、最讲究的；电影院里上映的是最新的片子。上海，似乎代表着中国文化生活的时代新潮流。更何况⑸，在这里有着他的家，妈妈、哥哥、弟弟、爸爸的亡灵……他噙着眼泪微笑了。为了归来，他什么都可以牺牲，都可以放弃。于是，一听说妈妈要退休，他立即行动起来，首先是要恢复知识青年的身份，至于上学、工作这一段历史，不要了，抹去吧！……反正⑹，他打了一仗，紧张而激烈，却是胜利了。

火车进站了，他把窗户推上去，他看见了弟弟。小家伙长大了，长得真高，真好看。弟弟也看见了他，跟着火车跑着，笑着叫："二哥！"他的心不由⑺缩了一下，升起了一丝歉意。可他立即想起十年前，火车开动时，哥哥这么追着火车，给他送行，他的心又平静了。

三

车停了，弟弟气喘吁吁地追上来了。

"大哥、大嫂和囡囡都来了，在外头。二哥，你东西多吗？"

"能对付，姆妈好吧？"

清洁	qīngjié	*adj.*	clean
讲究	jiǎng.jiu	*adj.*	exquisite; tasteful; particular
上映	shàngyìng	*v.*	show (a film); screen; be on 这部电影已经上映五天了。
片子	piān.zi	*n.*	film; movie
潮流	cháoliú	*n.*	trend
何况	hékuàng	*conj.*	moreover; besides; in addition

亡灵	wánglíng	*n.*	the soul of a deceased person
噙着眼泪	qín.zhe yǎnlèi	*v.-o.*	with tears in one's eyes
微笑	wēixiào	*v.*	smile
归来	guīlái	*v.*	return; come back
牺牲	xīshēng	*v.*	sacrifice
放弃	fàngqì	*v.*	give up; abandon
退休	tuìxiū	*v.*	retire
立即	lìjí	*adv.*	immediately; right away
行动起来	xíngdòng qǐlái	*v.-c.*	go into action
恢复	huīfù	*v.*	reinstate
身份	shēnfèn	*n.*	status; capacity; identity
抹去	mǒqù	*v.-c.*	wipe
反正	fǎnzhèng	*adv.*	anyway; anyhow
胜利	shènglì	*v.*	win; triumph
小家伙	xiǎo jiā.huo	*n.*	(informal) little chap; kid
不由	bùyóu	*adv.*	can't help; cannot but 她看见父母来了，不由高兴地叫了起来。
缩	suō	*v.*	contract; shrink
升	shēng	*v.*	rise
一丝歉意	yìsī qiànyì	*n.*	a tiny bit feeling of apology/regret
开动	kāidòng	*v.*	move; set in motion
追	zhuī	*v.*	run after; chase after
送行	sòngxíng	*v.*	see sb. off; say good-bye to sb.
平静	píngjìng	*v./adj.*	calm down
气喘吁吁	qìchuǎn xūxū	*adv.*	pant for breath; be short of breath 他气喘吁吁地从外面跑进来。
大嫂	dàsǎo	*n.*	one's eldest brother's wife
囡囡	nānnān	*n.*	(Shanghainese) little darling (used as a term of endearment for a child or a baby)
对付	duì.fu	*v.*	handle; deal with; cope with
姆妈	mǔ.ma	*n.*	(Shanghainese) mother

"还好，她在家里烧饭。今天早上三点钟她就去买菜。"弟弟说。

他还想说什么，可是鼻子酸酸的，嗓子眼儿被什么堵住了。于是便低下头，什么也不说了。他不说，弟弟也不说了。

他们这样默默地走过长长的站台，哥哥、嫂嫂、囡囡都在出口处等着，一拥而上抢走他的东西，可走了没几步便又还给了他，因为太重了。大家都笑了起来。大哥搂住他的肩膀，弟弟勾住他的胳膊。

"手续都齐了？"大哥问，"明天我请假陪你去劳动局。"

"我陪二哥去好了，我没事。"弟弟说。

陈信的心又是微微一动，他回头看看弟弟，微笑着说："好的，阿三陪我。"

转了两辆公共汽车，到家了。一进门，妈妈叫了声："阿信。"便低下头抹眼泪。三个儿子不知怎么安慰她，心中空有千种温情，无奈⑧不会表达，也不好意思表达。只是看着她，轮流地说："这有什么好哭的？这有什么好哭的？"

"吃饭，吃饭。"大家互相招呼着。饭桌临时从妈妈住的六平方米小间搬到了哥哥嫂嫂的大房间。陈信环视了一下房

烧饭	shāofàn	v.-o.	do the cooking; prepare a meal
鼻子酸酸的	bí.zi suānsuān.de	phr.	have a sting in the nose; feel like crying
嗓子眼儿	sǎng.zi yǎnr	n.	throat
堵住	dǔzhù	v.-c.	block up

默默地	mòmò.de	*adv.*	quietly; silently 他默默地坐着听大家辩论。
站台	zhàntái	*n.*	platform (in a railway station)
出口处	chūkǒuchù	*n.*	exit
一拥而上	yì yōng érshàng	*v.*	come forth with a rush; dash up
搂住	lǒuzhù	*v.-c.*	hug; embrace; cuddle
勾住	gōuzhù	*v.-c.*	secure with a hook; hook
胳膊	gē.bo	*n.*	arm
手续	shǒuxù	*n.*	procedures; formalities
齐	qí	*adj.*	all ready, all present; (here) complete; all done
请假	qǐngjià	*v.-o.*	ask for leave　请三天假
陪	péi	*v.*	accompany; keep sb. company
劳动局	Láodòngjú	*n.*	Labor Bureau
微微	wēiwēi	*adv.*	slightly; faintly
阿信	Ā Xìn	*n.*	陈信. In southern China, a mother usually calls her son using a prefix 阿 and one word of the name, such as 阿信，阿仿（陈信的哥哥）
安慰	ānwèi	*v.*	comfort; console
空有千种温情	kōngyǒu qiānzhǒng wēnqíng	*phr.*	cherishing tender feelings but unable to express in words
无奈	wúnài	*adv.*	but; however 我很想帮你们的忙，无奈实在没有时间。
表达	biǎodá	*v.*	express; convey; voice
轮流	lúnliú	*adv./v.*	do sth. in turn; take turns 轮流打扫房间/轮流烧饭
招呼	zhāo.hu	*v.*	notify; tell
临时	línshí	*adv./ adj.*	temporarily; at the last minute
平方米	píngfāngmǐ	*n.*	square meter
环视	huánshì	*v.*	look around

间，见这间以前他们三兄弟合住的屋子变了许多。墙上贴着淡绿的贴墙布，装饰着壁灯、油画。新添的一套家具十分漂亮。囡囡把个凳子搬到五斗橱前头，爬上去，熟练地按了一下录音机的键，屋子里立刻充满了节奏强烈的乐曲，把人的情绪一下子激起来了。

"生活得不错！"陈信兴奋地说。

大哥抱歉似的笑着，半天才答非所问地说："好了，你总算(9)回来了。"

嫂嫂端了菜进来，笑着说："回来了，该找对象结婚了。"

"嗨！我这把年纪，长得又丑，谁要我？"陈信说。

大家都笑了。

桌子上已经满满地摆了十几样菜：肉丁花生，酱排骨，鲫鱼汤……大家都给陈信夹菜，陈信碟子里的菜堆成了一座山，大家还是接连不断地夹菜，似乎为了补偿老二在外十年的艰辛。尤其是大哥，几乎把那碗阿信最爱吃的炒鳝丝扣在他盘子里。

淡绿	dànlǜ	n.	light green
装饰	zhuāngshì	v.	decorate; adorn
壁灯	bìdēng	n.	bracket light; wall lamp
油画	yóuhuà	n.	oil painting
添	tiān	v.	add
家具	jiājù	n.	furniture
凳子	dèng.zi	n.	stool
五斗橱	wǔdǒuchú	n.	chest of drawers
熟练	shúliàn	adj./adv.	skillful, skillfully

按	àn	*v.*	press; push down
键	jiàn	*n.*	key
节奏	jiézòu	*n.*	rhythm
强烈	qiángliè	*adj.*	strong; intense
情绪	qíngxù	*n.*	mood; feeling; sentiments
激起来	jī qǐlái	*v.-c.*	arouse; stimulate; excite
抱歉	bàoqiàn	*adj.*	apologetic
答非所问	dáfēisuǒwèn	*idm.*	give an irrelevant answer
总算	zǒngsuàn	*adv.*	at long last; finally 他想来想去，总算想出了一个好办法。
端	duān	*v.*	hold sth. level with both hands; carry
对象	duìxiàng	*n.*	marriage partner; prospective spouse
嗨	hāi	*intj.*	hi! (expressing sadness, regret or surprise)
这把年纪	zhèibǎniánjì	*phr.*	at such an (old) age
丑	chǒu	*adj.*	ugly
肉丁花生	ròudīng huāshēng	*n.*	diced pork and peanut
酱排骨	jiàng páigǔ	*n.*	spareribs cooked in soy sauce
鲫鱼汤	jìyú tāng	*n.*	crucian carp soup
夹菜	jiācài	*v.-o.*	pick up food with chopsticks
碟子	dié.zi	*n.*	small dish; saucer
堆	duī	*v.*	pile up; heap up
座	zuò	*AN.*	measure word for mountain, bridge, etc.
接连不断	jiēlián búduàn	*adv.*	continuously; incessantly
补偿	bǔcháng	*v.*	compensate; make up for
艰辛	jiānxīn	*n.*	hardships
炒鳝丝	chǎo shànsī	*n.*	fried shredded eel
扣	kòu	*v.*	pour; dump

他虽然要比陈信大三岁，可从来都受着弟弟的保护。他长得又高又细，小时候，外号叫"长豇豆"。功课虽然很好，玩起来却十分笨拙。跳长绳，绳到他脚下必定绊住；官兵捉强盗，有他的那方必定要输。因此，伙伴们都不要他一起玩。阿信就不答应了，他说："哥哥要不来，我也不来。我不来就要和你们捣蛋。"大家一则怕他捣蛋，二则⑩，少了他这个挺会玩挺会闹的角色，也的确有点可惜，于是就妥协了。后来，哥哥眼睛近视了，配了副眼镜，样子更像老夫子，外号便叫做"书呆子"。再后来，到了"文化大革命"，初中毕业的他和高中毕业的哥哥，同时面临分配。政策很明确，两丁抽一。这愁坏了妈妈，妈妈流着眼泪直说："手心手背，唉，这手心手背……"陈信看不下去了，说："我去插队。哥哥老实，出去要吃亏的。让哥哥留上海，我去！"他去了，哥哥送他，傻乎乎地站在送行的人群外边，一句话也不说，眼睛也不敢看他。

细	xì	adj.	thin; slender
外号	wàihào	n.	nickname
长豇豆	cháng jiāngdòu	n.	asparagus bean
笨拙	bènzhuó	adj.	clumsy
跳长绳	tiào chángshéng	v.-o.	rope skipping
绊住	bàn.zhu	v.-c.	be stumbled; be tripped
官兵捉强盗	guānbīng zhuō qiángdào	n.	the soldiers catch the bandits - a game played by children
输	shū	v.	lose; be beaten 我们输了。
伙伴	huǒbàn	n.	partner; mate

答应	dāyìng	v.	agree; consent
捣蛋	dǎodàn	v.	make trouble; do mischief 他上课时总是捣蛋，所以老师很生气。
角色	juésè	n.	role; part
妥协	tuǒxié	v.	compromise; come to terms
近视	jìnshì	v.	get nearsighted
配眼镜	pèi yǎnjìng	v.	have one's eyesight tested for glasses
副	fù	AN.	measure word for something in a pair such as glasses, gloves, etc.
老夫子	lǎofūzǐ	n.	unpractical old scholar
书呆子	shūdāi.zi	n.	bookworm; bookish
分配	fēnpèi	n / v.	job assignment on graduation, assign
明确	míngquè	adj.	clear and definite
两丁抽一	liǎngdīngchōu yī	phr.	draw one from every two men
愁坏	chóuhuài	v.-c.	seriously worry sb.
唉	āi	intj.	alas (expressing sadness, weariness, regret or disappointment)
手心手背	shǒuxīn shǒubèi	n.	手心: palm. 手背: the back of the hand A Chinese saying: 手心手背都是肉, meaning that both the elder and the younger are mother's sons – the mother is reluctant to let either one suffer
插队	chāduì	v.-o.	(a school graduate) be sent to live and work in the countryside as a member of a production team for a number of years (a practice during the 1960's and 1970's)
老实	lǎo.shi	adj.	modest; easily taken in
吃亏	chīkuī	v.-o.	suffer losses; to get picked on
傻乎乎地	shǎhūhū.de	adv.	simple-mindedly; silly; stupidly
人群	rénqún	n.	crowd; throng; multitude

当火车开动的时候，他却挤上前，抓住陈信的手，跟着火车跑。火车把他的手拉开了，他还跟着火车跑。现在，他终于回来了，彼此都有一肚子的感慨。可陈家兄弟是很不善于表达感情的，所有的情感都表现在具体的行动上。吃过饭，哥哥立即泡来了茶，嫂嫂去天井里的"违章建筑"为他整理床铺，弟弟到浴室帮他排队……。当他酒足饭饱，洗了个热水澡，躺在"违章建筑"那张同弟弟合睡的大床上时，他感到舒适得像醉了。干净暖和的被子发出一种好闻的气息，床头写字台上开着台灯，枕边有一叠期刊，不知是谁放的，反正家里人都知道陈信睡觉要靠小说催眠的。家，这就是家。他，漂流十年终于到家了。他感到一阵从未有过的安心，没有看书便合上眼睛睡着了。

　　一早就出门，去劳动局办手续，弟弟陪他一起去。车来了，弟弟挤进上车的人群里，回头叫他："二哥，快来！"

"等下一部吧。"陈信望着挤得满满的车厢和站上拥挤的人，犹豫着说。

"越往后越挤，上吧！"弟弟的声音像从很远的地方传来的。

挤吧，力气他是有的。他推开人，使劲往里钻，好容易⑾抓住

抓住	zhuāzhù	v.-c.	grab; seize; grasp
彼此	bǐcǐ	pron.	each other; one another
感慨	gǎnkǎi	v./n.	sigh with emotion, emotion
兄弟	xiōngdì	n.	brothers

具体	jùtǐ	*adj.*	concrete; specific; particular
泡茶	pàochá	*v.-o.*	make tea
天井	tiānjǐng	*n.*	small yard; courtyard
违章建筑	wéizhāng jiànzhù	*n.*	illegal building
床铺	chuángpù	*n.*	bedding
酒足饭饱	jiǔzú fànbǎo	*v.*	have dined and wined to one's heart's content
躺	tǎng	*v.*	lie; recline 躺在床上
醉	zuì	*v.*	become drunk
暖和	nuǎn.huo	*adj.*	warm; nice and warm
被子	bèi.zi	*n.*	quilt
好闻	hǎowén	*adj.*	pleasant to smell
气息	qìxī	*n.*	flavor; smell
床头	chuángtóu	*n.*	bedside
台灯	táidēng	*n.*	desk lamp; table lamp
枕	zhěn	*n.*	pillow
叠	dié	*AN.*	a pile of
期刊	qīkān	*n.*	journals; periodicals
催眠	cuīmián	*v.*	mesmerize; lull (to sleep)
漂流	piāoliú	*v.*	lead a wandering life; drift
阵	zhèn	*AN.*	a burst of; a fit of
安心	ānxīn	*adj.*	feel at ease; be relieved
望	wàng	*v.*	look; gaze
车厢	chēxiāng	*n.*	compartment; car
犹豫	yóuyù	*v.*	hesitate
传	chuán	*v.*	spread
力气	lìqì	*n.*	physical strength
使劲	shǐjìn	*v.*	exert all one's strength
钻	zuān	*v.*	go through; get into
好容易	hǎo róngyì	*adv.*	with great difficulty 我好容易才找到她，她却不肯帮我的忙。

了车门的栏杆上了车，又在一片哇哇乱叫声中挤到了窗口座位旁边。然而他感到十分不舒服，怎么站都站不好，一会儿碰前边人的头，一会儿碰后边人的腰。周围的乘客纷纷埋怨起来：

"你这人怎么站的！"

"外地人挤车子真是笨！"

"谁是外地人？"弟弟挤了过来，他十分愤怒，眼看着⑫要和人家吵起来了。

陈信赶紧拉住他："算了算了，挤成这样子还吵什么。"

弟弟轻声说："二哥，你这样：朝这边侧着身子。哎，对了对了，左手拉把手，这样就好了，是吧？"

确实好了许多，陈信吁了一口气，总算找到了个安定的位置。虽然还是挤，但究竟能站稳脚了。他扭头看看，见人们像是有个默契，全都向左侧着身子，一个紧挨一个。这种方法确实足以使车厢容纳量达到最大限度。上海人是十分善于在狭小的空间内生活的。

栏杆	lángān	n.	handrail; railing
哇哇乱叫	wāwā luànjiào	v.	cry out loudly
腰	yāo	n.	waist
周围	zhōuwéi	adj./n.	surrounding
乘客	chéngkè	n.	passenger
纷纷	fēnfēn	adv.	one after another; in succession
埋怨	mányuàn	v.	complain; blame; grumble

愤怒	fènnù	adj.	indignant; angry
笨	bèn	adj.	stupid
眼看着	yǎn kàn.zhe	adv.	soon; in a moment　眼看着要下雨了，我们快回家吧！
赶紧	gǎnjǐn	adv.	lose no time; hasten 考试的时间快到了，他赶紧跑到教室去。
拉住	lāzhù	v.-c.	stop sb. from doing sth. by pulling him back
朝	cháo	prep.	to; towards　朝外头看；朝里头走
哎	āi	intj.	(here): ya!ya!　(showing agreement)
侧着身子	cè.zhe shēn.zi	phr.	turning to one side
把手	bǎshǒu	n.	handle; holder
吁了一口气	xū.le yìkǒuqì	phr.	sigh (with a relief)
安定	āndìng	adj.	stable; settled
位置	wèi.zhi	n.	place; seat; location
究竟	jiūjìng	adv.	after all; finally
站稳脚	zhànwěnjiǎo	v.-o.	stand (or hold) one's ground
扭头	niǔtóu	v.-o.	turn one's head (to look over one's shoulder)　他一扭头，看见警察就站在他后头。
默契	mòqì	n.	tacit understanding; tacit agreement
紧挨	jǐn āi	v.	be closely next to
足以	zúyǐ	v.	be enough to; be sufficient to　这件事足以证明我是对的。
容纳量	róngnàliàng	n.	capacity
最大限度	zuìdà xiàndù	n.	maximum limit
十分	shífēn	adv.	very; fully; extremely 十分兴奋/十分高兴
狭小	xiáxiǎo	adj.	narrow; narrow and small
空间	kōngjiān	n.	space; room

271

下了车，弟弟带他穿过一条街，这街上是个热闹的自由市场，有菜、鱼、鸡、鸭；有羊毛衫、拖鞋、皮包、发夹；有卖小馄饨的，还有卖纸扎的灯笼和泥娃娃的，竖了一块牌子，上面写着"民间玩具"。陈信忍不住笑了，他没想到，大上海也会有这样的"集"。这集市，同前面繁华的现代的南京路相映成趣。

弟弟说："现在上海这种地方可多了，政府还鼓励待业青年自找出路呢！"

一提到待业青年，陈信的眉头不由皱了一下。他停了一会儿问道："阿三，今年你怎么搞的？又没考上学校。"

弟弟低下了头："我也不知怎么搞的，我读书好像很笨。"

"明年你还准备考吧？"

弟弟不说话，沉默了半天嗫嚅了一句："大概也还考不上。"

"你这么没信心还行吗？"陈信有点生气。

弟弟笑着："我读书怎么也读不进，我不是读书的料呀！"

"我和大哥想读书没有读，你有得读却不读。你是我们家唯一可以上大学的，却不争气。"

穿过	chuān.guo	v.-c.	pass through; cross; go through
			穿过马路
热闹	rè.nao	adj.	bustling with noise and excitement; lively
羊毛衫	yángmáo shān	n.	cardigan; woolen sweater

拖鞋	tuōxié	*n.*	slippers
发夹	fàqiǎ	*n.*	hairpin; bobby pin
馄饨	húndùn	*n.*	wonton
纸扎的灯笼	zhǐ zā.de dēng.long	*n.*	lantern made of paper and bamboo
泥娃娃	níwá.wa	*n.*	clay doll
竖	shù	*v.*	set upright ; erect; stand
民间玩具	mínjiān wánjù	*n.*	folk toys
忍不住	rěn.buzhù	*v.*	cannot hold back; cannot stand but to
集市	jíshì	*n.*	country fair; market; fair
繁华	fánhuá	*adj.*	flourishing; prosperous; bustling 最繁华的地区/越来越繁华
相映成趣	xiāngyìng chéngqù	*idm.*	contrast finely with each other; form a delightful contrast 湖边的红叶与湖中的水鸟相映成趣。
待业青年	dàiyè qīngnián	*n.*	young people waiting for job assignments; unemployed youth
自找出路	zìzhǎochūlù	*idm.*	find a way out by oneself
眉头	méitóu	*n.*	eyebrow; brow
皱	zhòu	*v.*	frown; wrinkle up
v. 道	dào		say (the words quoted)：她笑道："你说对了！"
怎么搞的	zěn.me gǎo.de	*phr.*	What have you done? What happened?
沉默	chénmò	*v.*	remain silent
嗫嚅	nièrú	*v.*	speak haltingly
不是读书的料	búshì dúshūde liào	*phr.*	料：makings; (here): sb. who has not got the makings of a scholar
争气	zhēngqì	*v.*	try to make a good showing 这个孩子争气，成绩总是特别好。

弟弟不响。

"你今后有什么打算呢？"

弟弟又笑笑，还是不响。这时，突然听见身后有人叫："陈信！"

回头一看，见是一个三十几岁的年轻女人，手里牵着一个很白很好看的男孩子。她烫着长波浪，穿着很时新。陈信一时想不起是谁了。

"不认识了？我就老成这样了吗？"

"哦，是你，袁小昕！真认不出了，但不是因为老，而是因为漂亮了。"陈信笑了起来。

袁小昕也笑了："真该死！一个集体户共事两年，居然会认不出来！"

"不，我是没想到会在这里遇到你。你不是第一批走的吗？现在还在淮北煤矿？"

"不，去年调回来了。"

"怎么回来的？"

"一言难尽。你呢？"

"我也调回来了，昨天刚到。"

"哦。"她的口气很平静，"张新虎、方芳也都调回来了。"

陈信兴奋地说："太好了！我们一个集体户回来了一大半，什么时候找个时间聚聚。唉，总算熬出头了。"

她没说话，只是淡淡一笑，眼角堆起了许多皱纹。

"舅舅，"忽然那孩子对着陈信发言了，"你头上有白头

不响	bùxiǎng	*v.*	remain silent; without saying a word
牵	qiān	*v.*	lead along (by holding the hand, the halter, etc.); pull 牵着狗散步
烫着长波浪	tàng.zhe cháng bōlàng	*phr.*	with a long wavy perm
时新	shíxīn	*adj.*	stylish; trendy
袁小昕	Yuán Xiǎoxīn	*n.*	personal name
真该死	zhēn gāisǐ	*phr.*	damn it!
集体户	jítǐhù	*n.*	collective household
共事	gòngshì	*v.*	work together (at the same organization)
第一批	dìyīpī	*n.*	the first group
淮北煤矿	Huáiběi méikuàng	*n.*	Huaibei Coal Mine
一言难尽	yìyán nánjìn	*idm.*	It would take too long to tell that in full; hard to explain it all in just a few words 我这几年的经历真是一言难尽。
口气	kǒu.qi	*n.*	tone; manner of speaking
聚	jù	*v.*	gather; get together
熬出头	áo chūtóu	*v.-c.*	go through years of suffering and finally come to an end 找到了工作，苦日子总算熬出头了。
淡淡一笑	dàndàn yíxiào	*v.*	smile indifferently; smile dryly
眼角	yǎnjiǎo	*n.*	the corner of the eye
堆起	duīqǐ	*v.-c.*	pile up; heap up
皱纹	zhòuwén	*n.*	wrinkle
舅舅	jiù.jiu	*n.*	mother's brother; (here): uncle (a polite address to mother's friend)
发言	fāyán	*v.-o.*	speak; make a statement

发，和外公一样的。"

陈信笑了，弯下腰握住孩子的手："儿子？"他问袁小昕。

"是我妹妹的。"她脸红了，赶忙解释，"我还没结婚呢。要结了婚，哪儿能回来。"

"啊！"陈信不由有点儿吃惊，他知道袁小昕是同大哥一届的，有三十三、四岁了吧？

"回来了，怎么还不抓紧解决？"

"怎么说呢，这种事是可遇而不可求的。"

陈信沉默了。

她抚摸着孩子毛茸茸的脑袋，轻声说："有时候，我觉得为了回上海，付出的代价有点不合算了。"

"不要这么说，能回来终究是好的。"陈信安慰她。

"大阿姨，看电影要迟到了。"孩子大声提醒道。

"噢，我们走了。"她抬起头对着陈信笑了，"对不起，扫了你的兴。你和我不一样，你是男的，又年轻，来日方长……会幸福的。"

陈信望着她的背影在人群中消失，心情不由有点沉重。

外公	wàigōng	n.	(maternal) grandfather
弯下腰	wānxiàyāo	v.-o.	bend down
握住	wò.zhu	v.-c.	hold; grasp; take by hand
赶忙	gǎnmáng	adv.	hurriedly; hastily 我看见她的行李那么重，赶忙去帮她拿。

解释	jiěshì	*v.*	explain
吃惊	chījīng	*v.-o.*	be startled; be shocked; be amazed 没想到他来了，我吃了一惊。
同大哥一届	tóng dàgē yí jiè	*phr.*	graduated the same year as his elder brother
抓紧	zhuājǐn	*v.-c.*	firmly grasp; pay close attention to 抓紧学习/ 抓紧解决
可遇而不可求	kěyùérbùkěqiú	*phr.*	sth. that can only be found by accident, and not through seeking
抚摸	fǔmō	*v.*	stroke; fondle
毛茸茸	máoróngróng	*adj.*	hairy; downy 毛茸茸的玩具/毛茸茸的小鸭子
脑袋	nǎo.dai	*n.*	head
合算	hésuàn	*adj.*	worthwhile 花了这么多钱，买了一幅很普通的画儿，太不合算了。
终究	zhōngjiū	*adv.*	in the end; after all 她终究是孩子的母亲，我们得让孩子回到她那儿去。
大阿姨	dà āyí	*n.*	aunt; auntie
提醒	tíxǐng	*v.*	remind
噢	o	*intj.*	oh! (expressing sudden realization)
抬头	táitóu	*v.-o.*	raise one's head
扫兴	sǎoxìng	*v.-o.*	have one's spirits dampened
来日方长	láirìfāngcháng	*idm.*	Many a day will come yet. There is ample time ahead. 来日方长，不必为眼前的失败难过。
背影	bèiyǐng	*n.*	the sight of one's back
消失	xiāoshī	*v.*	disappear; vanish
心情沉重	xīnqíng chénzhòng	*phr.*	with a heavy heart 听说打仗的消息，大家的心情都很沉重。

"三十几岁还没有朋友，没什么希望了。"弟弟说。

"袁小昕并不是找不到，她是有想法的。你没听她说，这是可遇而不可求的。你懂吧？"

不知弟弟是懂了还是没有懂，他不以为然地一笑："反正是个老大难，三十几岁不结婚的男人哪儿有？要么是有缺陷或者条件极差的，要么⑬就是条件极好，要求极高，这种人又是喜欢找年轻漂亮的。"

陈信想说：还有一种情况，是一直没寻找到爱情的。可又一想，这话和阿三说，他未必理解。这一批小青年和他这一代似乎大大两样了。他斜眼瞅瞅弟弟："你可真内行。"

弟弟自负地笑了，这小家伙，连哥哥话里的刺儿都听不出来。陈信又有点儿过意不去，便和缓了口气说："你现在每天的时间是怎样安排的呢？"

"也没什么，反正就是看看电视，听听收音机，睡睡觉。"

"你到底有什么打算呢？"陈信又提出了这个问题。

弟弟不响，一直走到劳动局大楼下，上了台阶，他才说："我蛮想工作的。"

陈信站住了脚，弟弟走了几级台阶回过头来说："走呀！"弟弟的眼睛是坦然而诚恳的，陈信却避开了他的眼睛。

不以为然	bùyǐwéirán	*idm.*	not think it right; disapprovingly
老大难	lǎodànán	*n.*	long-standing, big and difficult (problem)
要么⋯， 要么⋯	yào.me...yào.me...	*conj.*	either...or...
缺陷	quēxiàn	*n.*	defect; fault
寻找	xúnzhǎo	*v.*	seek; look for
未必	wèibì	*adv.*	may not; not necessarily 去过中国的人未必了解中国的情况。
理解	lǐjiě	*v.*	understand
两样	liǎngyàng	*adj.*	different
斜眼瞅瞅	xiéyǎn chǒuchǒu	*v.*	cast a sidelong glance at 瞅：(dialect) look at
内行	nèiháng	*adj.*	be expert at; know the ins and outs of
自负	zìfù	*adj.*	think highly of oneself; be conceited
话里的刺儿	huàlǐ.decìr	*n.*	the sting in one's words 刺：thorn; splinter
过意不去	guòyìbúqù	*v.*	feel apologetic; feel sorry 他自己那么忙，还花时间帮助我，我实在过意不去。
和缓	héhuǎn	*v./adj.*	relieve (the tone)
收音机	shōuyīnjī	*n.*	radio
台阶	táijiē	*n.*	footstep; step
蛮	mán	*adv.*	very; quite; pretty 蛮有意思的
级	jí	*AN.*	measure word for 台阶
坦然	tǎnrán	*adj.*	fully at ease
诚恳	chéngkěn	*adj.*	sincere; earnest
避开	bìkāi	*v.-c.*	avoid; evadc

四

上班了。妈妈的工厂很远，路上需要转三辆汽车，花一小时二十分钟。厂里分配他开车床，这是他从来没接触过的，一切都要从头学起。其实，难的倒并不是车床技术，而是要习惯和适应新的生活、新的节奏。

这里的节奏是快速的——下了第一辆汽车，必须跑步到第二个车站，正好赶上车到站；下了第二辆，又是跑步到第三个站……。三班倒的工作制也是他难以习惯的。一周夜班欠下的觉，下两个星期也还不掉。于是，他老感到睡不够。两个月下来，他的脸已瘦了一圈。不过，人家都说瘦了好，好看了。在外地的那种胖是虚胖，并非健康的象征。

不管怎么样，他总是回上海了，他心满意足。然而，满足之余⑭，有时他却又会感到心里空落落的，像是少了什么。十年中，他那无穷无尽的思念，现在是没有了。这思念叫人好苦，吃不下，睡不着。这思念叫他认准了目标，不屈不挠地为之奋斗；如今没有了，倒真有点不习惯。不过，回上海了，还有什么好说的？好好建立新的生活吧！至于，究竟是什么样的新生活，他尚未正式考虑。因为，一切才刚刚开始呢！

| 转车 | zhuǎnchē | v.-o. | change trains or buses |
| 车床 | chēchuáng | n. | lathe; turning machine |

接触	jiēchù	v.	contact; touch
技术	jì.shu	n.	technology; skill
适应	shì.ying	v.	adapt; get with it; fit
三班倒	sānbāndǎo	n.	works in three-shift rotation 三班：three shifts 倒：rotation
一周	yìzhōu	n.	one week
夜班	yèbān	n.	night shift
欠觉	qiànjiào	v.-o.	have not enough sleep 欠: not enough; lacking, owe (a debt)
还不掉	huán.budiào	v.-c.	cannot repay; be unable to repay; (here): cannot get enough sleep
瘦了一圈	shòu.le yìquānr	phr.	(the face) become smaller because of losing weight 圈：circle
虚胖	xūpàng	n.	puffiness
象征	xiàngzhēng	n.	symbol
心满意足	xīnmǎnyìzú	idm.	to one's heart's content; be fully satisfied and content
……之余	...zhīyú	adj.	in addition to doing…工作之余，他还坚持锻炼身体。
空落落	kōngluòluò	adj.	empty; open and desolate 空落落的院子/ 空落落的房子
无穷无尽	wúqióngwújìn	adj.	endless; boundless; everlasting
思念	sīniàn	v./n.	think of; long for; remember fondly
叫人好苦	jiàorénhǎokǔ	phr.	really give sb. a hard time
认准了目标	rènzhǔn.le mùbiāo	phr.	set one's mind on a target
不屈不挠	bùqūbùnáo	idm.	unyielding;　be unbending in struggle
为之奋斗	wèizhīfèndòu	phr.	strive after it; fight for it
尚未	shàngwèi	adv.	not yet 尚未成功/尚未完全解决

　　这天早班下班了，他拖着两条足足站了八小时的发麻的腿，走出厂门，到了汽车站。车站上人山人海，人行道上站不下了，漫了大半条马路。起码有三辆汽车脱班，才会造成这种局势。他等了十分钟，汽车连影儿都不见，大家牢骚满腹，议论纷纷，估计是出了交通事故。他等得心里发烦，一赌气⑮，转身离开了车站，走吧！走几站路，直接坐第二路汽车。他向前走去，穿过一条弄堂，走上一条路面窄窄的小街。街两边满满地坐着人，有的在洗刷马桶，有的烧饭炒菜，有的织毛线、缝衣服，有的看书、做作业，有的下棋、打乒乓，还有的在铺板上蒙头睡觉……，把小小的街面挤得更窄了。他转头左右看看，两边的屋子像是鸽子笼，又小又矮。从窗口望进去，里面尽是床。床，大的、小的、双层的、折叠的。因此一切娱乐、

早班	zǎobān	n.	morning shift
拖	tuō	v.	pull; drag
足足	zúzú	adv.	fully; as much as 足足用了两个小时/ 足足走了 5 个小时
发麻	fāmá	v.-o.	numb; tingle; have pins and needles
人山人海	rénshānrénhǎi	idm.	crowds of people; a sea of people
人行道	rénxíngdào	n.	side pavement; sidewalk
漫	màn	v.	overflow; brim over
起码	qǐmǎ	adv.	at least 参加考试的起码有三千人。
脱班	tuōbān	v.-o.	(of a bus, train, etc.) be behind schedule

局势	júshì	n.	situation
连影儿都不见	lián yǐngr dōu bújiàn	phr.	even cannot see the shadow of it – nothing can be seen 我等了她三个钟头，可她连影儿都不见。
牢骚满腹	láosāomǎnfù	phr.	be full of complaints 牢骚：complaint; grumble 腹：belly (of the body)
议论纷纷	yìlùnfēnfēn	phr.	discuss animatedly; give rise to much discussion
估计	gū.ji	v.	estimate; assess
交通事故	jiāotōng shìgù	n.	traffic accident
心里发烦	xīn.li fāfán	phr.	be vexed; be perturbed 他怎么做都做不好，免不了心里发烦。
赌气	dǔqì	v.	feel wronged and act rashly 他一赌气,连饭都不吃就走了。/这么一件小事，不值得你赌那么大的气。
弄堂	nòngtáng	n.	lane; alley
窄	zhǎi	adj.	narrow
洗刷	xǐshuā	v.	wash and brush; scrub
马桶	mǎtǒng	n.	night stool；chamber pot
炒菜	chǎocài	v.-o.	stir-fry the vegetable
织毛线	zhī máoxiàn	v.-o.	knit 毛线: woolen yarn
缝衣服	féng yī.fu	v.-o.	sew; make a dress
下棋	xiàqí	v.-o.	play chess
打乒乓	dǎ pīngpāng	v.-o.	play ping-pong (table tennis)
铺板	pùbǎn	n.	bed board
蒙头睡觉	méngtóu shuìjiào	phr.	sleep with the head under the quilt
鸽子笼	gē.zi lóng	n.	pigeon house; loft
双层	shuāngcéng	adj.	double deck
折叠	zhédié	v.	fold
娱乐	yúlè	n.	amusement; entertainment

一切工作、一切活动，不得不移到室外进行。原来⑯在五彩缤纷的橱窗、令人目眩的广告、光彩夺目的时装后面，却还有这么窄的街，这么挤的屋，这么可怜的生活。

走了有半小时，才到汽车站。当他回到家时，已经六点多钟了，又饿又累。原以为家里已有一桌热腾腾的饭菜在等他，却不知⑰连饭还没烧熟。原来妈妈下午去淮海路买东西，街上人多，店里人多，车上人更多，老太太如何挤得过人家，结果回来晚了。妈妈一边忙着洗菜切菜，一边埋怨弟弟："这个阿三呀！什么事也不干，一天到晚就是听听收音机睡睡觉。唉，这个阿三！"

陈信憋着一肚子火走进"违章建筑"，屋里黑洞洞的，简直伸手不见五指。他摸到床沿去，一下子绊在一条腿上，把他吓了一大跳。床上坐起一个人："二哥，下班了啊？"

陈信打开台灯，忍不住发火道："阿三，你日子过得太无聊了。整天在家没事，也帮妈妈干点家务嘛！"

"下午我去买了米，还拖了地板。"弟弟辩解道。

移	yí	v.	move
原来	yuánlái	adv.	as a matter of fact; as it turns out; actually
五彩缤纷	wǔcǎi bīnfēn	idm.	be riot with colors; blazing with color
橱窗	chúchuāng	n.	show window

目眩	mùxuàn	v.	feel dizzy and dazzled 灯光太强，令人目眩。
光彩夺目	guāngcǎi duómù	idm.	with dazzling brightness; brilliant
时装	shízhuāng	n.	fashionable dress
热腾腾	rèténgténg	adj.	steaming hot 热腾腾的汤面
熟	shú	adj.	(of rice, meat, etc.) cooked; done
如何	rúhé	pron.	怎么；how could
v. 得过	...deguò	comp.	(used after a verb plus 得 or 不 to indicate winning)打得过/ 比不过
人家	rén.jia	n.	别人；others
憋着一肚子火	biē.zhe yídù.zi huǒ	phr.	be filled with pent-up anger
黑洞洞	hēidōngdōng	adj.	pitch-dark 房子里没开灯，黑洞洞的。
伸手不见五指	shēnshǒu bújiàn wǔzhǐ	phr.	so dark that you can't see your hand in front of you 伸：stretch out 五指：five fingers
摸	mō	v.	feel for
床沿	chuángyán	n.	the edge of a bed
一下子	yíxià.zi	adv.	all of a sudden 不能希望人们把旧观念一下子都除掉。
吓了一大跳	xià.le yídàtiào	phr.	be greatly frightened; be greatly startled: 他突然跑进来，我吓了一跳。
发火	fāhuǒ	v.-o.	get angry; lose one's temper 听到这个消息，他发了火。
无聊	wúliáo	adj.	bored; boring
家务	jiāwù	n.	household duties
米	mǐ	n.	rice
拖地板	tuō dìbǎn	v.-o.	mop the floor
辩解	biànjiě	v.	explain away; try to defend oneself

"买米拖地板有什么了不起的，我像你这么大，在农村拉犁子，割麦子。"

弟弟不响了。

"你也二十岁了，脑子里该考虑点儿问题，干点儿正事儿了。起来起来，一个人，怎么生活得这么窝囊！"弟弟不声不响地走出了"违章建筑"。大哥也回来了，又冲着他说："阿三，你大了，该懂事了。哥哥嫂嫂在外工作了一天，回来总想好好休息，你应该帮帮忙啊！"

陈信在"违章建筑"里又接了上去："如果你每天在温习功课考大学，我们一点不会责备你不干家务……"弟弟仍然不响，妈妈过来打圆场了：

"好了好了，也怪我，走以前没和阿三交代。饭马上就好了，先吃点饼干吧！"七点半，饭菜终于烧好了。大家在妈妈睡觉的六平方小屋里围着饭桌吃饭。

因为饭前阿三引起的不愉快，气氛有点沉闷，谁都不想说话。大嫂也许为了使气氛活跃起来，挑开了话题："我们局里成立了'青少年之友'，其实就是婚姻介绍所呀。阿信，要不要我去帮你领张表格？"

"我吃饱饭没事干了！"陈信勉强笑着说，"我不想结婚。"

了不起	liǎo.buqǐ	*adj.*	amazing; terrific; extraordinary
拉犁子	lā lí.zi	*v-.o.*	work with a plough; pull a plough
割麦子	gē mài.zi	*v.-o.*	cut wheat
干正事儿	gàn zhèngshìr	*v.-o.*	do proper business 他什么正事也不干，整天玩儿。
窝囊	wō.nang	*adj.*	good-for-nothing; hopelessly stupid
不声不响	bùshēng bùxiǎng	*adv.*	make no reply; not utter a word 我问了他好几次，他只是不声不响地坐着，什么也不说。
冲着（人）	chòng.zhe	*prep.*	directed at sb.; aimed at sb.
接	jiē	*v.*	continue
温习	wēnxí	*v.*	review 温习功课
责备	zébèi	*v.*	reproach; blame
打圆场	dǎ yuánchǎng	*v.-o.*	mediate a dispute; smooth things over 他们两个人争执得很激烈，好在老师来打了圆场。
交代	jiāodài	*v.*	tell; leave words; order：我已经把工作交代得清清楚楚，他们都知道该怎么做了。
饼干	bǐnggān	*n.*	cookie; biscuit; cracker
气氛	qì.fen	*n.*	atmosphere; air
沉闷	chénmèn	*adj.*	depressed; in low spirits
活跃起来	huóyuè qǐlái	*v.-c.*	warm up; become lively
挑开话题	tiǎokāi huàtí	*v.-o.*	raise a new topic of conversation
婚姻介绍所	hūnyīn jièshàosuǒ	*n.*	matchmaking service center
领表格	lǐng biǎogé	*v.-o.*	get a form
吃饱饭没事干	chībǎo fàn méi shì gàn	*phr.*	have nothing to do after a good meal – do sth. really silly or senseless because there is actually nothing to do
勉强	miǎnqiǎng	*adv.*	manage with an effort; do with difficulty

"胡说！"妈妈说话了，"人怎么可以不结婚。我就不信像你这种相貌人品，会找不到老婆。"

"现在身高一米八十的最吃香了，小姑娘都喜欢高个子。"弟弟笑嘻嘻地说，把刚才受的责备全忘了，他是个没心眼儿的孩子。

"现在要找个对象也不容易。"嫂嫂说，"没有上千元办不了事。"

"儿子要结婚，哪怕⑱倾家荡产也要帮忙的。是吧，阿仿？"妈妈问大哥。

"哎哎。"大哥傻乎乎地应着。

"有了钱，要没有房子，还是一场空。"大嫂又说。

"实在没办法，我搬到弄堂里去睡，也要让儿子结婚的。是吧，阿仿？"

"对，对。"大哥应着。

"你们在开什么玩笑啊！"阿信放下了碗筷。虽然，妈妈和嫂嫂都是笑着，可骨子里却像是很认真的，又像是有些心照不宣的意味，使人感到很不愉快。

他在哥哥房间里看了一会儿电视，便觉得很困。想到明天还是早班，便站起来，睡觉去了。走进"违章建筑"，却见阿三已经睡在床上了。陈信照例看了几分钟小说，便关上了台灯。黑暗中突然响起弟弟的声音："二哥，要是爹爹还活着就好

胡说	húshuō	v.	talk nonsense; rubbish
相貌	xiàngmào	n.	facial features; looks
人品	rénpǐn	n.	moral quality
吃香	chīxiāng	adj.	be much sought after; be well-liked 现在到处需要英语老师，他们很吃香。
高个子	gāogè.zi	n.	tall person
笑嘻嘻	xiàoxīxī	adv.	giggling
没心眼儿	méi xīnyǎnr	adj.	simple and innocent
上…	shàng	v.	up to; as many as 上百辆汽车/ 上万人
哪怕	nǎpà	conj.	even; even if
倾家荡产	qīngjiā dàngchǎn	idm.	bring the family to ruin; family ruined and its property all lost
阿仿	Ā Fǎng	n.	陈仿，陈信的哥哥
应	yìng	v.	answer; respond
一场空	yìchǎng kōng	n.	all in vain; futile
骨子里	gǔ.zi lǐ	n.	in the bones – beneath the surface; in one's innermost nature 她说她不在乎，骨子里却在乎得要命。
心照不宣	xīnzhào bùxuān	idm.	both understand from their hearts what the matter is but do not choose to say so in public.; have a tacit (mutual) understanding
意味	yìwèi	n.	meaning; significance; implication
困	kùn	adj.	sleepy
照例	zhàolì	adv.	as a rule; as usual 虽然家里的情况不好，但过年的时候，母亲还是照例给孩子们买了新衣服。
黑暗	hēi'àn	adj.	dark
响	xiǎng	v.	sound; make a sound; ring 电话响了。/他一声不响地走了。
爹爹	diē.die	n.	dad; pa

了。我顶替妈妈，你顶替爹爹，爹爹的工作好，是坐办公室的。"

陈信突然鼻子发酸了，他很想将弟弟搂在怀里，可结果却只是翻了个身，粗声说："你应该说，考上学校就好了。"

过了一会儿，弟弟发出了轻轻的鼾声，陈信却一无睡意了。

妈妈退休，本来可以让弟弟顶替的，可就因为他……。他当即便打了长途电话回家，说："弟弟在上海，总有办法可想。这却是我唯一的途径了。"妈妈那边一声不吭，于是他便反反复复地说："妈妈，我十八岁出去，在外苦了十年。妈妈妈妈，我十八岁出去，苦了十年，十年哪！"妈妈那边仍是没有声音，但他知道，妈妈一定在哭，并且在心里直说："手心手背，哦，这手心手背……"结果，弟弟让了他，是应该的。十年前，他也让了哥哥。弟弟也和他一样，并没有怨言，也没有牢骚，同他亲亲热热的。

五

今天晚上，妈妈厂里的一个沈阿姨要带个姑娘来给陈信过目。这是妈妈一手主持的，陈信就不好太执拗了，可心里实在觉得又无聊又别扭。哥哥说："你现在应该着手建立新生活了。"他听了一震，新生活突然之间这么具体起来，他有点措手不及，难以接受。可他再想想，确也想不出来究竟还有什么更远大、更重要的新生活。也许，结婚，成家，抱儿子……这就是了。他摇摇头苦笑了一下，那种空落落的感觉又涌上心头，

顶替	dǐngtì	v.	replace; take sb.'s place
搂在怀里	lǒu zài huái.li	phr.	hold/cuddle someone in one's bosom
翻身	fānshēn	v.-o.	turn over
粗声	cūshēng	n./adv.	in a husky voice
鼾声	hānshēng	n.	snore
一无睡意	yīwú shuìyì	phr.	feel not sleepy at all
当即	dāngjí	adv.	at once; right away
途径	tújìng	n.	road; avenue; way; channel
一声不吭	yìshēng bùkēng	v.	without saying a word
反反复复	fǎnfǎn fùfù	adv.	repeatedly; again and again
让	ràng	v.	give way; yield
怨言	yuànyán	n.	complaint; grumble
亲亲热热	qīnqin rèrè	adj.	being affectionate
沈阿姨	Shěn āyí	n.	Auntie Shen, mother's friend
过目	guòmù	v.	look over (papers, lists, etc.) so as to check or approve; peruse
一手主持	yìshǒu zhǔchí	phr.	take charge of something single-handedly 这件事是父亲一手主持的，孩子们都不敢反对。
执拗	zhíniù	adj.	stubborn; pigheaded; willful
别扭	biè.niu	adj.	awkward; unnatural
着手	zhuóshǒu	v.	put one's hand to; set about 着手准备/着手处理这件事情
一震	yízhèn	v.	be shocked 他听到这个坏消息，心里一震。
措手不及	cuòshǒubùjí	idm.	be caught unprepared; be taken by surprise 你得先预备好，免得到时候措手不及。
摇头	yáotóu	v.-o.	shake one's head
苦笑	kǔxiào	v.	smile wryly
涌上心头	yǒngshàng xīntóu	phr.	well up in one's mind

一家人却都很起劲，从下午起便开始准备了，决定在哥哥房间里进行。嫂嫂把房间扫了一遍，抹了一遍。哥哥去买了点心水果。弟弟更是忙得不亦乐乎，建议妈妈晚上烧绿豆汤，又把自己最好的衣服拿出来让二哥穿。陈信发觉他的兴奋是由于极其无聊，生活中总算有了点新鲜内容，便开心得不得了，不免有点反感。

七点半左右，她们来了。那姑娘一直害羞地躲在沈阿姨身后，进了屋便坐在角落的沙发上，拿起一本书看着。正好是个黑影地，她又埋着头，看不清模样。

"阿信这孩子不错，厂里老师傅很夸奖他。到底⑲在外面吃过苦的，不像那些学校刚出来的小青年。"沈阿姨说。

"是啊，这孩子不容易，在外面苦了十年。"妈妈一面和沈阿姨聊天，眼睛却老瞟着角落里的姑娘。

"阿信，车床上的活儿做得惯吧？八小时站着，很吃力的噢？"沈阿姨又转向了陈信。

"还好。我不怕站，在农村什么活没干过！"陈信应付着，注意力却全在那个角落里。可惜看不清，只看得见一个轮廓，似乎是短短的卷发，宽宽的肩膀。

"阿仿，儿子呢？现在顽皮得不得了吧！"

"他睡觉了，还听话。"大哥心不在焉地回答。

起劲	qǐjìn	*adj.*	enthusiastic; in high spirits

点心	diǎnxīn	*n.*	light refreshments; pastry; dessert
不亦乐乎	búyìlèhū	*idm.*	terribly; extremely; awfully
建议	jiànyì	*v.*	suggest
绿豆汤	lǜdòutāng	*n.*	mung bean soup, a kind of dessert
极其……	jíqí	*adv.*	most; extremely; exceedingly: 极其顺利/极其深刻/极其困难
开心	kāixīn	*adj.*	happy; joyous; elated
反感	fǎn'gǎn	*adj.*	feel antipathy against; be averse to: 他不大诚实，我对他有些反感。
害羞地	hàixiū.de	*adv.*	bashfully; shyly
躲	duǒ	*v.*	hide (oneself)
角落	jiǎoluò	*n.*	corner
沙发	shāfā	*n.*	sofa
黑影地	hēiyǐngdì	*n.*	dark corner
埋着头	mái.zhe tóu	*v.-o.*	bury oneself (in books)
模样	múyàng	*n.*	appearance; look
老师傅	lǎoshīfu	*n.*	master worker (a qualified worker as distinct from an apprentice)
夸奖	kuājiǎng	*v.*	praise; commend; speak well of
到底	dàodǐ	*adv.*	after all; in the final analysis
吃苦	chīkǔ	*v.-o.*	bear/suffer/endure hardships
瞟	piǎo	*v.*	look sidelong at; glance sideways at: 他说完了，便瞟了她一眼。
活儿	huór	*n.*	work
吃力	chīlì	*adj.*	strenuous; laborious
应付	yìngfù	*v.*	do sth. perfunctorily
轮廓	lúnkuò	*n.*	outline; line
卷发	juǎnfà	*n.*	curly hair
宽	kuān	*adj.*	broad
顽皮	wánpí	*adj.*	naughty; mischievous
听话	tīnghuà	*adj.*	be obedient; behave

"听什么话！皮死了，我不要他了。"嫂嫂纠正道。

"这是讲讲的，人家想要还要不到呢。皮的小孩都聪明。"

"聪明倒是聪明……"嫂嫂转身向角落走去，"来，这儿坐，喝点绿豆汤呀！"

可有一个人抢在她前边走到角落里，说："这么暗，看书太吃力了吧！"说着便拉亮了落地灯。原来是弟弟，不知他什么时候进来的。现在，姑娘便全都被灯光笼罩了。大家不约而同都停止了说话，向她看去，又不约而同地回过头，相互望望。大家脸上都有一种失望的表情。还是嫂嫂比较沉得住气，她怔了一会儿便说："别看书了，喝点儿绿豆汤。"

姑娘扭扭捏捏地喝完一碗绿豆汤，用手绢擦擦嘴，便说要走了。大家也不留她，只客套了几句："以后来玩啊！""路上小心啊！"然后全家起立送她到门口便止了步，由沈阿姨一个人送出弄堂。

妈妈瞅空问陈信："阿信，你看怎么样？"

阿信不说话，却笑了起来。

"不行不行，颧骨高，要克男人的。"弟弟发言了。

"瞎三话四，又不问你。"

"形象是欠缺一点。"哥哥说。

"相貌是不好看，不知道人怎么样。"妈妈自己说。

交流只能暂时到此，沈阿姨回来了，笑着对陈信说："人家

皮	pí	*adj.*	顽皮; naughty; mischievous
纠正	jiūzhèng	*v.*	correct; put right; redress; rectify
转身	zhuǎnshēn	*v.-o.*	turn-back; turn round
抢	qiǎng	*v.*	rush over
拉亮了灯	lāliàng.le dēng	*phr.*	turn on the light (by pulling the chain)
落地灯	luòdìdēng	*n.*	floor lamp
笼罩	lǒngzhào	*v.*	envelop; shroud
不约而同	bùyuē értóng	*idm.*	take the same action or view without prior consultation
失望	shīwàng	*v./adj.*	disappointed, disappointing
表情	biǎoqíng	*n.*	facial expression
沉得住气	chén.de zhù qì	*v.-c.*	be able to keep calm; be able to stay steady
愣	lèng	*v.*	be in a daze
扭扭捏捏	niǔniǔ niēniē	*adv.*	be affectedly bashful
手绢	shǒujuàn	*n.*	handkerchief
留	liú	*v.*	ask sb. to stay; keep sb. where he is
客套	kètào	*v.*	make a few polite remarks
起立	qǐlì	*v.*	stand up; rise to one's feet
止步	zhǐbù	*v.-o.*	halt; stop
瞅空	chǒukòng	*v.*	wait for an opportunity 他瞅空出去打了一个电话。
颧骨	quángǔ	*n.*	cheekbone
克	kè	*v.*	bring bad luck to a man (a kind of superstition of old times)
瞎三话四	xiāsān huàsì	*idm.*	talking nonsense
形象	xíngxiàng	*n.*	appearance; image; figure;
欠缺	qiànquē	*v.*	deficient; lack; not good enough
交流	jiāoliú	*n./v.*	exchange; interchange
暂时	zànshí	*adv.*	temporarily; for the moment
人家	rénjiā	*n.*	he; she; they

说，看你的意思如何。小姑娘看样子蛮喜欢你的。"

陈信还是笑着，不回答。

沈阿姨似乎会意了一点儿什么，又说："这姑娘人品很好，老实厚道，今年二十八岁。家里条件蛮好的，她爸爸妈妈说：不看男方的条件，只要人好，要是没房子，可以住他们家。……好了，你们再商量商量，最好早点儿给我回信。阿信，沈阿姨不会骗你的，你放心。沈阿姨从小看你长大，最知道你了。"

全家把沈阿姨送至弄堂口，才回来。

"阿信，你对她印象究竟怎么样？"哥哥问。

"不佳。"阿信直截了当地说道。

"形象究竟是次要的，可以接触接触嘛！"嫂嫂说。

"嗯，形象可重要。要不，大哥为什么要找你。"陈信和嫂嫂开了个玩笑。

大家都笑了。

"阿信，我说你也可以接触接触，不能太以貌取人。"大哥说。

"靠介绍谈对象，外表当然很重要。否则，我凭什么[20]去和她交往下去，谈什么恋爱呢？"陈信有他的道理。

"姆妈，我看这姑娘还不错。"嫂嫂对妈妈说，"再说条件也好，有房子。上海的房子可是很要紧。"

陈信听见了，说："我是找人，又不是找房子。"

"可这也是很重要的呀。我看那姑娘也并不难看，就是面孔稍微阔了一点，眼睛眉毛都过得去。"

阿信不耐烦了，"什么眼睛眉毛，反正我看见这个人，一点儿激情都没有。"

看样子	kàn yàng.zi	*adv.*	it seems; it looks
会意	huìyì	*v.*	understand; know
厚道	hòu.dao	*adj.*	honest and kind; virtuous and sincere
不佳	bùjiā	*adj.*	not good
直截了当	zhíjiéliǎodàng	*idm.*	say without mincing words; come straight to the point
次要	cìyào	*adj.*	less important; secondary
嗯	ng/n	*intj.*	hey! (used to show surprise or disapproval)
以貌取人	yǐmàoqǔrén	*idm.*	judge people by outward appearance
介绍	jièshào	*n./v.*	introducing, introduce
谈对象	tán duìxiàng	*v.-o,*	look for a partner in marriage
外表	wàibiǎo	*n.*	outward appearance
凭什么	píng shén.me	*adv.*	base on what 他明明是个好人，你凭什么说他偷了东西？
谈恋爱	tán liàn'ài	*v.-o.*	be in love; date 他最近正跟一个女同学谈恋爱呢！
面孔	miànkǒng	*n.*	face
稍微	shāowēi	*adv.*	slightly
阔	kuò	*adj.*	wide; broad
眉毛	méi.mao	*n.*	eyebrow; brow
过得去	guò.dequ	*v.*	passable; not too bad 他的成绩不是太好，但还算过得去。
不耐烦	bú nàifán	*v./adj.*	impatient with
激情	jīqíng	*n.*	intense emotion; passion

“我也是为了你好，我看你将来能把‘激情’当饭吃！”嫂嫂说。

“对，对。”大哥附和。

妈妈开口了：“这是阿信的事，还是让他自己作主。”

“就是，就是。”大哥又附合道。

“好了，到此为止吧。”陈信感到无聊极了：“妈妈，以后你再别操这个心了。我自己找。有本事找个好老婆，没本事活该(21)打光棍。”说完，一头钻进“违章建筑”，睡觉去了。

睡梦中，有一双眼睛在对着他笑，这是一双黑黑的，弯弯的，月牙儿似的眼睛。哦，月牙儿般的眼睛，她在哪儿呢？她究竟是谁呢？在那里，每天早上，他去食堂吃饭回来，总是看见一辆自行车从校园驶过，老式笨重的车上坐着小巧纤细的她。她总是回过头看他。那眼睛，那眼睛……他自信，如果他问她：“你上哪儿去？”她一定会告诉他。可是他一直没问，因此也就一直无从知道。她一百次，一千次从他身边过去，他放过了她，心底里明明喜欢她的，他看到她便感到愉快。如今，终于回了上海，她却永远过去了，一去不回了。他又想起了他的学校，像是一个很宽阔的公园。可以说，上海还没有一所中学是这么大的。校园里有一条林荫道，一片小树林。他有一个班的学生，学生对他很忠实，常常把家里做的食物送给他。可他这次回来，为了避人耳目，生怕节外生枝，却是不告而别。

附和	fùhè	*v.*	chime in with
作主	zuòzhǔ	*v.-o.*	decide; take the responsibility for a decision
到此为止	dàocǐwéizhǐ	*phr.*	Let it end here.
操心	cāoxīn	*v.-o.*	worry about; trouble about
本事	běn.shi	*n.*	skill; ability; capability
活该	huógāi	*adv.*	serve sb. right; not wronged at all
打光棍	dǎ guānggùnr	*v.-o.*	stay single
钻进	zuānjìn	*v.-c.*	get into (a small space)
睡梦	shuìmèng	*n.*	sleep; slumber
弯弯的	wānwān.de	*adj.*	curved; crescent; bent
月牙儿	yuèyár	*n.*	crescent moon
笨重	bènzhòng	*adj.*	heavy; cumbersome
小巧纤细	xiǎoqiǎoxiānxì	*adj.*	slender and exquisite
自信	zìxìn	*v.*	believe in oneself
无从	wúcóng	*adv.*	have no way (of doing sth.) 事情太复杂，一时无从解释清楚。
放过	fàngguò	*v.*	let slip; let off
明明	míngmíng	*adv.*	obviously; undoubtedly
一去不回	yíqù bùhuí	*idm.*	gone forever
宽阔	kuānkuò	*adj.*	broad; wide; roomy; spacious
林荫道	línyīndào	*n.*	boulevard; avenue
树林	shùlín	*n.*	wood(s); grove
忠实	zhōngshí	*adj.*	true; faithful; loyal; reliable
避人耳目	bìréněrmù	*idm.*	avoid being noticed 耳目：ears and eyes
生怕	shēngpà	*v.*	for fear that; so as not to 他生怕考试考得不好，因此几天不睡觉地念书。
节外生枝	jiéwàishēngzhī	*idm.*	new problems crop up unexpectedly; deliberately complicate an issue
不告而别	búgào'érbié	*idm.*	leave without saying goodbye

299

六

这天早上，哥哥忽然向妈妈提出，把户口分开，他说："这，这么样，可，可以有两份，两份鸡蛋。按户头分配的东西，也都可以有，可以有两份了。"

妈妈没说话，抬起眼睛看着哥哥，哥哥却把脸避开了。

陈信觉得哥哥的想法挺不错，只是奇怪他为什么要这样吞吞吐吐、结结巴巴，似乎在说什么难于启齿的事。他在边上笑着说："这倒挺不错，亏(22)你们想得出。"

不想这句玩笑却叫哥哥红了脸，走了。而妈妈自始至终没有发言，眼睛却老盯着哥哥。

阿信走出门去上班，弟弟跟在他后面到了弄堂口。弟弟诡秘地压低声音说："你晓得大哥为什么要分户口吗？"

"鸡蛋……"

"什么鸡蛋！"弟弟打断了他的话，"是为房子。"

"房子？"陈信困惑了，停下了脚步。

"房子。"弟弟肯定了一句，"一分户口，这间二十二平方的客堂就归他们了。这一定是嫂嫂的主意。"

"归他就归他了！"陈信重又挪动了脚步，"你这个小鬼，正事上不用心，这种事倒内行得不得了！"

这一整天，陈信都有点心不在焉，常常有意无意地想起哥哥的话："分户口。"他隐隐地感觉到这"分户口"后面是有一点什么含意的。

户口	hùkǒu	*n.*	registered permanent residence, resident permit
户头	hùtóu	*n.*	household
吞吞吐吐	tūntūntǔtǔ	*adj.*	forbear from making a full explanation
结结巴巴	jiējiēbābā	*adj.*	hesitating in speaking
难于启齿	nányúqǐchǐ	*phr.*	find it difficult to bring the matter up
亏	kuī	*adv.*	fortunately; luckily; thanks to
盯着	dīng.zhe	*v.*	fix one's eyes on; gaze at
诡秘地	guǐmì.de	*adv.*	surreptitiously; secretively
压低声音	yādī shēngyīn	*phr.*	lower one's voice
打断	dǎduàn	*v.*	interrupt
困惑	kùnhuò	*v.*	perplexed; puzzled; bewildered
脚步	jiǎobù	*n.*	footstep; tread; step; pace
肯定	kěndìng	*v.*	affirm; approve; confirm
平方	píngfāng	*n.*	square meter 那间房有十平方。
客堂	kètáng	*n.*	drawing room; parlor
归	guī	*v.*	attribute to; belong to
主意	zhǔ.yi	*n.*	idea; plan
重	chóng	*adv.*	again; once more 第一次做得不好，我只好重做一遍。
挪动	nuódòng	*v.*	move
小鬼	xiǎoguǐ	*n.*	you little devil (used to address a child affectionately)
正事	zhèngshì	*n.*	one's proper business
用心	yòngxīn	*v.-o.*	be attentive; concentrate one's attention
隐隐地	yǐnyǐn.de	*adv.*	indistinctly; faintly
含意	hányì	*n.*	connotation; implication

　　下了班，回到家，他便听见妈妈在和大哥说："这户口不大好分。因为这房子有一半是阿信的。阿信在外苦了十年，要是他结婚，你们要让出半间，你说是吧？"

　　哥哥不响，妈妈又问了一遍："是吧？"他才附和着："是的，是的！"这时，嫂嫂端菜进来了，将菜碗放在桌子上。不知是有心还是无意，碗底发出很响的一声："砰！"

　　吃晚饭了，哥哥、嫂嫂的脸上像蒙了一层乌云。而妈妈却像是对他俩很抱歉似的，一个劲儿地往他们碗里夹菜。弟弟老是意味深长地向陈信递眼色，意思是："你看，你看！"陈信厌恶地转过脸，低下头，谁也不看。饭桌上的气氛十分沉闷，幸好有个囡囡，在凳子上一会儿站起一会儿坐下，一会儿要这一会儿要那，使空气活跃自然了一点。这会儿，他干脆丢了勺子，用手往碗里直接抓菜。奶奶捉住他的小手，摊开巴掌，在手心上打了三下。弟弟朝他做着幸灾乐祸的鬼脸："好极了，哈哈！"

　　囡囡高傲地说："一点儿都不痛！"大家都笑了，可嫂嫂一把(23)将囡囡从凳子上拖下来，嘴里训斥道："你不要脸皮厚，这么不识相。没把你赶出去是对你客气，不要当福气。"大家的笑容僵在脸上了，不知道该收回去，还是该放在那里。弟弟

| 有心 | yǒuxīn | *adv.* | deliberately; purposely |
| 响 | xiǎng | *adj.* | loud |

砰	pēng	onom.	sound of sth. falling heavily on the ground or striking against sth. else
蒙	méng	v.	cover; overspread
层	céng	AN.	layer
乌云	wūyún	n.	dark clouds
他俩	tāliǎ	pron.	the two of them
一个劲儿地	yí.gejìnr. de	adv.	continuously; persistently 无论我怎么说，他都一个劲儿地反对。
意味深长	yìwèi shēncháng	phr.	deep with meaning / implications
递眼色	dì yǎnsè	v.-o.	give a signal with the eyes 他向我递眼色，可是我实在不明白他的意思。
厌恶地	yànwù.de	adv.	disgustingly
干脆	gāncuì	adv.	simply; just; altogether 他说了半天，没有一个人相信，他就干脆不说了。
勺子	sháo.zi	n.	spoon
奶奶	nǎi.nai	n.	grandmother; grandma
摊开	tānkāi	v.-c.	spread out; unfold
巴掌	bā.zhang	n.	palm; hand
手心	shǒuxīn	n.	palm; the palm of the hand
幸灾乐祸	xìngzāilèhuò	idm.	take pleasure in other people's misfortune; be glad when other people are in difficulties
做鬼脸	zuò guǐliǎn	v.-o.	make a wry face; make faces
高傲地	gāo'ào.de	adv.	arrogantly; haughtily
训斥	xùnchì	v.	reprimand
脸皮厚	liǎnpí hòu	adj.	thick-skinned; shameless; cheeky
不识相	bù shíxiàng	v.	be insensitive; be untactful
赶出去	gǎn chū..qu	v.-c.	kick out
福气	fú.qi	n.	good fortune
僵	jiāng	v.	become rigid; become stiff

303

解嘲似的又轻轻说了一句："好极！"

妈妈沉下了脸："你这话是什么意思？"

"没有什么意思。"嫂嫂说。

"我知道你的意思。"妈妈干脆把话挑明了，"你是在为房子生气。"

"我不为房子生气，有没有房子我无所谓。不过，我儿子长大了，没有房子是不会让他娶人家女儿回家的。"

"你不用讲这种话来气我，我做婆婆的虽然穷，可是我心里疼孩子。三个儿子我要一样看待，手心手背都是肉。阿信出去，有一半是为了阿仿。你们不要忘恩负义。"妈妈哭了。

"我们怎么忘恩负义？人家小姑娘结婚，谁不是一套家具，沙发落地灯？我结婚时，阿仿有什么？我有过一句怨言吗？阿信在外地，逢年过节不都寄包裹寄钱？做媳妇做到了这种程度很可以了。"嫂嫂也哭了。

哥哥傻了眼，不知劝谁好。

"别哭了！"陈信烦躁地站了起来，"妈妈，我不要这房子，我不结婚。我们插队落户的，能有回上海的一天，就满足了。"

妈妈哭得更伤心了。嫂嫂看了他一眼，哭声低了下去。

晚上，大家都睡了，大哥抽着烟走进"违章建筑"，说："你别生你大嫂气，她就是这么个脾气，心并不坏。当时我们

结婚，我没有储蓄，只买了一张床。她并没抱怨。这几年，我

解嘲	jiěcháo	*v.*	try to explain things away when ridiculed; try to get out of a scrape when ridiculed
沉下脸	chén xià liǎn	*v.-c.*	straighten one's face; pull a long face
把话挑明	bǎ huà tiǎomíng	*phr.*	put all the cards on the table; no longer keep it back; bring it out into the open
婆婆	pó.po	*n.*	husband's mother; mother-in-law
疼	téng	*v.*	love dearly; be fond of
看待	kàndài	*v.*	treat; look on; regard　我把他当朋友看待。
忘恩负义	wàng'ēn fùyì	*idm.*	be ungrateful and act contrary to justice
逢年过节	féngnián guòjié	*idm.*	at every festival and at New Year
包裹	bāoguǒ	*n.*	package; parcel
媳妇	xí.fu	*n.*	son's wife; daughter-in-law
傻眼	shǎyǎn	*v.-o.*	be dumbfounded; be stunned　他一看考试，就傻了眼，他什么都不会。
烦躁地	fánzào.de	*adv.*	irritably; agitate
插队落户	chāduì luòhù	*v.*	go to live and work in a production team and settle down in the countryside. During the Great Cultural Revolution, many educated youth were sent to the countryside and be forced to settle down there.
伤心	shāngxīn	*v.*	sad; grieved; broken-hearted
抽烟	chōuyān	*v.-o.*	smoke (a cigarette or a pipe)
脾气	pí.qì	*n.*	temperament; disposition
储蓄	chǔxù	*n.*	savings
抱怨	bàoyuàn	*v.*	complain

们省吃俭用，买了家具，装修了房间，她心满意足，觉得苦了几年终于有了结果，自然要竭力保护。她心不坏，她也说，应该让给弟弟半间，只是舍不得，我慢慢劝她……"

"大哥，别说了。"他猝然说道，"我刚才不是说气话，我不要这半间，我发誓。你让她放心，只是不要分户口。妈妈要伤心的，老人家喜欢子孙团圆。"大哥哭了，抱住他肩膀。他也想抱住大哥的，可结果却一把推开他，钻进了被窝。

七

陈信过惯了独自一人省心的日子，如今感到真烦心。第二天是礼拜，他天不亮早饭没吃，谁也不告诉一声，便出了门。他想出去走走，找个开阔一点的地方。在空阔的北方过惯了，在上海总感到气闷。去哪儿呢？去外滩吧。

他下了汽车，向前走去。马路对面是黄浦江。看不见江面，只看见大大小小停泊着的轮船。江岸上绿树红花，老人在打太极拳，小孩子奔来跑去，年轻人在散步、照相。生活有了这些，就变得愉快、美好起来。他心情稍稍轻松了一点儿，他穿

省吃俭用	shěngchī jiǎnyòng	*idm.*	save money on food and expenses; be economical in everyday spending
装修	zhuāngxiū	*v.*	renovate
心满意足	xīnmǎnyìzú	*idm.*	be perfectly content
竭力	jiélì	*adv.*	do one's utmost; spare no efforts 竭力反对/竭力宣传/竭力保护

舍不得	shě.bu.de	v.	hate to part with or use 舍不得花钱/舍不得给她
猝然	cùrán	adv.	suddenly; abruptly; unexpectedly
气话	qìhuà	n.	words said in a fit of rage
发誓	fāshì	v.-o.	vow; pledge; swear
子孙团圆	zǐsūntuányuán	phr.	children and grandchildren reunite
被窝	bèiwō	n.	the sleeping bag formed by a folded quilt
独自	dúzì	adv.	alone; by oneself 他独自一人走向公园。
省心	shěngxīn	v.	have nothing to worry about
烦心	fánxīn	adj.	feel vexed; be troubled; vexatious
礼拜	lǐbài	n.	Sunday; 星期天
开阔	kāikuò	adv.	open; wide
空阔	kōngkuò	adv.	open; spacious
气闷	qìmèn	adv.	depressed; vexed; sad and silent
外滩	Wàitān	n.	the Bund, an area of Huangpu District in Shanghai which runs along the western bank of the Huangpu River, is one of the most famous tourist destinations
黄浦江	Huángpǔ jiāng	n.	Huangpu River, divides Shanghai into two regions: Pudong (east) and Puxi (west)
停泊	tíngbó	v.	anchor; berth
轮船	lúnchuán	n.	steamer; steamship; steamboat
太极拳	tàijíquán	n.	*taichi,* a system of physical exercise that emphasizes balance, coordination, and effortlessness in movements 打太极拳: practice *taijiquan*
奔来跑去	bēnláipǎoqù	v.	run around
散步	sànbù	v.-o.	take a walk; stroll
稍稍	shāoshāo	adv.	slightly; a little
轻松	qīngsōng	adv.	light; relaxed

过了马路。哦，黄浦江，这上海的象征。可它并不像记忆中和地图上那样是蓝色的。它是土黄色，并且散发出一股腥臭味儿。也许世界上一切东西都是只能远看，走近去一细看便要失望的。

他顺着江岸向前走去，前边是外滩公园，他买了门票进去了。一进去便是一个喷水池，水从假山顶上落下，落在池子里，激起一圈圈涟漪。记得很久很久以前，水不是这么直接落在水面上的，水珠子落在一把伞上。伞下是一个妈妈，搂着两个孩子，笑嘻嘻地挤在一起躲雨。他小时候第一次看见这座雕像时，是多么惊讶，多么喜欢。他看个没完没了，便赖着不肯走。他们，从来就是这么生活的。爹爹很早就死了，妈妈带着他们三个，相依为命，相濡以沫，什么苦都吃过了。可就因为大家挤在一起，再怎么(24)苦都是暖融融的。有一次刮龙卷风，四口人全挤在大床上，紧紧抱成一团。闪电，霹雳，呼啸的狂风，引得大家又害怕却又兴奋。弟弟夸张地尖叫着，妈妈笑着

象征	xiàngzhēng	n.	symbol
记忆	jìyì	n.	memory
地图	dìtú	n.	map
散发	sànfā	v.	send forth; diffuse; emit
股	gǔ	AN.	measure word used for smell, strength etc.闻到一股中国菜味儿
腥臭味儿	xīngchòuwèir	n.	stinking smell as of rotten fish; stench

细看	xìkàn	*v.*	examine carefully
顺着	shùn.zhe	*prep.*	along 顺着这条路走， 大约十分钟就到了。
喷水池	pēnshuǐchí	*n.*	fountain
假山	jiǎshān	*n.*	rockery; rockwork
顶	dǐng	*n.*	top; peak
落下	luòxià	*v.-c.*	fall; drop
圈	quān	*n.*	circle; ring
涟漪	liányī	*n.*	riffle; ripples
水珠子	shuǐzhū.zi	*n.*	drop of water; droplet
伞	sǎn	*n.*	umbrella
雕像	diāoxiàng	*n.*	statue; monument
惊讶	jīngyà	*adj.*	surprised; amazed; astonished
没完没了	méiwánméiliǎo	*adj.*	endless; without end 她没完没了地说， 真烦人。
赖	lài	*v.*	hang on in a place; hold on to a place 不交房租，房东是不会让我们赖在这里的。
相依为命	xiāngyī wéimìng	*idm.*	stick together and help each other in difficulties
相濡以沫	xiāngrúyǐmò	*v.*	mutual help and relief in time of poverty
暖融融	nuǎnróngróng	*adj.*	nice and warm
刮（风）	guā (fēng)	*v.-o.*	blow (of the wind)
龙卷风	lóngjuǎnfēng	*n.*	tornado
抱成一团	bàochéng yìtuán	*phr.*	huddle together
闪电	shǎndiàn	*n.*	lightning; flashing lightning
霹雳	pīlì	*n.*	thunderbolt; thunderclap
呼啸	hūxiào	*v.*	whistle; howl; roar
狂风	kuángfēng	*n.*	fiercc wind
夸张	kuāzhāng	*v.*	exaggerate
尖叫	jiānjiào	*v.*	scream

咒诅老天，雷打得真吓人，可真开心。是的，暖融融的。这温暖，吸引着他，吸引着他归来。

水，落在空荡荡的水面上，激起一个个单调而空洞的水圈。他是怎么了？当年离开上海，妈妈哭得死去活来，他却一滴泪不流。今天……他感到一种莫大的失望，好像有一样最美好最贵重的东西突然之间破裂了。他扭头走出了公园。

商店开门了，橱窗里的商品令人目眩。他走到一个橱窗前，不由自主地站住了脚，橱窗里是一些电动的装置：一个滑梯上，一个个大头胖娃娃鱼贯滑下，两个娃娃抱在一起荡秋千，后面几个少年在试飞机模型，一架架银色的飞机在蓝色的云幕上飞翔。他站在跟前，走不动了。他感到心里忽然有什么被唤回了，是的，被唤回了。

这是他的童年，他的少年，他离开上海时，心中留下的一片金色的记忆。这记忆在十年中被误认为是上海了。于是，他便拼命地争取回来。上海，是回来了，然而失去的，却仍是失去了。

咒诅	zhòuzǔ	v.	curse; swear
打雷	dǎléi	v.-o.	thunder
吓人	xiàrén	adj.	scary; terrible; frightening
温暖	wēnnuǎn	adj.	warm
空荡荡	kōngdàngdàng	adj.	empty; deserted 房间里空荡荡的，什么都没有。
单调	dāndiào	adj.	monotonous; dull

空洞	kōngdòng	*adj.*	empty; hollow; devoid of content
死去活来	sǐqùhuólái	*idm.*	have fainted and recovered consciousness several times; (sob) one's heart out
滴	dī	*AN.*	drop (measure word for liquid that is dropping) 一滴水
莫大	mòdà	*adj.*	greatest; utmost
贵重	guìzhòng	*adj.*	precious; valuable
破裂	pòliè	*v.*	break; fracture; burst; split
不由自主	bùyóuzìzhǔ	*idm.*	can't help; beyond one's control 他不由自主地流下了眼泪。
电动装置	diàndòng zhuāngzhì	*n.*	electrically operated device
滑梯	huátī	*n.*	children's slide
胖娃娃	pàng wá.wa	*n.*	chubby child
鱼贯	yúguàn	*adv.*	one following the other
滑下	huáxià	*v.*	slide down
荡秋千	dàng qiūqiān	*v.-o.*	play on the swing
模型	móxíng	*n.*	model
架	jià	*AN.*	measure word for plane, camera
银色	yínsè	*adj.*	silvery; silver-colored
云幕	yúnmù	*n.*	screen with the pattern of cloud
跟前	gēnqián	*n.*	in front of; near
飞翔	fēixiáng	*v.*	fly; circle in the air
唤回	huànhuí	*v.*	call back
童年	tóngnián	*n.*	childhood
少年	shàonián	*n.*	early youth (from about ten to sixteen)
误认为	wùrènwéi	*v.*	think mistakenly
拼命	pīnmìng	*adv.*	exerting the utmost strength; with all one's might 拼命赚钱
争取	zhēngqǔ	*v.*	strive for; fight for 争取时间/争取主动/争取胜利

人和人，肩挨肩，脚跟脚，这么密集地在一个世界里，然而彼此又是陌路人，不认识，不了解，彼此高傲地藐视着。哦，他忽然想起弟弟前几日录来的一首歌，歌词只有反反复复的两句："地上的人群就像天上的星星那样拥挤，天上的星星就像地上的人群那样疏远。"

他身不由己地跟随着人流向前走，自己也不知道走向哪里。他很茫然，十年里那点儿渗透他心灵的、苦苦的而又是甜甜的思念，消失了。他的目的地达到了，下一步，他该往哪儿走？人活着，总要有个目的地。完成西装革履、喇叭裤、录音机的装备，跟上时代新潮流？找对象、结婚、建立小家庭？……这些都可以开始了，只是还需要很多努力，很多辛苦。并且，如果时装里包裹着一颗沉重而不愉快的心灵，究竟又有什么幸福？为了建立家庭而结婚，终身伴侣却不是个贴心人，岂不(25)是给自己加了负荷？他不由又想起了月牙儿般的眼睛，唉，这是可遇而不可求的。人生的目的地，应该是幸福，而不是苦恼。他忽然感到，自己追求的目的地，应该再扩大一点儿，是的，再扩大一点儿。

他郁闷的心情开朗了一点儿，好像沉重的乌云开了一条缝，一

| 挨 | āi | v. | be close to; be next to 他家挨着一个公园。 |
| 密集 | mìjí | adv./adj. | densely; intensively, crowded together; dense; intensive |

陌路人	mòlùrén	n.	stranger
藐视	miǎoshì	v.	despise; look down upon
首	shǒu	AN.	measure word for songs
歌词	gēcí	n.	words of a song；lyrics
星星	xīng.xing	n.	star
疏远	shūyuǎn	adj.	drift apart; not in close touch
身不由己	shēnbùyóujǐ	idm.	involuntarily; have no command over oneself
人流	rénliú	n.	stream of people
茫然	mángrán	adj.	vacant; blank; in the dark; at a loss
渗透	shèntòu	v.	infiltrate
心灵	xīnlíng	n.	heart; soul; spirit
西装革履	xīzhuāng gélǚ	n.	Western dress and leather shoes
喇叭裤	lǎ.baikù	n.	bell-bottoms; flared trousers
装备	zhuāngbèi	n.	equipment；outfit
辛苦	xīnkǔ	n./adj.	hardship, hard; toilsome; laborious
包裹	bāoguǒ	v.	wrap up; bind up; enclose
颗	kē	AN.	measure word usually for anything small and roundish　一颗心/一颗牙
终身伴侣	zhōngshēn bànlǚ	n.	lifelong companion
贴心	tiēxīn	adj.	intimate; close
岂不	qǐbù	adv.	wouldn't it…; isn't it …(used to ask a rhetorical question)
负荷	fùhè	n.	burden; load
苦恼	kǔ'nǎo	n.	worry; distress; torment
扩大	kuòdà	v.	broaden; expand
郁闷	yùmèn	adj.	gloomy; depressed
开朗	kāilǎng	adj.	outgoing; optimistic
条	tiáo	AN.	measure word for long or narrow or thin things　一条鱼/一条毛巾
缝	fèng	n.	crack; crevice; fissure; slit

线朦朦胧胧的光透了进来。虽然是朦胧隐约的，但确实是光。

"阿信！"

他站住了，似乎有人叫他。

"阿信！"又是一声。他转脸一看，见马路上，熙熙攘攘的行人中间，无可奈何爬行着的一辆公共汽车窗户里，伸出大哥的半个身子，向他伸着手。他背后还有大嫂。他们脸上的表情很怪，似乎是十分惊慌恐惧。

他不知出了什么事，掉转身子追着汽车跑去。大哥一把抓住他的手，什么话也说不出来，只是呆呆地看着他。就像十年前，陈信坐在火车上，哥哥跟着火车跑的时候那神情一样。他心里一酸。大嫂也伸手抓住他："阿信，你可别想不开！"她又哭了。

"你们想到哪儿去了？！"陈信笑了，眼泪却也滚了出来。

"回家吧！"哥哥说。

"好的，回家。"回家，家毕竟(26)是家，就因为太贫困了，才会有这些不和。

他忽然感到羞愧，为自己把十年的艰辛当作王牌随时甩出去而感到羞愧。妈妈、哥哥、弟弟、嫂嫂，也都有十年的艰辛。当然，人生中还不仅是这些。还有很多很多的欢乐。真的，欢乐！比如，林荫道、小树林、天真无邪的学生、月牙儿般的眼睛……可全被他忽略了。好在，还有后十年、二十年、三十年，今后的日子还很长很长。该怎么过下去，真该好好想一想。

线	xiàn	*AN.*	line; (here) measure word for light
朦朦胧胧	méngméng lónglóng	*adj.*	dim; hazy
光	guāng	*n.*	light; ray
透	tòu	*v.*	penetrate; pass through
隐约	yǐnyuē	*adj.*	indistinct; faint
熙熙攘攘	xīxī rǎngrǎng	*idm.*	streams of people busily coming and going; bustling with activity
无可奈何	wúkěnàihé	*idm.*	helplessly
爬行	páxíng	*v.*	crawl; creep
惊慌	jīnghuāng	*adj.*	scared; panic-stricken
恐惧	kǒngjù	*adj.*	fear; dread; frightened
掉转	diàozhuǎn	*v.*	turn round
神情	shénqíng	*n.*	expression; look
想不开	xiǎng .bukāi	*v.*	take things too hard; take a matter to heart 别为这点小事想不开。/ 她一时想不开，就自杀了。
想到哪儿去了	xiǎng dào nǎr qù le	*phr.*	What are you thinking? (it is not the case at all.)
滚	gǔn	*v.*	roll down; shed (tears); drop (tears)
毕竟	bìjìng	*adv.*	after all; all in all
不和	bùhé	*n./v.*	discord, not get along well; be on bad terms
羞愧	xiūkuì	*adj.*	ashamed; abashed
王牌	wángpái	*n.*	trump card
甩出去	shuǎi chū.qu	*v.-c.*	throw; fling; toss
天真无邪	tiānzhēn wúxié	*idm.*	innocent; artless; naive
忽略	hūlüè	*v.*	ignore; neglect

315

又一次列车即将出站，目的地在哪里？他只知道，那一定要是更远、更大的，也许跋涉的时间不止是一个十年，要两个、三个、甚至整整一辈子。也许永远得不到安定感。然而，他相信，只要到达，就不会惶惑，不会苦恼，不会惘然若失，而是真正找到了归宿。

选自《上海文学》一九八一年第十期

即将	jíjiāng	*adv.*	be about to; soon; in no time 比赛即将开始。
出站	chūzhàn	*v.-o.*	leave the station (to set out on a journey)
跋涉	báshè	*v.*	trudge; make a long and difficult journey
惶惑	huánghuò	*adj.*	perplexed and alarmed
惘然若失	wǎngránruòshī	*idm.*	disconcertedly feel lost; feel disturbed as if having lost sth.

词语例句

1. 要（是）……还……吗？：if ..., how would / would sb. still...?
   (a rhetorical question)
   ❖ 要有还能回来？
   1) 要（是）我不会中国话，还能找到这个工作吗？
   2) 要（是）没有他帮忙，我还能做完吗？

2. 善于：be good at; be adept in
   ❖ 人，要善于从各种各样的生活里吸取乐趣。
   1) 他最大的优点就是善于解决纠纷。
   2) 我并不善于辩论，我看我还是不要参加这个辩论比赛。

3. ……似的：(used after a noun, pronoun, or verb to indicate similarity)
   ❖ 那是被细心分割成一小块一小块，绣花似的织上庄稼的田野。
   1) 他像个小孩似的，高兴得跳来跳去。
   2) 我大声叫他，他却没听见似的。

4. 何曾：didn't ever   (used in rhetorical questions)
   ❖ 十年前，他从这里离开，上海越来越远越来越渺茫的时候，他何曾想过回来。
   1) 我何曾不想结婚呢，但这是可遇而不可求的。
   2) 政府何曾不想保护环境，但是以目前来说，发展工业更重要。

5. 更何况：moreover; besides; in addition
   ❖ 上海，似乎代表着中国文化生活的时代新潮流。更何况，在这里有着他的家。
   1) 帮助人是应该的，更何况我们是老朋友。
   2) 我不喜欢那所房子，更何况价钱也太高。

6. 反正：anyway; anyhow (often used correlatively with 不管, 无论, etc.)
   ❖ 反正，他打了一仗，紧张而激烈，却是胜利了。
   1) 无论你怎么说，反正我绝不同意。
   2) 我不知道她有什么计划，反正我毕业以后是一定要出国留学的。

7. 不由：can't help; cannot but
   ❖ 弟弟也看见了他，跟着火车跑着，笑着叫："二哥！"他的心不由缩了一下，升起了一丝歉意。
   1）他说得这么清楚，不由你不相信。
   2）那个小乞丐那么可怜，他不由掏出几块钱给了他。

8. 无奈：but; however
   ❖ 心中空有千种温情，无奈不会表达，也不好意思表达。
   1）他本来是打算来的，无奈临时有事，来不了了。
   2）他急于要孩子，无奈太太不想这么年轻就生孩子。

9. 总算：at long last; finally
   ❖ 好了，你总算回来了。
   1）他失业半年，最近总算找到了工作。
   2）我跑了三家书店，总算买到了这本书。

10. 一则……，二则……：for one thing…, for another… ;
    firstly…secondly…
    ❖ 大家一则怕他捣蛋，二则，少了他这个挺会玩挺会闹的角色，也的确有点可惜。
    1）到中国去，一则可以实际使用你所学的中文，二则能亲身体验中国人的日常生活，好处是很多的。
    2）住在大城市里，一则工作机会比较多，二则人们的生活态度也比较多元化。

11. 好容易：with great difficulty
    ❖ 他推开人，使劲往里钻，好容易抓住了车门的栏杆上了车。
    1）路上的车一辆接着一辆，他好容易才过了街。
    2）他说得吞吞吐吐，结结巴巴，我好容易才明白了他的意思。

12. 眼看着：soon; in a moment
    ❖ 他十分愤怒，眼看着要和人家吵起来了。
    1）眼看着时间快要到了，考试才作了一半，真急死我了。
    2）眼看着客人就要到了，房间还这么乱，怎么办啊！

13．要么……，要么……：either...or...

❖ 要么是有缺陷或者条件极差的，要么就是条件极好，要求极高。

1）要么给她打个电话，要么给她发个电子邮件。

2）要么你来，要么我去，我们一定得见面谈谈。

14．……之余：in addition to doing sth.

❖ 满足之余，有时他却又会感到心里空落落的。

1）失望之余，他还是写了一封信表示自己的感谢之意。

2）读书之余，你都有些什么嗜好?

15．一赌气：feel wronged and act rashly

❖ 他等得心里发烦，一赌气，转身离开了车站，走吧!

1）说了半天，没有一个人同意，他一赌气，站起来走了。

2）丈夫坚持不买新车，太太一赌气，好几天不跟他说话。

16．原来：as a matter of fact; as it turns out (used when found sth. unexpected)

❖ 原来在五彩缤纷的橱窗、令人目眩的广告、光彩夺目的时装后面，却还有这么窄的街，这么挤的屋，这么可怜的生活。

1）原来是你啊! 我以为是别人呢!

2）原来他是这家公司的老板，难怪所有的职员都怕他。

17．原以为…，却不知…：thought previously…, but it turns out that …

❖ 原以为家里已有一桌热腾腾的饭菜在等他，却不知连饭还没烧熟。

1）我原以为戒烟很容易，却不知戒了好几次都没戒掉。

2）原以为上了英语辅导班，英语水平肯定能提高很多，却不知辅导班只是帮人考托福，对实际的应用一点儿帮助也没有。

18．哪怕：even; even if; no matter how

❖ 儿子要结婚，哪怕倾家荡产也要帮忙的。

1）节省资源是非常重要的。哪怕是一张纸也不该浪费的。

2）哪怕父母不同意，他还坚持选这个专业。

19．到底：after all; in the final analysis

❖ 到底在外面吃过苦的，不像那些学校刚出来的小青年。

1）他到底才来了一个月，对这儿的环境还不熟。

2）这个人到底是上过大学的，比那些高中毕业的成熟一些。

20．凭什么：base on what
　　❖ 外表当然很重要。否则，我凭什么去和她交往，谈什么恋爱呢?
　　1) 你凭什么得出这样的结论?
　　2) 你至少得上完大学。否则你凭什么跟人竞争呢?

21．活该：serve sb. right; not wronged at all
　　❖ 有本事找个好老婆，没本事活该打光棍。
　　1) 你不听我的话，吃了亏真是活该!
　　2) 我早就告诉你别开快车，现在被罚了钱，活该!

22．亏（人）v.：fortunately; luckily; thanks to sb.
　　❖ 这倒挺不错，亏你们想得出。
　　1) 这件事亏他帮忙，否则哪儿能办得这么好!
　　2) 亏你想出了这个主意，我立刻就去做!

23．一把 v.-c.：v.-c. to snatch (by hand) abruptly
　　❖ 嫂嫂一把将囡囡从凳子上拖下来.
　　1) 他把账单一把抢过去，说："今天我付账!"
　　2) 他走过来，一把拉住我的手，吓了我一跳。

24．再怎么 v 也/都：no matter how one v., still…
　　❖ 可就因为大家挤在一起，再怎么苦都是暖融融的。
　　1) 你得拿出证据来，否则再怎么说也没人相信。
　　2) 真没想到，我再怎么劝他都不听。

25．岂不：wouldn't it…; isn't it …(used to ask a rhetorical question)
　　❖ 终身伴侣却不是个贴心人，岂不是给自己加了负荷?
　　1) 你这样当面指责他，岂不是让他下不了台?
　　2) 你依靠父母生活，岂不给他们增加了负担?

26．毕竟：after all; all in all
　　❖ 家毕竟是家，就因为太贫困了，才会有这些不和。
　　1) 毕竟是母子，吵过架不久就和好了。
　　2) 他毕竟在美国住了二十年了，对美国人的习俗有不少了解。

练习

I. 填进最合适的词：

再怎么　毕竟　凭什么　一把　原来

1. 上海 _____ 是上海，百货公司的橱窗五彩缤纷，令人目眩。
2. 我听出他话里的刺儿，_____ 有些反感。
3. _____ 你是下乡插过队、吃过苦的，难怪比那些学校刚出来的小青年成熟多了。
4. 你又没跟他见过面，_____ 瞎三话四，说他相貌不好？
5. 我 _____ 想都没想到他居然过得这么窝囊！

II. 填进最合适的词：

自食其力	一望无际	直截了当	不亦乐乎
相映成趣	不屈不挠	一言难尽	熙熙攘攘

1. 他 _____ 地奋斗了好几年，终于有了成就。
2. 这件事 _____，电话里说不清楚，见面时我再详细地跟你说。
3. 面对着 _____ 的大海，他感到心情开朗多了。
4. 大学毕了业，还不能 _____，你大学岂不是白念了？
5. 他毫不客气，_____ 地说：你再怎么干也不会成功的。
6. 大街上 _____，完全看不出战争两个月前才刚刚结束。
7. 湖边的绿树和山上的建筑 _____，这儿的确风景优美。
8. 也许因为是星期天吧？生意特别好，把服务员忙得 _____。

酒足饭饱	节外生枝	措手不及	惘然若失
难于启齿	身不由己	兴致勃勃	不约而同

1. 到底是学历史的，一谈到这个古城的过去，他就 _____。
2. 尽管他心甘情愿在农村落户，看到老同学调回城里，仍不免 _____。
3. 这顿饭整整吃了两个小时，_____ 以后，主人才提到正事。
4. 他吞吞吐吐的，肯定有什么 _____ 的事儿。

321

5. 疾病很快地传染开来，医生面对大量的病人，未免有些 ＿＿＿＿＿＿＿。

6. 谈判原来进行得很顺利，但对方突然 ＿＿＿＿＿＿＿，最终导致了谈判失败。

7. 老师取消了考试，学生们都＿＿＿＿＿＿欢呼起来。

8. 找到既有意思工资又高的工作固然是最理想的，但在目前就业难的状况下，很多时候是 ＿＿＿＿＿＿＿，只求能养活自己。

III. 完成句子：

1. 他一赌气，＿＿＿＿＿＿＿＿＿＿＿＿＿＿＿＿＿＿＿＿＿＿＿。

2. 我早就看出来他不是做生意的料，果然，＿＿＿＿＿＿＿＿＿＿＿＿。

3. 来日方长，＿＿＿＿＿＿＿＿＿＿＿＿＿＿＿＿＿＿＿＿＿＿＿。

4. 只要 ＿＿＿＿＿＿＿＿＿＿＿＿＿＿＿＿＿＿＿＿ 我就心满意足了。

5. 你这个忘恩负义的家伙！你怎么可以 ＿＿＿＿＿＿＿＿＿＿＿＿＿！

6. 你不应该以貌取人，虽然他 ＿＿＿＿＿＿＿＿，可是＿＿＿＿＿＿＿。

7. 为了避人耳目，你最好＿＿＿＿＿＿＿＿＿＿＿＿＿＿＿＿＿＿＿＿＿。

8. 亏你＿＿＿＿＿＿＿＿＿＿＿＿＿＿，否则＿＿＿＿＿＿＿＿＿＿＿＿。

9. 这个比赛我们输了，可是我希望失望之余，大家也得 ＿＿＿＿＿＿＿＿。

10. 我何曾＿＿＿＿＿＿＿＿＿＿＿＿？ 但＿＿＿＿＿＿＿＿＿＿＿＿＿。

11. 我觉得你现在谈的这几个对象对你都不合适，要么 ＿＿＿＿＿＿＿＿＿＿ ，要么＿＿＿＿＿＿＿＿＿＿＿＿。

12. 反正这是我第一次来上海，＿＿＿＿＿＿＿＿＿＿＿＿＿＿＿＿＿＿＿。

13. 这姑娘人品好，老实厚道，更何况 ＿＿＿＿＿＿＿＿＿＿＿＿＿＿＿＿ 。

14. 他＿＿＿＿＿＿＿＿＿＿＿＿＿＿＿＿＿＿＿＿＿，我真觉得过意不去。

IV. 选出正确的意思：

1. 都已经这把年纪了，还讲究什么时髦！
   a. 因为年纪大了，所以得穿得时髦一点。
   b. 年纪不小了，不必在乎时髦不时髦了。
   c. 这个年纪的人都很讲究时髦。

2. 什么？你叫我去帮他的忙？我吃饱饭没事儿干了！
   a. 说话的人很愿意去帮忙。
   b. 说话的人要是有空就会去帮忙。
   c. 说话的人完全不愿意去帮忙。

3. 你想到哪儿去了？我怎么会那么不识相！
   a. 说话的人正在道歉，因为自己以前太不识相了。
   b. 说话的人在解释自己不识相的原因。
   c. 说话的人认为听话的人想错了。

4. 眼看着两个人就要吵起来，老张赶忙出来打圆场。

    a. 老张使紧张的局面缓和下来。

    b. 老张幸灾乐祸。

    c. 老张心不在焉，随便说了几句客套话。

5. 他好容易才从新疆调回北京，可在北京也没有安定感。

    a. 他很喜欢新疆，不想调回北京。

    b. 他总算回到了北京，不过对北京又有点不适应。

    c. 他没想到很容易就调回了北京，但是有一点儿后悔。

6. 哪怕他省吃俭用，到了月底还是剩不下钱。

    a. 他的收入不多，生活贫困。

    b. 因为他不节省，钱总是不够。

    c. 他生活得不错，不怕月底没有钱。

7. 我原以为他会来帮我办手续，无奈等了半天，他连个影儿都不见。

    a. 说话的人很失望。

    b. 说话的人很犹豫。

    c. 说话的人很不争气。

8. 要不使劲挤，还能挤得上车？

    a. 上车时很挤，下车就比较容易了。

    b. 虽然车挤，但是上车并不太难。

    c. 公车太挤了，非用力挤不可。

V. 讨论问题：

1. 这篇小说的题目为什么是"本次列车终点"？作者要用这篇小说表明什么？

2. 文革时期，有很多知识青年下乡插队，根据这篇小说中陈信的经历，请你说明知青下乡前后一般的情况。

3. 陈信的嫂嫂是不是这篇小说中的"坏人"？

4. 陈家三兄弟的感情好不好？请你举例说明。

5. 陈家三兄弟的个性各有什么特点？

6. 袁小昕说："有时候，我觉得为了回上海，付出的代价有点不合算了。"这话是什么意思？袁小昕付出了什么代价？陈信付出了什么代价？在你看来，合算不合算？

7. 从这篇小说你看得出来上海与其他地方有什么不同吗？为什么插队下乡的人想尽了办法要回上海？

8. 从50年代到70年代末，在毛泽东的号召下，上山下乡的知识青年总数估计在1200至1800万之间。规模这么大的一个运动，请你从社会和个人的角度，谈谈它所产生的影响。

握笔者

周大新

（一）

采访途中顺便⑴回趟老家。

近家时，日头还半挂西天。坡里不少人仍在做活，看见我在田埂上走过，先惊异地看了一阵我的西服，后辨认出原是范家老大，便呼，便叫，就有人放下手中正干的活路，跑到地头儿看我。有几位嫂子追问：娃子和娃子他妈怎不回？我一边给他们扔糖块，一边报告：娃子要上学，娃子他妈要上班。于是她们就一阵笑。

到家，爹、娘、弟、妹们自是欢喜。邻居们也来热闹，话说到很晚。人渐渐散去，爹和弟弟妹妹们也已睡下后，娘给我端来一盆温水，要我把脚洗洗。我脱鞋脱袜把脚伸进水里，

（一）

握	wò	v.	hold; grasp; take by the hand
采访	cǎifǎng	v.	interview; gather news
顺便	shùnbiàn	adv.	do something in addition to what one is already doing without much extra effort 你去图书馆的时候，顺便把我这本书还了吧。
日头	rìtóu	n.	the sun

Selected & prepared by: Joanne Chiang
Edited by: Joanne Chiang

半挂西天	bàn guà xītiān	v.	hanging half way in the sky, almost set
做活	zuòhuó	v.-o.	do manual labor; work
田埂	tiángěng	n.	a low bank of earth between fields; ridge
惊异地	jīngyì.de	adv.	surprisingly
辨认	biànrèn	v.	identify; recognize 这对双胞胎长得很像，很难辨认谁是姐姐，谁是妹妹。
范家老大	Fàn jiā lǎodà	n.	the oldest son of the Fan family
正干的活路	zhènggàn.de huólù	n.	the task that one is doing at the very moment
地头儿	dìtóur	n.	edge of a field 在地头休息
嫂子	sǎo.zi	n.	(here) a form of address for a married woman about one's own age
追问	zhuīwèn	v.	question closely 追问原因
娃子	wá.zi	n.	(dialect) baby; child; (here) your son
娃子他妈	wá.zi tā mā	n.	(your) son's mother; (your) wife
扔	rēng	v.	throw; toss; cast
爹	diē	n.	(informal) father; dad
娘	niáng	n.	ma; mom; mother
自是欢喜	zìshì huānxǐ	adj.	be very happy naturally 孩子成绩好，父母自是欢喜。要是成绩不好，父母肯定很担心。
散	sàn	v.	break up; disperse 开完会，大家就散了，很多人都回家了。
端	duān	v.	hold something level with both hands; carry 端进两杯茶来/ 端盘子
盆	pén	AN.	basin; tub. (here) measure word for things held in a basin; tub, or pot 几盆花/一盆热水
温水	wēnshuǐ	n.	lukewarm water
脱	tuō	v.	take off; strip
袜	wà	n.	socks; stockings
伸	shēn	v.	stretch; extend 不要把头伸出窗外

娘便拎着擦脚布站在面前，一副要替我倒洗脚水的样子⑵，我就催她也早点去睡，娘没理。正这当儿，院门被敲响，敲的声音不大，显出些迟疑。娘丢下擦脚布，边出去问是谁边开院门。我猜是哪家邻居又来问候，便急忙擦脚穿鞋。"老大，是你的同学。"娘领着一个高高瘦瘦的汉子进屋。灯光下，我看到一张陌生的脸，一时⑶竟想不起这同学的名字。

"怎么？记不起了？南庄的达宽，和你同岁，你们一块上小学的。"娘提醒我。

"哦，是达宽。"我握住他的手，脑子却在飞快地搜索旧时的记忆。一个名叫达宽的白胖少年被我从脑子深处翻拣出来，但那少年的影像和面前的汉子无论如何⑷也重叠不到一起。

"我们好多年不见了。"他握紧我的手说。我立刻感受出他掌上有两块硬茧。"我这些年很少回家，偶尔回家一次，也是住几天就走。同学、朋友处都未去拜访。"我一边解释一边让他坐下。我递给他香烟时注意到他的手指在抖，我意识到他这么晚来访一定有事。他住的南庄离我们庄有一里地远。"家里都好么？"我问。

拎	līn	v.	(dialect) carry
副	fù	AN.	measure word for facial expression
催	cuī	v.	urge; hurry; press
理	lǐ	v.	(usually used in the negative) pay attention; make a gesture or speak to

			别理那条狗。/他想跟我讲话，我没理他。
这当儿	zhèdāngr	*n.*	this very moment
敲响	qiāoxiǎng	*v.-c.*	knock and emit a sound 门被敲响了。
迟疑	chíyí	*v.*	hesitate 毫不迟疑
问候	wènhòu	*v.*	send one's respects (or regards) to; extend greetings to 请你替我问候她。
急忙	jímáng	*adv.*	in a hurry; in haste; hurriedly; hastily 他没吃饭就急忙去学校了。
领	lǐng	*v.*	lead; usher
汉子	hàn.zi	*n.*	man; fellow
陌生	mòshēng	*adj.*	strange; unfamiliar
南庄	nánzhuāng	*n.*	the south village
达宽	Dákuān	*n.*	personal name
提醒	tíxǐng	*v.*	remind
握住	wòzhù	*v.-c.*	hold; grasp
搜索	sōusuǒ	*v.*	search for; scout around 我在网上搜索到一些有关的信息。
记忆	jìyì	*n.*	recollection
翻拣	fānjiǎn	*v.*	look through and select from
影像	yǐngxiàng	*n.*	image
无论如何	wúlùn rúhé	*adv.*	in any case; at any rate 你无论如何也得收下这个礼物。
重叠	chóngdié	*v.*	place one upon another; overlap
掌	zhǎng	*n.*	palm
硬茧	yìngjiǎn	*n.*	callus
偶尔	ǒu'ěr	*adv.*	occasionally
拜访	bàifǎng	*v.*	visit
递	dì	*v.*	hand over; pass; give
手指	shǒuzhǐ	*n.*	finger
抖	dǒu	*v.*	tremble; shiver
意识到	yì.shidào	*v.*	be conscious (or aware) of; awake to; realize 他意识到自己的责任了。/这一点我当时还没有意识到。

他没有回答我的问话，仿佛在全心全意吸烟。过了一会儿才突然说："我知道你会写文章！"

"说不上会写，"我笑笑，"也算是凑个文人的数吧。"家乡人承认自己的才能不能不让人高兴。

"你能给俺们家写一篇吗？"他突然抬眼望定我。

"写什么？"我一怔。

"写写俺们家的冤情！"

"哦，什么冤情？"我这时才发现他的眉眼里和胡子遮掩的嘴角上隐藏着一种苦痛。

他又不语,又大口地吸烟，目光又重重地落在地上。

屋里很静，涌进院子的月光，已挤到了门槛外边，似乎还想向屋里逼来。

"知道葛炭永吧？" 他没有抬头。怎么能不知道？我还没有考上大学以前，葛炭永就当了大队干部，前几年又当了村长。一个精明强悍的汉子，今年大概有 50 岁了吧？

"就是这个老不要脸的东西！"

"怎么了？"

"他... 他戏弄俺娃子他妈..."他猛抬手把自己的头抱住："连着几次......"

仿佛	fǎngfú	*adv.*	seemingly; as if 这事他仿佛已经知道了。
全心全意	quánxīn quányì	*idm.*	whole-heartedly 全心全意为人民服务

凑个数	còu .ge shù	v.-o.	serve as a stopgap 他没什么经验，但是我们需要人， 只好找他来凑个数。
文人	wénrén	n.	man of letters; scholar
才能	cáinéng	n.	ability; capability; talent
俺们	ǎnmen	pron.	(dialect) my; our
抬眼	táiyǎn	v.-o.	raise one's eyes
怔	zhèng	v.	stare blankly; be in a daze 那消息使他怔住了。
冤情	yuānqíng	n.	facts of an injustice
眉眼	méiyǎn	n.	appearance; looks 眉: eyebrow
胡子	hú.zi	n.	beard, moustache or whiskers
遮掩	zhēyǎn	v.	cover; envelop
嘴角	zuǐjiǎo	n.	corners of the mouth
隐藏	yǐncáng	v.	hide; conceal; remain under cover 隐 藏很深的间谍往往很难被发现。
苦痛	kǔtòng	n.	pain; agony
目光	mùguāng	n.	sight; vision; view
涌进	yǒngjìn	v.-c.	pour into
门槛	ménkǎn	n.	threshold
逼	bī	v.	press on towards; press up to
葛炭永	Gě Tànyǒng	n.	personal name
大队	dàduì	n.	production brigade (of a rural people's commune)
干部	gàn.bu	n.	cadre
村长	cūnzhǎng	n.	village head
精明强悍	jīngmíng qiánghàn	adj.	intelligent and capable; able and efficient
不要脸	búyàoliǎn	adj.	(offensive) have no sense of shame; shameless
戏弄	xìnòng	v.	take liberties with (a woman); assail with obscenities
俺娃子他妈	ǎn wá.zi tā mā	n.	my kid's mother; my wife
猛	měng	adv.	suddenly; abruptly 千万别猛踩刹车。

我的心一搐，一时竟不知该说什么。我知道一个男人遇到这种事时心里的苦痛和屈辱。"你没有去上边告他？"

"告了，去乡上告了几回。可葛炭永同乡上的人熟，人家总推着不管，告不赢。葛炭永听说俺们在告他，还捎话来说，什么时候告赢了，他给俺 100 块钱！俺们咽不下这口气，这才想起了你，求你把俺们的冤情写写，也在报上登登，让世人评评理。反正(5)俺们也不怕丢人了……"

杂种！作了坏事还敢这样狂！你不就是一个村长么？我今日偏偏(6)要治治你这个家伙！我心里的火被陡然激起。我起身拍了拍达宽的肩说："你放心，我明儿就去你家里了解详情。我要先写篇内参，送给领导们看看，保准会替你把冤伸了！"

葛炭永，我就凭我这支笔，要同你较量较量。要让你知道，人做了恶就有报应！

我原计划在家要停两至三天，我有调查的时间！

(二)

第二天早饭后，我就骑了弟弟的自行车去了南庄。达宽

搐	chù	*v.*	jerk; twitch
屈辱	qūrǔ	*n.*	humiliation; mortification
上边	shàng.bian	*n.*	high authorities
赢	yíng	*v.*	win

捎话	shāohuà	v.-o.	take a message to somebody
咽不下这口气	yàn búxià zhèi kǒu qì	phr.	unable to swallow this offense
求	qiú	v.	ask; beg; request
评理	pínglǐ	v.-o.	judge between right and wrong; decide which side is right 顾客和服务员发生了争执，他们只好找商店的经理给他们评评理。
反正	fǎnzhèng	adv.	anyway; anyhow; in any case
丢人	diūrén	adj.	lose face; be disgraced
杂种	zázhǒng	n.	(offensive) bastard; son of a bitch
狂	kuáng	adj.	arrogant; unruly; wild
偏偏	piānpiān	adv.	willfully; insistently; persistently 我们劝她不要那样做，他偏偏不听。
治	zhì	v.	punish 这个孩子太淘气了，连老师也治不了他。
陡然	dǒurán	adv.	suddenly; unexpectedly 病人的血压陡然下降，情况非常危险。
激起	jīqǐ	v.-c.	arouse; stimulate; excite 他们的看法截然不同，激起了大家的讨论。
拍	pāi	v.	pat; beat; clap
肩	jiān	n.	shoulder
详情	xiángqíng	n.	detailed information; details
内参	nèicān	n.	short for 内部参考; confidential internal reference
领导	lǐngdǎo	n.	leader; leadership
保准	bǎozhǔn	v.	guarantee; ensure 这件事我保准办到。
把冤伸了	bǎ yuān shēn.le	phr.	redress an injustice; right a wrong
较量	jiàoliàng	v.	measure one's strength with; have a contest 他虽然输了，但是他还想再跟对方好好较量一次。
做恶	zuò'è	v.-o.	do evil
报应	bào.yìng	n.	due punishment

331

家在庄的东头，两间正屋是瓦房，但年代显然已经不少，瓦缝里长着一些杂草。一间偏房是草顶，安着锅灶。听到我的自行车响，达宽从正屋迎出来，把我让进去。屋里的摆设简陋得可怜，只有几把用木头做的矮凳，一张用木板钉成的矮饭桌。

"你坐吧，家里穷得实在不成样子(7)。"达宽边说边从口袋里摸出一盒显然是刚买来的香烟。

"出来吧！范辛兄弟来了。"一个少妇低了头从里间走出。达宽是在我考上大学以后结婚的，这是我第一次见他媳妇。她是一个看上去有些瘦弱的女子，穿得也很破旧。但若多看一眼就会发现，她的面孔和身材有一种娟秀和纤弱的美。

"灵芝，这是范辛。他会写文章，他帮我们告姓葛的。你把受他戏弄的事都说出来，他好写(8)！"

灵芝只向我看了一眼，就低了头，两只手卷着自己的衣角，半晌没有吭声。

"灵芝，坐下慢慢说吧！"她坐下时，抬手抹了一下眼睛，手背上便沾了泪水。

（二）

正屋	zhèngwū	n.	principal rooms (in a courtyard, usually facing south)
瓦房	wǎfáng	n.	tile-roofed house
年代	niándài	n.	age; years; time
缝	fèng	n.	crack; crevice; fissure
杂草	zácǎo	n.	weeds; rank grass
偏房	piānfáng	n.	wing-room

草顶	cǎodǐng	*n.*	thatch
安	ān	*v.*	install
锅灶	guōzào	*n.*	cooking stove; kitchen range
迎出来	yíng.chu.lai	*v.-c.*	come out (from a room) to meet a visitor
让进去	ràng.jin.qu	*v.-c.*	invite (the guest) into (a room)
摆设	bǎi.she	*n.*	decorations; ornaments
简陋	jiǎnlòu	*adj.*	simple and crude
矮凳	ǎidèng	*n.*	low stool
钉	dìng	*v.*	nail
不成样子	bùchéng yàng.zi	*adj.*	in no shape to be seen; unpresentable
口袋	kǒudài	*n.*	pocket
摸	mō	*v.*	feel for; grope for
盒	hé	*AN..*	a box of; a case of
范辛	Fàn Xīn	*n.*	personal name
兄弟	xiōng.di	*n.*	(informal) a familiar form of address for a man younger than oneself
媳妇	xí.fu	*n.*	wife
看上去	kàn.shang.qu	*v.-c.*	it looks
瘦弱	shòuruò	*adj.*	thin and weak; frail
面孔	miànkǒng	*n.*	face
身材	shēncái	*n.*	stature; figure
娟秀	juānxiù	*adj.*	beautiful; graceful
纤弱	xiānruò	*adj.*	slim and fragile; delicate
灵芝	Língzhī	*n.*	personal name
卷	juǎn	*v.*	roll up
衣角	yījiǎo	*n.*	corner/border/hem of an article of clothing
半晌	bànshǎng	*n.*	half of the day
吭声	kēngshēng	*v.-o.*	utter a sound or word
抹	mǒ	*v.*	wipe
手背	shǒubèi	*n.*	the back of the hand
沾	zhān	*v.*	be stained with

"哭什么？说吧！别怕丢人，反正脸已经丢了！"达宽又重声重气地朝灵芝叫。"这次非把他姓葛的告倒不可！"

我知道要求灵芝述说这样的事是难堪的，但事情不了解清楚又不行，也只好催道："说吧，灵芝。"

"去年秋里，"灵芝带着哭音开了口："我有天去南坡地里摘绿豆，葛炭永骑车经过，看见我一个人在地里，就到我身边，先是问了几句绿豆的长势，又弯腰去帮我摘豆，我当时很感激，说：'村长，你事情多，快去忙别的吧，不用帮我。'他笑着说：'再忙，帮你摘豆我也愿意⑼！'我听见这话有股不正经的味儿，就不再去理他。谁知⑽他摘了两把豆，来我身边，猛一下握住了我的手说：'去那边包谷地里歇歇！'我说：'俺不歇。'他抬手就拉开我的衣服，手伸过来...我低头咬了他的手..."

嗵！达宽忽然猛捶了一下那张木桌。

灵芝住了口，默默地抬手去抹眼里的泪。

我停住笔，低了头无言地等，我不忍心再去催。

"说嘛！"达宽双手抱了头，眼望着地嘶声说。

"...第二回，是年前。那天我背了一筐麦子去面粉厂换面，谁知管换面的人不在，我正要出门走，一个人猛从背后抱住了俺，俺回头一看，是姓葛的。我气极叫他放开，他却说：'让我亲一下就给你一筐面。'我手抓脚踢，总算从他手里

朝…叫	cháo… jiào	v.	cry or shout at (somebody)
述说	shùshuō	v.	state; recount; narrate
难堪	nánkān	adj.	embarrassed
道	dào	v.	say; talk; speak
摘	zhāi	v.	pick; take off 摘苹果、摘豆角、摘眼镜、摘围巾、摘帽子
南坡	nánpō	n.	the southern slope
绿豆	lǜdòu	n.	mung bean
长势	zhǎngshì	n.	the way a crop is growing 作物的长势良好。
弯腰	wānyāo	v.-o.	bend; flex
感激	gǎnjī	v.	feel grateful; be thankful
股	gǔ	AN.	measure word for strength, smell, etc. 一股香味
不正经	bú zhèng.jing	adj.	indecent
猛一下	měng yí.xia	adv.	suddenly; abruptly
包谷地	bāogǔdì	n.	corn field
歇	xiē	v.	have a rest 已经工作了四个钟头了，歇一会吧。
俺	ǎn	pron.	(dialect) I; me
咬	yǎo	v.	bite
嗵	tōng	onom.	sound of pounding the table
捶	chúi	v.	beat (with a stick or fist) 他的腰疼，所以他不停地用手捶腰。
住口	zhùkǒu	v.-o.	shut up; stop talking
默默地	mòmò.de	adv.	quietly; silently
嘶声	sīshēng	adv.	(speak) in a hoarse voice
筐	kuāng	AN.	a basket of
麦子	mài.zi	n.	wheat
面粉厂	miànfěn chǎng	n.	flour mill
亲	qīn	v.	kiss 睡觉前，妈妈总要亲一亲孩子。
手抓脚踢	shǒuzhuā jiǎotī	v.	cuff and kick

挣出来，他低声对我说：'只要我看上了你，你早晚(11)得乖乖地跟我睡觉.…'"

"第三回，是上月初。那天，达宽去城里买化肥没回来，天快黑的时候，有人敲院门，我开门一看，是葛炭永。我冷脸问他干什么？他说是来检查评比文明家庭，看俺们屋里扫得干净不干净。我说我不想当文明家庭，他说：'不当文明家庭，就当个聪明女人。老老实实听话，让我一个月来会你几夜，我保管让你男人进村办造纸厂，让你的孩子在村小免费读书。和我有来往的女人，哪个也没让她吃亏。'我没让他说下去，我说：'你走吧！'他面色难看，从我身边走过时，又猛地抱住我，乱亲，幸好邻居三婶这时过来借东西，他慌忙松开我跑了......"说完，灵芝嘤嘤地哭。

我说："别伤心，葛炭永做了坏事，是要受到惩罚的，我会替你把这股冤气出了，相信我！"

接下来，我又问了他们去乡上告状的经过，又找了他们叫三婶的那个中年妇女，问了她所看见的情景，交待了以后请她作证的事，我便往回走了。

（三）

原想下午就把内参稿子写成，接着让人捎到镇上邮局寄

挣出来	zhèng chūlái	v.-c.	struggle to get free
看上	kàn.shang	v.-c.	take a fancy to
			他看上了一位漂亮的姑娘。

乖乖地	guāiguāi.de	*adv.*	obediently; well-behaved
化肥	huàféi	*n.*	short for 化学肥料：chemical fertilizer
评比	píngbǐ	*v.*	compare and assess
文明家庭	wénmíng jiātíng	*n.*	Civilized Family, an activity initiated and launched by 中华全国妇女联合会
会	huì	*v.*	meet; see
保管	bǎoguǎn	*v.*	assure; guarantee 只要你花时间，保管你学得好。
村办造纸厂	cūnbàn zàozhǐchǎng	*n.*	village-run paper mill
免费	miǎnfèi	*v.*	be free of charge
三婶	Sānshěn	*n.*	"3rd aunt", a woman whose husband is the third eldest in his family. (here): polite address to a neighbor woman
慌忙	huāngmáng	*adv.*	in a great rush; in a flurry
松开	sōngkāi	*v.-c.*	let go; release
嘤嘤	yīngyīng	*onom.*	sound of sobbing, chirping, or whispering
伤心	shāngxīn	*v.*	sad; grieved; broken-hearted
冤气	yuānqì	*n.*	resentment 要是不把这个杀人犯送进监狱，受害人家的冤气就出不来
告状	gàozhuàng	*v.-o.*	bring a law suit against somebody; go to law against somebody 他们告状已经告了一年了，但是就是告不倒欺负他们的人。
情景	qíngjǐng	*n.*	scene; sight; circumstances
交待	jiāodài	*v.*	make clear; brief
作证	zuòzhèng	*v.-o.*	testify; bear witness

（三）

稿子	gǎo.zi	*n.*	draft; sketch
接着	jiē.zhe	*adv.*	and then; after that 我们先总结了今年的工作，接着又讨论了明年的计划。
捎	shāo	*v.*	take along sth. to or for sb.

回报社，不料刚吃过午饭，舅家表弟来了。表弟小我一岁，如今也已是两个孩子的父亲了。我俩寒暄了一阵以后，表弟说："表哥，今日来，一来是为了看望姑父、姑姑和你，二来(12)，是想求你帮我办一件事。"我急忙应道："只要我能办到，只管(13)说。"

"我这几年一直想盖几间房子。如今总算把砖瓦、木料买齐了，可在宅基地上遇到了麻烦。我们原来的旧房不能拆，我爹和弟弟妹妹还要住，那新房就得另选新宅。可如今土地管理严格，占地必须经过村长批准。我去找了葛村长几回，他都推说忙而没有答应。其间送了一回礼，也只允许我在老宅上挤挤。老宅子你也知道，原本就不大，哪有盖三间房的地方？我正愁着，听说你回来，我就赶紧来了。你在外边混出了名堂(14)，求你去找葛村长说说，我想这个面子他一定会给你的。"

"让我去找葛炭永？"我惊得站了起来。

"对呀！他这个人聪明，绝不会驳你的面子！"

"这个忙我还真不能帮。"我断然地摆手。让我去求这个坏蛋，到他面前说好话，绝不干！

"怎么了？"表弟跳了起来："去帮我说句话都不肯？出去混出名堂了，不认我这个穷表弟了？"

| 报社 | bàoshè | n. | general office of a newspaper |
| 不料 | búliào | adv. | unexpectedly 本来想周末带孩子出去玩，不料孩子发烧了，所以，只能 |

			呆在家里。
舅家表弟	jiùjiā biǎodì	*n.*	younger male cousin who is the son of one's mother's brother
寒暄	hánxuān	*v.*	exchange of conventional greetings
姑父	gū.fu	*n.*	the husband of one's father's sister
姑姑	gū.gu	*n.*	one's father's sister
砖瓦	zhuānwǎ	*n.*	brick and tile
木料	mùliào	*n.*	timber; lumber
买齐	mǎiqí	*v.-c.*	everything needed has been bought
宅基地	zháijīdì	*n.*	the site of a house; the foundations of a house
拆	chāi	*v.*	pull down; dismantle
新宅	xīnzhái	*n.*	new site
批准	pīzhǔn	*v.*	approve; ratify; sanction 市政府批准了他们的设计方案，他们马上进行施工
推说	tuīshuō	*v.*	offer as an excuse (for not doing something)我问他为什么没来，他却推说工作忙。
其间	qíjiān	*n.*	during this or that time
送礼	sònglǐ	*v.-o.*	give somebody a present; present a gift to somebody
老宅	lǎozhái	*n.*	old site
赶紧	gǎnjǐn	*adv.*	hastily; without losing time
混出了名堂	hùn chū.le míng.tang	*phr.*	(informal) have earned some reputation; have accomplished something
驳…的面子	bó...de miàn.zi	*phr.*	not spare somebody's sensibilities; not show due respect for somebody's feelings
断然	duànrán	*adv.*	absolutely; flatly
摆手	bǎishǒu	*v.-o.*	shake one's hand in admonition or disapproval
坏蛋	huàidàn	*n.*	bad egg; scoundrel; bastard
说好话	shuō hǎohuà	*v.-o.*	say something pleasant to hear; say some fine words
认	rèn	*v.*	recognize somebody as one's relatives 他有了钱以后，就不认以前的那些穷朋友了。

"不，不是。"我急忙摇头。有心想把写内参的事给表弟说出，又担心把达宽家的事张扬开来。毕竟，灵芝还要在村里做人。"我以后再把原因给你说清楚。"

"我不听！"表弟朝地上吐了一口唾沫，起身就走，娘拉他也没拉住。表弟走远之后，娘抱怨我："其实你帮他去说说也没什么。"我苦笑着说："我一边写材料告葛炭永，一边又去找他求情，这事你让我怎么做？"

娘叹一口气说："唉，只怕(15)要惹你舅生气了。"

娘的判断没错。没过多久，舅便提着他的长杆烟袋进了院门。我看见后急忙迎出去招呼："舅来了。"舅脸阴着，理也没理便进了屋。娘见舅来，倒了一杯水端过去说："哥，你喝。"舅连看也不看。舅在一张椅子上坐好，我赶紧把一支香烟递过去。舅哼了一声说："俺们是让人瞧不起的穷人，吸不起这纸烟！"我朝娘无声地笑笑，娘瞪我一眼。

我知道我该向舅做个解释，于是便把我不去找葛炭永要宅基地的原因说了。我原以为舅听了就会消了气，没料到舅听后反而气得更狠，瞪大眼叫："你这不是存心要让我们今年盖不成房子吗？"

我愣在那里，嗫嚅着反问："这怎么叫成心..."

"你想想嘛，你不过是一个耍笔杆的记者，你说告就能把人家告倒？人家做了几十年官，上上下下人都熟。在你之前

有心	yǒuxīn	v.	have a mind to; set one's mind on 我有心去看看他，又怕打扰他。
张扬	zhāngyáng	v.	make widely known; make public
毕竟	bìjìng	adv.	after all; all in all
吐	tǔ	v.	spit
唾沫	tuò.mo	n.	saliva; spittle
抱怨	bàoyuàn	v.	complain
苦笑	kǔxiào	v.	force a smile; make a wry smile
材料	cáiliào	n.	data; material
求情	qiúqíng	v.-o.	plead; intercede; ask for a favor; beg for leniency 向他求情/为某人求情
叹一口气	tànyīkǒu qì	v.-o.	heave a sigh
唉	ai	intj.	alas (expressing sadness, weariness, regret or disappointment)
惹	rě	v.	offend; provoke 别惹她生气。
判断	pànduàn	n./v.	judgment, judge; decide
提	tí	v.	carry (in one's hand with the arm down)
长杆烟袋	chánggǎn yāndài	n.	long-stemmed pipe
招呼	zhāo.hu	v.	greet; hail; say hello to
脸阴着	liǎn yīn.zhe	phr.	have a sombre countenance; look glum
哼	hēng	v.	give a snort of contempt
瞧不起	qiáo.buqǐ	v.	same as 看不起; look down upon
瞪我一眼	dèng wǒ yìyǎn	phr.	give me an angry stare
消气	xiāoqì	v.-o.	cool down; be mollified
狠	hěn	adj.	(here) very; same as 很
存心	cúnxīn	adv.	intentionally; deliberately; on purpose 我不是存心这么做的。
愣	lèng	v.	dumbfounded; stupefied 他一问，大家都愣了。
嗫嚅	nièrú	v.	speak haltingly
反问	fǎnwèn	v.	ask a question in reply
耍笔杆	shuǎ bǐgǎn	v.-o.	wield a pen; be skilled in literary tricks 他光会耍笔杆，不会干别的。

也不是没人告过，告成了吗？你要告不成，风声又传到人家耳朵里，你是我外甥，村长他不迁怒到我身上？还能给我批宅基地？"

"我要告就要把他告倒，让上级另换一个村长！"舅舅的话让我也有些生气。

"好，退一万步讲，就算你把葛炭永告倒了，可村上具体管宅基地分配的是葛炭永的堂弟。他见你把他堂哥告倒，会善罢甘休？我去申请宅基地他会顺顺利利地给我？今年我们还能盖成房子？"

"那你说怎么办？"我不想和舅舅争下去。

"怎么办？你要是还看得起你舅，心里还想着你舅要盖房子，你就别惹人家，就带上盒烟去看看人家。你在外边做事，他也许会给你面子，痛痛快快把我要的宅基地批了！"

舅舅说完，起身就走了。

我进了自己的房间往床上一躺，我的心情很坏。那天我没有动笔。

（四）

早饭吃罢，我去几个邻居家做了礼貌性的拜会之后，决定还是把那篇内参写出。舅家的房子可以晚盖几天，可达宽家的冤不能不伸。我定下神刚写了一段，院里响起了大妹妹和妹夫的声音。我刚到家时已经见过他们，所以就不想再出去招呼，仍坐在桌前写自己的。但妹妹却边喊着哥边走进了我屋里，进屋开口就问："哥，你是不是在帮着达宽告人家葛村长？"

"你怎么知道？" 消息传得这样快？

"我怎么知道？我不光知道，还已经受了报答哩！" 大妹妹气哼哼地在床边坐下。

风声	fēngshēng	*n.*	rumor; talk; news
外甥	wài.sheng	*n.*	nephew
迁怒	qiānnù	*v.*	vent one's anger on somebody who is not to blame; take it out on somebody
批	pī	*v.*	write instructions or comments on (a report from a subordinate, etc.) (here) ratify; approve
上级	shàngjí	*n.*	higher authorities
退一万步讲	tuìyíwànbùjiǎng	*adv.*	even in the infinitesimal possibility
具体	jùtǐ	*adv.*	in the concrete; specifically
分配	fēnpèi	*v./n.*	distribute; allot, distribution
堂弟	tángdì	*n.*	male younger cousin on the paternal side
善罢甘休	shànbà gānxiū	*idm.*	(usually used in the negative) leave the matter at that; let it go at that

（四）

礼貌性	lǐmàoxìng	*adj.*	courteous; by courtesy
拜会	bàihuì	*n./v.*	(usually used on a diplomatic occasion) call, pay an official call
定下神	dìng.xia shén	*v.-o.*	collect oneself; compose oneself 一开始她吓坏了，后来才定下神来。
传	chuán	*v.*	spread 消息在网上传得很快。
报答	bàodá	*n./v.*	repay; requite; (here) revenge
气哼哼	qìhēnghēng	*adv.*	in a huff; panting with rage

"报答？"我不解。

"我们小二和小三，不是超生的吗？按村上的规定，一年是要罚八百块钱的。早些日子，我和小三他爹到葛村长家又是送礼又是求情的，总算让葛村长答应，以俺们家困难为理由不罚了。可今早起来，村妇女部主任却到家执意要罚，而且限我们五天内交出罚款，怎么求都不行。我当时就猜一定是咱家有谁做了什么对不住葛家的事。果然，妇女主任刚走，邻居一个嫂子就告诉我，说你正帮着达宽告村长！"

"欺人太甚！"我霍地立起，将手中的笔掷到桌上。报复竟这么快就来了！

"哥，你办事得想想俺们。俺们住在这儿，属人家管。"妹妹的话里夹了哭音。这当儿，妹夫领着他们的三个孩子进了屋。老大是女孩，六岁；老二也是女孩，四岁；老三是个男孩，三岁。姐弟仨一个比一个高，站在那儿像楼梯一样。

"你们当初也真不该要这么多孩子！"我抱怨地叹口气："如今让人家抓住了把柄。"

妹妹用泪眼瞪着我："俺们总得要个男娃吧？没有男娃，闺女们日后嫁出门，俺们老了谁照应？俺们老了又不像你那样，有养老金！"

我不愿同妹妹在这问题上说下去，就挥了挥手说："你们走吧！既然葛炭永要报复，我来替你们交这八百元罚款。"

　　"你说得倒轻巧，"妹妹撇撇嘴："有黑娃是年年要罚

的，你今年替俺们交了，明年呢？明年还不是照样(16)罚？再

说，八百块钱不是一个小数，你替俺们交，我嫂子能愿意？她

不解	bùjiě	*v.*	not understand
超生	chāoshēng	*v.*	bear a child over the permitted quota
答应	dā.ying	*v.*	agree; promise; comply with
执意	zhíyì	*adv.*	insist on; be determined to
限⋯天内	xiàn...tiānnèi	*v.*	within the stipulated X days
猜	cāi	*v.*	guess
欺人太甚	qīrén tàishèn	*idm.*	what a beastly bully; that's going too far; push people too hard
霍地	huò.de	*adv.*	suddenly
掷	zhì	*v.*	throw; cast
报复	bào.fu	*n./v.*	make reprisals; retaliate
属⋯管	shǔ... guǎn	*v..*	be under the management of; be subordinate to
仨	sā	*n.*	(informal) (not used with measure word) three people　我们仨
楼梯	lóutī	*n.*	stairs; staircase; stairway
当初	dāngchū	*adv.*	in the first place; originally
抓住把柄	zhuā.zhu bǎbǐng	*v.-o.*	catch sb. tripping; have sth. on sb.
闺女	guī.nü	*n.*	(informal) daughter
照应	zhào.ying	*v.*	look after; take care of
养老金	yǎnglǎojīn	*n.*	pension
挥手	huīshǒu	*v.-o.*	wave one's hand
说得轻巧	shuō.de qīng.qiao	*phr.*	talk as if it were a simple matter
撇嘴	piězuǐ	*v.-o.*	curl one's lip (in contempt, disbelief or disappointment)
黑娃	hēiwá	*n.*	children born over the permitted quota
照样	zhàoyàng	*adv.*	as before; in the same old way
嫂子	sǎo.zi	*n.*	elder brother's wife

那心胸你知道，俺和娘去城里看你，多住两天她都给我们脸色看，能给你八百块钱来替我们交罚款？"

我被妹妹说得有点脸热。不过我心里也承认她说得有理。

"明年他葛炭永想罚你们也罚不成了。不到明年，我就能把他告倒！"葛炭永的报复行为激得我越发下了告倒他的决心。

"说那大话干嘛(17)？一个村干部是那样好告倒的？就算你把村长告倒了，可村妇女主任是村长的外甥媳妇，她明年不是照样罚我？你能把人家妇女主任也告倒？人家又没犯什么错！"

"那你们说怎么办？"我没想到还有这一层。

"怎么办？别管达宽家的闲事！你在家住两天，就快回城里享你的福去！"

"那不行！"我想起达宽那副痛苦的模样。

"不行？"妹妹的眼圈又红了："好吧，你不可怜你妹妹，你总(18)该可怜可怜你这些外甥吧？大妞、二妞、小三，给你舅跪下！"老大、老二被她按跪在地，小三不肯跪，她便打了他的屁股一下，于是哇哇的哭声便在屋里响得惊天动地。妹夫呆立在那儿，不知所措。

娘在外间听见屋里的哭声，推门进来，一见这个场面，也掉下了眼泪，一边叫道："这干什么？干什么？"一边上前，一手抱住一个往外走，妹夫也赶紧抱了剩下的一个出门，妹妹捂着脸哭着跑出去。

我久久站在那儿，心乱如麻……

心胸	xīnxiōng	*n.*	breadth of mind
给…脸色看	gěi…liǎnsè kàn	*phr.*	convey displeasure or disapproval to sb. through facial expression
脸热	liǎnrè	*adj.*	blush (with shame or embarrassment)
越发	yuèfā	*adv.*	even more
下决心	xià juéxīn	*v.-o.*	make up one's mind; be determined 下定决心要完成工作
说大话	shuō dàhuà	*v.-o.*	brag; boast; talk big
层	céng	*AN.*	a component part in a sequence
管闲事	guǎn xiánshì	*v.-o.*	be meddlesome; be a busybody 这是他们的问题，你别管闲事。
享福	xiǎngfú	*v.-o.*	enjoy a happy life; live in ease and comfort
眼圈	yǎnquān	*n.*	rim of the eye
大妞	dàniū	*n.*	the elder girl
跪下	guì.xia	*v.*	kneel down
按跪在地	àn guì zàidì	*v.*	forcefully press somebody to kneel down
屁股	pì.gu	*n.*	(informal) buttocks (of human)
哇哇	wāwā	*onom.*	sound of crying child
惊天动地	jīngtiān dòngdì	*idm.*	shaking heaven and earth; earth-shaking
不知所措	bùzhī suǒcuò	*idm.*	be at a loss; be at one's wits' end
场面	chǎngmiàn	*n.*	scene; occasion
捂着脸	wǔ.zhe liǎn	*v.-o.*	cover one's face with one's hand
心乱如麻	xīnluàn rúmá	*idm.*	have one's mind all in a tangle; be utterly confused and disconccrted

（五）

下午，我独自去北坡的麦田田埂上走走，想平静一下纷乱的思绪。我缓缓地走着，视而不见地望着麦田，心里仍在想着那条内参究竟怎么办。写了，舅家的房子今年可能盖不成，妹妹家每年都要被罚款 800 块；不写，达宽的冤气就无法伸！我感觉我的决心已不如当初的那么坚决，但我想了一阵之后仍然决定：写！我不能让达宽和灵芝骂我！

远远地，我看见村里走出一个妇女，很快地向这片麦地走来。我估计是谁家的女人来田里干活，便也没有在意，直到脚步声到了身后不远处时，才又扭头去看。这一看让我吃了一惊，来者原来是南庄达宽的那个邻居三婶。

"你是…"我猜她是来找我，莫非 ⑲ 达宽家又出了什么事？

"来找你！"那三婶一边喘气抹汗一边说。

"有事？"

"我没有看见！"她望着我忽然这样坚决地说。

我一时没明白她的意思，茫然地问："你没看见什么？"

"就是葛村长和灵芝的事，我一点也没看见！"她扭开脸，把目光对着那些嫩绿的麦苗。

我顿时明白了她的话："可你前天不是亲口向我证明说，你看见了葛炭永抱住灵芝的事么？"

"我没有看见！我一点也没有看见！"

"你仔细想想..."

"我没有看见！"她打断了我的话，又说了一遍后，便快速地转身沿着来路回去了。

（五）

独自	dú.zì	*adv.*	alone; by oneself
北坡	běipō	*n.*	north slope
平静	píngjìng	*v.*	calm down
纷乱	fēnluàn	*adj.*	numerous and disorderly
思绪	sīxù	*n.*	train of thought; thinking
缓缓	huǎnhuǎn	*adv.*	slowly
视而不见	shì ér bújiàn	*idm.*	pretend not to notice; turn a blind eye to
坚决	jiānjué	*adj.*	firm; resolute; determined
估计	gū.ji	*v.*	estimate; reckon
在意	zàiyì	*v.*	care about; mind; take to heart
扭头	niǔtóu	*v.-o.*	turn one's head
吃了一惊	chīle yì jīng	*v.-o.*	be startled; be shocked
莫非	mòfēi	*adv.*	can it be that; is it possible that 他没来，莫非生病了？
喘气	chuǎnqì	*v.-o.*	breathe deeply; pant; gasp
抹汗	mǒhàn	*v.-o.*	wipe the sweat
茫然	mángrán	*adv.*	ignorant; in the dark
嫩绿	nènlǜ	*adj.*	light green; soft green
麦苗	màimiáo	*n.*	wheat seedling
顿时	dùnshí	*adv.*	immediately; at once
亲口	qīnkǒu	*adv.*	(say something) personally
仔细	zǐ.xi	*adv.*	carefully; attentively
打断	dǎduàn	*v.*	interrupt; cut short
转身	zhuǎnshēn	*v.*	turn around
沿着	yán.zhe	*prep.*	along 沿着公路一直走

我呆呆地看着她的背影。她这个举动令我发慌：即使我把内参写了，上级领导批了，调查组也成立了，可是调查时没有证人，只是灵芝一个人揭发，若葛炭永坚决否认，这件事就难办。那位三婶，一定是受了什么恐吓！我原本定下来的心重又变乱...

（六）

晚饭我吃得心绪不宁。正吃时，院门外响起了一声洪亮的叫声："听说范辛兄弟回来了，可是真的？"这声音有些陌生，娘听了先是一怔，继而慌张地对我说："是村长！"跟着就和爹一块急急地迎出去："是村长来了，快进屋！"跟着又转向我叫："老大，快！村长来看你了！"

我不情愿地放下饭碗。高高壮壮的葛炭永已经走到门口："果然是范辛兄弟回来了，这一向弟妹和孩子可好？"

"好。"我应酬地回答。屋里的灯光虽暗，但仍能让我看出他脸上的红润和精神。

"回来了怎么也不告诉一声？是怕我来吸你带来的好烟吧？"他在椅子上坐了，双眼笑望着我。

爹早惶恐地把我带回来的好烟递了过去，我看见爹的手有些颤。我想叫爹继续吃他的饭，话还没出口，葛炭永已抓了爹的手又望着娘极亲热地叫："大叔，婶子，我得代表全村人感谢你们二老啊，你们养了一个多么聪明有为的孩子，又是记者又是作家，这是我们村值得炫耀的光荣啊！"

背影	bèiyǐng	n.	a view of somebody's back
举动	jǔdòng	n.	movement; act
发慌	fāhuāng	v.	feel nervous; get flustered
调查组	diàocházǔ	n.	investigation group
证人	zhèng.ren	n.	witness
揭发	jiēfā	v.	expose; unmask; bring to light
恐吓	kǒnghè	v./n.	threaten; intimidate
重	chóng	adv.	again; once more 重写/重做

（六）

心绪不宁	xīnxùbùníng	idm.	in a disturbed state of mind
洪亮	hóngliàng	adj.	loud and clear; sonorous
继而	jì'ér	adv.	then; afterwards
慌张	huāngzhāng	adv.	in a flurried manner
不情愿	bù qíngyuàn	adv.	unwillingly
弟妹	dìmèi	n.	one's younger brother's wife
应酬	yìngchóu	adv./v.	exchange words perfunctorily
红润	hóngrùn	adj.	ruddy; rosy
惶恐	huángkǒng	adv.	in a state of alarm (or trepidation)
颤	chàn	v.	quiver; tremble
抓	zhuā	v.	grab; seize
亲热	qīnrè	adv.	affectionately; intimately
大叔	dàshū	n.	uncle (a polite form of address for a man about one's father's age)
婶子	shěn.zi	n.	aunt
有为	yǒuwéi	adj.	promising
炫耀	xuànyào	v.	show off; make a display of 她常常在朋友面前炫耀自己的丈夫有多爱她。
光荣	guāngróng	n.	honor; glory; credit

娘和爹被这串奉承话压得不知如何是好。我微笑着望定姓葛的，等着他摊牌。如果你姓葛的今天想来吓唬、威胁我，你算走错门儿了！在这一刹，我心中原有的那股犹豫反而飞走，我一定要替达宽把状告下去！

"兄弟怎么不把娃子也带回来玩玩？"葛炭永仍然谈着家常，语调极是亲切。

"孩子已经上三年级了，不放假不好带他。"我只好应付这种谈话。

"范辛兄弟，今晚听说你回来，我特意登门，是因为有一件事相求啊！" 葛炭永长长地吸了一口烟说。我估计这是他道明真实来意的时候了，我看见爹和娘的眼中都露出了紧张。我淡淡一笑，点了点头：

"说吧！"我已做好了当面批驳的准备。想吓唬我？没那么容易！

"你可能不晓得，我的大娃子都上高中了，偏偏也喜欢学写东西，整天看这报纸看那杂志。听说你回来了，非要让我领来拜你为师不可！你可千万得收下这个徒弟呀！大河！"他说着扭头朝院门外喊。随着这声喊，一个十六七岁的小伙子腼腆地走进院子走进屋门。

我一时呆住了，没想到事情会这样发展。同时看见爹和娘都长舒了一口气，刚才脸上的那份紧张都没有了。

串	chuàn	AN.	a string of; a bunch of 一串钥匙
奉承话	fèng.cheng huà	n.	flattery
压	yā	v.	suppress; daunt; intimidate
不知如何是好	bùzhīrúhé shìhǎo	phr.	don't know what to do; to be at a loss
微笑	wēixiào	v.	smile
摊牌	tānpái	v.-o.	lay one's card on the table; have a showdown
吓唬	xià.hu	v.	frighten; scare; intimidate
威胁	wēixié	v.	threaten
走错门儿	zǒu cuò ménr	phr.	come to a wrong door – no way to get what one wants
一刹	yíchà	n.	instant; a split second
犹豫	yóuyù	n./v.	hesitation, hesitate
家常	jiācháng	n.	the daily life of a family
语调	yǔdiào	n.	intonation
亲切	qīnqiè	adj.	cordial; kind
特意	tèyì	adv.	for a special purpose; specially 特意来看你
登门	dēngmén	v.-o.	visit somebody's house
相求	xiāngqiú	v.	beg; request; entreat; beseech
道明来意	dàomíng láiyì	phr.	make clear what one has come for
露出	lùchū	v.	show; reveal 脸上露出了笑容
淡淡一笑	dàndàn yí xiào	v.	smile indifferently
点头	diǎntóu	v.-o.	nod
批驳	pībó	v.	refute; criticize; rebut
拜师	bàishī	v.-o.	formally become a pupil to a master
徒弟	túdì	n.	apprentice; disciple
扭头	niǔtóu	v.-o.	turn one's head
腼腆	miǎntiǎn	adj.	bashfully
长舒一口气	cháng shū yì kǒu qì	phr.	relax; have a breathing space

"大河，这就是你那个当记者、作家的范叔。你不是想学写东西吗？以后他就是你的老师。快，拜师学艺，给你范叔磕头！"

那小伙子犹豫了一下真要下跪，我急忙上前扶住他说："可别磕头！你既然要学写作，我教你就是。"

"也是，如今不时兴这礼节了，就免了也行。可是大河，你总不能拜了师对老师一点心意也不表吧？"葛炭永坐在那里笑着对他的儿子说。

那小伙子被提醒了似地涨红着脸跑出去，片刻后便背了一个装得满满的麻袋进屋。麻袋显然不轻，把小伙子压得身子乱晃。我一看便知这是礼物，急忙上前拦住说："这可不能放下！"

"拜师学艺，徒弟当然得给师傅送点礼物！他还能拿什么好东西？还不就是 (20) 点土产！"葛炭永起身拉起他儿子向门外走，高声说道:"师生如父子,从今以后，你把他当儿子看就是！""不，不行！"我扯紧那孩子的另一只手，想把那麻袋塞过去。但爹这时过来，以少见的力气推开我说："还不快谢谢村长！"

我没有开口，只是呆望着爹娘送葛家父子走出院门。

"送礼不收等于打脸啊！"爹回屋后瞪着我训："再说，这么多年你见村长给谁家送过礼？逢年过节，都是村上人给他送礼，这是看得起咱啊！"

娘慢慢地解开麻袋口去掏里边的东西：先是两块布料，

接着是一大包黑木耳，足有五斤；再接着是四瓶酒，跟着是

拜师学艺	bàishī xuéyì	idm.	become a pupil to a master and learn a craft or trade
磕头	kētóu	v.-o.	kowtow
扶住	fú.zhu	v.-c.	strengthen somebody up
时兴	shíxīng	v./adj.	be in style/popular; in vogue
礼节	lǐjié	n.	courtesy; etiquette; ceremony
表心意	biǎo xīnyì	v.-o.	express one's regard; show one's kindly feelings
涨红脸	zhàng hóngliǎn	v.-o.	redden or flush the face (with anger or shy)
片刻	piànkè	n.	a short while; a moment
麻袋	mádài	n.	gunny bag; gunnysack
乱晃	luàn huàng	v.	shake; sway
拦住	lán.zhu	v.-c.	stop (somebody) 他刚要说，我把他拦住了。
土产	tǔchǎn	n.	local product
扯紧	chějǐn	v.-c.	pull somebody (by the hand)
塞	sāi	v.	fill in; squeeze
力气	lì.qi	n.	strength
打脸	dǎ liǎn	v.-o.	(informal) do not show due respect for somebody's feelings
训	xùn	v.	give somebody a lecture
逢年过节	féngnián guòjié	idm.	on New Year's Day or other festivals
解开	jiěkāi	v.-c.	untie; undo
掏	tāo	v.	draw out; pull out; fish out
布料	bùliào	n.	cloth
黑木耳	hēimù'ěr	n.	edible black fungus
足	zú	adv.	fully; as much as 路上足足走了两个钟头。

烟，接下来是两桶香油，都是十斤一桶的，最底层是绿豆。

"天哪！多么重的礼物啊！"娘惊叹着。

爹看定娘，叹息着说："当村长的能给咱送这样重的礼，咱范家也算活得值了！"

"值了！"娘轻轻点了下头。然后看定我，以轻微得我几乎听不见的声音说："老大，算了，别难为村长了。"

我知道娘的意思，我什么也没说，只是缓缓地在椅子上坐了……

（七）

晨起，我去洗脸时，娘进屋叠被扫地，待我洗漱完回屋，发现娘把我摊放在桌上的稿纸收起来了。我懂得娘的心意。其实她不收我也不准备写那内参了。我昨晚想了一夜，眼下如果坚持写，势必要给爹和娘增添很重的心理负担，而且万一因为无证人而没把葛炭永告倒，那么接下来便是自己的家人倒霉了。爹娘辛辛苦苦地供我上学，我毕业工作后，因为工资低平日并没给家里多少照应，要是为了这内参的事再给爹娘的晚年带来不快和不幸，可真是不该。还有，葛炭永也许会反告我诬陷，那样，我就可能陷进一桩官司里，时间和声誉都会因此而受损失，这也有点犯不着 (21)。再说，葛炭永虽然三次欺侮灵芝，却都没有得逞。经过这次我要告他的虚惊，以后可能收敛一点，不敢再做这样的坏事了。

桶	tǒng	*AN.*	barrel; bucket
香油	xiāngyóu	*n.*	sesame oil
惊叹	jīngtàn	*v.*	wonder at; marvel at; exclaim (with admiration)
活得值	huó.de zhí	*v.-c.*	have led a worthwhile life with no regrets
难为	nán.wei	*v.*	embarrass; press 他不会唱歌，你就别难为他了。

（七）

叠被	diébèi	*v.-o.*	fold up a quilt; make the bed
洗漱	xǐshù	*v.*	wash (the face) and rinse (the mouth)
摊放	tānfàng	*v.*	spread out
稿纸	gǎozhǐ	*n.*	standardized writing paper with squares or lines
眼下	yǎnxià	*n.*	at the moment; at present
势必	shìbì	*adv.*	certainly will; be bound to
倒霉	dǎoméi	*v.*	have bad luck; be out of luck
辛辛苦苦	xīnxīnkǔkǔ	*adv.*	take a lot of trouble; take great pains 他每天辛辛苦苦地工作。
照应	zhào.ying	*n./v.*	look after; take care of
晚年	wǎnnián	*n.*	old age; one's later years
不快	búkuài	*n./adj.*	be unhappy; be displeased
不幸	búxìng	*n./adj.*	misfortune; adversity
反告	fǎn gào	*v.*	countercharge
诬陷	wūxiàn	*v.*	frame a case against; frame somebody
桩	zhuāng	*AN.*	measure word for matter, affair, etc. 一桩大事
声誉	shēngyù	*n.*	reputation; fame; prestige
欺侮	qīwǔ	*v.*	bully and humiliate
得逞	déchěng	*v.*	(derog.) have one's way; prevail; succeed
虚惊	xūjīng	*n.*	false alarm 受了一场虚惊
收敛	shōuliǎn	*v.*	restrain oneself

如此这样一想，我的心在天亮之前其实已经平静，我准备吃过早饭后，照原来的计划，去十几里外一家国营化纤厂采访。

吃过早饭，正准备出门，在村办纸厂当厂长的我最要好的中学同学何向突然来了。"干什么去？"明白了我的去向后，他说："干嘛先去那儿而不来我的纸厂采访？走吧，先到我的纸厂！"说着推了车便先出门。我解释了一阵，他不理，只管走。我想想再拖一天也问题不大，便只好跟了他走。

纸厂设在一条河边，主要生产包装纸箱。厂子不大，我在何向的带领下整个看了一遍。我这双外行人的眼睛也能看出，厂子的方向虽对，但管理太差，效益可能不好。果然，回到办公室何向介绍生产情况时说厂子盈利不大，并说要我帮忙让厂子有所发展。我急忙笑着摆手："我又不懂企业管理，能帮什么忙？"

"你能帮！"何向的语气坚定："就看 ㉒ 你愿不愿帮！"

"嗨！"我无可奈何："你真是病急乱投医。我能帮你什么？"

"你给我们写篇文章！"

"文章？"我愕然。

"你写篇文章吹吹我们这个厂，吹吹我们的创业精神，吹吹我们产品的质量，这对我们厂子的发展不大有帮助？"

"老天，你怎么想出这个主意？"

"你写不写吧！你要是还看得起我这个老同学，你要是
还想着家乡父老，你就该写！我们没钱做广告，你的文章就是
好广告啊！"

"你是在逼我？"

"你只是动动你手中的笔，用不了两三个小时，就能帮

国营化纤厂	guóyíng huàxiān chǎng	*n.*	state-run chemical fiber factory
要好	yàohǎo	*adj.*	be close friends
去向	qùxiàng	*n.*	the direction in which somebody or something has gone
拖	tuō	*v.*	delay; drag on; procrastinate
生产	shēngchǎn	*v.*	produce; manufacture
包装纸箱	bāozhuāng zhǐxiāng	*n.*	packing box
带领	dàilǐng	*v.*	lead; guide
外行人	wàihángrén	*n.*	layman; nonprofessional
效益	xiàoyì	*n.*	beneficial result
盈利	yínglì	*n.*	profit; gain
企业管理	qǐyè guǎnlǐ	*n.*	business management
嗨	hāi	*intj.*	What? ; Darn it! (sigh expressing sadness, regret or surprise)
无可奈何	wúkě nàihé	*idm.*	have no way out
病急乱投医	bìngjí luàn tóuyī	*idm.*	men at death's door will turn in desperation to any doctor – men in a desperate plight will try anything
愕然	è'rán	*v./adv.*	stunned; astounded
吹	chuī	*v.*	boast; brag
创业	chuàngyè	*v.*	start an undertaking; do pioneering work
家乡父老	jiāxiāng fùlǎo	*n.*	elders in one's hometown
逼	bī	*v.*	force; press

我们很大的忙！当初为了办它，我们吃了多少苦费了多少力，你就不心疼俺们？”

“好吧！”我叹了口气，“那就说说你们当初创业的情况和当前的进展，以及下一步的打算…”

“我们领导和工人一开始就认为…”何向开始向我介绍。他说得滔滔不绝，似乎早有准备，而且多次使用“我们领导”这个词组。我觉得有些好笑，但也只把这些理解为上报纸心切 (23)，并没去想别的。

何向一直说到中午，午饭我和他就在厂里吃。吃过饭稍休息了一会，我便决定为他们写一篇报导，尽快把这事应付过去。何向听说我要动笔，高兴得急忙给我端茶倒水。

这篇报导主要是肯定他们办企业的方向，以及为办企业所做的努力，顺便介绍了一下他们的产品，也根据何向的介绍写了他们厂领导如何廉洁正派。我用了两个小时写完了，然后交给何向看。何向看后眉开眼笑，连说：“好，好！”跟着就把稿子装进了他的口袋，又说：“我们厂明天有人去省城，就把你这篇报导捎到报社去，早登早高兴。”

我起身告辞要回家，他扯住我的手不放：“这哪里行？你这样帮我们，我们哪有不谢之理(24)？今晚必须在这里吃饭！”

再三推辞不允，便只好随他去。晚饭是在厂子食堂隔

壁的小房间里开的。何向又叫来了五个少时的伙伴。我们说说
笑笑地走进那个小房间时，桌上的酒菜让我大吃一惊。 酒是一
瓶茅台和一瓶五粮液，热菜还没上，但冷盘的做工和用料都和
城里宾馆的不相上下。

　　"你这一桌得花多少钱？"我指着那瓶茅台，真有些生

吃苦	chīkǔ	v.-o.	bear hardships; suffer
心疼	xīnténg	v.	feel sorry; be distressed
滔滔不绝	tāotāo bùjué	idm.	pouring out words in a steady flow
词组	cízǔ	n.	phrase
好笑	hǎoxiào	adj.	funny; ridiculous
…心切	xīnqiè	adj.	anxious; eager 出国心切/望子成龙心切
稍	shāo	adv.	a little; a bit 稍知道一点儿/稍看了一下
应付	yìng.fu	v.	do something perfunctorily
廉洁正派	liánjié zhèngpài	adj.	upright and honest
眉开眼笑	méikāi yǎnxiào	idm.	be all smiles; beam with joy
告辞	gàocí	v.	take leave (of one's host)
扯	chě	v.	pull; hold onto
推辞	tuīcí	v.	decline (an invitation, appointment, etc.)
不允	bùyǔn	v.	refuse to consent
伙伴	huǒbàn	n.	pal; partner
茅台	Máotái	n.	Maotai (a famous Chinese spirit)
五粮液	Wǔliángyè	n.	Wuliangye (a famous Chinese spirit)
冷盘	lěngpán	n.	cold dish
做工	zuògōng	n.	workmanship
用料	yòngliào	n.	ingredient
不相上下	bùxiāng shàngxià	idm.	equally matched; about the same 跟第一流的大学不相上下

361

气，我想到了达宽家的可怜样子："我们老朋友见面何必非要喝这种酒？一百多块钱一瓶，你真舍得！你厂子赚几个钱？"

"嗨！这也不全是我的意思。再说，两年了你不才回来一次？你要时常回来我就不这样了！"何向笑着辩解。

我当时并没有留意他前半句话。我被伙伴们推到上座，只得坐下。这时我发现身边空着一个座位，我让他们过来坐，但无论怎么说，他们都不来，我就不再啰嗦。酒席开始，照例是碰杯、敬酒。喝得面红耳热之时，门外突然有个声音叫："嗬，这儿有酒香！"我还没有反应过来，何向已经跑去拉开了门。门外站着满面笑容的葛炭永。

"哈哈，看来我的鼻子还行！"葛炭永在门口大声笑着。

"快来坐，村长！"身边的几个伙伴起身去拉他，他也没有推让，径直走到我身边的空位上坐了。我有些发窘。我虽然已不打算写内参告他，但也从来没想到要和他坐在一起喝酒。我拿不高兴的目光去看何向，但何向不瞧我，只管倒酒。

"我既是碰上这酒宴，就要借这机会，敬范辛老弟一杯！"葛炭永笑着高高将酒杯举过来。我迟疑了一下，似乎没有不应之理，便也举起杯子，碰了过去。

"你们两个碰一杯不行！"

何向这时开口："葛村长，你不知道，范辛刚为咱们厂写了篇报导，为了这篇文章，你这村长兼厂长不该再敬范辛两杯？"

"兼厂长？"我压不住自己的吃惊。

"对呀，对呀！"何向笑着向我解释："葛村长一直兼我们纸厂的正厂长，我只是个副厂长，在葛村长的指挥下办点具体事情。"

我的心猛一沉。这么说，我其实是在为葛炭永写歌颂文章？

辩解	biànjiě	*v.*	try to defend oneself
留意	liúyì	*v.*	pay attention to; keep one's eyes open
上座	shàngzuò	*n.*	the seat of honor
啰嗦	luō.suo	*v.*	talk on and on
酒席	jiǔxí	*n.*	feast; banquet
照例	zhàolì	*adv.*	as usual; as a rule; usually
碰杯	pèngbēi	*v.-o.*	clink glasses
敬酒	jìngjiǔ	*v.-o.*	propose a toast; toast
嗬	he	*intj.*	ah, oh
推让	tuīràng	*v.*	decline (a position, favor, etc. out of modesty)
径直	jìngzhí	*adv.*	straight; directly; straightaway
发窘	fājiǒng	*v.*	feel embarrassed; be ill at ease
酒宴	jiǔyàn	*n.*	banquet
借机会	jiè jīhuì	*v.*	take the opportunity to
敬	jìng	*v.*	offer politely 敬你一杯/敬酒/敬茶
兼	jiān	*v.*	hold two or more jobs concurrently
副厂长	fùchǎng zhǎng	*n.*	vice director of a factory
指挥	zhǐhuī	*v.*	direct; command; conduct
猛一沉	měng yì chén	*phr.*	(heart) sink suddenly
歌颂	gēsòng	*v.*	sing the praises of; extol; eulogize

"来来，为了范辛兄弟对纸厂建设的关心，我再敬你两杯！"我边咽酒边在心里骂何向：你小子为什么早不说葛炭永兼着这纸厂的厂长？

"现在我有个提议，"何向站起来，照例是那副笑脸："范辛这报导中凡是写着'厂领导'的地方，干脆都改成葛村长的名字算了，要不，外人看了，会误认为我们有好多领导干部，其实领导就一个：葛村长！"

"对，对！"其余几个伙伴立即附和，只有葛炭永笑着摆手："改什么，改什么！功劳其实都是群众的！"

"改一下吧，范辛？"何向直直望着我。杂种！我真想一拳朝他脸上打过去。我现在才明白，这一切都是事先设计好的。

我默默地捏着酒杯，屋子里突然变得很静。我知道我必须作出个回答。如果我答不必改，实际上就把这桌上所有的人得罪了！既然文章实际上写的是他，既然已不打算告他，那就不必再结怨了。"你拿笔改改吧！"我朝何向说罢，端起自己面前的酒便又喝了。

我听见葛炭永在夸我海量，我感到一股灼热的东西向腹里刺去……

（八）

我一直到第二天中午才从酒醉中醒过来。我从床上坐起身时，看见娘正在床前洗我吐脏的衣服。"怎么喝成这

样？" 娘心疼地责怪。我没说话，坐在那里回想昨晚回家的

咽	yàn	v.	swallow
小子	xiǎo.zi	n.	(derog.) bloke; fellow; guy
提议	tíyì	n.	motion; proposal
干脆	gāncuì	adv.	simply; just; altogether 别犹豫了，你干脆说"行"还是"不行"！
外人	wàirén	n.	stranger; outsider
误认为	wù rènwéi	v.	mistake one thing for another 他误认为明天考试，所以今天没来。
其余	qíyú	adj.	all the other (persons or things); the rest
附和	fùhè	v.	echo; chime in with 附和别人的意见
功劳	gōngláo	n.	credit; meritorious service; contribution
群众	qúnzhòng	n.	the masses
拳	quán	n.	fist
设计	shèjì	v.	design; plan
捏	niē	v.	holding between the finger and thumb; pinch
得罪	dézuì	v.	offend; displease
结怨	jiéyuàn	v.-o.	contract enmity; incur hatred
说罢	shuōbà	v.	finish saying
夸	kuā	v.	praise
海量	hǎiliàng	adj.	great capacity for liquor
灼热	zhuórè	adj.	scorching hot
腹	fù	n.	belly (of the body); abdomen
刺	cì	v.	stab; prick

（八）

酒醉	jiǔzuì	v.	be drunk
醒过来	xǐng.guo.lai	v.-c.	regain consciousness
吐脏	tù zāng	v.-c.	become filthy from vomit
责怪	zéguài	v.	blame

经过，但记不起来，脑子里一片空白。

外间传来舅舅说话的声音。我估计他又是来让我替他要宅基地的，不由得心里一阵烦躁。我心里想好，只要舅舅再提起宅基地的事，我就告诉他，我立刻要去化纤厂采访，没时间管这事了。

未料到的是，我刚走出里屋，舅舅一看见我就站起身说："辛儿，上回舅舅不该那样怪你，你对舅舅盖房的事这样挂心，舅舅不会忘记！"

"我觉得莫名其妙，不知舅舅说的是什么。

你的话还真管用！"舅舅笑得脸上都是皱纹："今儿早上村上的干部就去通知，说已给俺家批了盖四间房的宅基地。要的是三间，给批了四间。这要是没有你的面子，能行？"原来如此。回报也来得这样快！我叹了一口气，对舅舅说："既然批了，那你就抓紧盖吧！"

"盖，盖，三几天后就动工。"舅舅边说边从身后拉过一个竹篮，"这是自家做的黄酒，喝着养人。你写东西的人每早喝上一碗，比什么都好。"篮子里放着一个黄澄澄的乡下酒坛，舅舅把它放到我的面前。

这时候，随着一阵脚步响，我看见妹妹、妹夫拉着他们那三个小儿女，也走进了院里。

"二妞，小三，快，来给你舅磕头！"

"你干什么？"我是真的火了。干嘛非用这法逼我不可？我真想朝她吼：你的事我就是不管！

"感谢你呀！"妹妹朝我笑道："没有你，俺二妞、小三做梦也不敢想能分到责任田。"

"责任田？"娘替我惊问。

空白	kòngbái	*n.*	blank space
不由得	bùyóu.de	*adv.*	can't help; cannot but 他说得很不清楚，我不由得有点儿怀疑。
烦躁	fánzào	*adj.*	fidgety; agitated
挂心	guàxīn	*v.*	be on one's mind
莫名其妙	mòmíng qímiào	*idm.*	be unable to make head or tail of something; be baffled
管用	guǎnyòng	*adj.*	(informal) of use; effective
皱纹	zhòuwén	*n.*	wrinkle
通知	tōngzhī	*v.*	notify; inform; give notice
回报	huíbào	*n./v.*	repay; reciprocate
抓紧	zhuājǐn	*v.*	firmly grasp; pay close attention to
动工	dònggōng	*v.-o.*	begin construction; start building
竹篮	zhúlán	*n.*	bamboo basket
黄酒	huángjiǔ	*n.*	yellow rice or millet wine
养人	yǎngrén	*adj.*	nutritious; beneficial to one's health
黄澄澄	huáng chéngchéng	*adj.*	glistening yellow; golden
酒坛	jiǔtán	*n.*	wine jar
火	huǒ	*v.*	get angry; get mad
吼	hǒu	*v.*	roar; howl
做梦也不敢想	zuòmèngyě bùgǎnxiǎng	*phr.*	dare not to even dream about it
责任田	zérèntián	*n.*	field distributed to a family (by the government) that it is responsible for

"是啊！今儿早上，妇女主任亲自跑到家告诉说，不仅超生小二、小三那八百块钱不罚了，今年还要给小二、小三分一份责任田哩。你说，这样的好事，没有哥的脸面，能落到俺们头上？"

我长长地吁了一口气，默然坐下去。

（九）

我原本想下午就去完成原定的采访任务，而且采访完就直接由那里回城里，娘听说我采访完了不再回来，坚持让我再住一夜。可没想到，天黑的时候，达宽来了。我看见他进院，一时不知该说什么好。他手里提着一串小鱼，有五六条，大的不过二三两重。

"大娘，这是俺用渔网在水塘里逮的，不多，表示俺和灵芝的一点心意。你把他们炸炸让范辛兄弟尝尝。他整日写文章，吃这东西好。"他把鱼递给娘，然后转向我，不好意思地笑笑："实在拿不出别的东西。"

我张了张嘴，但没说出话来。达宽还不知道我已经变了主意，我说什么呢？

"快坐吧！达宽，你今晚就在这里吃饭。"娘亲热地让着。

"不了，灵芝还在外头。我们说好一块来看看你的，可到了院子外边，她又不好意思进来。"达宽说着便向门口走。

"你等等。"娘急忙拉住他的手，示意他停一下。她急步走进屋里，片刻后走出来，手上拎了一大包红枣，还有一块我带回来的布料。"拿着，达宽！"

"不，大娘，你这是……"

"拿着！"娘把那包东西塞在达宽怀里。我知道，娘这是在替我向达宽表示歉意。

我和娘送达宽出门。在院门外，我看见灵芝站在几十步外的一棵树下。月亮刚升上来，光很弱很暗，我只能看见灵

| 脸面 | liǎnmiàn | *n.* | face; somebody's feelings |
| 吁一口气 | xūyìkǒuqì | *v.* | heave a sigh |

（九）

任务	rènwù	*n.*	mission; assignment; task
两	liǎng	*AN.*	a traditional unit of weight, about 50 grams
渔网	yúwǎng	*n.*	fishnet; fishing net
水塘	shuǐtáng	*n.*	pond; pool
逮	dǎi	*v.*	capture; catch 警察逮住了那个小偷。
尝	cháng	*v.*	taste; try the flavor of
张嘴	zhāngzuǐ	*v.-o.*	open one's mouth
主意	zhǔ.yi	*n.*	decision, idea
让	ràng	*v.*	invite; offer
示意	shìyì	*v.*	signal; hint; motion
红枣	hóngzǎo	*n.*	red date
大娘	dàniáng	*n.*	aunt (a respectful form of address used for an elderly woman)
怀	huái	*n.*	bosom
歉意	qiànyì	*n.*	apology; regret
棵	kē	*AN.*	measure word for plants

芝那纤细的身影，看不清她的面容，看不清她的神情。不知道她的眼中是不是还含着耻辱的眼泪。

我和达宽握别。达宽喃喃地说道："范辛兄弟，俺们一辈子不会忘记你……"

"我…尽力吧…" 我说完这句模棱两可的话，慌忙把手松开，我害怕他还会说出什么。娘走过去和灵芝说话，我没有过去，我没有和灵芝说话的勇气。我只是站在院门前，默默地望着达宽和灵芝一高一低的两个身影，在暗淡的月光下向远处移动，直到他们变成两个若有若无的黑点……

选自《瓦解》，长江文艺出版社，2001 年 5 月

纤细	xiānxì	*adj.*	very thin; slender; fine
身影	shēnyǐng	*n.*	a person's silhouette; figure
面容	miànróng	*n.*	facial features; face
神情	shénqíng	*n.*	expression; look
含	hán	*v.*	contain; (here): with tears in one's eyes
耻辱	chǐrǔ	*n.*	shame; disgrace; humiliation
握别	wòbié	*v.*	shake hands at parting; part
喃喃	nánnán	*onom.*	mutter; murmur
一辈子	yíbèi.zi	*n.*	all one's life; a life time
尽力	jìnlì	*v.*	do all one can; try one's best
模棱两可	móléng liǎngkě	*idm.*	equivocal; ambiguous
勇气	yǒngqì	*n.*	courage
移动	yídòng	*v.*	move; shift
若有若无	ruòyǒu ruòwú	*idm.*	faintly discernible

词语例句：

（一）

1. 顺便: conveniently; while you are at it; without extra effort
   ❖ 采访途中顺便回趟老家。
   1) 你上图书馆的时候，请你顺便把我的书还了。
   2) 他在去北京的途中，顺便经过香港去看一个老朋友。

2. 一副……的样子: with a look of…
   ❖ 娘便拎着擦脚布站在面前，一副要替我倒洗脚水的样子。
   1) 他听了这个消息，气得变了脸色，一副要动手打人的样子。
   2) 他瞪大了眼睛看着我，一副不相信的样子。

3. 一时 : temporarily; momentarily
   ❖ 灯光下，我看到一张陌生的脸，一时竟想不起这同学的名字。
   1) 他突然问我一个这样复杂的问题，我一时不知怎么回答。
   2) 我一时不小心，说错了话，请你原谅。

4. 无论如何: in any case; at any rate; by all possible means
   ❖ 那少年的影像和面前的汉子无论如何也重叠不到一起。
   1) 无论如何，我要让孩子受到最好的教育。
   2) 这么荒唐的做法，我无论如何也无法理解。

5. 反正: anyway; anyhow; all the same; in any case
   ❖ 求你把俺们的冤情写写，也在报上登登，让世人评评理。反正俺们也不怕丢人了。
   1) 不管怎么样，反正我们今天必须完成这项工作。
   2) 那本书你拿去吧，反正我没时间看。

6. 偏偏: deliberately; just; only
   ❖ 我今日偏偏要治治你这个家伙！
   1) 正当我坐下吃晚饭时，偏偏电话来了。
   2) 他来看我，偏偏我不在家。

（二）

7. adj. 得不成样子: adj. to the point of ridiculousness (derogatory)
   ❖ 你坐吧，家里穷得实在不成样子。

1）他好像从来不整理，屋子里乱得不成样子。

2）那个孩子懒得不成样子，难怪谁都不喜欢他。

8. 好：so as to; so that

❖ 你把受他戏弄的事都说出来，他好写！

1）把她的电话号码告诉我，我好打电话找她。

2）快把这些事做完，好早点儿回家。

9. 再 adj.，也……：no matter how adj., still …

❖ 再忙，帮你摘豆我也愿意！

1）天气再坏，课也得上。

2）过去的农人，再穷也不愿意离开自己的土地。

10. 谁知：who knows that …; unexpectedly

❖ 谁知他摘了两把豆，来我身边，猛一下握住了我的手。

1）我去图书馆借书，谁知那天图书馆不开门。

2）我去劝他，谁知他坚持己见，完全不听别人的意见。

11.早晚：sooner or later

❖ 只要我看上了你，你早晚得乖乖地跟我睡觉。

1）你的专业那么好，早晚能找到工作，你着什么急?

2）这件事你早晚得做，为什么不早点开始?

（三）

12. 一来……，二来……：firstly …; secondly …

❖ 今日来，一来是为了看望姑父、姑姑和你，二来，是想求你帮我办一件事。

1）我反对这个婚事，一来他没有稳定的工作，二来他以前离过婚。

2）一来投资股票风险太大，二来你也快退休了，我看，你还是把钱存在银行里吧!

13. 只管 v.：v. by all means; not hesitate to v.

❖ 只要我能办到，只管说。

1）有什么问题，只管问。

2）你只管干下去，别理他。

14. 混出了名堂：have earned some reputation; have accomplished something
    ❖ 你在外边混出了名堂，求你去说说，这个面子他一定会给你的。
    1) 他从农村到城市住了几年，还是没混出什么名堂。
    2) 他现在混出名堂了，看不起人了。

15. 只怕：be afraid of only one thing; I am afraid that …
    ❖ 唉，只怕要惹你舅生气了。
    1) 办学校是件好事，只怕资金不够。
    2) 我很同意你的看法，只怕你父母有意见。

（四）

16. 照样：all the same; as before
    ❖ 你今年替俺们交了，明年呢？明年还不是照样罚？
    1) 他受到了惩罚，却还是照样犯错。
    2) 无论刮风下雨，她总是照样上班，从来不迟到。

17. ……干嘛？：why on earth
    ❖ 说那大话干嘛？
    1) 你干嘛那么瞧不起人？他虽然现在不行，将来一定有成就。
    2) 你生气干嘛？生气能解决问题吗？

18. 总……？：definitely; certainly (indicates a very sure inference)
    ❖ 你不可怜你妹妹，你总该可怜可怜你这些外甥吧？
    1) 借100块钱不行，借10块钱总可以吧？
    2) 上班的时候不能给朋友打电话，现在下了班了，总可以打了吧？
    3) 她总不会当面对他这样讲吧？

（五）

19. 莫非：can it be that...?; is it possible that...?
    ❖ 莫非达宽家又出了什么事？
    1) 他今天没来，莫非又病了不成？
    2) 这几句话完全没有道理，莫非他写错了？

（六）

20. 还不就是……!? : after all; it's only...
   ❖ 他还能拿什么好东西？还不就是点土产！
   1) 只有 10 分钟的时间，哪儿能多谈？还不就是随便说几句话！
   2) 一个月就赚几百块钱，哪儿能送孩子上私立学校？还不就是在家附近的学校随便念点书！

（七）

21. 犯不着： not worthwhile; it won't pay
   ❖ 我可能陷进一桩官司里，时间和声誉都会因此而受损失，这有点犯不着。
   1) 犯不着在小问题上花这么多时间。
   2) 为了这么一件小事，得罪了那么多人，实在犯不着。

22. 就看……： it all depends on ...
   ❖ 你能帮！就看你愿不愿帮！
   1) 这个厂子能不能赚钱，就看管理好不好。
   2) 能不能把那个坏蛋告倒，就看证人怎么说。

23. ……心切： eager; anxious
   ❖ 我觉得有些好笑，但也只把这些理解为上报纸心切，并没去想别的。
   1) 她望子成龙心切，不免给孩子很大的压力。
   2) 由于出国心切，他居然买了假证件。

24. 哪儿有不 v.……之理？ : How can one not v.?
   ❖ 你这样帮我们，我们哪有不谢之理？
   1) 这么要紧的事，哪有不管之理？
   2) 申请到了这么好的大学，哪儿有不上之理？

练习

I. 选择合适的四字词填进去：

> 精明强悍，善罢甘休，欺人太甚，惊天动地，不知所措，
> 心绪不宁，无可奈何，病急乱投医，滔滔不绝，眉开眼笑，
> 不相上下，模棱两可

1. 我请他帮忙，他却喃喃地说了几句 _____ 的话就走了。我失望极了。

2. 1911 年，在中国发生了一场 _____ 的革命，把中国几千年来的政治制度彻底改变了。

3. 他谈到他的研究，_____ 地说了两个钟头。

4. 你这不是 _____ 吗？怎么找一个外行人来帮忙呢！

5. 没想到这家乡下馆子的菜跟城里宾馆的 _____。

6. 他 _____！我非打死他不可！

7. 这个人 _____，才几年的工夫，不但把工厂的经营权都抢过来，而且做得很好，盈利年年提高。

8. 他向来廉洁正派，因此收了那份礼物以后就整天 _____，不知如何是好。

9. 一谈到他那个聪明有为的儿子，他就 _____。

10. 他双眼笑望着我，语调极为亲切，我 _____，只好应酬他几句。

11. 他是个出了名的坏蛋，吃了亏，是不会 ____ 的，你得小心一点儿。

12. 他的举动令我发慌，一时之间竟 _____。

II. 完成下面的句子：

1. _____，这是我们值得炫耀的光荣啊！

2. 我意识到 _____，所以 _____。

3. 他 _____，我这才发现 _____。

4. 你不就是一个 _____ 吗？别以为你现在混出了名堂，就 _____ 。

我偏偏要跟你较量较量，要让你知道 _____ 。

5. 只要 _____ ，早晚 (sooner or later) _____ 。

6. 你还是给他这个面子吧！毕竟 _____ 。

7. 如果 _____ ，你算走错门了！

8. 他还能 _____ ？还不就是 _____ ！

9. 他听说 _____ ，便非要 _____ 不可，你可千万 _____ 啊！

10. 我原想 _____ ，不料 _____ 。

III. 用提供的词语完成下面的对话：

1. A: 既然他亲自登门相求，你就答应吧！
   B: 不行，（无论如何）

2. A: 这么丢脸的事，还是不要张扬出去。
   B: （反正）

3. A: 他是领导，他的话人人都附和，你何必得罪他呢？
   B: （偏偏）

4. A: 你非得今天把那篇稿子写完吗？
   B: （好：so as to; so that）

5. A: 我一想到得写一篇歌颂领导的文章，心里就一阵烦燥。
   B: （再 adj., 也……）

6. A: 你知道他为什么到你家去吗？
   B: （一来……，二来……）

7. A: 那个证人已经坚决表示不愿意作证了。
   B: 真的？（莫非）

8. A: 为什么范辛决定不告葛炭永了？

　　B:（再说）

9. A: 既然你知道他说的都是奉承话，你干吗还理他？

　　B:（总：definitely; certainly）

10. A: 你看他到底能不能毕业？

　　B:（就看……）

11. A: 我还是很犹豫，不知道该不该提这件事。

　　B:（只管）

12. A: 我想请他吃一桌做工和用料都第一流的酒席。

　　B:（只怕）

IV. 用提供的词语回答问题：

1. 范辛和达宽是小学同学，长大后有了什么样的不同？

　　(记者，白胖，文人，显然，不成样子，简陋，再三，戏弄，屈辱)

2. 达宽为什么愿意把家里丢脸的事登在报上？

　　(告，赢，狂，咽不下这口气，难堪，决心)

3. 表弟对范辛的要求是什么？

　　(盖，土地，批准，答应，送礼，混出了名堂，给面子)

4. 范辛的妹妹有什么困难？

　　(超生，抓住把柄，求情，罚款，迁怒，报复，别管闲事)

5. 葛炭永用什么办法送礼给范辛？

　　(拜师学艺，写作，表示心意，背，土产，重，活得值，难为)

6. 范辛决定不帮达宽告葛炭永了，理由是什么？

　　(揭发，势必，心理负担，证人，辛辛苦苦，不快，诬陷，声誉，损失，得逞，犯不着)

7. 范辛的老同学何向请范辛喝酒，目的是什么？
    (报导，借机会，歌颂，事先设计，得罪)

8. 作者怎么描写灵芝这个人？
    (看上去，瘦弱，破旧，多看一眼，娟秀，耻辱，丢人)

V. 讨论问题：
1. 从这个故事中，你能看出记者在乡下人的眼中有什么样的地位？乡下人对记者的要求合理不合理？

2. 你对故事中的村长葛炭永有什么样的印象？

3. 记者范辛是不是太懦弱了？他最后没帮达宽告葛炭永的理由，你认为合理不合理？

4. 这个故事所描写的社会是一个什么样的社会？有什么特点？有什么严重的缺点？

5. 你认为作者用这个故事表达了什么？

6. 这是不是一篇好小说？为什么？

Pinyin Index

拼音索引

A

Ā Fǎng, 阿仿, *n.*, personal name, L. 11, p. 289

āsǎo, 阿嫂, *n.*, informal way to address a middle-aged woman, L. 3, p. 36

Ā Xìn, 阿信, *n.*, personal name, L. 11, p. 263

āi, 挨, *v.*, get close to, L. 10, p. 193, L. 11, p. 312

āi, 哎, *intj.*, ya!ya! , L. 11, p. 271

ai, 唉, *intj.*, alas, L. 11, p. 267, L. 12, p. 341

āichóu, 哀愁, *n.*, sorrow; sad, L. 10, p. 239

āikū, 哀哭, *n.*, wail, L. 10, p. 213

āiqiú, 哀求, *v.*, beseech; implore, L. 9, p. 175

āishāng, 哀伤, *v./n.*, distressed; sad; grieved, L. 10, p.187

āi.zhe, 挨着, *v.*, close to ; next to, L. 10, p. 233

ái, 挨, *v.* , suffer; endure, L. 10, p. 235

ái'è, 挨饿, *v.-o.*, suffer from hunger, L. 9, p. 161

ǎidèng, 矮凳, *n.*, low stool, L. 12, p. 333

àibùzháo, 碍不着, *v.-c.*, not in the way, L. 10, p. 197

àifǔ, 爱抚, *n./v.*, caress; show tender care for, L. 3, p. 31 , L. 6, p. 85

àihù, 爱护, *v.*, cherish; treasure; take good care of, L. 6, p. 89

ān, 安, *v.*, install, L. 12, p. 333

āndìng, 安定, *adj.*, stable; settled, L. 11, p. 271

āndìnggǎn, 安定感, *n.*, sense of stability, L. 11, p. 258

ānfèn, 安分, *adj.*, be contented with one's lot, L. 10, p. 223

ānfèn shǒujǐ, 安分守己, *idm.*, abide by the law and behave oneself, L. 7 , p. 111

ānpái, 安排, *v.*, arrange; plan; settle, L. 11, p. 255

ānshēn, 安身, *v.-o.*, make one's home; take shelter, L. 9, p. 161

ānwèi, 安慰, *n./v.*, consolation; comfort, L. 2, p. 17, L. 6, p. 87, L. 7, p. 109, L. 10, p. 211, L. 11, p. 263

ānxīn, 安心, *adj.*, feel at ease; be relieved, L. 11, p. 269

ānxiáng, 安祥, *adj.*, composed; be resolute and serene, L. 10, p. 213

ǎn, 俺, *pron.*, (dialect) I; me, L. 12, p. 335

ǎn wá.zi tā mā, 俺娃子他妈, *n.*, my kid's mother; my wife, L. 12, p. 329

ǎnmen, 俺们, *pron.*, (dialect) my; our, L. 12, p. 329

àn, 按, *v.*, press; push down, L. 9, p. 175, L. 11, p. 265

àn guì zàidì, 按跪在地, *v.*, forcefully press somebody to kneel down, L. 12, p. 347

àndàn, 黯淡, *adj.*, dim; faint; gloomy, L. 10, p. 239

ànjiàn, 按键, *n.*, key; button, L. 4, p. 47

ànshí, 按时, *adv.*, on time; on schedule, L. 9, p. 173

ànshuō, 按说, *adv.*, in the ordinary course of events; normally, L. 4, p. 47

ànsuǒ, 暗锁, *n.*, built-in lock, L. 8, p. 139

ànzhào, 按照, *prep.*, according to, L. 8, p. 133

ángrán, 昂然, *adv.*, upright and unafraid, L. 6, p. 97

áo, 熬, *v.*, endure; go through (difficult times), L. 4, p. 47

áo chūtóu, 熬出头, *v.-c.*, go through years of suffering and finally come to an end, L. 11, p. 275

àonǎo, 懊恼, *adj.*, chagrined; annoyed, L. 10, p. 223

àosàng, 懊丧, *adj.*, feel dejected or depressed, L. 9, p. 177

àoshì, 傲视, *v.*, turn up one's nose at; show disdain for, L. 11, p. 259

B

bā.zhang, 巴掌, *n.*, palm; hand, L. 11, p. 303

báshè, 跋涉, *v.*, trudge; make a long and difficult journey, L. 11, p. 316

bǎ huà tiǎomíng, 把话挑明, *phr.*, put all the cards on the table; bring it out into the open, L. 11, p. 305

bǎshǒu, 把手, *n.*, handle; holder, L. 11, p. 271

bǎ yuān shēn.le, 把冤伸了, *phr.*, redress an injustice; right a wrong, L. 12, p. 331

báicài, 白菜, *n.*, Chinese cabbage, L. 9, p. 157

báifà cāngcāng, 白发苍苍, *idm.*, white-haired , L. 5, p. 75

báiguǒ, 白果, *n.*, ginkgo tree, L. 10, p. 190

báixī, 白皙, *adj.*, white-skinned; fair-complexioned, L. 10, p. 204

bǎidòng, 摆动, *v.*, swing; sway , L. 5, p. 75

bǎifēnr, 百分儿, *n.*, a popular card game, L. 10, p. 201

bǎi.she, 摆设, *n.*, decorations; furnishings, L. 5, p. 75, L. 12, p. 333

bǎishǒu, 摆手, *v.-o.*, shake one's hand in admonition or disapproval, L. 7, p. 115, L. 9, p. 161, L. 12, p. 339

bǎituō, 摆脱, *v.*, break away; cast off; get rid of, , L. 8, p. 143, L. 10, p. 209

bǎizhèng, 摆正, *v.-c.*, settle; arrange; set in order, L. 4, p. 49

bàifǎng, 拜访, *v.*, visit, L. 12, p. 327

bàihuì, 拜会, *n./v.*, call, pay an official call, L. 12, p. 343

bàishī, 拜师, *v.-o.*, formally become a pupil to a master, L. 12, p. 353

bàishī xuéyì, 拜师学艺, *idm.*, become a pupil to a master and learn a craft or trade, L. 12, p. 355

bān, 搬, *v.*, move, L. 6, p. 83

bān, 般, *n.*, sort; kind; like, L. 10, p. 205

bānzhǔ, 班主, *n.*, owner of the circus, L. 4, p. 55

bānzhǎng, 班长, *n.*, class monitor, L. 7, p. 107

bǎnlì, 板栗, *n.*, Chinese chestnut, L. 10, p. 190

bànbèi.zi, 半辈子, *n.*, half a lifetime, L. 3, p. 33

bàn guà xītiān, 半挂西天, *v.*, hanging half way in the sky, L. 12, p. 325

bànjiér, 半截儿, *AN.*, half, L. 10, p. 204

bànlǐ, 办理, *v.*, handle , L. 1, p. 5

bànshǎng, 半晌, *n.*, half of the day, L. 12, p. 333

bàn.zhu, 绊住, *v.-c.*, be stumbled; be tripped, L. 11, p. 266

bǎngtuǐ, 绑腿, *n.*, leg wrappings; puttee, L. 5, p. 71

bǎngyàng, 榜样, *n.*, example; model, L. 10, p. 237

bāo.fu, 包袱, *n.*, cloth-wrapper, a bundle wrapped in cloth, L. 9, p. 157

bāo.fu, 包袱, *n.*, millstone round one's neck; burden; weight, L. 7 , p. 111

bāogǔdì, 包谷地, *n.*, corn field, L. 12, p. 335

bāoguǒ, 包裹, *n./v.*, package; parcel; wrap up, L. 2, p. 21, L. 11, p. 305, L. 11, p. 313

bāozhuāng zhǐxiāng, 包装纸箱, *n.*, packing box, L. 12, p.359

báo, 薄, *adj.*, thin; flimsy, L. 9, p. 159

báo, 薄, *adj.*, lacking in warmth (usually used in the negative form), L. 3, p. 36

bǎo.bei, 宝贝, *n.*, darling; baby, L. 10, p. 187

bǎoguǎn, 保管, *v.*, assure; guarantee, L. 12, p. 337

bǎoguǎnyuán, 保管员, *n.*, storekeeper; stockman, L. 10, p. 195

bǎohán, 饱含, *v.*, be filled with; contain (certain emotion, feelings, etc.), L. 4, p. 53, L. 10, p. 239

bǎomǔ, 保姆, *n.*, maid; housekeeper, L. 3, p. 36

bǎozhǔn, 保准, *v.*, guarantee; ensure, L. 12, p. 331

bào, 抱, *v.*, cradle; hold with both arms; embrace, L. 3, p. 31, L. 4, p. 55

bàochéng yìtuán, 抱成一团, *phr.*, huddle together, L. 11, p. 309

bàodá, 报答, *n./v.*, repay; requite; (here) revenge, L. 12, p. 343

chánggōng, 长工, *n.,* long-term laborer; farm hand by the year, L. 10, p. 236

cháng jiāngdòu, 长豇豆, *n.,* asparagus bean, L. 11, p. 266

chángmián, 长眠, *v.,* sleep eternally; die, L. 2, p. 21

chángmíng, 长鸣, *n.,* a booming sound, L. 9, p. 165

cháng shū yì kǒu qì, 长舒一口气, *phr.,* relax; have a breathing space, L. 12, p. 353

chǎngkāi, 敞开, *v.-c.,* open wide, L. 7, p. 103

chǎngmiàn, 场面, *n.,* scene; occasion, L. 12, p. 347

chàngkuài, 畅快, *adj.,* free from inhibitions and happy; carefree, L. 9, p. 173

chāoqǐ, 抄起, *v.,* take up; grab, L. 10, p. 197

chāoshēng, 超生, *v.,* bear a child over the permitted quota, L. 12, p. 345

chāozhī, 超支, *v.,* live beyond one's income; overspend, L. 10, p. 193

cháo, 朝, *prep. ,* to; towards, L. 1, p. 3, L. 4, p. 43, L. 11, p. 271

cháo… jiào, 朝…叫, *v.,* cry or shout at , L. 12, p. 335

cháofēng, 嘲讽, *v.,* satirize; mock, L. 10, p. 239

cháoliú, 潮流, *n.,* trend, L. 11, p. 260

cháoshī, 潮湿, *adj.,* moist; damp; humid, L. 5, p. 67, L. 7, p. 113

chǎocài, 炒菜, *v.-o.,* stir-fry the vegetable, L. 11, p. 283

chǎorǎng, 吵嚷, *v.,* shout in confusion; make a racket, L. 10, p. 207

chǎo shànsī, 炒鳝丝, *n.,* fried shredded eel, L. 11, p. 265

chēchuáng, 车床, *n.,* lathe; turning machine, L. 11, p. 280

chētóu, 车头, *n.,* the front of the train; the engine, L. 1, p. 7

chēxiāng, 车厢, *n.,* compartment; car; carriage, L. 6, p. 81, L. 11, p. 269

chě, 扯, *v.,* pull; hold onto, L. 12, p. 361

chěduàn, 扯断, *v.-c.,* rip out; disconnect, L. 8, p. 145

chějǐn, 扯紧, *v.-c.,* pull somebody (by the hand), L. 12, p. 355

chè, 撤, *v.,* dismiss sb. from a post , L. 6, p. 83

chèzhí, 撤职, *v.-o.,* remove sb. from office, L. 10, p. 191

chén.de zhù qì, 沉得住气, *v.-c.,* be able to keep calm; be able to stay steady, L. 11, p. 295

chénjìn, 沉浸, *v.,* immerse; steep , L. 5, p. 69, L. 10, p. 241

chénliè, 陈列, *v.,* display; exhibit, L. 7, p. 119

chénmèn, 沉闷, *adj.,* depressed; in low spirits, L. 11, p. 287

chénmò guǎyán, 沉默寡言, *idm.,* of few words; reticent; reserved, L. 6, p. 93

chénmò, 沉默, *v.,* remain silent, L. 10, p. 215, L. 11, p. 273

chénsī, 沉思, *n.,* meditation; contemplation, L. 6, p. 93

chén xià liǎn, 沉下脸, *v.-c.,* straighten one's face; pull a long face, L. 11, p. 305

Chén Xìn, 陈信, *n.,* personal name, L. 11, p. 253

chénzhòng, 沉重, *adj.,* heavy, L. 10, p. 217

chènchū, 衬出, *v.-c.,* set off by contrast; serve as a foil to, L. 7, p. 119

chènjī, 趁机, *adv.,* take the opportunity to; seize the chance to, L. 1, p. 7, L. 8, p. 133

chēng, 撑, *adj.,* full to the point of bursting, L. 4, p. 49

chēnggǔ, 撑鼓, *v.-c.,* full to the point of bursting, L. 8, p. 133

chéng, 乘, *v.,* take advantage of , L. 9, p. 157

chéng, 成, *adj. ,* all right; okay, L. 10, p. 197

chéng, 盛, *v.,* fill; ladle; fill a bowl, L. 9, p. 159, L. 10, p. 233

chéng diàntī, 乘电梯, *v.-o.,* take the elevator, L. 8, p. 131

chéngjiàn, 成见, *n.,* prejudice, L. 10, p. 241

chéngkè, 乘客, *n.,* passenger, L. 11, p. 270

chéngkěn, 诚恳, *adj.,* sincere; earnest, L. 11, p. 279

chénglì, 成立, *v.,* establish, L. 5, p. 69

chéngqīn, 成亲, *v.-o.,* get married, L. 10, p. 237

chéngrèn, 承认, *v.,* admit; acknowledge; recognize, L. 7, p. 111, L. 10, p. 237, L. 11, p. 257

chéngshòu, 承受, *v.,* bear; sustain, L. 10, p. 217

chéngshú, 成熟, *adj.,* ripe; mature, L. 10, p. 241

chéngtiān, 成天, *n.,* all day long, L. 2, p. 15

chéngxíng, 成形, *v.,* take shape, L. 10, p. 210

chéngyī, 成衣, *n.,* ready-to-wear, L. 7, p. 119

chībǎo fàn méi shì gàn, 吃饱饭没事干, *phr.,* have nothing to do after a good meal – do sth. really silly or senseless because there is actually nothing to do, L. 11, p. 287

chīchī.de, 痴痴地, *adv.,* stupidly; senselessly, L. 4, p. 58

chī, 嗤, *onom.,* sound of chuckling, L. 10, p. 201

chījīng, 吃惊, *v.-o.,* be startled; be shocked; be amazed, L. 11, p. 277

chīkǔ, 吃苦, *v.-o.,* bear/suffer/endure hardships, L. 11, p. 293, L. 12, p. 361

chīkuī, 吃亏, *v.-o.,* suffer losses; at a disadvantage; to get picked on, L. 7 , p. 111, L. 11, p. 267

chīle yì jīng, 吃了一惊, *v.-o.,* be startled; be shocked, L. 12, p. 349

chīlì, 吃力, *adj.,* strenuous; laborious, L. 11, p. 293

chīxiāng, 吃香, *adj.,* be much sought after; be well-liked, L. 11, p. 289

chítáng, 池塘, *n.,* pond; pool, L. 7 , p. 111

chíyí, 迟疑, *v.,* hesitate, L. 10, p. 217, L. 12, p. 327

chǐrǔ, 耻辱, *n.,* shame; disgrace; humiliation, L. 6, p. 85, L. 10, p. 217, L. 12, p. 371

chǐxiào, 耻笑, *v.,* sneer at; ridicule, L. 10, p. 209

chìjiǎo, 赤脚, *v.-o.,* barefoot, L. 10, p. 211

chōng, 冲, *v.,* charge; rush; dash, L. 4, p. 55

chōng, 冲, *v.,* wash away; flush, L. 10, p. 195

chōngdòng, 冲动, *n.,* impulse; impulsive motion , L. 10, p. 213

chōngjǐng, 憧憬, *v./n.,* long for; look forward to, L. 10, p. 189

chōngpò, 冲破, *v.-c.,* break through, L. 10, p. 237

chōngyù, 充裕, *adj.,* abundant; ample, L. 11, p. 259

chóng, 重, *adv.,* again; once more, L. 11, p. 301, L. 12, p. 351

chóngdié, 重叠, *v.,* place one upon another; overlap, L. 12, p. 327

chóngxīn, 重新, *adv.,* again, L. 6, p. 82

chǒng'ài, 宠爱, *v.,* fond of (pets, children), L. 3, p. 29

chǒngwù, 宠物, *n.,* pet, L. 3, p. 31

chòng.zhe, 冲着（人）, *v.,* directed at sb. ; targeted at sb., L. 11, p. 287

chōu, 抽, *v.,* take out, select, L. 8, p. 133

chōudǎ, 抽打, *v.,* whip; lash, L. 10, p. 209

chōukòngr, 抽空儿, *v.-o.,* manage to find time, L. 10, p. 188

chōuqì, 抽泣, *v.,* sob, L. 10, p. 239

chōu.ti, 抽屉, *n.,* drawer, L. 2, p. 19

chōuyān, 抽烟, *v.-o.,* smoke (a cigarette or a pipe), L. 11, p. 305

chóu, 愁, *n.,* worry, L. 10, p. 193

chóubèi, 筹备, *v.,* arrange, prepare, L. 8, p. 127

chóuhèn, 仇恨, *n.,* hatred; hostility, , L. 1, p. 9, L. 10, p. 225

chóuhuài, 愁坏, *v.-c.,* seriously worry sb., L. 11, p. 267

chóukǔ, 愁苦, *n.,* anxiety; distress, L. 10, p. 233

chǒu, 丑, *adj.,* ugly, L. 11, p. 265

chǒukòng, 瞅空, *v.,* wait for an opportunity, L. 11, p. 295

chūchāi, 出差, *v.-o.,* go on a business trip, L. 7, p. 115, L. 11, p. 259

chūchāifèi, 出差费, *n.*, allowances for a business trip, L. 7, p. 119

chūgōng, 出工, *v.-o.*, go to work, L. 9, p. 159, L. 10, p. 229

chūkǒuchù, 出口处, *n.*, exit, L. 11, p. 263

chūmiàn, 出面, *v.-o.*, act in one's own capacity or on behalf of somebody , L. 7, p. 107

chūqí, 出奇, *adv.*, unusually; extraordinarily, L. 9, p. 177

chūshǒu, 出手, *v.*, take out (money; property; etc.), L. 3, p. 29

chūshì, 出事, *v.-o.*, meet with a mishap; have an accident, L. 1, p. 5

chūshén, 出神, *v.-o.*, be in a trance; be lost in thought, L. 11, p. 255

chūxí, 出席, *v.*, attend; be present (at a meeting, social gathering, etc.), L. 7, p. 119

chūyár, 出芽儿, *v.-o.*, bud, L. 10, p. 197

chūzhàn, 出站, *v.-o.*, leave the station (to set out on a journey), L. 11, p. 316

chūzhú.yi, 出主意, *v.-o.*, offer advice; make suggestions, L. 10, p. 241

chú, 锄, *v.*, hoe, L. 10, p. 206

chúchuāng, 橱窗, *n.*, display window; shop window, L. 7, p. 119, L. 11, p. 284

chúwài, 除外, *v.*, be an exception; apart from, L. 2, p. 15

chúxī, 除夕, *n.*, New Year's Eve, L. 9, p. 169

chǔbiàn bùjīng, 处变不惊, *idm.*, with presence of mind in the face of disasters, L. 4, p. 45

chǔjìng, 处境, *n.*, unfavorable situation; plight, L. 4, p. 47

chǔlǐ, 处理, *v.*, handle; deal with, L. 3, p. 33

chǔxù, 储蓄, *n.*, savings, L. 11, p. 305

chù, 搐, *v.*, jerk; twitch, L. 12, p. 330

chùdiàn, 触电, *v.-o.*, get an electric shock, L. 10, p. 203

chuān.guo, 穿过, *v.-c.*, pass through; cross; go through, L. 10, p. 199, L. 11, p. 272

chuán, 传, *v.*, spread, L. 11, p. 269, L. 12, p. 343

chuánshén, 传神, *adj.*, vivid; lifelike; expressive , L. 4, p. 53

chuándá, 传达, *v.*, pass on; relay; convey, L. 10, p. 229

chuándáshì, 传达室, *n.*, reception office, L. 7, p. 103

chuǎnqì, 喘气, *v.-o.*, breathe deeply; pant; gasp, L. 4, p. 55, L. 12, p. 349

chuàn, 串, *AN.*, a string of; a bunch of , L. 12, p. 353

chuānglián chā.zi, 窗帘叉子, *v.*, curtain pole (for opening curtains), L. 4, p. 43

chuáng, 床, *AN.*, measure word for bedding, L. 7, p. 119

chuángpù, 床铺, *n.*, bedding, L. 11, p. 269

chuángtóu, 床头, *n.*, bedside, L. 11, p. 269

chuángtóuguì, 床头柜, *n.*, nightstand, L. 6, p. 91

chuángyán, 床沿, *n.*, the edge of a bed, L. 11, p. 285

chuǎngdàng, 闯荡, *v.*, make a living wandering from place to place, L. 4, p. 54

chuàngyè, 创业, *v.*, start an undertaking; do pioneering work, L. 12, p. 359

chuī, 吹, *v.*, boast; brag, L. 12, p. 359

chuīshì yuán, 炊事员, *n.*, a cook or a kitchen staff, L. 9, p. 167

chúi, 捶, *v.*, beat (with a stick or fist) , L. 12, p. 335

chuí, 垂, *v.*, hang down; droop; let fall, L. 4, p. 49, L. 9, p. 173, L. 10, p. 185

chuítóu, 垂头, *v.-o.*, lower one's head , L. 5, p. 67

chuítóu sàngqì, 垂头丧气, *idm.*, be crestfallen; be dejected, L. 5, p. 73

chuíxiōng dùnzú, 捶胸顿足, *idm.*, beat one's breast and stamp one's feet (in deep sorrow); etc), L. 10, p. 239

Chūnjié, 春节, *n.*, Spring Festival; Chinese New Year, L. 2,

p. 17, L. 7, p. 113, L. 9, p. 157

chúncuì, 纯粹, *adv./ adj.*, pure; purely, L. 3, p. 31, L. 8, p. 129

chǔn, 蠢, *adj.*, stupid; clumsy, L. 10, p. 231

chuòqì, 啜泣, *v.*, sob; whimper, L. 10, p. 235

chuòxué, 辍学, *v.*, discontinue one's studies; drop out, L. 4, p. 47, L. 10, p. 219

císhàn, 慈善, *adj.*, charitable; benevolent, L. 3, p. 29

cízǔ, 词组, *n.*, phrase, L. 12, p. 361

cǐkè, 此刻, *n.*, at the moment, L. 10, p. 205

cì, 刺, *v.*, stab; prick, L. 6, p. 81, L. 12, p. 365

cì.hou, 伺候, *v.*, serve; wait on, L. 3, p. 36

cìrù, 刺入, *v.*, stab, L. 8, p. 149

cìshāng, 刺伤, *v.-c.*, jab and hurt, L. 10, p. 235

cìyǔ, 赐予, *v.*, bestow; grant, L. 10, p. 213

cìyào, 次要, *adj.*, less important; secondary, L. 11, p. 297

cōngmáng, 匆忙, *adv.*, hastily; in a hurry, L. 6, p. 95

cóngcóng xīshuǐ, 淙淙溪水, *n.*, gurgling stream, L. 10, p. 229

cóng rénjiān zhēngfā, 从人间蒸发, *phr.*, evaporate from the world -- vanish without a trace , L. 4, p. 57

cóngtóu shuōqǐ, 从头说起, *v.*, relate (the story) from the very beginning, L. 7, p. 105

cóngwèi, 从未, *adv.*, have never, L. 6, p. 83, L. 8, p. 135

còu .ge shù, 凑个数, *v.-o.*, serve as a stopgap, L. 12, p. 329

còuqián, 凑钱, *v.-o.*, pool money; raise a fund, L. 1, p. 7

còu.zhe, 凑着, *v.*, move close to, L. 10, p. 207

cūcāo, 粗糙, *adj.*, (of skin) rough, L. 11, p. 253

cūshēng, 粗声, *n./adv.*, in a husky voice, L. 11, p. 291

cūxì, 粗细, *n.*, thickness, L. 10, p. 191

cūzhuàng, 粗壮, *adj.*, sturdy; thickset; brawny, L. 5, p. 73, L. 10, p. 187

cùrán, 猝然, *adv.*, suddenly; abruptly; unexpectedly, L. 11, p. 307

cùsǐ, 猝死, *n.*, sudden death, L. 3, p. 32

cùxīn, 簇新, *adj.*, brand new, L. 10, p. 233

cuànquán, 篡权, *v.*, usurp the power, L. 6, p. 95

cuī, 催, *v.*, urge; hurry; press, L. 12, p. 326

cuīmián, 催眠, *v.*, mesmerize; lull (to sleep), L. 11, p. 269

cuìruò, 脆弱, *adj.*, fragile; delicate, L. 6, p. 85

cūnbàn zàozhǐchǎng, 村办造纸厂, *n.*, village-run paper mill, L. 12, p. 337

cūnkǒu, 村口, *n.*, the entrance to a village, L. 2, p. 15

cūntóu, 村头, *n.*, the entrance of the village, L. 9, p. 159

cūnzhǎng, 村长, *n.*, village head, L. 2, p. 16, L. 12, p. 329

cūnzhuāng, 村庄, *n.*, village, L. 2, p. 15

cúnxīn, 存心, *adv.*, intentionally; deliberately; on purpose, L. 12, p. 341

cúnzài, 存在, *v.*, exist, L. 3, p. 31

cúnzhé, 存折, *n.*, bankbook, L. 8, p. 141

cuòshāng, 挫伤, *v.*, be injured; be wounded, L. 10, p. 210

cuòshǒubùjí, 措手不及, *idm.*, be caught unprepared; be taken by surprise, L. 11, p. 291

D

dā.shan, 答讪, *v.*, strike up a conversation with sb., L. 10, p. 197

dā.ying, 答应, *v.*, agree; promise; comply with, L. 11, p. 267, L. 12, p. 345

dǎr, 打儿, *AN.*, a dozen, L. 3, p. 29

dáchéng xiédìng, 达成协定, *v.-o.*, come to an agreement; come to terms, L. 10, p. 227

dádào...de mùdì, 达到…的目的, *v.-o.*, achieve or attain the goal of…, L. 6, p. 95

dáfēisuǒwèn, 答非所问, *idm.*, give an irrelevant answer,

duǒ, 躲, v., hide (oneself), L. 11, p. 293

duǒkāi, 躲开, v., avoid; dodge, L. 10, p. 199

duǒshǎn, 躲闪, v., dodge; evade, L. 10, p. 203

dūn, 蹲, v., squat on the heels, L. 9, p. 169, L. 10, p. 197

dùnshí, 顿时, adv., immediately; at once (used for past events), L. 2, p. 17, L. 8, p. 141, L. 10, p. 203, L. 12, p. 349

E

étóu, 额头, n., forehead, L. 7, p. 115

ézhà, 讹诈, v., blackmail; extort, L. 8, p. 126

è'rán, 愕然, v./adv., stunned; astounded, L. 12, p. 359

èzuòjù, 恶作剧, v., play practical jokes, prank, L. 7, p. 117

ēndé, 恩德, n., favor; kindness, L. 9, p. 177

ěrguāng, 耳光, n., a slap on the face, L. 2, p. 21

F

fādāi, 发呆, v., stare blankly, L. 8, p. 139, L. 10, p. 207

fādǒu, 发抖, v., shiver; shake; tremble, L. 10, p. 209

fāfēng, 发疯, v., go crazy; become insane, L. 10, p. 212

fāfēngshì.de, 发疯似地, adv., as if going crazy, L. 6, p. 97

fāhàoshīlìng, 发号施令, idm., issue orders; order people about, L. 7, p. 117

fāhuǒ, 发火, v.-o., get angry; lose one's temper, L. 11, p. 285

fāhuāng, 发慌, v., feel nervous; get flustered, L. 12, p. 351

fāhuī zuòyòng, 发挥作用, v.-o., give full scope to; play a role in, L. 10, p. 229

fājiǒng, 发窘, v., feel embarrassed; be ill at ease,, L. 12, p. 363

fājué, 发掘, v., scout for; excavate; unearth; explore, L. 11, p. 255

fālèng, 发愣, v., stupefied; dazed, L. 8, p. 141, L. 10, p. 233

fāmá, 发麻, v.-o., numb; tingle; have pins and needles, L. 11, p. 282

fāméi, 发霉, v.-o., go moldy; become mildewed, L. 7, p. 113

fāshì, 发誓, v.-o., vow; pledge; swear, L. 3, p. 29, L. 8, p. 137, L. 11, p. 307

fāyù, 发育, v., develop physically (in puberty), L. 10, p. 192

fāyán, 发言, v.-o., speak; make a statement, L. 11, p. 275

fāzhàng, 发胀, v., swell, L. 10, p. 219

fákuǎn, 罚款, v.-o., impose a fine, L. 4, p. 55

fàqiǎ, 发夹, n., hairpin; bobby pin, L. 11, p. 273

fān, 番, AN., a course; a turn, L. 8, p. 127

fān, 番, AN., measure word for actions, deeds, etc., L. 1, p. 3, L. 7, p. 105

fān'àn, 翻案, v.-o., reverse a verdict, L. 10, p. 225

fānbiàn, 翻遍, v.-c., rummage all over, L. 1, p. 5

fānchē, 翻车, v.-o., (of a car) turn over, L. 9, p. 171

fāngài, 翻盖, v., renovate (a house), L. 10, p. 235

fān.guo, 翻过, v., cross over; climb over, L. 10, p. 199

fānjiǎn, 翻拣, v., look through and select from, L. 12, p. 327

fānshēn, 翻身, v.-o., turn over, L. 11, p. 291

fāntāo, 翻掏, v., turn inside out, L. 4, p. 44

fānzhǎo, 翻找, v., rummage; search, L. 1, p. 3, L. 2, p. 16

fān.zhe, 翻着, v., browse; look over, L. 6, p. 91

Fán gāo, 凡高, n., Vincent Van Gogh, L. 4, p. 53

fánhuá, 繁华, adj., flourishing; prosperous, L. 11, p. 273

fánxīn, 烦心, adj., feel vexed; be troubled; vexatious, L. 11, p. 307

fánzào, 烦躁, adj., fidgety; agitated, L. 12, p. 367

fánzào.de, 烦躁地, adv., irritably; agitate, L. 11, p. 305

fǎnbǎng, 反绑, v., with one's hands tied behind one's back, L.10, p. 208

fǎnfǎn fùfù, 反反复复, adv., repeatedly; again and again, L. 11, p. 291

fǎnfù, 反复, adv., repeatedly; again and again, L. 9, p. 167

fǎn'gǎn, 反感, adj., feel antipathy; be averse to, L. 10, p. 241, L.11, p. 293

fǎn gào, 反告, v., countercharge, L. 12, p. 357

fǎn gémìng fènzǐ, 反革命分子, n., a counterrevolutionary, L.5, p. 73

fǎnkàng, 反抗, v., resist, L. 10, p. 205

fǎnwèn, 反问, v., ask a question in reply, L. 6, p. 86, L. 8, p.143, L. 12, p. 341

fǎnyòu dòuzhēng, 反右斗争, n., the Anti-Rightist Campaign (1957), L. 7, p. 107

fǎnzhèng, 反正, adv., anyway; anyhow; in any case, , L. 11, p.261, L. 12, p. 331

fàn, 泛, v., float; drift, L. 10, p. 223

fàncuò, 犯错, v.-o., make a mistake, L. 9, p. 165

Fàn jiā lǎodà, 范家老大, n., the oldest son of Fan family, L.12, p. 325

Fàn Xīn, 范辛, n., personal name, L. 12, p. 333

fāng'àn, 方案, n., scheme; plan, L. 11, p. 253

fāngbiànmiàn, 方便面, n., instant noodles, L. 4, p. 49

fāngxīn, 芳馨, n., fragrance; sweet-smelling aroma, L. 10, p. 213

fángbèi, 防备, v./n., precautions, guard against, L. 4, p. 43, L.10, p. 211

fángdàomén, 防盗门, n., burglar-proof door, L. 4, p. 45

fǎngfú, 仿佛, adv., as if; seem, L. 4, p. 49, L. 6, p. 81, L. 8, p.133, L. 10, p. 190, L. 12, p. 328

fàng.guo, 放过, v., let off; let slip , L. 1, p. 7, L. 11, p. 299

fàngqì, 放弃, v., abandon; give up, L. 10, p. 217, L. 11, p. 261

fàngyǎn sìgù, 放眼四顾, v., look all around, L. 10, p. 227

fàngyáng, 放羊, v.-o., herd sheep, L. 10, p. 229

fàngzhì, 放置, v., lay aside; place, L. 4, p. 45

fēibēn, 飞奔, v., dash, L. 10, p. 215

fēichí, 飞驰, v., speed along; dash forward, L. 10, p. 199

fēifèn, 非分, adj., presumptuous; overstepping one's bounds, L.7, p. 113

fēihóng, 绯红, adj./v., bright red, L. 10, p. 185

fēixiáng, 飞翔, v., fly; circle in the air, L. 11, p. 311

fèilì, 费力, adj., need or use great effort; be strenuous, L. 10, p.187

fèixīn láoshén, 费心劳神, idm., take a lot of care; take a lot of trouble, L. 8, p. 131

fēngē, 分割, v., cut apart; break up, L. 11, p. 256

fēnbiàn, 分辩, v., defend against a charge, L. 10, p. 223

fēnbié, 分别, adv., respectively, L. 3, p. 33

fēnbié, 分别, v., leave each other, L. 6, p. 97

fēnchéng, 分成, v., divide into, L. 3, p. 33

fēnfēn, 纷纷, adv., one after another; in succession, L. 11, p. 270

fēngōng, 分工, v., divide work, L. 4, p. 45

fēnhóng, 分红, v.-o., share out profits, L. 10, p. 193

fēnluàn, 纷乱, adj., numerous and disorderly, L. 12, p. 349

fēnmiǎn, 分娩, v., deliver; give birth, L. 8, p. 135

fēnmíng, 分明, adj./adv., be clear; be distinct, clearly; evidently, L. 7, p. 103, L. 8, p. 149, L. 9, p. 167

fēnpèi, 分配, v./n., distribute; allot, distribution, job assignment on graduation, L. 2, p. 14, L. 3, p. 35, L. 8, p. 129, L.11, p. 267, L. 12, p. 343

fēnshǒu, 分手, v.-o., break up, L. 2, p. 15

fén, 坟, n., grave; tomb, L. 10, p. 215

fénshān, 坟山, n., cemetery hill, L. 2, p. 21

fěnshuāyìxīn, 粉刷一新, phr., be painted anew, L.10, p. 239

L. 12, p. 337

gē, 搁, v., put; (here): hang up, L. 8, p. 141

gē.bo, 胳膊, n., arm, L. 9, p. 175, L. 11, p. 263

gē.da, 疙瘩, n., lump, knot, L. 10, p. 203

gēcǎo, 割草, v.-o., cut grass, L. 10, p. 219

gēcí, 歌词, n., words of a song; lyrics, L. 11, p. 313

gējù, 歌剧, n., opera, L. 10, p. 236

gē mài.zi, 割麦子, v.-o., cut wheat, L. 11, p. 287

gēsòng, 歌颂, v., sing the praises of; extol; eulogize, L. 12, p.363

gē.zi lóng, 鸽子笼, n., pigeon house; loft, L. 11, p. 283

gé, 隔, v., be separated by, L. 10, p. 217

géwài, 格外, adv., especially, L. 6, p. 85, L. 10, p. 199

Gě Tànyǒng, 葛炭永, n., personal name, L. 12, p. 329

gěi...liǎnsè kàn, 给⋯脸色看, phr., convey displeasure or disapproval to sb. through facial expression, L. 12, p. 347

gěi...qǔmíng, 给⋯取名, v., name someone, L. 3, p. 31

gēnqián, 跟前, n., in front of; near, L. 11, p. 311

gēnyuán, 根源, n., root; source; origin, L. 10, p. 194

Gēnzhù, 根柱, n., personal name, L. 9, p. 157

gěngyè, 哽咽, v., choke with sobs, L. 9, p. 169

gōng'ān yuán, 公安员, n., policeman, L. 10, p. 213

gōng bó, 攻博, v.-o., study for a Ph.D, L. 8, p. 135

gōngdì, 工地, n., work site; construction site, L. 1, p. 5, L. 10, p. 195

gōngfèi, 公费, adv., at public expense; at state expense, L. 8, p. 135

gōngfēnr, 工分儿, n., work point, L. 10, p. 193

gōng.gong, 公公, n., husband's father, L. 9, p. 159

gōnggōng jìngjìng, 恭恭敬敬, adv., with the utmost respect, L. 10, p. 215

gōngguān, 公关, n., public relations, L. 8, p. 129

gōnghán, 公函, n., official letter, L. 6, p. 95

gōnghòu liángjiǔ, 恭候良久, idm., wait respectfully for a long time, L. 8, p. 141

gōngjī, 攻击, v., attack, L. 10, p. 191

gōngjiāncāo, 工间操, n., work-break exercises, L. 7, p. 103

gōngláo, 功劳, n., credit; meritorious service; contribution, L. 8, p. 131, L. 12, p. 365

gōnglì, 功利, n., material gain, L. 3, p. 31

gōngliáng, 公粮, n., agricultural tax paid in grain, L. 10, p.189

gōngrán, 公然, adv., brazenly; openly, L. 10, p. 237

gōngshè, 公社, n., commune, L. 6, p. 87, L. 10, p. 185

gōngshì gōngbàn, 公事公办, idm., do business according to official principles., L. 10, p. 223

gōngxiāodiàn, 供销店, n., store, L. 10, p. 187

gōngzhèng rén, 公证人, n., notary public, L. 3, p. 33

gōngzuòduì, 工作队, n., work team, L. 10, p. 236

gòngchǎn zhǔyì, 共产主义, n., Communism, L. 10, p. 189

gòngrèn búhuì, 供认不讳, idm., confess everything, L. 8, p.147

gòngshì, 共事, v., work together (at the same organization), L. 11, p. 275

gòngzhí, 供职, v., serve; work at, L. 8, p. 126

gōuzhù, 勾住, v.-c., secure with a hook; hook, L. 11, p. 263

gǒufèi, 狗吠, n., dog bark, L. 10, p. 208

gūdūgūdū, 咕嘟咕嘟, onom., sound of water bubbling or a person gurgling, L. 4, p. 49

gūdú, 孤独, adj., lonely, L. 6, p. 81

gū.fu, 姑父, n., the husband of one's father's sister, L. 9, p.173, L. 12, p. 339

gū.gu, 姑姑, n., one's father's sister, L. 12, p. 339

gū.ji, 估计, v., estimate; assess, reckon, L. 11, p. 283, L. 12, p. 349

gū.niang, 姑娘, n., girl; miss, L. 3, p. 31

gūpì, 孤僻, adj., unsociable and eccentric, L. 10, p. 217

gú.tou bàng.zi gè yá, 骨头棒子硌牙, phr., (robber's idiom) refers to a place which is well guarded and difficult to steal from, L. 4, p. 45

gǔ, 股, AN., measure word for strength, smell, etc., L. 11, p. 308, L. 12, p. 335

gǔ, 股, AN., a gust of (wind), a burst of L. 6, p. 81, L. 9, p. 173

gǔfèn gōngsī, 股份公司, n., publicly-traded company, L. 8, p. 127

gǔlì, 鼓励, v., encourage, L. 6, p. 89

gǔzhǎng, 鼓掌, v.-o., clap one's hands; applaud, L. 10, p. 221

gǔ.zi lǐ, 骨子里, n., in the bones – beneath the surface; in one's innermost nature, L. 2, p. 22, L. 11, p. 289

gǔzú yǒngqì, 鼓足勇气, phr., muster up the courage, pluck up one's courage L. 7, p. 105, L. 10, p. 202

gù.bushàng, 顾不上, v.-c., have no time for, L. 10, p. 207

gù.ji, 顾忌, n./v., scruple; apprehension; worry, L. 10, p. 187

gùxiāng, 故乡, n., native place; hometown, L. 11, p. 255

gùyōng móushā, 雇佣谋杀, n., orchestrated murder; hiring someone to kill someone else, L. 8, p. 147

guā (fēng), 刮(风), v.-o., blow (of the wind), L. 11, p. 309

guāguā zhuìdì, 呱呱坠地, idm, (of a child) be born, L. 10, p. 191

guāzǐliǎn, 瓜子脸, n., oval face; pretty face with an oval shape, L. 6, p. 85

guā zuǐ.ba, 刮嘴巴, v.-o., slap one's face, L. 10, p. 209

guàduàn, 挂断, v.-c., hang up the phone, L. 8, p. 147

guàpái, 挂牌, v.-o., listed (on the market), L. 8, p. 127

guàtú, 挂图, n., hanging banner; wall chart, L. 10, p. 237

guàxīn, 挂心, v., be on one's mind, L. 12, p. 367

guà.zhe, 挂着, v., hang; put up; (here) wear certain expression on one's face, L. 6, p. 93

guāi, 乖, adj., well-behaved (child), L. 9, p. 159

guāiguāi.de, 乖乖地, adv., obediently; well-behaved, L. 12, p. 337

guāiqiǎo, 乖巧, adj., cute; lovely, L. 3, p. 31

guàiwù, 怪物, n., monster, a freak, L. 4, p. 49

guānbīng zhuō qiángdào, 官兵捉强盗, n., the soldiers catch the bandits - a game played by children, L. 11, p. 266

guǎnchī guǎn zhù, 管吃管住, v., provide food and accommodation, L. 4, p. 47

guǎnlǐ, 管理, v., manage; administer, L. 2, p. 15

guǎnyòng, 管用, adj., (informal) of use; effective, L. 12, p. 367

guǎn xiánshì, 管闲事, v.-o., be meddlesome; be a busybody, L. 12, p. 347

guàn.le, 惯了, v., used to it, L. 4, p. 47

guāng, 光, n., light; ray, L. 11, p. 315

guāng, 光, adj.. naked; stripped, L. 10, p. 203

guāngcǎi, 光彩, n., luster; splendor; brilliance, L. 9, p. 161

guāngcǎi duómù, 光彩夺目, idm. with dazzling brightness; brilliant, L. 11, p. 285

guāngjǐng, 光景, n., about; around, L. 7, p. 103

guāngmáng, 光芒, n., brilliant rays, L. 10, p. 229

guāngróng, 光荣, n., honor; glory; credit, L. 12, p. 351

guāngzé, 光泽, n., luster; gloss, L. 10, p. 219

Guǎngzhōu, 广州, n., Guangzhou, capital of Guangdong Province, L. 11, p. 255

guàng.guang, 逛逛, v., stroll around, L. 10, p. 217

guī, 归, v., attribute to; belong to, L. 11, p. 301

guīfàn, 规范, adj., orthodox; conforming with the norm, L. 8, p. 133

guī.ju, 规矩, n., rule; custom; established practice, L. 10, p.221

guīlái, 归来, v., return; come back, L. 11, p. 261

guīlù, 规律, n., regulation; regular pattern, L. 2, p. 17

guī.nü, 闺女, n., (informal) daughter, L. 12, p. 345

guīsù, 归宿, n., destination of one's life voyage, L. 11, p. 258

guī...suǒyǒu, 归…所有, v., be turned over to sb. to verb, L. 3, p. 33

guǐdào, 轨道, n., track, L. 7, p. 115

guǐmì.de, 诡秘地, adv., surreptitiously; secretively, L. 11, p.301

guì, 跪, v., kneel, L. 2, p. 22

guì.xia, 跪下, v., kneel down, L. 10, p. 209, L. 12, p. 347

guìzhòng, 贵重, adj., valuable; precious, L. 3, p. 31, L. 11, p.311

guì.zi, 柜子, n., cupboard; cabinet, L. 9, p. 157

gǔn, 滚, v., roll down; shed (tears); drop (tears), L. 10, p. 237, L. 11, p. 315

guōzào, 锅灶, n., cooking stove; kitchen range, L. 12, p. 333

guóyíng, 国营, v., state-operated; state-run, L. 10, p. 193

guóyíng huàxiān chǎng, 国营化纤厂, n., state-run chemical fiber factory, L. 12, p. 359

guǒ, 裹, v., wrap, L. 10, p. 187

guǒrán, 果然, adv., as expected; as things turn out, L. 10, p.202

guò.dequ, 过得去, v., passable; not too bad, L. 11, p. 297

guòchèng, 过秤, v., weigh on a scale, L. 10, p. 195

guòjié, 过节, v.-o., celebrate a festival, L. 7, p. 107

guòménr, 过门儿, v., move in to one's husband's household upon marriage, L. 10, p. 235

guòmù, 过目, v., look over (papers, lists, etc.) so as to check or approve; peruse, L. 11, p. 291

guòshāi, 过筛, v., sift out, L. 10, p. 197

guòwèn, 过问, v., inquire about; take an interest in, L. 2, p. 15

guòyìbúqù, 过意不去, v., feel apologetic; feel sorry, L. 11, p. 279

H

hā.bagǒu, 哈巴狗, n., Pekingese, L. 3, p. 35

Hā'ěrbīn, 哈尔滨, n., Harbin, capital of Heilongjiang Province, L. 11, p. 255

hāi, 嗨, intj., hi! What? ; Darn it! (expressing sadness, regret or surprise), L. 11, p. 265, L. 12, p. 359

hǎijiāng, 海疆, n., coastal areas and territorial waters, L. 10, p.227

hǎiliàng, 海量, adj., great capacity for liquor, L. 12, p. 365

hǎiyáng, 海洋, n., sea; ocean, L. 10, p. 227

hàisào, 害臊, v.-o., feel ashamed; be bashful , L. 5, p. 67

hàixiū.de, 害羞地, adv., bashfully; shyly, L. 11, p. 293

hānhòu, 憨厚, adj., be simple and honest, L. 10, p. 197

hānshēng, 鼾声, n., snore, L. 11, p. 291

hānshuì, 酣睡, v., sleep soundly, L. 8, p. 133

hānxiào, 憨笑, v., smile openly, smile artlessly, L. 10, p. 227

hán, 含, v., contain; (here): with tears in one's eyes, L. 12, p.371

hánhùn, 含混, adj., indistinct; vague, L. 10, p. 211

hánjìn, 寒噤, n., shiver (with cold or fear), L. 10, p. 233

hánlěng, 寒冷, adj., cold, L. 2, p. 19

hánqíng mòmò, 含情脉脉, idm., (soft eyes) exuding tenderness and love, L. 5, p. 73

hánsuān, 寒酸, adj., shabby and miserable, L. 7, p. 115

hánxiào, 含笑, v.-o., have a smile on one's face, L. 7, p. 117

hánxuān, 寒暄, v., exchange of conventional greetings, L. 12, p. 339

hányì, 含义, n., meaning; connotation, L. 10, p. 237

hányì, 含意, n., connotation; implication, L. 11, p. 301

hán.zhe, 含着, v., have/fill with (tears in the eyes), L. 2, p. 17

hán.zhe lèishuǐ, 含着泪水, v.-o., with tears in the eyes, L. 6, p.87

hǎn, 喊, v., call (a person); yell, L. 7, p. 117, L. 10, p. 195

hàn, 汗, n., sweat, L. 9, p. 163

hànshuǐ, 汗水, n., sweat; perspiration, L. 10, p. 233

hànwèir, 汗味, n., stink with perspiration, L. 4, p. 53

hàn.zi, 汉子, n., man; fellow, L. 12, p. 327

háofàng, 豪放, adj., bold and uninhibited, L. 11, p. 253

háotáodàkū, 嚎啕大哭, idm., cry one's eyes out; wail, L. 10, p. 208

háotáodàkū, 号啕大哭, idm., cry loudly; cry one's eyes out, L. 2, p. 22

hǎo, 好, adj., be easy (to do); be convenient, L. 7, p. 105

hǎobǎ.shi, 好把式, n., person skilled in a trade, L. 10, p. 229

hǎo bù róngyì, 好不容易, adv., with great difficulty; have a hard time (doing sth.), L. 4, p. 53

hǎochù, 好处, n., gain; profit, L. 10, p. 225

hǎojǐng bùcháng, 好景不长, idm., Good times don't last long., L. 2, p. 21

hǎo róngyì, 好容易, adv., with great, L. 11, p. 269

hǎo shāng.liang, 好商量, adj., can be settled through discussion, L. 4, p. 43

hǎowén, 好闻, adj., pleasant to smell, L. 11, p. 269

hǎoxiào, 好笑, adj., funny; ridiculous, L. 12, p. 361

hàoqí, 好奇, adj., curious, L. 4, p. 49

hé, 盒, AN., a box of; a case of, L. 7, p. 119, L. 12, p. 333

hébāo dàn, 荷包蛋, n., poached egg, L. 9, p. 163

hébì, 何必, adv., why must, L. 7, p. 115

hécéng, 何曾, adv., did ever (used in rhetorical questions), L.8, p. 135, L. 11, p. 257

héděng, 何等, adv., how, what, L. 6, p. 81

héfǎ, 合法, adj., legal; lawful; legitimate, L. 3, p. 33

héhuǎn, 和缓, v. /adj., relieve (the tone), L. 11, p. 279

hékuàng, 何况, conj., moreover; besides; in addition, L. 8, p.129, L. 11, p. 260

Hélán, 荷兰, n., the Netherlands; Holland, L. 4, p. 52

hé.shang, 合上, v.-c., close; shut, L. 5, p. 69, L. 6, p. 93

héshēn, 合身, adj., fit, L. 9, p. 159

hésuàn, 合算, adj., worthwhile, L. 11, p. 277

héyǐ, 何以, pron., why, L. 8, p. 149

héyì, 合意, adj., agreeable; to one's liking, L. 3, p. 35

héyǐng, 合影, v./n., take a group photo; group photo, L. 10, p.227

hézuòshè, 合作社, n., co-op; cooperative, L. 10, p. 189

hèxǐ, 贺喜, v., congratulate on a happy occasion, L. 10, p. 189

hè.zhe, 喝着, v., shout an order, L. 10, p. 215

he, 嗬, intj., ah, oh, L. 12, p. 363

hēi'àn, 黑暗, adj., dark, L. 6, p. 83, L. 11, p. 289

hēidǐ.zi, 黑底子, n., black background, L. 4, p. 43

hēidōngdōng, 黑洞洞, adj., pitch-dark, L. 11, p. 285

hēimù'ěr, 黑木耳, n., edible black fungus, L. 12, p. 355

hēiwá, 黑娃, n., children born over the permitted quota, L. 12, p. 345

hēiyāyā, 黑压压, adv., with a dense mass of people, L. 10, p.209

Pinyin Index

jìn, 尽, *v.*, exert one's utmost effort, L. 3, p. 36

jìn, 浸, *v.*, soak; saturate, L 4, p. 55

jìnhū, 近乎, *v.*, approach; be close to, L. 6, p. 93

jìnlì, 尽力, *v.*, do all one can; try one's best, L. 12, p. 371

jìnqíng, 尽情, *adv.*, to one's heart's content; as much as one likes, L. 11, p. 255

jìnr, 劲儿, *n.*, physical strength, L. 10, p. 192

jìnshī, 浸湿, *v.*, soaked, L. 10, p. 211

jìnshì, 近视, *v.*, get nearsighted, L. 11, p. 267

jìnsì, 近似, *adj.*, similar, L. 5, p. 67

jìntóur, 尽头儿, *n.*, the end, L. 10, p. 217

jīngchà, 惊诧, *adj.*, surprised; amazed; astonished, L. 3, p.35, L. 4, p. 57, L. 10, p. 194

jīngcóng, 荆丛, *n.*, thistles and thorns, L. 10, p. 215

jīnghuāng, 惊慌, *adj.*, scared; panic-stricken, L. 11, p. 315

jīnghún wèidìng, 惊魂未定, *v.*, be still suffering from the shock, L. 4, p. 51

jīngléi, 惊雷, *n.*, a sudden clap of thunder, L. 4, p. 51

jīnglǐ, 经理, *n.*, manager, L. 8, p. 127

jīnglì, 经历, *n.*, experience, L. 5, p. 67

jīngmíng, 精明, *adj.*, shrewd, L. 3, p. 33

jīngmíng qiánghàn, 精明强悍, *adj.*, intelligent and capable; able and efficient, L. 12, p. 329

jīngqí, 惊奇, *adj./adv.*, be surprised; be amazed, L. 2, p. 18, L.4, p. 47

jīngrǎo, 惊扰, *v.*, disturb, L. 10, p. 211

jīngtàn, 惊叹, *v.*, wonder at; marvel at; exclaim (with admiration), L. 12, p. 357

jīngtiān dòngdì, 惊天动地, *idm.*, shaking heaven and earth; earth-shaking, L. 12, p. 347

jīngtiáo, 荆条, *n.*, twigs of the chaste tree , L. 10, p. 229

jīngtōng, 精通, *adj.*, good at, L. 8, p. 133

jīngxǐng, 惊醒, *v.*, wake up with a start, L. 6, p. 81, L. 9, p.169

jīngyà, 惊讶, *adj.*, surprised; amazed; astonished, L. 11, p. 309

jīngyì.de, 惊异地, *adv.*, surprisingly, L. 12, p. 325

jīngyíng, 经营, *v.*, operate; run a business, L. 3, p. 28

jīngzhì xiǎoqiǎo, 精致细巧, *adj.*, fine; exquisite; delicate, L. 11, p. 256

jǐng, 井, *n.*, pit; mine, L. 4, p. 55

jǐngdí, 警笛, *n.*, siren, L. 4, p. 55

jǐngkuàng, 景况, *n.*, circumstances, L. 10, p. 189

jǐngtì.de, 警惕地, *adv.*, vigilantly, L. 10, p. 217

jǐngxiàng, 颈项, *n.*, neck, L. 10, p. 203

jìng, 净, *adv.*, only; merely; nothing but, L. 4, p. 51

jìng, 敬, *v.*, offer politely, L. 12, p. 363

jìngjiǔ, 敬酒, *v.-o.*, propose a toast; toast, L. 12, p. 363

jìngrán, 竟然, *adv.*, surprisingly, L. 2, p. 18

jìngzhí, 径直, *adv.*, straight; directly; straightaway, L. 8, p. 137, L. 12, p. 363

jiǒng, 窘, *adj.*, embarrassed, L. 10, p. 221

jiūjìng, 究竟, *adv.*, after all; finally, L. 3, p. 29, L. 11, p. 271

jiūzhèng, 纠正, *v.*, correct; put right; redress; rectify, L. 10, p.201, L. 11, p. 295

jiǔjīng shāchǎng, 久经沙场, *idm.*, have fought many battles; be a veteran of many wars, L. 4, p. 45

jiǔtán, 酒坛, *n.*, wine jar, L. 12, p. 367

jiǔxí, 酒席, *n.*, feast; banquet, L. 12, p. 363

jiǔyàn, 酒宴, *n.*, banquet, L. 12, p. 363

jiǔzú fànbǎo, 酒足饭饱, *v.*, have dined and wined to one's heart's content, L. 11, p. 269

jiǔzuì, 酒醉, *v.*, be drunk, L. 12, p. 365

jiùbiàn, 就便, *adv.*, at somebody's convenience, L. 7, p. 113

jiùjiā biǎodì, 舅家表弟, *n.*, younger male cousin who is the son of one's mother's brother, L. 12, p. 339

jiù.jiu, 舅舅, *n.*, mother's brother; uncle (a polite address to mother's friend), L. 9, p. 159, L. 11, p. 275

jiùrén, 救人, *v.-o.*, Help!, L. 10, p. 211

júhóngsè, 桔红色, *n./adj.*, tangerine (color), reddish orange (color), L. 10, p. 187

júshì, 局势, *n.*, situation, L. 11, p. 283

júwàirén, 局外人, *n.*, stranger, outsider, L. 8, p. 127

jǔdòng, 举动, *n.*, move; movement, L. 9, p. 175, L. 12, p. 351

jǔsàng, 沮丧, *n./adj.*, depression; dejection; depressed; dejected, L. 2, p. 21, L. 8, p. 141

jù, 聚, *v.*, gather; get together, L. 11, p. 275

jùdà, 巨大, *adj.*, huge, L. 3, p. 28

jùdǎo, 锯倒, *v.-c.*, cut down with a saw, L. 10, p. 190

jùjí, 聚集, *v.*, gather; assemble; collect, L. 10, p. 207

jùjué, 拒绝, *v.*, refuse; reject, L. 4, p. 48

jùtǐ, 具体, *adj./adv.*, concrete; specific, specifically, L. 3, p. 33, L. 11, p. 257, L. 11, p. 269, L. 12, p. 343

juānkuǎn, 捐款, *v.-o.*, donate, L. 3, p. 29

juānxiù, 娟秀, *adj.*, beautiful; graceful, L. 12, p. 333

juǎn, 卷, *v.*, roll up, L. 12, p. 333

juǎnfà, 卷发, *n.*, curly hair, L. 11, p. 293

juànyì, 倦意, *n.*, feeling of exhaustion, L. 6, p. 81

juēshé, 撅折, *v.-c.*, break, L. 10, p. 195

juēzuǐr, 撅嘴儿, *v.*, pout one's lips, L. 10, p. 203

juéchá, 觉察, *v.*, detect; perceive, L. 10, p. 223

juédī, 决堤, *v.-o.*, (of a dike) be breached; burst, L. 10, p. 211

juéjiàng, 倔强, *adj.*, stubborn; unbending, L. 10, p. 241

juéliè, 决裂, *v.*, break with, L. 6, p. 85

juésè, 角色, *n.*, role; part, L. 11, p. 267

jūnjiàn, 军舰, *n.*, warship, L. 10, p. 228

K

kāichéng bùgōng, 开诚布公, *idm.*, speak frankly and sincerely, L. 8, p. 139

kāidòng, 开动, *v.*, move; set in motion, L. 11, p. 261

kāiēn, 开恩, *v.-o.*, grant leniency; have mercy, L. 4, p. 55

kāi hòuménr, 开后门儿, *v.-o.*, buy things in short supply through improper channels, L. 10, p. 201

kāikuò, 开阔, *adv.*, open; wide, L. 11, p. 307

kāilǎng, 开朗, *adj.*, outgoing; optimistic, L. 11, p. 313

kāimén jiànshān, 开门见山, *idm.*, The door opens on a view of mountains - go straight to the point, L. 8, p. 141

kāimǒ, 揩抹, *v.*, wipe, L. 10, p. 203

kāitiānpìdì, 开天辟地, *idm.*, since the beginning of history , L.10, p. 189

kāitóur, 开头儿 , *v.-o.*, begin; start; at the beginning of, L. 4, p.52

kāiwài, 开外, *suffix* , ...and above; and beyond, L. 10, p. 217

kāixiāo, 开销, *n.*, expense, L. 9, p. 163

kāixīn, 开心, *adj.*, happy; joyous; elated, L. 11, p. 293

kǎn, 砍, *v.*, chop, L. 10, p. 229

kàn.buguàn, 看不惯, *v.-c.*, cannot bear the sight of; hate to see, L. 1, p. 7

kàndài, 看待, *v.*, treat; look on; regard, L. 11, p. 305

kàn.shang, 看上, *v.-c.*, take a fancy to, L. 12, p. 336

kàn.shang.qu, 看上去, *v.-c.*, it looks, L. 12, p. 333

kàn yàng.zi, 看样子, *adv.*, it seems; it looks, L. 11, p. 297

kànzhòng, 看中, *v.*, take a fancy to; settle on, L. 10, p. 237

kāngkǎi, 慷慨, *adj.*, generous, L. 8, p. 143

káng, 扛, v., carry on the shoulder, L. 4, p. 55

kàng, 炕, n., kang - a heatable brick bed, L. 9, p. 157

kàngyán, 炕沿, n., the edge of a kang, L. 9, p. 175

kàngyì, 抗议, v., protest; object, L. 10, p. 213

kào…wéi shēng, 靠…为生, v., make a living by…, L. 4, p.48

kàobèi, 靠背, n., back of a chair, L. 10, p. 223

kàolǐyícè, 靠里一侧, n., the side away from the door, L. 4, p.45

Kàoshānzhuāng, 靠山庄, n., place name, L. 10, p. 189

kē, 棵, AN., measure word for plants, L. 12, p. 369

kē, 颗, AN., measure word usually for anything small and roundish, L. 11, p. 313

kēhuài, 磕坏, v.-c., knocked (against sth. hard) and broken, L.4, p. 51

kētóu, 磕头, v.-o., kowtow, L. 10, p. 215, L. 12, p. 355

kě, 渴, adj., thirsty, L. 4, p. 49

kěchǐ, 可耻, adj., shameful; disgraceful, L. 6, p. 83

kělián, 可怜, adj., miserably; pitifully, L. 2, p. 15

kělián, 可怜, v., pity; have pity on, L. 6, p. 85

kěwàng, 渴望, v., thirst for; long for , L. 5, p. 71

kěyùěrbùkěqiú, 可遇而不可求, phr., sth. that can only be found by accident, and not through seeking, L. 11, p. 277

kè, 克, v., bring bad luck to a man (a kind of superstition of old times), L. 11, p. 295

kètáng, 客堂, n., drawing room; parlor, L. 11, p. 301

kètào, 客套, v., make a few polite remarks, L. 11, p. 295

kěndìng, 肯定, adj., positive; affirmative, L. 7, p. 115

kěndìng, 肯定, v., affirm; approve; confirm, L. 11, p. 301

kēngshēng, 吭声, v.-o., utter a sound or word, L. 12, p. 333

kōngdàngdàng, 空荡荡, adj., spacious and deserted, L. 6, p.97, L. 11, p. 310

kōngdòng, 空洞, adj., empty; hollow; devoid of content, L. 11, p. 311

kōngjiān, 空间, n., space; room, L. 11, p. 271

kōngkuò, 空阔, adv., open; spacious, L. 11, p. 307

kōngluòluò, 空落落, adj., empty; open and desolate, L. 11, p.281

kōngshǒu, 空手, adv., empty-handed, L. 9, p. 163

kōngwúyìrén, 空无一人, phr., empty; nobody there, L. 6, p.91

kōngxū, 空虚, adj., hollow; void, L. 7, p. 119

kōngyǒu qiānzhǒng wēnqíng , 空有千种温情, phr., cherishing tender feelings but unable to express in words, L. 11, p. 263

kǒngbù, 恐怖, n., terror; horror, L. 10, p. 235

kǒnghè, 恐吓, v./n., threaten; intimidate, L. 12, p. 351

kǒngjù, 恐惧, adv./ n., be frightened, fear; dread, L. 8, p. 147, L. 9, p. 169, L. 10, p. 217, L. 11, p. 315

Kǒng lǎo fūzǐ, 孔老夫子, n., (informal) Confucius, L. 10, p.195

kòngbái, 空白, n., blank space, L. 5, p. 71, L. 12, p. 367

kòngzhì, 控制, v., control, L. 4, p. 51

kōu, 抠, v., dig with a finger, L. 10, p. 215

kǒudài, 口袋, n., pocket, L. 1, p. 5, L. 12, p. 333

kǒukě, 口渴, v., thirsty, L. 9, p. 173

kǒuqì, 口气, n., tone; manner of speaking, L. 7, p. 115, L. 9, p.169, L. 11, p. 275

kǒuzhuó shébèn, 口拙舌笨, idm., be awkward in speech; inarticulate, L. 8, p. 137

kòu, 扣, v., button up, L. 9, p. 175

kòu, 扣, v., pour; dump, L. 11, p. 265

kòumén, 叩门, v.-o., knock at the door, L. 6, p. 97

kūchái, 枯柴, n., dry wood; dry branch, L. 3, p. 29

kūgān, 枯干, adj., withered; haggard, L. 10, p. 212

kūháo, 哭嚎, v., cry loudly, L. 10, p. 212

kūqiāng, 哭腔, n., tearful tone, L. 1, p. 5

kūsè, 枯涩, adj., be dull and heavy, L. 10, p. 219

kūxiàobùdé, 哭笑不得, idm., be able neither to cry nor to laugh, L. 4, p. 45

kǔguāliǎn, 苦瓜脸, n., facial expression of bitterness, L. 1, p. 5

kǔkǔ.de, 苦苦地, adv., painstakingly; piteously, L. 9, p. 175

kǔláo, 苦劳, n., toil, L. 8, p. 131

kǔmèn, 苦闷, adj./n., depressed; depression, L. 6, p. 89

kǔmìng, 苦命, n., hard lot, L. 10, p. 239

kǔ'nǎo, 苦恼, n., worry; distress; torment, L. 11, p. 313

kǔsè, 苦涩, adj., pained; agonized; anguished, bitter and astringent, L. 9, p. 173

kǔtòng, 苦痛, n., pain; agony, L. 12, p. 329

kǔxiào, 苦笑, n./v., forced smile, smile wryly, L. 6, p. 89, L. 7, p. 115, L. 10, p. 191, L. 11, p. 291, L. 12, p. 341

kùdōu, 裤兜, n., trouser pocket, L. 4, p. 44

kùtuǐ, 裤腿, n., trouser legs, L. 1, p. 3

kuā, 夸, v., praise, L. 12, p. 365

kuājiǎng, 夸奖, v., praise; commend; speak well of, L. 11, p.293

kuāzhāng, 夸张, v., exaggerate, L. 11, p. 309

kuài.ji, 会计, n., accountant, L. 8, p. 126, L. 10, p. 201

kuàrù, 跨入, v., stride into, L. 10, p. 185

kuān, 宽, adj., broad , L. 11, p. 293

kuānchǎng, 宽敞, adj., spacious; roomy, L. 8, p. 145

kuāndù, 宽度, n., width; breadth, L. 4, p. 47

kuānguǎng, 宽广, adj., broad; extensive; vast, L. 10, p. 227

kuānkuò, 宽阔, adj., broad; wide; roomy; spacious, L. 11, p.299

kuānshù, 宽恕, n./v., pardon; forgive; excuse, L. 6, p. 82

kuǎndài, 款待, v., treat cordially; entertain, L. 9, p. 171

kuāng, 筐, AN/ n., a basket of, basket, L. 10, p. 219, L. 12, p.335

kuáng, 狂, adj., arrogant; unruly; wild , L. 10, p. 223, L. 12, p.331

kuángfēng, 狂风, n., fierce wind, L. 11, p. 309

kuàngyě, 旷野, n., wilderness, L. 9, p. 177

kuàngzhǔ, 矿主, n., owner of the mine, L. 4, p. 55

kuī, 亏, adv., fortunately; luckily; thanks to, L. 11, p. 301

kuílùsè, 葵绿色, n., grass green, L. 10, p. 199

kuìjiù, 愧疚, v./adj., have a guilty conscience, L. 10, p. 231

kǔn, 捆, AN., bundle; bunch, a bundle of, L. 8, p. 139, L. 9, p. 159

kùn, 困, adj., sleepy, L. 11, p. 289

kùnhuò, 困惑, v., perplexed; puzzled; bewildered, L. 11, p.301

kuò, 阔, adj., wide; broad, L. 11, p. 297

kuòdà, 扩大, v., broaden; expand, L. 11, p. 313

L

lā, 拉, v., pull, L. 1, p. 3

lā.che, 拉扯, v., take great pains to bring up (a child), L. 4, p.53

lālí, 拉犁, v.-o., pull the plough; plough (the field), L. 11, p.257

lā lí.zi, 拉犁子, v.-o., work with a plough; pull a plough, L. 11, p. 287

lāliàn, 拉链, n., zipper, L. 8, p. 139

lāliàng.le dēng, 拉亮了灯, phr., turn on the light (by pulling the chain), L. 11, p. 295

lāzhù, 拉住, v.-c., stop sb. from doing sth. by pulling him back, L. 11, p. 271

lǎ.bakù, 喇叭裤, *n.,* bell-bottoms; flared trousers, L. 11, p. 313

làjiāo, 辣椒, *n.,* hot pepper, L. 9, p. 157

làròu, 腊肉, *n.,* bacon; cured meat, L. 2, p. 19

làyuè, 腊月, *n.,* the twelfth month of the lunar year, L. 2, p. 19, L. 9, p. 169

lái.bují, 来不及, *v.-c.,* there is not enough time (to do something); too late (to do something), L. 7, p. 117

lái.dejí, 来得及, *v.,* there's still time; be able to do in time, L.10, p. 213

láilín, 来临, *v.,* arrive; to come, L. 9, p. 177, L. 10, p. 207

láirìfāngcháng, 来日方长, *idm.,* Many a day will come yet. There is ample time ahead. , L. 11, p. 277

lài, 赖, *v.,* hang on in a place; hold on to a place, L. 11, p. 309

lándǐ báihuā, 蓝底白花, *n.,* white flower on a blue background, L. 9, p. 159

lángān, 栏杆, *n.,* handrail; railing, L. 11, p. 270

Lánhuā, 兰花, *n.,* orchid; (here) personal name, L. 5, p. 64

lán.zhu, 拦住, *v.-c.,* stop (somebody); bar; block, L. 5, p. 69, L.9, p. 161,L. 12, p. 355

lǎn.de, 懒得, *adv.,* not feel like; not be in the mood to, L. 4, p.44

làn, 烂, *v.,* worn out, L. 10, p. 201

làngtāo, 浪涛, *n.,* wave , L. 5, p. 71

lāo huílái, 捞回来, *v.,* gain back, L. 10, p. 235

láo.dao, 唠叨, *v.,* chatter; be garrulous, L. 5, p. 69, L. 10, p.195

Láodòngjú, 劳动局, *n.,* Labor Bureau, L. 11, p. 263

láojià, 劳驾, *v.,* excuse me; May I trouble you?, L. 2, p. 15

láoláo, 牢牢, *adv.,* firmly; safely, L. 8, p. 147, L. 10, p. 191

láolì, 劳力, *n.,* manpower, L. 10, p. 195

láosāomǎnfù, 牢骚满腹, *phr.,* be full of complaints, L. 11, p.283

lǎo, 老, *adv.,* very, L. 2, p. 15

lǎobànr, 老伴儿, *n.,* one's dear old companion – one's spouse in old age, L. 3, p. 29, L. 8, p. 135

lǎobàntiān, 老半天, *n.,* quite a while, L. 10, p. 233

lǎodànán, 老大难, *n.,* long-standing, big and difficult (problem), L. 11, p. 279

lǎofūzǐ, 老夫子, *n.,* unpractical old scholar, L. 11, p. 267

lǎo gànbù, 老干部, *n.,* old cadre, L. 6, p. 91

lǎojiā, 老家, *n.,* native place; old home, L. 1, p. 5

lǎoliúmáng, 老流氓, *n.,* old hooligan, L. 8, p. 145

lǎo.po, 老婆, *n.,* (informal) wife, L. 11, p. 255

lǎo.shi, 老实, *adj.,* honest, modest; easily taken in, L. 10, p.231, L. 11, p. 267

lǎoshīfu, 老师傅, *n.,* master worker (a qualified worker as distinct from an apprentice), L. 11, p. 293

lǎotàipó, 老太婆, *n.,* old woman, L. 7, p. 109

lǎo tóngzhì, 老同志, *n.,* old comrade, L. 1, p. 7

lǎotóu, 老头, *n.,* old man, L. 7, p. 103

lǎoxiāng, 老乡, *n.,* fellow-townsman; fellow-villager, L. 1, p. 7

lǎoxiǔ, 老朽, *adj./n.,* decrepitude, old and useless, L. 3, p. 29

lǎozhái, 老宅, *n.,* old site, L. 12, p. 339

lào, 烙, *v.,* bake in a pan, L. 9, p. 159

lèguān, 乐观, *adj.,* optimistic; hopeful; bright, L. 10, p. 189

lèhēhē, 乐呵呵, *adj.,* buoyant; happy and gay, Ι. 10, p. 193

lèqù, 乐趣, *n.,* delight; pleasure; joy, L. 11, p. 255

lēi, 勒, *v.,* tie or strap something tight, L. 9, p. 171

lèiguāng, 泪光, *n.,* the shine of tears in someone's eyes, L. 4, p. 57

lèishuǐ, 泪水, *n.,* tears, L. 1, p. 9

lèisì, 类似, *adj.,* similar, L. 8, p. 141

lèizhū, 泪珠, *n.,* teardrops, L. 6, p. 91

lěngbīngbīng, 冷冰冰, *adj.,* ice cold; icy; frosty, L. 2, p. 19

lěngdàn, 冷淡, *adj./n,* cold; indifferent, L. 10, p. 223

lěnglěng qīngqīng, 冷冷清清, *adj.,* cold and cheerless; desolate, L. 9, p. 177

lěngmò, 冷漠, *adj.,* be cold and detached; unconcerned; indifferent, L. 10, p. 215

lěngpán, 冷盘, *n.,* cold dish, L. 12, p. 361

lěngxiào, 冷笑, *v.,* sneer; laugh scornfully, L. 1, p. 3

lěngyù, 冷遇, *n.,* cold shoulder; cold reception, L. 6, p. 83

lèng, 怔, *v.,* be in a daze, L. 11, p. 295

lèng, 愣, *v.,* blank; stupefied, be struck dumb, L. 1, p. 7, L. 2, p. 21, L. 8, p. 131, L. 10, p. 185, L. 12, p. 341

lènglèng.de, 愣愣地, *adv.,* blankly, L. 6, p. 85

límǐ, 厘米, *n.,* cm. (centimeter), L. 4, p. 46

límíng, 黎明, *n.,* dawn; daybreak , L. 5, p. 65

líxiū, 离休, *v.,* retire , L. 5, p. 75

lǐ, 理, *v.,* pay attention; make a gesture or speak to , L. 12, p.326

lǐbài, 礼拜, *n.,* Sunday, L. 11, p. 307

lǐcǎi, 理睬, *v.,* pay attention to; show interest in, L. 10, p. 225

lǐjiào, 礼教, *n.,* the Confucian ethical code, L. 10, p. 205

lǐjié, 礼节, *n.,* courtesy; etiquette; ceremony, L. 7, p. 115, L. 12, p. 355

lǐjiě, 理解, *v.,* understand, L. 11, p. 279

lǐmàoxìng, 礼貌性, *adj.,* courteous; by courtesy, L. 12, p. 343

lǐtáng, 礼堂, *n.,* auditorium, L. 10, p. 185

lǐzhì, 理智, *n.,* reason; sense, L. 10, p. 204

lì, 立, *v.,* make/set up (a will), L. 3, p. 33

lìjí, 立即, *adv.,* immediately; right away, L. 11, p. 261

lì.liang, 力量, *n.,* physical strength, L. 10, p. 189

lìmà, 詈骂, *v.,* curse, L. 10, p. 209

lì.qi, 力气, *n.,* strength, L. 11, p. 269, L. 12, p. 355

lì.yi, 利益, *n.,* advantage; interest; profit, L. 8, p. 127

lián, 联, *v.,* be connected; be related, L. 10, p. 231

liándāo, 镰刀, *n.,* sickle, L. 10, p. 219

liánjié, 廉洁, *adj.,* honest; integrity, L. 8, p. 129

liánjié zhèngpài, 廉洁正派, *adj.,* upright and honest, L. 12, p. 361

liánlādàichě, 连拉带扯, *v.,* dragging and pulling, L. 9, p. 163

liánlèi, 连累, *v.,* implicate; get sb. into trouble, L. 6, p. 93, L. 7, p. 105

liánlián, 连连, *adv.,* repeatedly; again and again, L. 2, p. 17

liánmǐn, 怜悯, *v.,* take pity on; have compassion for, L. 11, p.259

liánshuōdàiquàn, 连说带劝, *v.,* talking and urging, L. 9, p.163

liántóng, 连同, *conj.,* together with; along with, L. 10, p. 190

liánxì, 联系, *v.,* contact; touch, L. 11, p. 253

liányè, 连夜, *n.,* that very night; the same night, L. 10, p. 190

liányī, 涟漪, *n.,* riffle; ripples, L. 11, p. 309

lián yǐngr dōu bújiàn, 连影儿都不见, *phr.,* even cannot see the shadow of it – nothing can be seen, L. 11, p. 283

liǎnmiàn, 脸面, *n.,* face; somebody's feeling, L. 12, p. 369

liǎnpáng, 脸庞, *n.,* face, L. 10, p. 199

liǎnpí hòu, 脸皮厚, *adj.,* thick-skinned; shameless; cheeky, L.11, p. 303

liǎnrè, 脸热, *adj.,* blush (with shame or embarrassment), L. 12, p.347

liǎn yīn.zhe, 脸阴着, *phr.,* have a sombre countenance; look glum, L. 12, p. 341

liàngāng chǎng, 炼钢厂, *n.,* steel plant, L. 10, p. 190

liànliànbùshě, 恋恋不舍, *idm.,* be reluctant to part with, L. 9, p. 163

liáng, 粮, *n.,* grain; food, L. 9, p. 161

liángxīn, 良心, *n.,* conscience, L. 3, p. 35

liángxīnfāxiàn, 良心发现, *idm.,* be stung by conscience, L. 2, p. 17

liǎng, 两, *AN.,* a traditional unit of weight, about 50 grams, L.7, p. 113, L. 12, p. 369

liǎngdīngchōu yī, 两丁抽一, *phr.,* draw one from every two men, L. 11, p. 267

liǎngjiétóu, 两节头, *n.,* with two cars, L. 7, p. 117

liǎngxiǎo wúcāi, 两小无猜, *idm.,* (of a little boy and a little girl) be innocent playmates, L. 5, p. 69

liǎngyàng, 两样, *adj.,* different, L. 11, p. 279

liàngkāi, 晾开, *v.-c.,* dry by spreading out, L. 10, p. 198

liáokuò, 辽阔, *adj.,* vast; extensive, L. 11, p. 257

Liáoníng, 辽宁, *n.,* Liaoning Province, L. 6, p. 87

liǎo.buqǐ, 了不起, *adj.,* amazing; terrific; extraordinary, L. 11, p. 287

liàolǐ, 料理, *v.,* arrange; manage; take care of , L. 5, p. 73

liàoxiǎng, 料想, *v.,* expect; presume, L. 10, p. 202

liě.zhezuǐ, 咧着嘴, *v.-o.,* grin, L. 10, p. 201

lièchē, 列车, *n.,* train, L. 11, p. 252

lièchēyuán, 列车员, *n.,* attendant (on a train), L. 1, p. 3

lièchēzhǎng, 列车长, *n.,* head of a train crew; conductor, L. 1, p. 5

lièhuǒ, 烈火, *n.,* raging flames, L. 10, p. 237

lièshǒu, 猎手, *n.,* hunter, L. 8, p. 135

līn, 拎, *v.,* carry; lift, L. 7, p. 112, L. 8, p. 137, L. 12, p. 326

Lín Biāo, 林彪, *n.,* Lin Biao, 1907-1971, named as Mao's successor in 1966, L. 6, p. 91

lín.ju, 邻居, *n.,* neighbor, L. 4, p. 51

línchǎng, 林场, *n.,* tree farm, L. 10, p. 193

línchuāng, 临窗, *adj.,* by the window, L. 7, p. 103

línmó, 临摹, *v.,* copy (a picture) , L. 4, p. 52

línshěng, 邻省, *n.,* neighboring province, L. 9, p. 159

línshí, 临时, *adv./adj.,* temporarily; at the last minute, L. 11, p. 263

línxiàn, 邻县, *n.,* neighboring county, L. 10, p. 199

línyīndào, 林荫道, *n.,* boulevard; avenue, L. 11, p. 299

línghuāqián, 零花钱, *n.,* pocket money, L. 10, p. 229

língluàn, 凌乱, *adj.,* in disorder; in a mess, L. 10, p. 229

língsǎn, 零散, *adj.,* scattered, L. 2, p. 19

líng.tou, 零头, *n.,* fractional amount, L. 8, p. 133

Língzhī, 灵芝, *n.,* personal name, L. 12, p. 333

lǐng, 领, *v.,* lead; usher, L. 12, p. 327

lǐng biǎogé, 领表格, *v.-o.,* get a form, L. 11, p. 287

lǐngdǎo, 领导, *v./n.,* lead; exercise leadership, leader; leadership, L. 6, p. 95，L. 12, p. 331

lǐngkǒur, 领口儿, *n.,* collar band; neckband, L. 10, p. 203

lǐng.zi, 领子, *n.,* collar, L. 7, p. 119

liū, 溜, *v.,* sneak off, L. 10, p. 207

liūbīng, 溜冰, *v.-o.,* skate; skating, L. 11, p. 255

liú, 留, *v.,* ask sb. to stay; keep sb. where he is, L. 11, p. 295

liú, 留, *v.,* leave behind, L. 3, p. 34

liúbù, 留步, *v.-o.,* don't bother to see me out, L. 7, p. 117

liúlàng, 流浪, *v.,* roam about; lead a vagrant life, L. 4, p. 48

liúliàn, 留恋, *v.,* be reluctant to leave (a place); can't bear to part from sb., L. 10, p. 213

liúluò, 流落, *v.,* drift about; wander about , L. 3, p. 35

Liú Qiǎo ér, 刘巧儿, *n.,* a person's name, L. 10, p. 237

liúshī, 流失, *v.,* drained away; depleted, L. 8, p. 133

liúyì, 留意, *v.,* pay attention to; keep one's eyes open, L. 12, p.363

liúshù, 柳树, *n.,* willow, L. 9, p. 159

lóngjuǎnfēng, 龙卷风, *n.,* tornado, L. 11, p. 309

lǒngzhào, 笼罩, *v.,* envelop; shroud; hover over, L. 4, p. 57, L.8, p. 127, L. 11, p. 295

lóutī, 楼梯, *n.,* stairs; staircase; stairway, L. 4, p. 57, L. 12, p.345

lǒu, 搂, *v.,* hug; cuddle; embrace, L. 9, p. 165, L. 10, p. 187

lǒu zài huái.li, 搂在怀里, *phr.,* hold/cuddle someone in one's bosom, L. 11, p. 291

lǒuzhù, 搂住, *v.-c.,* hug; embrace; cuddle, L. 11, p. 263

lòuyǔ, 漏雨, *v.-o.,* (of a house) rain leaking in, L. 7, p. 113

Lǔ Xùn, 鲁迅, *n.,* Lu Xun, 1881-1936, L. 5, p. 68

lùchū, 露出, *v.,* reveal; show, L. 9, p. 161, L. 10, p. 191, L. 12, p. 353

lùxiàn, 路线, *n.,* route, L. 6, p. 91

lùzhū, 露珠, *n.,* dewdrop, L. 10, p. 219

lǚkè, 旅客, *n.,* passenger, L. 9, p. 177

lǚshè, 旅社, *n.,* hotel; hostel, L. 11, p. 253

lǜdòu, 绿豆, *n.,* mung bean, L. 12, p. 335

lǜdòutāng, 绿豆汤, *n.,* mung bean soup, a kind of dessert, L.11, p. 293

luànhuàng, 乱晃, *v.,* shake; sway, L. 12, p. 355

luànzāozāo, 乱糟糟, *adj.,* chaotic, L. 10, p. 207

luàn.zi, 乱子, *n.,* disturbance; trouble, L. 3, p. 32

lüè, 略, *adv.,* briefly, L. 10, p. 215

lüèguò, 掠过, *v.,* sweep past; fly past, L. 6, p. 86, L. 11, p. 255

lüèlüè, 略略, *adv.,* slightly; briefly, L. 5, p. 75

lüèwēi, 略微, *adv.,* slightly; a little, L. 10, p. 217

lún, 轮, *v.,* take turns, L. 8, p. 147

lúnchuán, 轮船, *n.,* steamer; steamship; steamboat, L. 5, p. 71, L. 11, p. 307

lúnkuò, 轮廓, *n.,* outline; contour, L. 7, p. 103, L. 11, p. 293

lúnliú, 轮流, *adv./v.,* do sth. in turn; take turns, L. 11, p. 263

luō.suo, 啰嗦, *v.,* talk on and on, L. 12, p. 363

luógǔshēng, 锣鼓声, *n.,* the sound of gong and drum, L. 10, p. 219

luó.ji, 逻辑, *n.,* logic, L. 8, p. 137

luòdào, 落到, *v.,* befall; fall upon, L. 10, p. 207

luòdì, 落地, *v.,* fall to the ground; be born, L. 10, p. 188

luòdìdēng, 落地灯, *n.,* floor lamp, L. 11, p. 295

lùoxià, 落下, *v.-c.,* fall; drop, L. 11, p. 309

M

mābù, 抹布, *n.,* rag for wiping   , L. 5, p. 69

mā.de, 妈的, *intj.,* damn! , L. 8, p. 147

mádài, 麻袋, *n.,* gunny bag; gunnysack, L. 10, p. 197, L. 12, p.355

má.fan, 麻烦, *v./adj.,* trouble somebody; bother sb. to do sth., L. 2, p. 17

málì, 麻利, *adj.,* quick and neat; dexterous, L. 4, p. 44

mámù, 麻木, *adj.,* numb; apathetic; be dead to all feeling, L. 2, p. 22, L. 6, p. 93

mǎbùtíngtí, 马不停蹄, *idm.,* make a hurried journey without stop; without a single halt, L. 2, p. 21

mǎtǒng, 马桶, *n.,* night stool; chamber pot, L. 11, p. 283

mà, 骂, *v.,* curse, L. 3, p. 35

mái, 埋, *v.,* bury, L. 4, p. 55

mái.zhe tóu, 埋着头, *v.-o.,* bury oneself (in books), L. 11, p.293

mó, 磨, *v.*, grind, L. 7, p. 113, L. 9, p. 157

módēng, 摩登, *adj.*, modern; fashionable, L. 11, p. 259

mófàn, 模范, *n.*, an exemplary person or thing; model, L. 8, p.135

móléng liǎngkě, 模棱两可, *idm.*, equivocal; ambiguous, L. 12, p. 371

móxíng, 模型, *n.*, model, L. 11, p. 311

mǒ, 抹, *v.*, wipe, L. 4, p. 51, L. 9, p. 163, L. 12, p. 333

mǒhàn, 抹汗, *v.-o.*, wipe the sweat, L. 12, p. 349

mǒlèi, 抹泪, *v.-o.*, wipe away tears, L. 10, p. 207

mǒqù, 抹去, *v.-c.*, wipe, L. 11, p. 261

mǒshā, 抹杀, *v.*, obliterate , L. 5, p. 73

mò bú zuòshēng, 默不作声, *idm.*, hold one's tongue; keep silence, L. 3, p. 35

mòcè gāoshēn, 莫测高深, *idm.*, too profound to be understood, L. 8, p. 127

mòdà, 莫大, *adj.*, greatest; utmost, L. 6, p. 83, L. 11, p. 311

mòfēi, 莫非, *adv.*, can it be that; is it possible that , L. 12, p.349

mòlùrén, 陌路人, *n.*, stranger, L. 11, p. 313

mòmíng qímiào, 莫名其妙, *idm.*, be unable to make heads or tails of something; absurd, L. 10, p. 231, L. 12, p. 367

mòmò, 默默, *adv.*, silently, L. 7, p. 117

mòmò.de, 默默地, *adv.*, quietly; silently, L. 11, p. 263, L. 12, p. 335

mòmòwúyán, 默默无言, *idm.*, keep silent; without saying a word, L. 8, p. 129, L. 10, p. 213

mòqì, 默契, *n.*, tacit understanding; tacit agreement, L. 11, p.271

mòshēng, 陌生, *adj.*, unfamiliar; strange, L. 6, p. 81, L. 10, p.185, L. 12, p. 327

mòshēngrén, 陌生人, *n.*, stranger, L. 11, p. 259

múyàng, 模样, *n.*, appearance; look, L. 1, p. 3, L. 4, p. 45, L. 9, p. 161, L. 10, p. 201, L. 11, p. 293

mǔ.ma, 姆妈, *n.*, (Shanghainese) mother, L. 11, p. 261

mǔyè, 母业, *n.*, mother's job, L. 5, p. 69

mù, 木, *adj.*, numb; wooden, L. 9, p. 177

mùdìdì, 目的地, *n.*, destination, L. 11, p. 258

mùdōng, 暮冬, *n.*, late winter, L. 10, p. 239

mùguāng, 目光, *n.*, sight; vision; gaze; look, L. 7, p. 103, L.12, p. 329

mùliào, 木料, *n.*, timber; lumber, L. 12, p. 339

mùrán, 木然, *adj.*, stupefied, L. 10, p. 233

mùsòng, 目送, *v.*, follow somebody with one's eyes, watch sb. go, L. 7, p. 117, L. 10, p. 223

mùxiān, 木锨, *n.*, wooden shovel, L. 10, p. 197

mùxuàn, 目眩, *v.*, feel dizzy and dazzled, L. 11, p. 285

N

nǎpà, 哪怕, *conj.*, even; even if; even though, L. 7, p. 103, L.11, p. 289

nǎi.nai, 奶奶, *n.*, grandmother; grandma, L. 11, p. 303

nàixīn, 耐心, *adj./adv.*, patient, patiently, L. 2, p. 17, L. 8, p.139, L. 9, p. 165

nài.zhe xìng.zi, 耐着性子, *adv.*, restrain oneself; patiently do sth., L. 3, p. 35

nānnān, 囡囡, *n.*, (Shanghainese) little darling (used as a term of endearment for a child or a baby), L. 11, p. 261

nándé, 难得, *adv.*, seldom; rarely, L. 7, p. 117

nánkān, 难堪, *adj.*, embarrassed, L. 12, p. 335

nánnán, 喃喃, *onom.*, mutter; murmur, L. 12, p. 371

nánnán zìyǔ, 喃喃自语, *v.* , mutter sth. to oneself, L. 10, p.239

nánpō, 南坡, *n.*, the southern slope, L. 12, p. 335

nán.wei, 难为, *v.*, embarrass; press , L. 10, p. 211, L. 12, p.357

nányán, 难言, *adj.*, difficult to describe, indescribable, L. 6, p.93

nányúqǐchǐ, 难于启齿, *phr.*, find it difficult to bring the matter up, L. 11, p. 301

nánzhuāng, 南庄, *n.*, the south village, L. 12, p. 327

nǎo.dai, 脑袋, *n.*, (informal) head, L. 5, p. 75, L. 9, p. 177, L.11, p. 277

nǎonù, 恼怒, *v./adv.*, angry; indignant, L. 8, p. 145

nǎorén, 恼人, *adj.*, annoying; irritating, L. 2, p. 20

nàorǎng, 闹嚷, *v.*, raise clamor; din, L. 4, p. 55

nào.teng, 闹腾, *v.*, be rowdy; create a disturbance, L. 10, p. 211

nènè, 呐呐, *v.*, murmur, L. 7, p. 115

nèicān, 内参, *n.*, short for 内部参考；confidential internal reference , L. 12, p. 331

nèidōu, 内兜, *n.*, inside pocket, L. 8, p. 141

nèiháng, 内行, *adj.*, be expert at; know the ins and outs of , L.11, p. 279

nèikē, 内科, *n.*, internal medicine, L. 6, p. 97

nèixīn, 内心, *n.*, inward; heart, L. 6, p. 91, L. 10, p. 189

nènlǜ, 嫩绿, *adj.*, light green; soft green, L. 12, p. 349

nènmiáo, 嫩苗, *n.*, tender seedling, L. 9, p. 167

ng/n, 嗯, *intj.*, hey! (used to show surprise or disapproval), L.11, p. 297

níwá.wa, 泥娃娃, *n.*, clay doll, L. 11, p. 273

nì, 溺, *v.*, drown, L. 8, p. 135

niándài, 年代, *n.*, age; years; time, decade, L. 10, p. 185, L. 12, p. 332

niánhuò, 年货, *n.*, special purchases for the Spring Festival, L.2, p. 17

niánqīng màoměi, 年轻貌美, *idm.*, young and pretty, L. 3, p.31

niánxià, 年下, *n.*, the Chinese lunar New Year holidays, L. 10, p. 193

niǎn, 撵, *v.*, drive away; oust, L. 10, p. 229

niǎnliàng, 捻亮, *v.*, turn up the wick (of a lamp), L. 10, p. 208

niáng, 娘, *n.*, ma; mom; mother, L. 12, p. 325

niáng.jia, 娘家, *n.*, a married woman's parents' home, L. 9, p.157, L. 10, p. 237

niào, 尿, *n./v.*, urine, urinate, L. 5, p. 65

niē, 捏, *v.*, holding between the finger and thumb; pinch, L. 1, p. 3, L. 4, p. 57, L. 12, p. 365

nièrú, 嗫嚅, *v.*, speak haltingly, L. 11, p. 273, L. 12, p. 341

níngjìng, 宁静, *n./adj.*, tranquility; peace, tranquil; peaceful, L. 5, p. 69

níngshì, 凝视, *v.*, gaze fixedly; stare, L. 10, p. 199

níngwàng, 凝望, *v.*, gaze , L. 10, p. 186

nǐngkāi, 拧开, *v.-c.*, twist open; screw open, L. 4, p. 49

niǔ, 扭, *v.*, sprain; twist, L. 10, p. 197

niǔdòng, 扭动, *v.*, sway; writhe, L. 5, p. 73

niǔ .guo tóu, 扭过头, *v.* , turn one's head, L. 6, p. 91

niǔkāi, 扭开, *v.-c.*, wrench the door open, L. 8, p. 139

niǔniǔ niēniē, 扭扭捏捏, *adv.*, be affectedly bashful, L. 11, p.295

niǔtóu, 扭头, *v.-o.*, turn one's head, L. 11, p. 271, L. 12, p. 349, L. 12, p. 353

nóng, 浓, *adj.*, great; strong, L. 8, p. 131

nóngmì, 浓密, *adj.*, dense, L. 10, p. 219

nóngxián, 农闲, *n.*, slack season (in farming), L. 9, p. 157

nóngzhuó, 浓浊, *adj.*, thick and turbid, L. 10, p. 239

nòng, 弄, *n.,* alley, L. 6, p. 97

nòngtáng, 弄堂, *n.,* lane; alley, L. 11, p. 283

nù chōngchōng, 怒冲冲, *adv.,* furiously; in a rage, L. 9, p.175

nùhuǒ, 怒火, *n.,* flames of fury; fury, L. 9, p. 173

nǚ.xu, 女婿, *n.,* son-in-law, L. 8, p. 135

nǚyōng, 女佣, *n.,* woman servant; maid, L. 5, p. 65

nuǎn.huo, 暖和, *adj.,* warm; nice and warm, L. 11, p. 269

nuǎnróngróng, 暖融融, *adj.,* nice and warm, L. 11, p. 309

nuó, 挪, *v.,* move; shift, L. 4, p. 47, L. 8, p. 127

nuódòng, 挪动, *v.,* move, L. 11, p. 301

O

o, 哦!, *intj.,* Oh!; Hi!, L. 5, p. 75, L. 11, p. 257

o, 噢, *intj.,* oh! (expressing sudden realization), L. 7, p. 105, L.11, p. 277

ǒu'ěr, 偶尔, *adv.,* occasionally, L. 12, p. 327

ǒurán, 偶然, *adj.,* accidental; by chance, L. 10, p. 194

P

páxíng, 爬行, *v.,* crawl; creep, L. 11, p. 315

pāi, 拍, *v.,* clap; pat; beat, L. 11, p. 254, L. 12, p. 331

pāi, 拍, *v.,* take (a picture), L. 7, p. 109

pāi diànbào, 拍电报, *v.-o.,* send a telegram, L. 6, p. 97

pài, 派, *AN.,* measure word used with scenery, sight, sound, etc., L. 4, p. 57

pài, 派, *v.,* assign (a duty; task), L. 10, p. 197

pàn, 盼, *v.,* hope for; long for, L. 7, p. 107

pànbiàn, 叛变, *v.,* turn traitor, L. 6, p. 83

pànduàn, 判断, *n./v.,* judgment, judge; decide, L. 12, p. 341

pàntú, 叛徒, *n.,* traitor, L. 6, p. 81

pànwàng, 盼望, *v.,* look forward to; long for, L. 6, p. 95, L. 11, p. 258

pànxíng, 判刑, *v.-o.,* sentence, L. 10, p. 225

pàng wá.wa, 胖娃娃, *n.,* chubby child, L. 11, p. 311

pāodào jiǔxiāo yúnwài, 抛到九霄云外, *phr.,* recede from one's mind far into the ninth celestial sphere, L. 2, p. 20

pāosǎ, 抛洒, *v.,* throw; toss, L. 10, p. 237

pǎo.le, 跑了, *v.,* run away; elope, L. 4, p. 53

pào, 泡, *v.,* pour boiling water on, L. 4, p. 49

pàochá, 泡茶, *v.-o.,* make tea, L. 11, p. 269

pàohuǒ, 炮火, *n.,* artillery fire; gunfire, L. 6, p. 83

pēi, 呸, *intj.,* pah; bah (used to express disdain, annoyance or stern disapproval), L. 10, p. 203

péi, 陪, *v.,* accompany; keep sb. company, L. 11, p. 263

péitóng, 陪同, *v.,* go with; accompany, L. 10, p. 227

pèijǐ, 配给, *v.,* ration, L. 7, p. 113

pèi yǎnjìng, 配眼镜, *v.,* have one's eyesight tested for glasses, L. 11, p. 267

pēnchū, 喷出, *v.,* spurt out, L. 10, p. 191

pēnshuǐchí, 喷水池, *n.,* fountain, L. 11, p. 309

pén, 盆, *AN,* basin; tub, measure word for things held in a basin, L. 5, p. 75, L. 12, p. 325

pēng, 砰, *onom.,* sound of sth. falling heavily on the ground or striking against sth. else, L. 11, p. 303

pēng.deyíxià, 砰地一下, *phr.,* with a big bang, L. 6, p. 97

pēngpēng, 怦怦, *onom.,* (of the heart) pit-a-pat, L.10, p. 227

pēngpōng.de, 怦怦地, *adv.,* thump; go pit-a-pat, L. 11, p. 257

pěng, 捧, *v.,* hold or carry in both hands, L. 2, p. 22, L. 4, p. 51

pěng.zhe, 捧着, *v.,* carrying in both hands, L. 10, p. 237

pèngbēi, 碰杯, *v.-o.,* clink glasses, L. 12, p. 363

pèngbēi zhùjiǔ, 碰杯祝酒, *v.,* clink glasses and drink a toast, L. 8, p. 145

pī, 批, *v.,* criticize; refute, L. 10, p. 195

pī, 批, *v.,* ratify; approve, L. 6, p. 87, L. 12, p. 343

pībó, 批驳, *v.,* refute; criticize; rebut, L. 12, p. 353

pīgǎi, 批改, *v.,* correct (students' homework), L. 6, p. 95

pīlì, 霹雳, *n.,* thunderbolt; thunderclap, L. 11, p. 309

pīpàn, 批判, *v./n.,* criticize; criticism, L. 6, p. 85, L. 10, p. 231

pīpànhuì, 批判会, *n.,* criticism meeting, L. 7, p. 107

pītóu sànfà, 披头散发, *idm.,* disheveled hair; with hair hanging loose, L. 10, p. 208

pīzhǔn, 批准, *v.,* approve; ratify; sanction, L. 12, p. 339

pí, 皮, *adj.,* naughty; mischievous, L. 11, p. 295

pífū, 皮肤, *n.,* skin, L. 11, p. 253

píjuàn, 疲倦, *n./adj.,* tired; weary; exhausted, L. 5, p. 69, L. 6, p. 81

pí.qi, 脾气, *n.,* temperament; disposition, L. 9, p. 165, L. 11, p.305

pì.gu, 屁股, *n.,* (informal) buttocks (of human), L. 12, p. 347

piān, 偏, *adv.,* deliberately; contrary to what is expected, L. 4, p. 51

piān.zi, 片子, *n.,* film; movie, L. 11, p. 260

piānfáng, 偏房, *n.,* wing-room, L. 12, p. 332

piānpiān, 偏偏, *adv.,* willfully; insistently; persistently, L. 12, p. 331

piānqiǎo, 偏巧, *adv.,* it so happened that; as luck would have it, L. 4, p. 53

piānyuǎn, 偏远, *adj.,* remote; faraway, L. 2, p. 14

piànkè, 片刻, a short while; a moment, L. 6, p. 87, L. 12, p.355

piāofú, 漂浮, *v.,* float, L. 5, p. 67

piāohàn, 剽悍, *adj.,* agile and strong, L. 10, p. 195

piāoliú, 漂流, *v.,* lead a wandering life; drift, L. 11, p. 269

piāoyáng, 飘扬, *v.,* fly; wave; flutter, L. 5, p. 65

piǎo, 瞟, *v.,* glance sideways at, L. 10, p. 233, L. 11, p. 293

piē, 瞥, *v.,* glance at, L. 10, p. 221

piězuǐ, 撇嘴, *v.-o.,* curl one's lip (in contempt, disbelief or disappointment), L. 12, p. 345

pīn.jinr, 拼劲, *n.,* great zeal; hard working spirit, L. 10, p. 195

pīnmìng, 拼命, *adv.,* exerting the utmost strength; with all one's might, L. 11, p. 311

pínfá, 贫乏, *adj.,* poor; short; lacking, L. 10, p. 205

pínxiàzhōngnóng, 贫下中农, *n.,* 贫农: lower class peasants; 下中农: lower-middle peasants, L. 6, p. 89

pìnlǐ, 聘礼, *n.,* betrothal gifts (from the bridegroom's to the bride's family), L. 9, p. 161

pìnqǐng, 聘请, *v.,* invite; hire, L. 3, p. 31

píng, 凭, *prep.,* base on; according to, on the basis of, L. 8, p.143, L. 10, p. 239

píngbǐ, 评比, *v.,* compare and assess, L. 12, p. 337

píngdànwúqí, 平淡无奇, *idm.,* very ordinary; appear trite and insignificant, L. 10, p. 194

píngdìng, 评定, *v./n.,* evaluate; evaluation, L. 1, p. 5

píngfǎn, 平反, *v.,* redress (a mishandled case), L. 7, p. 111

píngfāng, 平方, *n.,* square meter, L. 11, p. 301

píngfāngmǐ, 平方米, *n.,* square meter, L. 11, p. 263

pínggài, 瓶盖, *n.,* bottle cap, L. 4, p. 49

píngjūn, 平均, *adj./v.,* equally; share and share alike, L. 3, p.33

píngjìng, 平静, *adj./v.,* calm; quiet, calm down, L. 1, p. 9, L.10, p. 233, L. 11, p. 261, L. 12, p. 349

pínglǐ, 评理, *v.-o.,* judge between right and wrong, L. 12, p.331

píngpíng'ān'ān, 平平安安, *adj.,* safe and sound, L. 7, p. 111

píng shén.me, 凭什么, *adv.,* base on what, L. 11, p. 297

pō, 颇, *adv.,* pretty, quite, rather, L. 8, p. 133

pōlà, 泼辣, *adj.*, bold and forceful, L. 10, p. 192

pó.po, 婆婆, *n.*, husband's mother; mother-in-law, L. 11, p.305

pòhài, 迫害, *v.*, persecute, L. 6, p. 91

pòlàn, 破烂, *adj.*, tattered; ragged; worn-out, L. 5, p. 75

pòlì, 破例, *v.*, break a rule; make an exception, L. 2, p. 17

pòliè, 破裂, *v.*, break; fracture; burst; split, L. 11, p. 311

pò.zhan, 破绽, *n.*, burst seam; flaw, L. 8, p. 135

pū, 铺, *v.*, spread , L. 10, p. 198

pūdǎo, 扑倒, *v.*, throw oneself on, L. 10, p. 208

pū.gaijuǎnr, 铺盖卷儿, *n.*, bedding roll; bedroll; luggage roll, L. 7, p. 112

pū jìn...de huáilǐ, 扑进…的怀里, *v.*, throw oneself into someone else's arms, L. 6, p. 82

pútáo jiǔ, 葡萄酒, *n.*, wine, L. 8, p. 131

pù, 铺, *n.*, plank bed, L. 6, p. 93

pùbǎn, 铺板, *n.*, bed board, L. 11, p. 283

Q

qīdài, 期待, *v.*, expect, L. 7, p. 103

qī.fu, 欺负, *v.*, bully with, L. 9, p. 165

qīkān, 期刊, *n.*, journals; periodicals, L. 11, p.269

qīliáng, 凄凉, *adj.*, lonely and desolate, L. 6, p. 81, L. 10, p.213

qī.qiao, 蹊跷, *adj.*, odd; queer, L. 10, p. 194

qīqīng, 凄清, *adj.*, lonely and sad, L. 10, p. 239

qīrén tàishèn, 欺人太甚, *idm.*, what a beastly bully; that's going too far; push people too hard, L. 12, p. 345

qīshǒu bājiǎo, 七手八脚, *idm.*, seven hands and eight feet –hussle and bustle; disorderly, L. 10, p. 211

qīwǔ, 欺侮, *v.*, bully and humiliate, L. 10, p. 219, L. 12, p. 357

qīzuǐbāshé, 七嘴八舌, *idm.*, with seven mouths and eight tongues -- all sorts of gossip; all talking at once, L. 10, p. 209

qí, 齐, *adj.*, all ready, all present; (here) complete; all done, L.11, p. 263

qíjiān, 其间, *n.*, during this or that time, L. 12, p. 339

qímiào, 奇妙, *adj.*, marvelous; wonderful, L. 10, p. 191

qíshì, 歧视, *n./v.*, discrimination; discriminate, L. 6, p. 83

qítā, 其他, *adj.*, other, L. 3, p. 35

qíyú, 其余, *adj.*, all the other (persons or things); the rest, L. 12, p. 365

qǐbù, 岂不, *adv.*, wouldn't it…; isn't it …(used to ask a rhetorical question), L. 11, p. 313

qǐ chuòhào, 起绰号, *v.-o.*, give somebody a nickname, L. 7, p.117

qǐgài, 乞丐, *n.*, beggar , L. 5, p. 65

qǐjìn, 起劲, *adj.*, enthusiastic; in high spirits, L. 11, p. 292

qǐlì, 起立, *v.*, stand up; rise to one's feet, L. 11, p. 295

qǐmǎ, 起码, *adv.*, at least, L. 8, p. 129, L. 11, p. 282

qǐ míng.zi, 起名字, *v.-o.*, give a name, L. 10, p. 189

qǐshēn, 起身, *v.-o.*, stand up, L. 7, p. 115

qǐshì, 启示, *n.*, inspiration; enlightenment, L. 10, p. 239

qǐtú, 企图, *v./n.*, attempt; try, L. 8, p. 133, L. 10, p. 205

qǐyè, 企业, *n.*, enterprise, L. 3, p. 28

qǐyè guǎnlǐ, 企业管理, *n.*, business management , L. 12, p.359

qì, 砌, *v.*, build by laying bricks or stones, L. 5, p. 67

qìchuǎn xūxū, 气喘吁吁, *adv.*, pant for breath; be short of breath, L. 4, p. 57, L. 9, p. 165, L. 11, p. 261

qì.fen, 气氛, *n.*, atmosphere; air, L. 8, p. 127, L. 11, p. 287

qìhēnghēng, 气哼哼, *adv.*, in a huff; panting with rage, L. 12, p. 343

qìhuà, 气话, *n.*, words said in a fit of rage, L. 11, p. 307

qìmèn, 气闷, *adv.*, depressed; vexed; sad and silent, L. 11, p.307

qìpài, 气派, *n.*, manner; style; air, L. 10, p. 221

qìxī, 气息, *n.*, flavor; smell, L. 11, p. 269

qìzhòng, 器重, *v.*, think highly of (one's juniors or subordinates), L. 7, p. 119

qiān, 牵, *v.*, lead along (by holding the hand, the halter, etc.); pull, L. 11, p. 275

qiān, 签, *v.* , sign, L. 3, p. 36

qiānlián, 牵连, *v.*, involve (in trouble); implicate (in a crime), L.8, p. 143

qiānnù, 迁怒, *v.*, vent one's anger on somebody who is not to blame; take it out on somebody, L. 12, p. 343

qiānwàn fùwēng, 千万富翁, *n.*, billionaire , L. 8, p. 147

qiánfāng, 前方, *n.*, the place ahead, L. 11, p. 252

qiántí, 前提, *n.*, premise, L. 8, p. 143

qiántú, 前途, *n.*, future; prospects, L. 6, p. 93, L. 10, p. 237

qián.zi, 钳子, *n.*, tongs; pincers; (here): nickname of one of the thieves, L. 4, p. 44

qiǎnfǎn, 遣返, *v.*, repatriate, L. 4, p. 47

qiànjiào, 欠觉, *v.-o.*, have not enough sleep, L. 11, p. 281

qiànquē , 欠缺, *v.*, deficient; lack; not good enough, L. 11, p.295

qiànyì, 歉意, *n.*, regret; apology, L. 7, p. 105, L. 12, p. 369

qiángdiào, 强调, *v.*, emphasize; stress, L. 6, p. 89

qiángjiā, 强加, *v.*, impose, L. 6, p. 95

qiángjiān, 强奸, *v./n.*, rape, L. 10, p. 215

qiángjiǎo, 墙脚, *n.*, the foot of a wall, L. 9, p. 163

qiángjiǎo, 墙角, *n.*, corner of the wall, L. 10, p. 186

qiángjiàn, 强健, *adj.*, strong and healthy, L. 10, p. 205

qiángliè, 强烈, *adj.*, strong; intense; violent, L. 2, p. 22, L. 5, p. 71, L. 10, p. 187, L. 11, p. 265

qiǎng, 抢, *v.*, rush over, L. 11, p. 295

qiǎng, 强, *adv.*, make an effort; by force, L. 6, p. 82

qiǎngjiù, 抢救, *v.*, rescue; save, L. 6, p. 83

qiāo, 敲, *v.*, knock, L. 5, p. 75

qiāoqiāo, 悄悄, *adv.*, quietly, L. 3, p. 33, L. 5, p. 65

qiāoqiāo.de, 悄悄地, *adv.*, without being noticed, L. 10, p.228

qiāoxiǎng, 敲响, *v.-c.*, knock and emit a sound, L. 12, p. 327

qiāoyǔ, 悄语, *v.*, speak in a low voice, L. 8, p. 139

qiáo, 瞧, *v.*, look; see, , L. 2, p. 21, L. 6, p. 81, L. 10, p. 197

qiáo.buqǐ, 瞧不起, *v.-c.*, look down upon, L. 11, p. 259, L. 12, p. 341

qiáocuì, 憔悴, *adj.*, haggard; thin and pallid, L. 4, p. 53

qiáoliáng, 桥梁, *n.*, bridge, L. 10, p. 189

qiáoshǒu qìpàn, 翘首企盼, *phr.*, raise one's head and stand on tiptoe – eagerly looking forward to/awaiting, L. 2, p. 21

qiàokāi, 撬开, *v.-c.*, pry open, L. 4, p. 43

qiàolì, 俏丽, *n.*, (of a young woman) handsome; pretty, L. 6, p.91

qiērù, 切入, *v.*, cut to; cut through to , L. 8, p. 131

qièzéi, 窃贼, *n.*, thief; burglar, L. 4, p. 53

qīn, 亲, *v.*, kiss, L. 6, p. 81, L. 12, p. 335

qīnfàn, 侵犯, *v.*, disturb; encroach on , L. 4, p. 45

qīnkǒu, 亲口, *adv.*, (say something) personally, L. 12, p. 349

qīnnì.de, 亲昵地, *adv.*, intimately, L. 8, p. 131

qīnniáng, 亲娘, *n.*, mother, L. 9, p. 159

qīnqiè, 亲切, *adj./adv.*, tender; kind, L. 3, p. 31, L. 12, p. 353

qīnqinmìmì, 亲亲密密, *adv.*, intimately, L. 8, p. 139

qīnqin rèrè, 亲亲热热, *adj.*, being affectionate, L. 11, p. 291

qīnrè, 亲热, *adv.*, affectionately; intimately, L. 9, p. 171, L. 12, p. 351

qīnrén, 亲人, *n.*, one's family member, L. 6, p. 89

qīnzuǐr, 亲嘴儿, v.-o., kiss, L. 10, p. 202

qíncài, 芹菜, n., celery, L. 9, p. 157

qín.kuai, 勤快, adj., diligent; hardworking, L. 10, p. 197

qín.zhe yǎnlèi, 噙着眼泪, v.-o., with tears in one's eyes, L. 11, p. 261

qīngchūn, 青春, n., youth; youthfulness, L. 5, p. 69, L. 6, p. 91, L. 10, p. 213

qīngjiā dàngchǎn, 倾家荡产, idm., bring the family to ruin; family ruined and its property all lost, L. 11, p. 289

qīngjié, 清洁, adj., clean, L. 11, p. 260

qīngkuài, 轻快, adj., relaxed, L. 7 , p. 111

qīngmiè, 轻蔑, adj., scornful; disdainful, L. 10, p. 215

qīngmíng, 清明, adj., clear and bright, L. 4, p. 52

qīngniántuán, 青年团, n., Communist Youth League, L. 7, p. 107

qīng.qiao, 轻巧, adj., easy; simple, L. 10, p. 197

qīngróu, 轻柔, adj., soft; gentle, L. 10, p. 241

qīngsōng, 轻松, adj., light; relaxed, L. 6, p. 93, L. 11, p. 307

qīngtāng, 清汤, n., clear soup, L. 9, p. 167

qīngtǔ, 倾吐, v., pour; exchange ideas without reservation, L.6, p. 89

qīngwā, 青蛙, n., frog, L. 7 , p. 111

qīngxīn, 清新, adj., pure and fresh, L. 11, p. 257

qīngyì, 轻易, adv., lightly; rashly; easily, L. 10, p. 211

qīngxǐng, 清醒, v., be wide-awake , L. 5, p. 71

qīngzhuān, 青砖, n., black brick , L. 5, p. 67

qíngjié, 情节, n., circumstances; plot, L. 8, p. 137

qíngjǐng, 情景, n., scene; sight; circumstances , L. 5, p. 65, L.12, p. 337

qíngláng, 情郎, n., lover, L. 10, p. 237

qíngxù, 情绪, n., mood; feeling; sentiments, L. 11, p. 265

qíng.yi, 情谊, n., friendly feelings; affection, L. 6, p. 89

qíngyuàn, 情愿, v., be willing to, L. 2, p. 21

qǐngjià, 请假, v.-o., ask for leave, L. 6, p. 93, L. 11, p. 263

qǐngqiú, 请求, v., ask; request; beg, L. 4, p. 57

qìng.jia, 亲家, n., parents of one's daughter-in-law or son-in-law, L. 9, p. 159

qìnghè, 庆贺, v., celebrate, L. 8, p. 145, L. 9, p. 171

qióngxiāng pìrǎng, 穷乡僻壤, idm., remote, backward place, L. 2, p. 15

qiú, 求, v., ask; beg; request , L. 1, p. 7, L. 4, p. 51, L. 8, p. 143, L. 12, p. 331

qiúqíng, 求情, v., plead; ask for a favor, L. 10, p. 211, L. 12, p.341

qiúráo, 求饶, v.-o., beg for mercy, L. 9, p. 175

qūjiě, 曲解, v., misunderstand, L. 8, p. 137

qūqūzhīshù, 区区之数, n., a small amount; a pittance, L. 8, p.135

qūrǔ, 屈辱, adj. / n., humiliated, humiliation, L. 10, p. 209, L.12, p. 330

qūsàn, 驱散, v., disperse; dispel; break up, L. 10, p. 211

qǔyìyú, 取意于, v., derive its meaning from, L. 10, p. 189

qùshì, 去世, v., pass away, L. 3, p. 29, L. 5, p. 73

qùxiàng, 去向, n., direction in which somebody or something has gone, L. 12, p. 359

quān, 圈, n., circle; ring, L. 7, p. 117, L. 8, p. 141, L. 11, p.309

quān.zi, 圈子, n., circle, L. 4, p. 55

quángǔ, 颧骨, n., cheekbone, L. 11, p. 295

quán, 拳, n., fist, L. 12, p. 365

quánbù, 全部, adj., entire; full, L. 3, p. 33

quánrán, 全然, adv., completely; entirely, L. 10, p. 221

quán.tou, 拳头, n., fist, L. 9, p. 175

quánxīn quányì, 全心全意, idm., whole-heartedly, L. 12, p.328

quányízhījǔ, 权宜之举, n., expedient act, L. 8, p. 143

quànwèi, 劝慰, v., console; soothe, L. 10, p. 211

quēxiàn, 缺陷, n., defect; fault, L. 11, p. 279

quèhū, 确乎, adv., really; indeed, L. 8, p. 133

qúnzhòng, 群众, n., the masses, L. 12, p. 365

R

ránqǐ, 燃起, v.-c., burn; ignite , L. 5, p. 67

ránshāo, 燃烧, v., burn, L. 9, p. 173, L. 10, p. 205

rǎn, 染, v., dye, L. 7, p. 119

rǎng, 嚷, v., shout; yell, L. 4, p. 51

ràng, 让, v., give way; yield, L. 11, p. 291

ràng, 让, v., invite; offer, L. 12, p. 369

ràng.jin.qu, 让进去, v.-c., invite (the guest) into (a room), L.12, p. 333

ràngzuò, 让座, v.-o., offer one's seat to somebody, L. 7, p.115

rě, 惹, v., offend; provoke, L. 4, p. 51, L. 12, p. 341

rè.nao, 热闹, adj./n., fun; lively; bustling with activity, L. 10, p. 197, L. 11, p. 272

rèlàlà, 热辣辣, adj., burning hot, L. 10, p. 199

rèqì téngténg, 热气腾腾, idm., steaming hot, L. 10, p. 233

rèqiè, 热切, adj., fervent; earnest, L. 6, p. 81

rèqíng, 热情, n., enthusiasm; zeal; warmth, warmly, L. 5, p. 67, L. 6, p. 85, L. 10, p. 228

rèténgténg, 热腾腾, adj., steaming hot, L. 11, p. 285

rénjiā, 人家, pron., they; he; she, L. 1, p. 5, L. 11, p. 295

rén.jia, 人家, n., others, L. 11, p. 285

rénlìchē, 人力车, n., rickshaw , L. 5, p. 65

rénliú, 人流, n., stream of people, L. 11, p. 313

rénmín gōngshè, 人民公社, n., People's Commune, L. 10, p.189

rénpǐn, 人品, n., moral quality, L. 11, p. 289

rénqún, 人群, n., crowd; throng; multitude, L. 11, p. 267

rénshānrénhǎi, 人山人海, idm., crowds of people; a sea of people, L. 11, p. 282

rénshēng, 人生, n., life , L. 11, p. 255

rénxíngdào, 人行道, n., side pavement; sidewalk, L. 11, p.282

rénzàomáo, 人造毛, n., artificial wool, L. 7, p. 119

rénzhèng, 人证, n., testimony of a witness; (here) "certificate of human-ness", L. 1, p. 3

rěn, 忍, v. , bear; put up with, L. 6, p. 83

rěn.buzhù, 忍不住, v., cannot hold back; cannot stand but to, L. 11, p. 273

rěnshòu, 忍受, v., endure; to bear , L. 5, p. 65

rěnxīn, 忍心, v., be hardhearted enough to, L. 9, p. 169

rèn, 认, v., recognize somebody as one's relatives, L. 12, p.339

rèn...dōu..., 任⋯都⋯, conj., no matter (how/what/ etc.) , L.2, p. 21

rènjiào, 任教, v., teach, L. 6, p. 91

rènpíng, 任凭, v., allow; let (sb. do as he pleases), L.10, p. 209

rènwù, 任务, n., mission; assignment; task, L. 12, p. 369

rènzhèng bú rènrén, 认证不认人, phr., only recognize/accept identification, and not the person himself/herself, L. 1, p. 5

rènzhǔn.le mùbiāo, 认准了目标, phr., set one's mind on a target, L. 11, p. 281

rēng, 扔, v., throw; toss; cast, L. 12, p. 325

rēngxià, 扔下, v., abandon; leave behind, L. 9, p. 169

réngjiù, 仍旧, adv., still; yet; as before, L. 6, p. 81

rìtóu, 日头, n., the sun, L. 12, p. 324

rónghuà, 融化, *v.*, thaw, L. 2, p. 20

róngmào, 容貌, *n.*, appearance; looks, L. 6, p. 85

róngnàliàng, 容纳量, *n.*, capacity, L. 11, p. 271

róu, 揉, *v.*, rub, L. 4, p. 55

róuhé, 柔和, *adj.*, soft; gentle; mild, L. 10, p. 219

róuqíng, 柔情, *n.*, tender feelings, L. 10, p. 223

róushù, 柔术, *n.*, contortionism, L. 4, p. 47

ròudīng huāshēng, 肉丁花生, *n.*, diced pork and peanut, L.11, p. 265

rúhé, 如何, *pron.*, 怎么；how could, L. 11, p. 285

rújīn, 如今, *n.*, nowadays; now, L. 3, p. 36, L. 7, p. 111

rúshù, 如数, *adv.*, exactly the number or amount, L. 7, p. 119

rútóng, 如同, *v.*, like, L. 3, p. 29

rǔfáng, 乳房, *n.*, breast, L. 10, p. 204

rùtuán, 入团, *v.-o.*, join the Chinese Communist Youth League, L. 6, p. 87

ruǎnruò, 软弱, *adj.*, weak; feeble, L. 6, p. 83

ruǎnruò wúlì, 软弱无力, *adj.*, weak and feeble, L. 4, p. 57

ruòyǒu ruòwú, 若有若无, *idm.*, faintly discernible, L. 12, p.371

ruòyǒu suǒshī, 若有所失, *idm.*, feel as if sth. were missing, L.4, p. 57

S

sā, 仨, *n.*, (informal) three people, L. 12, p. 345

sāhuǎng, 撒谎, *v.-o.*, tell a lie; lie, L. 4, p. 55

sā niào, 撒尿, *v.-o.*, urinate; pee, L. 5, p. 65

sǎ, 撒, *v.*, spill; drop, L. 10, p. 197

sāi, 塞, *v.*, fill in; squeeze, L. 12, p. 355

sānbāndǎo, 三班倒, *n.*, works in three-shift rotation, L. 11, p.281

Sānmǔ táng, 三亩塘, *n.*, name of the local pond, L. 10, p.211

Sānshěn, 三婶, *n.*, "3rd aunt", a woman whose husband is the third eldest in his family; (here) polite address to a neighbor woman, L. 12, p. 337

sǎn, 伞, *n.*, umbrella, L. 11, p. 309

sàn, 散, *v.*, break up; disperse, L. 12, p. 325

sànbù, 散步, *v.-o.*, take a walk; stroll, L. 11, p. 307

sànfā, 散发, *v.*, send forth; diffuse; emit, L. 5, p. 67, L. 11, p.308

sànhuì, 散会, *v.-o.*, meeting is adjourned; meeting ends, L. 10, p. 187

sāngmù, 桑木, *n.*, mulberry, L. 10, p. 192

sǎngyīn, 嗓音, *n.*, voice, L. 10, p. 227

sǎng.zi yǎnr, 嗓子眼儿, *n.*, throat, L. 11, p. 262

sàngfū, 丧夫, *v.-o.*, lose a husband; be widowed, L. 2, p. 16

sàngshī, 丧失, *v.*, lose; forfeit, L. 5, p. 73

sǎoxìng, 扫兴, *v.-o.*, have one's spirits dampened, L. 11, p.277

sǎo.zi, 嫂子, *n.*, elder brother's wife, a form of address for a married woman about one's own age, L. 12, p. 325,L. 12, p.345

shāfā, 沙发, *n.*, sofa, L. 11, p. 293

shāshǒu, 杀手, *n.*, killer, L. 8, p. 137

shātān, 沙滩, *n.*, beach, L. 6, p. 89

shá, 啥, *n.*, what, L. 4, p. 44

shǎ, 傻, *v.*, be dumbfounded; be stunned, L. 3, p. 36

shǎhūhū.de, 傻乎乎地, *adv.*, simple-mindedly; silly; stupidly, L. 11, p. 267

shǎyǎn, 傻眼, *v.-o.*, be dumbfounded; be stunned, L. 11, p.305

Shǎpàng, 傻胖, *n.*, nickname of one of the thieves, L. 4, p. 44

shǎxiào, 傻笑, *v.*, laugh foolishly; to giggle; to smirk, L. 7, p.105

shài, 晒, *v.*, (of the sun) shine upon, L. 9, p. 167

shài tài.yang, 晒太阳, *v.-o.*, sun-bathe, L. 5, p. 75

shān, 扇, *v.*, slap, L. 2, p. 21

shān'ào, 山坳, *n.*, mountain ridge, L. 10, p. 217

shāngē, 山歌, *n.*, folk song, L. 10, p. 193

shāngōu, 山沟, *n.*, remote mountain valley, L. 2, p. 20

shānhóng, 山洪, *n.*, mountain torrents, L. 10, p. 195

shānlí, 山梨, *n.*, mountain pear, L. 10, p. 189

shānpō, 山坡, *n.*, hillside; mountain slope, L. 10, p. 189

shānyù, 山芋, *n.*, sweet potato, L. 10, p. 191

shānyùgān, 山芋干, *n.*, dried sweet potato, L. 10, p. 197

shānzhāshù, 山楂树, *n.*, hawthorn tree, L. 7, p. 107

shǎn, 闪, *v.*, flash past, L. 4, p. 57

shǎn, 闪, *v.*, sparkle; shine, L. 10, p. 229

shǎndiàn, 闪电, *n.*, lightning; flashing lightning, L. 11, p. 309

shǎnshǎn fāguāng, 闪闪发光, *idm.*, sparkle; glitter, L. 10, p.213

Shǎnxī, 陕西, *n.*, Shaanxi Province, L. 9, p. 169

shàn, 扇, *AN.*, measure word for door, window, etc., L. 4, p. 43, L. 5, p. 65

shànbà gānxiū, 善罢甘休, *idm.*, (usually used in the negative) leave the matter at that; let it go at that, L. 12, p. 343

shànliáng, 善良, *adj.*, kind-hearted; good and honest, L. 7, p.109

shànshàn.de, 讪讪地, *adv.*, looking embarrassed, L. 10, p.203

shànyú, 善于, *v.*, be good at; be adept in, L. 11, p. 255

shānghén, 伤痕, *n.*, scar, L. 6, p. 81

shāngrén, 商人, *n.*, businessman, L. 3, p. 29

shāngtòng, 伤痛, *n.*, pain, sadness, L. 6, p. 91

shāngxīn, 伤心, *v./ adj.*, hurt, sad; grieved; broken-hearted, L.6, p. 85, L. 11, p. 305, L. 12, p. 337

shāngyuán, 伤员, *n.*, the wounded, L. 6, p. 83

shàng, 上…, *v.*, up to; as many as, L. 11, p. 289

shàng.bian, 上边, *n.*, high authorities, L. 12, p. 330

shàngjí, 上级, *n.*, higher authorities, L. 12, p. 343

shàngshān xiàxiāng, 上山下乡, *idm.*, (of educated urban youth) go and work in the countryside and mountain areas, L. 6, p. 83

shàngshì, 上市, *v.-o.*, go on the market, L. 8, p. 127

shàngwèi, 尚未, *adv.*, not yet, L. 11, p. 281

shàngyìng, 上映, *v.*, show (a film); screen; be on, L. 11, p.260

shàngyóu, 上游, *n.*, upper reaches (of a river), L. 9, p. 159

shàngzuò, 上座, *n.*, the seat of honor, L. 12, p. 363

shāo, 捎, *v.*, bring to sb., L. 2, p. 17, L. 12, p. 337

shāo, 稍, *adv.*, a little; a bit, L. 12, p. 361

shāofàn, 烧饭, *v.-o.*, do the cooking; prepare a meal, L. 11, p.262

shāohuà, 捎话, *v.-o.*, take a message to somebody, L. 12, p.331

shāohuǐ, 烧毁, *v.*, burn down; burn up, L. 10, p. 237

shāoshāo, 稍稍, *adv.*, slightly; a little, L. 11, p. 307

shāoshuǐ, 烧水, *v.-o.*, heat water, L. 9, p. 173

shāowēi, 稍微, *adv.*, slightly, L. 11, p. 297

sháo.zi, 勺子, *n.*, spoon, L. 11, p. 303

shàonián, 少年, *n.*, early youth (from about ten to sixteen), L.11, p. 311

shào.ye, 少爷, *n.*, young master of the house, L. 5, p. 65

shēchǐpǐn, 奢侈品, *n.*, luxury goods; luxuries, L. 10, p. 199

shě.bu.de, 舍不得, *v.*, hate to part with or use, L. 11, p. 307

shè, 设, *v.*, set up; establish, L. 10, p. 219

shèfǎ, 设法, *v.*, try; think up a method, L. 5, p. 75

shèjì, 设计, *v.*, design; plan, L. 12, p. 365

shēn, 伸, *v.*, stretch; extend, L. 12, p. 325

shēnbùyóujǐ, 身不由己, *idm.*, involuntarily; have no command over oneself, L. 11, p. 313

shēncái, 身材, *n.*, stature; figure, L. 12, p. 333

shēnfèn, 身份, *n.*, status; capacity; identity, L. 5, p. 73, L. 6, p.93, L. 11, p. 261

shēnhòu, 深厚, *adj.*, deep; profound, L. 6, p. 89

shēn lǎn.yao, 伸懒腰, *v.-o.*, stretch oneself, L. 10, p. 201

shēnqíng, 深情, *n.*, deep affection, L. 6, p. 83

shēnqū, 身躯, *n.*, body; stature , L. 5, p. 69

shēnshān, 深山, *n.*, remote mountains; deep in the mountains, L. 2, p. 15

shēnshǒu bújiàn wǔzhǐ, 伸手不见五指, *phr.*, so dark that you can't see your hand in front of you, L. 11, p. 285

shēnsīshúlǜ, 深思熟虑, *idm.*, consider carefully, L. 7, p. 115

shēnxìnbùyí, 深信不移, *idm.*, believe firmly, L. 10, p. 241

shēnyāo, 身腰, *n.*, waistline; waist, L. 7, p. 119

shēnyǐng, 身影, *n.*, figure; a person's silhouette, L. 10, p. 197, L. 12, p. 371

shēnyuān, 伸冤, *v.-o.*, redress an injustice; right a wrong, L.10, p. 225

shēnyuān, 深渊, *n.*, abyss; chasm, L. 10, p. 213

shéncǎi fēiyáng, 神采飞扬, *idm.*, in high spirits, L. 10, p. 233

shéncǎi huànfā, 神采焕发, *idm.*, glowing with health and radiating vigor, L. 7, p. 109

shénjīngzhì.de, 神经质地, *adv.*, nervously, L. 7, p. 103

shénmì, 神秘, *adj.*, mysterious, L. 10, p. 185

shén.qi, 神气, *n.*, expression; air; manner, L. 11, p. 259

shénqíng, 神情, *n.*, expression; look, L. 2, p. 17, L. 11, p. 315, L. 12, p. 371

shénsè, 神色, *n.*, facial expression, L. 8, p. 137

Shěn āyí, 沈阿姨, *n.*, Auntie Shen，mother's friend, L. 11, p.291

shěnshì, 审视, *v.*, look at carefully; examine, L. 6, p. 85

shěn.zi, 婶子, *n.*, aunt , L. 12, p. 351

shèntòu, 渗透, *v.*, infiltrate, L. 11, p. 313

shēng, 升, *v.*, rise, L. 11, p. 261

shēngchǎn, 生产, *v.*, produce; manufacture, L. 12, p. 359

shēngpà, 生怕, *v.*, for fear that; so as not to, L. 11, p. 299

shēngpíng, 生平, *n.*, all one's life; life-time, L. 3, p. 35, L. 10, p. 221

shēngqián, 生前, *n.*, during one's lifetime, L. 6, p. 83

shēngxiǎng, 声响, *n.*, sound; noise , L. 5, p. 65

shēngyù, 声誉, *n.*, reputation; fame; prestige, L. 12, p. 357

shéngsuǒ, 绳索, *n.*, rope, L. 6, p. 93

shěngchī jiǎnyòng, 省吃俭用, *idm.*, save money on food and expenses; be economical in everyday spending, L. 11, p. 306

shěngxīn, 省心, *v.*, have nothing to worry about, L. 11, p. 307

shènglì, 胜利, *v.*, win; triumph, L. 11, p. 261

shī, 诗, *n.*, poem; poetry, L. 5, p. 69

shīfàn zhuānkē xuéxiào, 师范专科学校, *n.*, teachers college; teachers training college, L. 11, p. 257

shīlūlū, 湿漉漉, *adj.*, wet, L. 10, p. 213

shīmián, 失眠, *v./n.*, insomnia; inability to sleep, L. 8, p. 139

shīrùn, 湿润, *adj.*, moist, L. 10, p. 205

shīshén, 失神, *v.-o.*, dejected; in low spirits, L. 10, p. 212

shīwàng, 失望, *v./adj.*, disappointed, disappointing, L. 11, p.295

shífēn, 十分, *adv.*, very; fully; extremely, L. 11, p. 271

shíkè, 时刻, *n.*, a point of time; hour; moment, L. 7, p. 107

shíláifēnzhōng, 十来分钟, *n.*, a couple of minutes; 10 to 20 minutes, L. 7, p. 103

shímáo, 时髦, *adj.*, fashionable; stylish, L. 11, p. 259

shí.tou, 石头, *n.*, stone; rock, L. 9, p. 159

shíxīn, 时新, *adj.*, stylish; trendy, L. 11, p. 275

shíxīng, 时兴, *v./adj.*, be in style; in vogue, L. 12, p. 355

shíyù, 食欲, *n.*, appetite, L. 9, p. 173

shíyǐn shíxiàn, 时隐时现, *phr.*, appear at times, disappear at times, L. 6, p. 81

shízhuāng, 时装, *n.*, fashionable dress, L. 7, p. 119, L. 11, p.285

shǐ, 驶, *v.*, (of a vehicle, etc.) drive；speed; speed by, L. 6, p. 97, L. 7, p. 117, L. 11, p. 257

shǐjìn, 使劲, *v.*, exert all one's strength, L. 11, p. 269

shǐzhōng, 始终, *adv.*, from beginning to end; all along, L. 6, p.93, L. 7, p. 117

shìbì, 势必, *adv.*, certainly will; be bound to, L. 12, p. 357

shì.de, *n./pron./v.* 似的, *part.*, similar to; like, L. 11, p. 256

shì ér bújiàn, 视而不见, *idm.*, pretend not to notice; turn a blind eye to, L. 12, p. 349

shìgān, 拭干, *v.-c.*, wipe dry, L. 10, p. 241

shì.gu, 事故, *n.*, accident; mishap, L. 4, p. 55

shìjì, 世纪, *n.*, century, L. 10, p. 185

shìjiè guān, 世界观, *n.*, worldview, L. 6, p. 91

shìqū, 市区, *n.*, downtown area, L. 11, p. 257

shìxiàn, 视线, *n.*, line of sight, L. 6, p. 82

shìyì, 示意, *v.*, signal; hint; motion, L. 12, p. 369

shì.ying, 适应, *v.*, adapt; get with it; fit, L. 11, p. 281

shōuhuò, 收获, *n.*, results; gains; (here) loot, L. 4, p. 49

shōuliǎn, 收敛, *v.*, restrain oneself, L. 7, p. 107, L. 12, p. 357

shōuliú, 收留, *v.*, take somebody in, L. 9, p. 161

shōumài, 收麦, *v.-o.*, harvest the wheat, L. 11, p. 257

shōu.shi, 收拾, *v.*, pack, L. 6, p. 95

shōuyǎng, 收养, *v.*, adopt, L. 3, p. 34

shōuyīnjī, 收音机, *n.*, radio, L. 11, p. 279

shǒu, 首, *AN.*, measure word for songs, L. 11, p. 313

shǒubèi, 手背, *n.*, the back of the hand, L. 12, p. 333

shǒubì, 手臂, *n.*, arm , L. 5, p. 75

shǒudiàntǒng, 手电筒, *n.*, flashlight, L. 10, p. 209

shǒujuàn, 手绢, *n.*, handkerchief, L. 11, p. 295

shǒutíbāo, 手提包, *n.*, handbag, L. 8, p. 131

shǒutóur, 手头儿, *n.*, one's financial condition at the moment, L. 3, p. 28

shǒuwàn, 手腕, *n.*, wrist, L. 10, p. 213

shǒuxīn, 手心, *n.*, palm; the palm of the hand, L. 11, p. 303

shǒuxīn shǒubèi, 手心手背, *n.*, palm and the back of the hand, L. 11, p. 267

shǒuxù, 手续, *n.*, procedures; formalities, L. 11, p. 263

shǒuzhǐ, 手指, *n.*, finger, L. 12, p. 327

shǒuzhuā jiǎotī, 手抓脚踢, *v.*, cuff and kick, L. 12, p. 335

shòubābā, 瘦巴巴, *adj.*, thin; emaciated, L. 10, p. 206

shòuchǒng ruòjīng, 受宠若惊, *idm.*, feel extremely flattered, L. 8, p. 131

Shòugānláng, 瘦干狼, *n.*, nickname of the thief, L. 4, p. 47

shòugǔ línxún, 瘦骨嶙峋, *idm.*, thin and bony; skin and bones, L. 4, p. 49

shòu.le yìquānr, 瘦了一圈, *phr.*, (the face) become smaller because of losing weight, L. 11, p. 281

shòupiàoyuán, 售票员, *n.*, booking-office clerk; ticket seller, L. 1, p. 3

shòuruò, 瘦弱, *adj.*, thin and weak; frail, L. 12, p. 333

shū, 输, v., lose; be beaten, L. 11, p. 266

shū.ji, 书记, n., Secretary of the Communist Youth Committee, L. 10, p. 185

shūcài, 蔬菜, n., vegetable, L. 7 , p. 111, L. 10, p. 229

shūdāi.zi, 书呆子, n., bookworm; bookish, L. 11, p. 267

shūjì, 书记, n., party secretary, L. 6, p. 87

shūyuǎn, 疏远, adj., drift apart; become estranged, L. 11, p.259, L. 11, p. 313

shú, 熟, adj., (of rice, meat, etc.) cooked; done, L. 11, p. 285

shúliàn, 熟练, adj./adv., skillful, skillfully, L. 11, p. 264

shúrén, 熟人, n., a familiar face; friend, L. 11, p. 259

shǔ… guǎn, 属…管, v.., be under the management of; be subordinate to, L. 12, p. 345

shǔ.luo, 数落, v., rebuke; scold sb. by enumerating his/her wrongdoings, L. 10, p. 235

shǔyú… zhī liè, 属于…之列, v., be part of; pertain to, L. 10, p. 201

shù, 竖, v., set upright ; erect; stand, L. 11, p. 273

shùlì, 竖立, v., set upright; stand, L. 4, p. 51

shùlín, 树林, n., wood(s); grove, L. 11, p. 299

shùshuō, 述说, v., state; recount; narrate, L. 12, p. 335

shùyè, 树叶, n., tree leaf, L. 10, p. 192

shùzhī, 树枝, n., branch; twig, L. 10, p. 209

shùzhuāng, 树桩, n., stump, L. 10, p. 212

shuā.de, 刷地, adv., with a swish, L. 10, p. 203

shuāshuā, 唰唰, onom., sound of swishing, L. 5, p.75

shuǎ bǐgǎn, 耍笔杆, v.-o., wield a pen; be skilled in literary tricks, L. 12, p. 341

shuāilǎo, 衰老, v., grow old, L. 10, p. 233

shuǎi, 甩, v., swing, L. 7, p. 107

shuǎi chū.qu, 甩出去, v.-c., throw; fling; toss, L. 11, p. 315

shuǎikāi, 甩开, v.-c., throw off; shake off, L. 10, p. 233

shuàilǐng, 率领, v., lead; head, L. 2, p. 19

shuāngcéng, 双层, adj., double deck, L. 11, p. 283

shuǐkù, 水库, n., reservoir, L. 10, p. 195

shuǐtáng, 水塘, n., pond; pool, L. 12, p. 369

shuǐwāngwāng, 水汪汪, adj., (of children's or young women's eyes) bright and intelligent, L. 10, p. 219

shuǐzhū.zi, 水珠子, n., drop of water; droplet, L. 11, p. 309

shuìmèng, 睡梦, n., sleep; slumber, L. 11, p. 299

shuìshú, 睡熟, v.-c., in deep sleep, L. 9, p. 163

shuìyì, 睡意, n., sleepiness, L. 6, p. 81

shùnbiàn, 顺便, adv., do something in addition to what one is already doing without much extra effort, L. 7, p. 115, L. 12, p.324

shùn.dang, 顺当, adj., smoothly; without a hitch, L. 10, p. 188

shùnlǐ chéngzhāng, 顺理成章, idm. , follow as a matter of course , L. 8, p. 133

shùnshuǐ dāchuán, 顺水搭船, idm., sail with the wind; go with the flow, L. 8, p. 127

shùn.zhe, 顺着, prep., along, L. 11, p. 309

shuōbà, 说罢, v., finish saying, L. 12, p. 365

shuōbáile, 说白了, phr., frankly speaking; in short, L. 2, p. 15

shuō dàhuà, 说大话, v.-o., brag; boast; talk big, L. 12, p. 347

shuō.de qīng.qiao, 说得轻巧, phr., talk as if it were a simple matter, L. 12, p. 345

shuō hǎohuà, 说好话, v.-o., say something pleasant to hear; say some fine words, L. 12, p. 339

shuōmíng, 说明, v/n., explain; illustrate, L. 3, p. 33

shuòshì, 硕士, n., Master's degree, L. 8, p. 135

sī, 丝, AN., a thread of, L. 9, p. 167

sīdiào, 撕掉, v.-c., tear up, L. 6, p. 95

sīháo, 丝毫, adv., in the slightest degree (usually used in the negative), L. 5, p. 73

sīmì, 私密, adj., personal; private; not to be divulged, L. 4, p.53

sīniàn, 思念, v./n., think of; long for, L. 7, p. 113, L. 11, p. 281

sīshēng, 嘶声, adv., (speak) in a hoarse voice, L. 12, p. 335

sīxù, 思绪, n., train of thought; thinking, L. 12, p. 349

sīyǎ, 嘶哑, adj., hoarse, L. 10, p. 212

sīzhái, 私宅, n., private house, L. 4, p. 48

sǐqùhuólái, 死去活来, idm., have fainted and recovered consciousness several times；(sob) one's heart out, L. 11, p. 311

sìchù, 四处, adv., all around; everywhere, L. 5, p. 65

sìliào, 饲料, n., fodder; food, L. 10, p. 235

Sìrénbāng, 四人帮, n., Gang of Four, L. 6, p. 93, L. 7 , p. 111, L. 11, p. 258

sōngchí, 松弛, adj., limp; flabby; slack, L. 7, p. 105

sōngkāi, 松开, v.-c., let go; release, L. 12, p. 337

sōng kǒuqì, 松口气, v., let out one's breath; relax, L. 7, p. 105

sōngmáo, 松毛, n., pine needles , L. 10, p. 193

sōngsǎn, 松散, adj., loose; lax, L. 2, p. 15

sōng yìkǒu qì, 松一口气, v.-o., let out a breath; sigh (of relief), L. 4, p. 47

sǒng, 耸, v., rise straight up, L. 4, p. 55

sòng, 送, v., see somebody off or out, L. 7, p. 117

sònglǐ, 送礼, v.-o., give somebody a present; present a gift to somebody, L. 12, p. 339

sòngxíng, 送行, v., see sb. off; say good-bye to sb., L. 11, p.261

sōu, 艘, AN., measure word for boats or ships, L. 5, p. 71

sōusuǒ, 搜索, v., search for; scout around, L. 12, p. 327

Sū Xiǎolín, 苏小林, n., person's name, L. 6, p. 86

sùliàobù, 塑料布, n., plastic cloth, L. 5, p. 73

suíshí, 随时, adv., at all times; any time, L. 6, p. 89

suíshǒu, 随手, adv., conveniently; without extra trouble, L. 6, p. 91

suítāqùba , 随他去吧, phr., Do as he pleases., L. 10, p. 225

suíyì, 随意, adv., casually; randomly; informally, L. 11, p. 253

suízhī, 随之, adv., following this, L. 2, p. 15

suìhuā guà.zi, 碎花褂子, n., short gown made of printed calico, L. 5, p. 69

suìxiè, 碎屑, n., crumb, L. 10, p. 203

suìyì, 遂意, adj., to one's liking; fulfill one's desire, L. 2, p. 22

suìyuè, 岁月, n., years; time , L. 5, p. 67

suō, 缩, v., contract; shrink, L. 11, p. 261

suǒ, 锁, v., lock, L. 2, p. 19

Suǒwá, 锁娃, n., personal name, L. 9, p. 167

T

tā, 塌, v., collapse, L. 5, p. 75, L. 10, p. 235

tāliǎ, 他俩, pron., the two of them, L. 11, p. 303

tàdǎo, 踏倒, v., step down, L. 10, p. 215

tái, 抬, v., (of two or three persons) carry, lift; raise , L. 5, p. 71

táidēng, 台灯, n., desk lamp; table lamp, L. 11, p. 269

táijiē, 台阶, n., footstep; a flight of steps, L. 5, p. 65, L. 7, p. 117, L. 11, p. 279

tái.ju, 抬举, v., praise or promote sb. to show favor, L. 8, p.129

táitóu, 抬头, v.-o., raise one's head , L. 5, p. 67, L. 11, p. 277

táiyǎn, 抬眼, v.-o., raise one's eyes, L. 12, p. 329

Tàigē'ěr, 泰戈尔, n., Rabindranath Tagore, 1861-1941, L. 5, p. 69

tàijíquán, 太极拳, *n., taichi,* a system of physical exercise that emphasizes balance, coordination, and effortlessness in movements, L. 11, p. 307

tàipíng, 太平, *adj.,* peaceful, L. 9, p. 171

tān, 贪, *adj.,* greedy, L. 8, p. 149

tānfàng, 摊放, *v.,* spread out, L. 12, p. 357

tānkāi, 摊开, *v.-c. ,* spread out; unfold, L. 4, p. 44, L. 11, p.303

tānpái, 摊牌, *v.-o.,* lay one's card on the table; have a showdown, L. 12, p. 353

tānruǎn, 瘫软, *v.,* (of arms and legs) become weak and limp, L. 10, p.205

Tánbó, 谭博, *n.,* personal name, L. 5, p. 64

tán duìxiàng, 谈对象, *v.-o.,* look for a partner in marriage, L.11, p. 297

tánfēng hěn jiàn, 谈锋很健, *phr.,* in high spirits to talk, L. 11, p. 253

tán liàn'ài, 谈恋爱, *v.-o.,* be in love; date, L. 11, p. 297

tántiàoérqǐ, 弹跳而起, *v.,* spring up, L. 8, p. 137

tánxìng, 弹性, *n.,* elasticity; resilience, L. 10, p. 204

tǎnrán, 坦然, *adj.,* have no misgiving; fully at ease, L. 10, p.213, L. 11, p. 279

tǎnshuài, 坦率, *adj.,* candid; straightforward, L. 8, p. 145

tàn kǒu qì, 叹口气, *v.-o.,* sigh; heave a sigh, L. 4, p. 47

tànqīn, 探亲, *v.-o.,* go home to visit one's family or go to visit one's relatives, L. 6, p. 81, L. 11, p. 259

tànshì, 探视, *v.,* visit, L. 5, p. 71

tànshǒu, 探手, *v.,* reach into, L. 8, p. 141

tànxī, 叹息, *v.,* sigh, L. 7, p. 105

tànxún, 探寻, *v.,* seek, L. 10, p. 241

tàn yīkǒu qì, 叹一口气, *v.-o.,* heave a sigh, L. 12, p. 341

tànzhī, 探知, *v.,* find out by inquiry, L. 8, p. 137

tángdì, 堂弟, *n.,* male younger cousin on the paternal side, L.12, p. 343

táng'ér huángzhī, 堂而皇之, *idm.,* openly and legally, L. 7, p.107

tǎng, 躺, *v.,* lie; recline, L. 11, p. 269

tàng.zhe cháng bōlàng, 烫着长波浪, *phr.,* with a long wavy perm, L. 11, p. 275

tāo, 掏, *v.,* draw out; pull out; fish out, L. 4, p. 43, L. 12, p.355

tāotāo bùjué, 滔滔不绝, *idm.,* pouring out words in a steady flow, L. 12, p. 361

táo, 逃, *v.,* run away; flee, L. 4, p. 45

táohuāng, 逃荒, *v.-o.,* flee from famine, L. 9, p. 161

táosū, 桃酥, *n.,* a kind of shortbread, L. 4, p. 55

tǎofàn, 讨饭, *v.-o.,* beg for food, L. 10, p. 191

tǎojià huánjià, 讨价还价, *idm.,* haggle over the price of sth., L. 10, p. 227

tàoshàng, 套上, *v.,* harness; (metaphor): impose a burden, L.6, p. 93

tèdì, 特地, *adv.,* specially, L. 9, p. 159

tèyì, 特意, *adv.,* for a special purpose; specially, L. 12, p. 353

téng, 疼, *v.,* love dearly; be fond of, L. 11, p. 305

tí, 提, *v.,* carry (in one's hand with the arm down), L. 12, p.341

tíjí, 提及, *v.,* mention; speak of, L. 3, p. 31

tíqián, 提前, *v.,* in advance; ahead of time, L. 2, p. 19

tíxǐng, 提醒, *v.,* remind, L. 11, p. 277, L. 12, p. 327

tíyì, 提议, *n.,* motion; proposal, L. 12, p. 365

tǐcāo, 体操, *n.,* gymnastics, setting-up exercises to radio music, L. 7, p. 103

tǐgé, 体格, *n.,* physique; build, L. 10, p. 194

tǐpò, 体魄, *n.,* physique; build, L. 10, p. 205

tǐwēn, 体温, *n.,* body temperature, L. 10, p. 213

tǐzhì, 体制, *n.,* system of organization, L. 8, p. 127

tì…jiěwéi, 替…解围, *v.,* help somebody out of a predicament, L. 1, p. 7

tìdài, 替代, *v.,* substitute for; replace, L. 3, p. 33

tì .zhe guāngtóu, 剃着光头, *v.-o.,* with shaved head, L. 4, p.43

tiān, 添, *v.,* add, L. 10, p. 199, L. 11, p. 264

tiāndìliángxīn, 天地良心, *idm.,* speak the truth; from the bottom of one's heart, L. 8, p. 145

tiāngāo dìhòu, 天高地厚, *idm.,* high as heaven, deep as earth – the complexity of things, L. 10, p. 225

tiānjǐng, 天井, *n.,* (here)天窗; skylight, L. 4, p. 57

tiānjǐng, 天井, *n.,* small yard; courtyard, L. 11, p. 269

tiānkōng, 天空, *n.,* sky, L. 5, p. 65

tiān.na, 天哪, *intj.,* Good Heavens!, L. 4, p. 51

tiāntáng, 天堂, *n.,* heaven; (here) a place name , L. 10, p. 185

tiānzhēn, 天真, *adj.,* innocent; naive, L. 6, p. 85

tiānzhēn wúxié, 天真无邪, *idm.,* innocent; artless; naive, L.11, p. 315

tiánbǎo dù.zi, 填饱肚子, *v.-o.,* fill oneself with food, L. 10, p.197

tiángěng, 田埂, *n.,* a low bank earth between fields; ridge, L.12, p. 325

tiánjiān, 田间, *n.,* field; farm, L. 6, p. 91

tiánmì, 甜蜜, *adj.,* sweet, L. 10, p. 223

tiánsīsī, 甜丝丝, *adj.,* pleasantly sweet, L. 10, p. 223

tiánxiě, 填写, *v.,* fill in (a form), L. 6, p. 87, L. 7, p. 103

tiányě, 田野, *n.,* field; open country, L. 11, p. 256

tiāo máobìng, 挑毛病, *v.-o.,* find fault; pick at, L. 9, p. 165

tiāoqǐ, 挑起, *v.,* carry on the shoulder, L. 10, p. 192

tiáo, 条, *AN.,* measure word for long or narrow or thin things, L. 11, p. 313

tiáojí, 调级, *v.-o.,* adjust a wage scale (usually upwards); promote, L. 7, p. 111

tiáopí, 调皮, *adj.,* naughty; mischievous, L. 7 , p. 111, L. 10, p.185

tiǎokāi huàtí, 挑开话题, *v.-o.,* raise a new topic of conversation, L. 11, p. 287

tiào chángshéng, 跳长绳, *v.-o.,* rope skipping, L. 11, p. 266

tiē, 贴, *v.,* nestle up to; snuggle up to, L. 10, p. 193

tiēxīn, 贴心, *adj.,* intimate; close, L. 11, p. 313

tiěgē.da, 铁疙瘩, *n.,* iron lump, L. 10, p. 191

tiěguǐ, 铁轨, *n.,* rail, L. 9, p. 177

tiěqīng, 铁青, *adj.,* ashen; ghastly pale, L. 10, p. 209

tiězhà, 铁栅, *n.,* iron bars, L. 4, p. 46

tīnghuà, 听话, *adj.,* be obedient; behave, L. 11, p. 293

tíngbó, 停泊, *v.,* anchor; berth, L. 11, p. 307

tōng, 嗵, *onom.,* sound of pounding the table, L. 12, p. 335

tōngdá, 通达, *adj.,* be reasonable; be sensible, L. 7, p. 109

tōnghóng, 通红, *adj.,* very red, L. 2, p. 19

tōngzhī, 通知, *v.,* notify; inform; give notice, L. 5, p. 75, L. 12, p. 367

tóng, 同, *prep.,* with, L. 11, p. 259

tóng dàgē yí jiè, 同大哥一届, *phr.,* graduated the same year as his elder brother, L. 11, p. 277

tóngnián, 同年, *adj.,* of the same age, L. 10, p. 194

tóngnián, 童年, *n.,* childhood, L. 11, p. 311

tóngyǎngxí, 童养媳, *n.,* a girl taken into the family as a daughter-in-law to be, L. 10, p. 237

tǒng, 桶, *AN.,* barrel; bucket, L. 12, p. 357

tǒngtǒng, 统统, *adv.,* wholly; completely, L. 10, p. 190

wēiwǔ, 威武, *adj.*, mighty, L. 10, p. 221

wēixiǎn, 危险, *n./adj.*, danger, dangerous, L. 10, p. 205

wēixiào, 微笑, *v./n.*, smile, L. 10, p. 197, L. 11, p. 261, L. 12, p. 353

wēixié, 威胁, *n./v.*, threaten; menace, L. 4, p. 51, L. 12, p. 353

wéi, 围, *v.*, enclose; surround; encircle, L. 9, p. 159, L. 10, p.209

wéidú, 唯独, *adv.*, only, L. 4, p. 46

wéifǎ, 违法, *adj./v.*, illegal, break the law, L. 4, p. 51, L. 10, p.205

wéinán, 为难, *adj.*, feel awkward; be in a quandary, L. 6, p. 89, L. 8, p. 143

wéiqiáng, 围墙, *n.*, closure; wall; fence, L. 11, p. 257

wéiqún, 围裙, *n.*, apron, L. 9, p. 171

wéirào, 围绕, *v.*, encircle; go round, L. 5, p. 75

wéiyī, 唯一, *adj.*, single; only; sole, L. 2, p. 16

wéizhāng jiànzhù, 违章建筑, *n.*, illegal building, L. 11, p.269

wěi.qu, 委屈, *adj /n.*, feel wronged; be misunderstood, the feeling of being wronged, L. 1, p. 9, L. 10, p. 225

wěishēng, 尾声 *n.*, the end, L. 8, p. 137

wěiwěi, 娓娓, *adv.*, tirelessly, L. 8, p. 147

wèibì, 未必, *adv.*, may not; not necessarily, L. 11, p. 279

Wèihé, 渭河, *n.*, Weihe River, L. 9, p. 159

wèilái, 未来, *n.*, future, L. 10, p. 189

wèishēngjiān, 卫生间, *n.*, bathroom, L. 4, p. 43

wèizhǐfèndòu, 为之奋斗, *phr.*, strive after it; fight for it, L. 11, p. 281

wèi.zhi, 位置, *n.*, place; seat; location, L. 11, p. 271

wēnnuǎn, 温暖, *adj.*, warm, L. 6, p. 87, L. 11, p. 310

wēnshuǐ, 温水, *n.*, lukewarm water, L. 12, p. 325

wēnshùn, 温顺, *adj.*, docile; tame, L. 3, p. 31

wēnxí, 温习, *v.*, review, L. 11, p. 287

wēnxīn, 温馨, *adj./n.*, warmth, coziness, L. 2, p. 20

wéngōng tuán, 文工团, *n.*, song and dance ensemble; art troupe; cultraul troupe, L. 5, p. 71

wénjiàn, 文件, *n.*, file; record, document, L. 3, p. 36, L. 10, p.229

wénmíng jiātíng, 文明家庭, *n.*, Civilized Family, an activity initiated and launched by 中华全国妇女联合会, L. 12, p. 337

wénrén, 文人, *n.*, man of letters; scholar, L. 12, p. 329

wénxùn érlái, 闻讯而来, *phr.*, hear the news and come, L. 1, p. 5

wényì yǎnchū, 文艺演出, *n.*, entertainment performance, L. 8, p. 131

wènhòu, 问候, *v.*, send one's respects (or regards) to; extend greetings to, L. 12, p. 327

wēngwēng, 嗡嗡, *onom.*, drone; buzz; hum, L. 10, p. 233

wō.nang, 窝囊, *adj.*, good-for-nothing; hopelessly stupid, L.11, p. 287

wò, 握, *v.*, hold; grasp; take by the hand, L. 12, p. 324

wòbié, 握别, *v.*, shake hands at parting; part, L. 12, p. 371

wòtǔ, 沃土, *n.*, fertile soil, L. 11, p. 257

wò.zhu, 握住, *v.-c.*, hold; grasp; take by hand, L. 11, p. 276, L.12, p. 327

wū, 呜, *onom.*, toot; hoot; zoom , L. 9, p. 165

wūwā wūwā, 呜哇呜哇, *onom.*, sound of siren, L. 4, p. 55

wūwūyèyè, 呜呜咽咽, *adv.*, sobbingly, L. 9, p. 175

wūxiàn, 诬陷, *v.*, frame a case against; frame somebody, L. 12, p. 357

wūyā zuǐ, 乌鸦嘴, *n.*, a person who always says something inauspicious, L. 2, p. 21

wūyè, 呜咽, *v.*, sob; whimper, L. 10, p. 209

wūyún, 乌云, *n.*, dark clouds, L. 11, p. 303

wúcháng, 无偿, *adj.*, gratuitous; free, L. 10, p. 221

wúcháng.de, 无偿的, *adj.*, gratuitous; done without compensation, L. 3, p. 35

wúcóng, 无从, *adv.*, have no way (of doing sth.), L. 7, p. 113, L. 11, p. 299

wúgōng shòulù, 无功受禄, *idm.*, get a reward without deserving it, L. 8, p. 139

wúkěnàihé, 无可奈何, *idm.*, have no way out, helplessly, L.11, p. 315, L. 12, p. 359

wúliáo, 无聊, *adj.*, bored; boring, L. 11, p. 285

wúlùn rúhé, 无论如何, *adv.*, in any case; at any rate , L. 12, p.327

wúnài, 无奈 *n./adj.*, feeling of helpless; have no choice, helpless, L. 8, p.141

wúnài, 无奈, *adv.*, but; however, L. 11, p. 263

wúqióngwújìn, 无穷无尽, *adj.*, endless; boundless; everlasting, L. 11, p. 281

wúquán, 无权, *adv.*, has no right, L. 8, p. 128

wúshù, 无数, *adj.*, countless; innumerable, L. 10, p. 199

wúxīn, 无心, *v.*, not in the mood for, L. 2, p. 15

wúyányǐdá, 无言以答, *v.*, unable to answer, L. 8, p. 143

wúyì.shi, 无意识, *adv.*, unconsciously, L. 7, p. 117

wúyōu wúlǜ, 无忧无虑, *idm.*, carefree; without sorrow and anxiety, L. 10, p. 207

wǔ, 舞, *v.*, move; wave (hand), L. 6, p. 81

wǔ, 捂, *v.*, cover (with hand) , L. 8, p. 139

wǔ.zhe liǎn, 捂着脸, *v.-o.*, cover one's face with one's hand, L. 10, p. 209, L. 12, p. 347

wǔcǎi bīnfēn, 五彩缤纷, *idm.*, be blazing with color; colorful, L. 6, p. 81, L. 11, p. 284

wǔdǒuchú, 五斗橱, *n.*, chest of drawers, L. 11, p. 264

wǔhuì, 舞会, *n.*, dance; ball, L. 7, p. 107

Wǔliángyè, 五粮液, *n.*, Wuliangye (a famous Chinese spirit), L. 12, p. 361

wǔtái, 舞台, *n.*, stage, L. 10, p. 237

wǔxiū, 午休, *v.*, noon break, midday rest, L. 8, p. 139

wǔyè, 午夜, *n.*, midnight, L. 4, p. 42

wǔzhù, 捂住, *v.-c.*, cover or seal with one's hand, L. 5, p. 67

wùjiě, 误解, *v.*, misunderstand, L. 8, p. 137

wùrènwéi, 误认为, *v.*, think mistakenly , L. 11, p. 311, L. 12, p. 365

wùyùhéngliú, 物欲横流, *idm.*, material desires overflow, L. 3, p. 31

wù.zhì, 物质, *n.*, material, L. 10, p. 205

X

xī, 嘻, *onom.*, hehe, L. 10, p. 201

xīcān, 西餐, *n.*, Western-style food or meal, L. 11, p. 253

xīfú, 西服, *n.*, suit, L. 8, p. 141

xī.li huālā, 稀里哗啦, *onom.*, sound of rushing water, L. 10, p. 195

xīluò, 奚落, *v.*, scoff at; taunt; jeer at, L. 10, p. 209

xīqǔ, 吸取, *v.*, absorb; draw, L. 11, p. 255

xīshēng, 牺牲, *v.*, sacrifice, L. 11, p. 261

xīshū, 稀疏, *adj.*, few and scattered; thin, L. 10, p. 206

xīxīrǎngrǎng, 熙熙攘攘, *adj./idm.*, bustling with activity, L. 7, p. 11 5, L. 11, p. 315

xīxīsūsū, 窸窸窣窣, *onom.*, a succession of slight, soft sounds, as of leaves, silks, papers. etc. L. 4, p. 43

xīxīn, 悉心, *v.*, with the entire mind, L. 3, p. 34

xīyáng wúxiàn hǎo; zhǐshì jìn huánghūn, 夕阳无限好只是近黄昏, *idm.*, A sunset may be infinitely brilliant, nonetheless night follows its heels, L. 3, p. 32

xiàomīmī.de, 笑眯眯地, *adv.*, with a smile on one's face, L. 2, p. 19

xiàoróng, 笑容, *n.*, smile; smiling expression, L. 6, p. 91, L. 7, p. 112

xiàowén, 笑纹, *n.*, laugh line, L. 6, p. 93

xiàoxīxī, 笑嘻嘻, *adv.*, giggling , L. 11, p. 289

xiàoxīn, 孝心, *n.*, filial piety, L. 2, p. 17

xiàoyì, 效益, *n.*, beneficial result, L. 12, p. 359

xiàoyòng, 效用, *n.*, effectiveness; usefulness, L. 10, p. 191

xiàoyǔ xuānhuá, 笑语喧哗, *idm.*, uproarious talk and laughter, L. 10, p. 221

xiē, 歇, *v.*, have a rest, L. 12, p. 335

xiēsīdǐlǐ, 歇斯底里, *adj./n.*, hysterical, hysteria, L. 3, p. 35

xiē.zhe, 歇着, *v.*, stop (work, etc.); knock off; at roost, L. 10, p. 197

xiéyǎn, 斜眼瞧, *v.*, look sideways at sb., L. 8, p. 137

xiéyǎn chǒuchǒu, 斜眼瞅瞅, *v.*, cast a sidelong glance at, L.11, p. 279

xiéyǎn kàn, 斜眼看, *v.*, look at someone sideways, L.1, p. 4

xiéyìn, 鞋印, *n.*, footprint, L. 4, p. 43

xiézhù, 协助, *v.*, help; assist, L. 8, p. 133

xièzhuāng, 卸妆, *v.-o.*, take off a costume; remove makeup, L.4, p. 47

xīn'ānlǐdé, 心安理得, *idm.*, feel at ease and justified , L. 8, p.133

xīnbúzàiyān, 心不在焉, *idm.*, be absent-minded, L. 11, p. 255

xīnfù, 心腹, *n.*, trusted subordinate, L. 8, p. 129

Xīnjiāng, 新疆, *n.*, Xinjiang Province, in the northeast part of China, L. 11, p. 253

xīnkǔ, 辛苦, *n./adj.*, hardship, hard; toilsome; laborious, L. 11, p. 313

xīn.li fāfán, 心里发烦, *phr.*, be vexed; be perturbed, L. 11, p.283

xīnlíng, 心灵, *n.*, soul; heart, L. 2, p. 22, L. 10, p. 207, L. 11, p.313

xīnluàn rúmá, 心乱如麻, *idm.*, have one's mind all in a tangle; be utterly confused and disconcerted, L. 12, p. 347

xīnmǎnyìzú, 心满意足, *idm.*, be perfectly content; be completely satisfied, L. 3, p. 32, L. 7 , p. 111, L. 10, p. 200, L.11, p. 281, L. 11, p. 306

xīnmù, 心目, *n.*, mind; mental view, L. 10, p. 185

xīnqiè, ⋯心切, *adj.*, anxious; eager, L. 12, p. 361

xīnqín, 辛勤, *adj.*, hardworking; industrious, L. 10, p. 239

xīnqíng, 心情, *n.*, mood, L. 2, p. 15

xīnqíng chénzhòng, 心情沉重, *phr.*, with a heavy heart, L. 11, p. 277

xīnruǎn, 心软, *v.*, be softhearted; be tenderhearted, L. 9, p. 175

xīnshì, 心事, *n.*, sth. weighing on one's mind; cares; concerns, , L. 4, p. 57, L. 10, p. 241

xīnsuì, 心碎, *v.*, be broken-hearted, L. 9, p. 175

xīnténg, 心疼, *v./adj.*, feel sorry; be distressed, L. 3, p. 31, L.12, p. 361

xīn wǎng xià yìchén, 心往下一沉, *phr.*, worried; one's heart sinks, L. 4, p. 43

xīnxīnkǔkǔ, 辛辛苦苦, *adv.*, take a lot of trouble; take great pains, L. 12, p. 357

xīnxiōng, 心胸, *n.*, breadth of mind, L. 12, p. 347

xīnxū, 心虚, *adj.*, with a guilty conscience , L. 8, p. 139

xīnxùbùníng, 心绪不宁, *idm.*, in as disturbed state of mind, L.12, p. 351

xīnyì, 心意, *n.*, kindly feelings; regard, L. 3, p. 36

xīnzàngbìng, 心脏病, *n.*, heart disease, L. 3, p. 29

xīnzhái, 新宅, *n.*, new site, L. 12, p. 339

xīnzhào bùxuān, 心照不宣, *idm.*, both understand from their hearts what the matter is but do not choose to say so in public, L. 11, p. 289

xīnzhōng yǒushù, 心中有数, *idm.*, know what's what, L. 8, p.128

xìnhào, 信号, *n.*, signal, L. 4, p. 51

xìnlài, 信赖, *v.*, trust; have faith in, L. 3, p. 29, L. 6, p. 89

xìnrèn, 信任, *v./n.*, trust, L. 3, p. 33

xìnyòngshè, 信用社, *n.*, credit cooperative, L. 10, p. 188

xīng, 兴, *v.*, become popular, L. 10, p. 201

xīngbàn, 兴办, *v.*, initiate; set up, L. 10, p. 190

xīngchòuwèir, 腥臭味儿, *n.*, stinking smell as of rotten fish; stench, L. 11, p. 308

xīng.xing, 星星, *n.*, star, L. 11, p. 313

xíngdān yǐngzhī, 形单影只, *idm.*, a solitary form, a single shadow -- extremely lonely, L. 3, p. 30

xíngdòng, 行动, *n.*, action; operation, L. 3, p. 31

xíngdòng qǐlái, 行动起来, *v.-c.*, go into action, L. 11, p. 261

xínghuì, 行贿, *v.*, bribe, L. 8, p. 133

xíng.li, 行李, *n.*, luggage; baggage, L. 1, p. 5, L. 11, p. 253

xínglǐjià, 行李架, *n.*, luggage rack, L. 6, p. 85

xíngxiàng, 形象, *n.*, image; form; figure, L. 5, p. 73, L. 11, p. 295

xǐng.guo.lai, 醒过来, *v.-c.*, regain consciousness, L. 12, p. 365

xìnggé, 性格, *n.*, nature; disposition, L. 11, p. 253

xìngzāilèhuò, 幸灾乐祸, *idm.*, take pleasure in other people's misfortune, L. 11, p. 303

xìngzhìbóbó, 兴致勃勃, *adj.*, be in the best of spirits; be in high spirits, L. 11, p. 253

xiōngdì, 兄弟, *n.*, brothers, L. 11, p. 268

xiōng.di, 兄弟, *n.*, (informal) address for a man younger than oneself, L. 12, p. 333

xiōngjī, 胸肌, *n.*, chest muscle; pectoral, L. 10, p. 203

xiōngpú, 胸脯, *n.*, chest; breast, L. 9, p. ,171 L. 10, p. 193

xiūdādā, 羞答答, *adj.*, coy; shy; bashful , L. 5, p. 73

xiūchǐ, 羞耻, *adj.*, shame, L. 8, p. 149

xiūchǐxīn, 羞耻心, *n.*, sense of shame, L. 10, p. 205

xiūhóng, 羞红, *v.*, blush from shyness, L. 5, p. 67

xiūjià, 休假, *v.-o.*, have a holiday; take a vacation, L. 11, p.259

xiūkuì, 羞愧, *adj.*, ashamed; abashed, L. 5, p. 67, L. 11, p. 315

xiūkuì nánróng, 羞愧难容, *phr.*, extremely ashamed, L. 10, p.209

xiūrǔ, 羞辱, *v./n.*, put to the shame; insult, L. 10, p. 187

xiūsè, 羞涩, *adj.*, shy; bashful, L. 6, p. 85, L. 10, p. 185

xiūyú chūkǒu, 羞于出口, *v.*, too shy to talk about, L. 10, p.185

xiù, 绣, *v.*, embroider, L. 10, p. 187

xiùhuā, 绣花, *v.-o.*, embroider; do embroidery, L. 11, p. 256

xiùkǒu, 袖口, *n.*, wrist; cuff of a sleeve, L. 10, p. 199

xiùlì, 秀丽, *adj.*, beautiful; handsome; pretty, L. 11, p. 257

xiù.qi, 秀气, *adj.*, delicate; elegant, L. 10, p. 186

xūjīng, 虚惊, *n.*, false alarm, L. 12, p. 357

xū.le yìkǒuqì, 吁了一口气, *phr.*, sigh (with a relief), L. 11, p.271

xūpàng, 虚胖, *n.*, puffiness, L. 11, p. 281

xūruò, 虚弱, *adj.*, weak; debilitated, L. 9, p. 161

xūyìkǒuqì, 吁一口气, *v.*, heave a sigh, L. 12, p. 369

xù, 蓄, *v.*, harbor; retain; full of, L. 1, p. 9

xùjiù, 叙旧, *v.-o.*, talk about the old days, L. 7, p. 117

xùshù, 叙述, *v.*, narrate; recount; relate , L. 5, p. 67

xuānbù, 宣布, *v.*, declare; announce, L. 3, p. 33, L. 8, p. 145

Pinyin Index

xuānchuán bù, 宣传部, *n.*, publicity department, L. 6, p. 91

xuānxiāo, 喧嚣, *n.*, noise, L. 10, p. 207

xuánguà, 悬挂, *v.*, hang , L. 4, p. 53

xuànyūn, 眩晕, *n.*, dizziness, L. 10, p. 205

xuànyào, 炫耀, *v.*, show off; make a display of , L. 12, p. 351

xuéshēnghuì, 学生会, *n.*, student union; student association, L. 7, p. 107

xuěliàng, 雪亮, *adj.*, bright as snow, L. 10, p. 209

xuèyè, 血液, *n.*, blood, L. 10, p. 205

xuèyìn, 血印, *n.*, bloodstain, L. 10, p. 209

xūn bí.zi, 熏鼻子, *adj.*, stinking; foul-smelling, L. 4, p. 53

xúnshēng, 循声, *adv.*, follow the sound, L. 4, p. 43

xúnwèn, 询问, *v.*, ask about; inquire, L. 1, p. 5, L. 5, p. 67

xúnzhǎo, 寻找, *v.*, seek; look for , L. 5, p. 65, L. 11, p. 279

xùn, 训, *v.*, lecture; teach; train, L. 4, p. 47, L. 12, p. 355

xùnchì, 训斥, *v.*, reprimand, L. 11, p. 303

xùnwèn, 讯问, *v.*, interrogate; question, L. 4, p. 45

Y

yā, 压, *v.*, suppress; daunt; intimidate, L. 12, p. 353

yā, 押, *v.*, escort, L. 10, p. 208

yādī shēngyīn, 压低声音, *phr.*, lower one's voice, L. 11, p.301

yāpò, 压迫, *v.*, oppress; press down upon, L. 6, p. 81

yà, 轧, *v.*, run over (by a car, train, etc.), L. 1, p. 5

yānxiāo yúnsàn, 烟消云散, *idm.*, disappear (vanish) like mist and smoke, L. 10, p. 205

yānyè, 烟叶, *n.*, tobacco leaf, L. 9, p. 159

Yán'ān, 延安, *n.*, Yan'an, the base of Communist Party in 1937-1947, L. 5, p. 71

yánjùn, 严峻, *adj.*, stern; severe; rigorous, L. 10, p. 215

yánshēn, 延伸, *v.*, extend; stretch , L. 5, p. 71

yántīng jìcóng, 言听计从, *idm.*, always follow sb.'s advice; act upon whatever sb. says, L. 8, p. 147

yányánshíshí, 严严实实, *adv.*, tightly, closely, L. 2, p. 19

yán.zhe, 沿着, *prep.*, along, L. 6, p. 89, L. 10, p. 219, L. 12, p.349

yǎnjiǎn, 眼睑, *n.*, eyelid , L. 4, p. 49

yǎnjiǎo, 眼角, *n.*, the corner of the eye, L. 4, p. 45, L. 9, p. 177, L. 11, p. 275

yǎn kàn.zhe, 眼看着, *adv.*, soon; in a moment, L. 11, p. 271

yǎnkuàng, 眼眶, *n.*, eye socket, L. 9, p. 165

yǎnpí, 眼皮, *n.*, eyelid, L. 9, p. 173

yǎnquān, 眼圈, *n.*, rim of the eye, L. 9, p. 163, L. 12, p. 347

yǎnshén, 眼神, *n.*, expression in one's eyes, L. 4, p. 51, L. 5, p. 69, L. 7, p. 109

yǎnxì, 演戏, *v.-o.*, act in a play; play act; pretend, L. 4, p. 47

yǎnxià, 眼下, *n.*, at the moment; at present, L. 12, p. 357

yàn, 咽, *v.*, swallow, L. 12, p. 365

yàn búxià zhèi kǒu qì, 咽不下这口气, *v.-o.*, unable to swallow this offense, L. 12, p. 331

yànwù, 厌恶, *v.*, detest, L. 6, p. 87

yànwù.de, 厌恶地, *adv.*, disgustingly, L. 11, p. 303

yángguāng, 阳光, *n.*, sunlight; sunshine, L. 5, p. 64, L. 10, p.199

yángmáoshān, 羊毛衫, *n.*, cardigan; woolen sweater, L. 11, p.272

yǎnglǎojīn, 养老金, *n.*, pension, L. 12, p. 345

yǎngrén, 养人, *adj.*, nutritious; beneficial to one's health, L.12, p. 367

yǎngsīsī, 痒丝丝, *adj.*, itchy, L. 10, p. 199

yǎngtóu, 仰头, *v.-o.*, raise one's head, L. 4, p. 43

yǎngwàng, 仰望, *v.*, look up at, L. 10, p. 239

yāo, 腰, *n.*, waist, L. 11, p. 270

yāoshēn, 腰身, *n.*, waistline; waist, L. 9, p. 171

yāo.zi bìng, 腰子病, *n.*, kidney disease, L. 10, p. 207

yáohàn, 摇撼, *v.*, shake something violently, L. 6, p. 97

yáotóu, 摇头, *v.-o.*, shake one's head, L. 1, p. 7, L. 10, p. 223, L. 11, p. 291

yǎo, 咬, *v.*, bite, L. 12, p. 335

yǎoyáqièchǐ, 咬牙切齿, *idm.*, gnash the teeth in anger, L. 3, p.35, L. 8, p. 147

yàohǎo, 要好, *adj.*, be close friends, L. 12, p. 359

yào.me...yào.me..., 要么···，要么···, *conj.*, either...or..., L. 11, p. 279

yào.shi, 钥匙, *v.*, key, L. 4, p. 45, L. 8, p. 139

yēzhù, 噎住, *v.-c.*, choked up; throat closed up, L. 10, p. 235

yérsā, 爷儿仨, *n.*, three men of two or more generations, L. 9, p. 159

yěbào, 野豹, *n.*, wild leopard; wild panther, L. 10, p. 204

yěcài, 野菜, *n.*, edible wild herbs, L. 9, p. 161

Yěmǎ gē, 野马哥, *n.*, nickname of one of the thieves, L. 4, p.49

yèbān, 夜班, *n.*, night shift, L. 11, p. 281

yīdōu, 衣兜, *n.*, pocket, L. 4, p. 43

yījiǎo, 衣角, *n.*, corner/border/hem of an article of clothing, L.12, p. 333

yī.shang, 衣裳, *n.*, clothes, L. 10, p. 235

yīrán, 依然, *adv.*, still; as before, L. 7, p. 109

yīwú shuìyì, 一无睡意, *phr.*, feel not sleepy at all, L. 11, p.291

yí, 移, *v.*, move, L. 11, p. 284

yíbèi.zi, 一辈子, *n.*, all one's life; a life time, L. 12, p. 371

yícè, 一侧, *n.*, one side, L. 6, p. 81

yíchà, 一刹, *n.*, instant; a split second, L. 12, p. 353

yíchǎn, 遗产, *n.*, legacy; inherited goods, L. 3, p. 34

yídàn, 一旦, *adv.*, now that; once, L. 10, p. 191

yídòng, 移动, *v.*, move; shift, L. 4, p. 51, L. 12, p. 371

yígài, 一概, *adv.*, without exception, L. 3, p. 29

yí.gejìnr.de, 一个劲儿地, *adv.*, continuously; persistently, L.11, p. 303

yíhàn, 遗憾, *n./adj.*, regret; sorrow, L. 3, p. 29

yíliùyānr, 一溜烟儿, *adv.*, (run away) swiftly, L. 4, p. 57

yíqù bùhuí, 一去不回, *idm.*, gone forever, L. 11, p. 299

yíshùnjiān, 一瞬间, *n.*, in the twinkling of an eye, L. 3, p. 35

yíwàng, 遗忘, *v.*, forget; lethe, L. 10, p. 185

yíwàng wújì, 一望无际, *idm.*, stretch as far as the eye can see, L. 9, p. 167, L. 11, p. 257

yíxià.zi, 一下子, *adv.*, all of a sudden, L. 11, p. 285

yíxiàng, 移向, *v.*, shift to, L. 6, p. 82

yízài, 一再, *adv.*, repeatedly; again and again, L. 7, p. 117

yízhèn, 一震, *v.*, be shocked, L. 11, p. 291

yízhèn, 一阵, *n.*, a period of time, L. 4, p. 47

yízhèn.zi, 一阵子, *n.*, a period of time; a spell, L. 7, p. 119

yízhǔ, 遗嘱, *n.*, last words; will, L. 3, p. 28

yǐ, 倚, *v.*, lean on or against, L. 9, p. 163

yǐ...míngyì, 以···名义, *n.*, in the name of, L. 8, p. 147

yǐ...zhùchēng, 以···著称, *v.*, be celebrated for; be famous for, L. 3, p. 35

yǐliáng wéigāng, 以粮为纲, *v.*, take food production as the key link, L. 10, p. 197

yǐmàoqǔrén, 以貌取人, *idm.*, judge people by outward appearance, L. 11, p. 297

yì, 溢, *v.*, overflow; spill, L. 4, p. 57

414

yìchǎng kōng, 一场空, *n.*, all in vain; futile, L. 11, p. 289

yìdòng, 异动, *n.*, unusual movement, L. 4, p. 43

yì huǒr.zi, 一伙儿子, *n.*, partners; group, L. 4, p. 44

yìjiàn, 意见, *n.*, idea; opinion, L. 3, p. 35

yìlùn, 议论, *v.*, talk; discuss, L. 8, p. 145

yìlùnfēnfēn, 议论纷纷, *phr.*, discuss animatedly; give rise to much discussion, L. 11, p. 283

yì nián yí dù, 一年一度, *adj.*, once a year; yearly, L. 10, p. 193

yìrújìwǎng, 一如既往, *idm.*, just as in the past; continue as always, L. 8, p. 131, L. 10, p. 223

yì sǎo ér guāng, 一扫而光, *idm.*, wipe out completely, make a clean sweep of; (here) finish off all the food, L. 4, p. 49

yìshēn, 一身, *adv.*, the whole body, L. 7 , p. 111

yìshēng, 一生, *n.*, lifetime , L. 2, p. 14

yìshēng bùkēng, 一声不吭, *v.*, without saying a word, L. 11, p. 291

yìshí, 一时, *adv.*, for the time being, for a while, L. 1, p. 7, L. 8, p. 137

yì.shi, 意识, *n.*, sense; consciousness, L. 4, p. 52

yì.shidào, 意识到, *v.*, be conscious (or aware) of; awake to; realize, L. 5, p. 69, L. 11, p. 259, L. 12, p. 327

yìshǒu zhǔchí, 一手主持, *phr.*, take charge of something single-handedly, L. 11, p. 291

yìsī qiànyì, 一丝歉意, *n.*, a tiny bit feeling of apology/regret, L.11, p. 261

yìwèi, 意味, *n.*, meaning; significance; implication, L. 10, p.233, L. 11, p. 289

yìwèi shēncháng, 意味深长, *phr.*, deep with meaning / implications, L. 11, p. 303

yìwù láodòng, 义务劳动, *n.*, voluntary labor, L. 1, p. 7

yìxīn, 一心, *adv.*, whole heartedly, L. 8, p. 149

yìyán nánjìn, 一言难尽, *idm.*, It would take too long to tell that in full; hard to explain it all in just a few words, L. 11, p. 275

yì yōng érshàng, 一拥而上, *v.*, come forth with a rush; dash up, L. 11, p. 263

yìzhōu, 一周, *n.*, one week, L. 11, p. 281

yínsè, 银色, *adj.*, silvery; silver-colored, L. 11, p. 311

yínsī, 银丝, *n.*, grey hair, L. 7, p. 109

yínyuán, 银元, *n.*, silver dollar, L. 10, p. 237

yǐncáng, 隐藏, *v.*, hide; conceal; remain under cover, L. 12, p. 329

yǐnchū, 引出, *v.*, give rise to; draw forth; lead to, L. 3, p. 32

yǐnmì, 隐秘, *adj.*, secret; concealed, L. 10, p. 219

yǐnyǐn.de, 隐隐地, *adv.*, faintly; vaguely, L. 10, p. 207, L. 11, p. 301

yǐnyuē, 隐约, *adj.*, indistinct; faint, L. 10, p. 223, L. 11, p. 315

yìn, 印, *v.*, print, L.1, p. 4, L. 10, p. 239

yīngjùn, 英俊, *adj.*, handsome and spirited, L. 10, p. 236

yīngmíng, 英明, *adj.*, wise; brilliant, L. 6, p. 95

yīngyīng, 嘤嘤, *onom.*, sound of sobbing, chirping, or whispering, L. 12, p. 337

yīngzī huànfā, 英姿焕发, *idm.*, dashing and spirited, L. 5, p. 73

yíng, 赢, *v.*, win, L. 12, p. 330

yíng, 迎, *v.*, greet; go to meet, L. 10, p. 233

yíng.chu.lai, 迎出来, *v.-c.*, come out (from a room) to meet a visitor, L. 12, p. 333

yíngjiē, 迎接, *v.*, meet; greet, L. 2, p. 17

yínglì, 盈利, *n.*, profit; gain, L. 12, p. 359

yíngrào, 萦绕, *v.*, hover; linger, L. 7, p. 119

yíng.shang.lai, 迎上来, *v.-c.*, go to meet, L. 2, p. 15

yíngyǎng, 营养, *n.*, nutrition, L. 10, p. 192

yíngzhǎng, 营长, *n.*, battalion commander, L. 10, p. 208

yǐngxiàng, 影像, *n.*, image, L. 12, p. 327

yìng, 应, *v.*, answer; respond, L. 11, p. 289

yìng, 映, *v.*, mirror; reflect, L. 10, p. 213

yìng, 硬, *adv.*, obstinately, L. 10, p. 207

yìngchóu, 应酬, *adv./v.*, exchange words perfunctorily, L. 12, p. 351

yìngduì, 应对, *v.*, reply; answer, L. 1, p. 7

yìngfù, 应付, *v.*, do sth. perfunctorily, L. 11, p. 293, L. 12, p. 361

yìngjiǎn, 硬茧, *n.*, callus, L. 12, p. 327

yǒngjǐ, 拥挤, *adj.*, crowded, L. 11, p. 257

yǒng, 涌, *v.*, well up; surge, L. 6, p. 87, L. 9, p. 165

yǒngchū, 涌出, *v.*, gush; well up, L. 2, p. 17, L. 10, p. 239

yǒngjìn, 涌进, *v.-c.*, pour into, L. 12, p. 329

yǒngqì, 勇气, *n.*, courage; nerve, L. 7, p. 109, L. 10, p. 189, L.12, p. 371

yǒngshàng xīntóu, 涌上心头, *phr.*, well up in one's mind, L.11, p. 291

yǒngyuǎn, 永远, *adj.*, forever; ever; for good , L. 2, p. 22

yòng.dezháo, 用得着, *v.-c.*, find sth. useful; need , L. 10, p. 201

yòngliào, 用料, *n.*, ingredient , L. 12, p. 361

yòngxīn, 用心, *v.-o.*, be attentive; concentrate one's attention, L. 11, p. 301

yōu'àn, 幽暗, *adj.*, dim; gloomy, L. 10, p. 233

yōulíng, 幽灵, *n.*, ghost; spirit, L. 8, p. 141

yōushēn, 幽深, *adj.*, remote and quiet, L. 5, p. 67

yōuxīn chōngchōng, 忧心忡忡, *idm.*, care-laden; heavyhearted , L. 5, p. 75

yōuxiù, 优秀, *adj.*, outstanding; excellent, L. 8, p. 135

yōuyù, 忧郁, *adj./n.*, melancholy, dejection, L. 4, p. 53, L. 6, p. 93, L. 10, p. 186

yōuyuè, 优越, *adj.*, superior; advantageous, L. 11, p. 259

yóuchāi, 邮差, *n.*, mailman, L. 2, p. 14

yóudàng, 游荡, *v.*, wander; stray, L. 9, p. 177

yóudiàn xuéxiào, 邮电学校, *n.*, school of post and telecommunications, L. 2, p. 14

yóuhuà, 油画, *n.*, oil painting, L. 4, p. 51, L. 11, p. 264

yóu.shui, 油水, *n.*, profit; (improper) fringe benefit, L. 4, p. 45

yóuxiāng mǎxì bān.zi, 游乡马戏班子, *n.*, traveling circus, L .4, p. 47

yóuyìn.zi, 油印子, *n.*, oil stains, marks made by oil, L. 4, p. 55

yóuyǒng, 游泳, *v.-o.*, swim, L. 11, p. 255

yóuyù, 犹豫, *n./v.*, hesitation, hesitate, L. 9, p. 169, L.11, p. 269, L. 12, p. 353

yóuyùbùjué, 犹豫不决, *idm.*, hesitate; dubious; remain undecided, L. 6, p. 95

yǒu juéxīn, 有决心, *v.-o.*, be resolute; be determined, L. 11, p. 255

yǒu yǎnfú, 有眼福, *n.*, have the good fortune of seeing sth. rare or beautiful, L. 10, p. 201

yǒufènr, 有份儿, *v.-o.*, have one's share in, L. 8, p. 129

yǒujiǎ, 有假, *v.*, there is falsification , L. 1, p. 7

yǒukǒu wúxīn, 有口无心, *idm.*, speak good words but be unsympathetic; say what one does not mean, L. 10, p. 196

yǒuwéi, 有为, *adj.*, promising, L. 12, p. 351

yǒuxīn, 有心, *adv.*, deliberately; purposely, L. 11, p. 302

yǒuxīn, 有心, *v.*, have a mind to; set one's mind on, L. 10, p. 239, L. 12, p. 341,

yǒuyì, 有意, *adv.*, purposely; deliberately, L. 6, p. 93